John Lord Peck

The Kingdom of the Unselfish, or Empire of the Wise

John Lord Peck

The Kingdom of the Unselfish, or Empire of the Wise

ISBN/EAN: 9783337171766

Printed in Europe, USA, Canada, Australia, Japan

Cover: Foto ©Thomas Meinert / pixelio.de

More available books at **www.hansebooks.com**

THE

KINGDOM OF THE UNSELFISH,

OR

EMPIRE OF THE WISE.

BY

JOHN LORD PECK.

NEW YORK:
EMPIRE BOOK BUREAU,
28 LAFAYETTE PLACE.

PREFACE.

THIS book makes its appearance because the existing stage of social evolution demands something not yet possessed; and it is one of the many things evolved to supply that demand. But it may not prove well suited to the present state of opinion. In that case it will be better adapted to a later one, and if not read in this century may be in the next.

That it will meet with hostile criticism from those who fail to apprehend its best meaning is quite likely. That it can do any serious harm, however, is not probable; not only because its motive is good, and because it is better to know the truth than to believe the unreal, but also because the human mind seems disposed to appropriate what is adapted to its condition of growth, and to refuse all that is beyond. There are other persons who will be able to appreciate the most of it; and these too, in all kindness, may find much to criticise adversely. The author has been continually conscious of such imperfection, and in excuse must reply that the work undertaken needed to be done; there was no one else to do it; and he has done the best he could. Whatever comments, friendly or unfriendly, may point out unseen faults, will be accepted, and turned to good account in the future, when there shall be opportunity.

Regarding the various dogmatic statements that will be found throughout the following pages, it must be said there was no time for proving everything, and these were left to prove themselves; while the justification of the book as a whole is trusted to justify this mode of proceeding. Whatever failure there is to give credit for ideas used that are not original has the same reason for a partial excuse; another part will be found on page 139, and in the whole of the succeeding chapter; while it may also be said that they are mostly such as are already familiar to persons acquainted with the progress and present condition of Science. For similar reasons, no better claim is made for anything else that is here presented.

Those who possess facts bearing upon any of the peculiar theories here advanced, or who, after sufficient reading and thought, shall be animated by a desire to take some steps toward the ideal "Kingdom" described, are invited to correspond with the author, addressing communications in care of the publishing company named on title page. J. L. P.

CONTENTS.

CHAPTER I.   INTRODUCTORY.   THE RELIABLE AND THE UNRELIABLE IN THOUGHT.

CHAP. II.   THE EVOLUTION OF MORALITY.

CHAP. III.   THE EVOLUTION OF MORALITY *(Continued)*.

CHAP. IV.   INDEPENDENCE.

CHAP. V.   VANITY AND PRIDE.

CHAP. VI.   INTELLECTUAL IMMORALITY.

CHAP. VII.   CONCEIT AND SELF-RIGHTEOUSNESS.

CHAP. VIII.   NATURAL AND SOCIAL SELECTION.

CHAP. IX.   NATURAL AND SOCIAL SELECTION *(Continued)*.

CHAP. X.   NATURAL AND SOCIAL SELECTION *(Continued)*.

CHAP. XI.   NATURAL AND SOCIAL SELECTION *(Continued)*.

CHAP. XII.   NATURAL AND SOCIAL SELECTION *(Continued)*.

CHAP. XIII.   LOVE.

CHAP. XIV.   LOVE *(Continued)*.

CHAP. XV.   RELIGIOSITY AND RELIGION.

CHAP. XVI.   CONVERSION AND SALVATION.

CHAP. XVII.   ARTOSITY AND ART.

CHAP. XVIII.   GOD.

CHAP. XIX.   IMMORTALITY.

CHAP. XX.   HUMAN PERFECTIBILITY.

CHAPTER I.

THE RELIABLE AND UNRELIABLE IN THOUGHT.

INTRODUCTORY.

IF we take all the different sorts of ideas or conceptions that enter the human mind, either as knowledge, opinion, doctrine, dogma, philosophy, revelation, myth or tradition, and put them into two contrasted classes regarding the point of their reliability or certainty, one of these classes will naturally be called Science and the other Nescience, or one Knowledge and the other Conjecture. Under the head of Conjecture or Nescience will be included all tradition, myth, revelation, doctrine, dogma, speculation and opinion, as the more uncertain part; while under that of Knowledge or the Reliable will be positive science only. Science will stand over against all the rest as the only certainty. Indeed, science and certainty are almost exchangeable words. All those things classed as Nescience contain so much of that which is doubtful that doubt, skepticism or criticism is their great enemy, the one thing they all dread, and which is really dangerous to them; whereas, Science has no fear of criticism, and boldly challenges it to do its worst. For, whatever cannot endure criticism is not science, and until it can will not become such. And the point is to be noted that although what passes for science is not yet all positively certain, it is in the process of becoming certain—is having its doubtful material constantly reduced in amount, unlike the opposite class of conceptions, in which the uncertain matter increases or becomes more prominent under the application of criticism. The authority and influence of the latter is continually being weakened, while the matter composing science is continually going forward to a point where it can be received by every one alike as beyond question. Thus it was in the old contest over Astronomy, in the later one over Geology, and so it is in the present disputes concerning Biology and the philosophy of Evolution.

At the same time that there is more or less of doubt attached to everything outside of positive science, there is also more or less of truth mixed with the falsity, both together waiting for that final sifting process to be ultimately applied by the Scientific Method, which shall separate one from the other, and leave to us the clear grain of knowledge unmixed with any chaff of superstition, misrepresentation, or misconception. Moreover, I here willingly venture the opinion, to be supported more or less farther on, that little of what passes for truth is *wholly* false, and that Science will yet discover some solid rocks of certainty where it now sees only the marsh and swamp of superstition and folly.

In claiming so much for Science, however, it is not forgotten that at the bottom of all Science, as we now commonly understand the word, there remain some questions of a philosophical character, such as the ultimate test of truth, the nature of the Absolute, the nature of force, of intelligence and of cause, with definitions of space, time, matter and motion, to be definitively settled before Science can finally conquer its whole domain from its opponents. This done we shall then at last be able to speak of a scientific Ontology.

To a mature mind the theory or philosophy of a subject seems the first thing that ought to be learned; and the fact that Science has not yet fully reached its philosophical basis—that these great questions are still undecided—is and will be a hindrance to its progress. But though it will hinder, it will not prevent, the acceptance of any ordinary scientific truth when supported by evidence in sufficient amount. Nobody can escape from his own instincts, nor always refuse to believe his own senses; and so positive truth makes its way notwithstanding all philosophy or lack of philosophy. We may trust philosophy to the final outcome, well believing that it, like all the subordinate departments of knowledge, will at last take on the positive and unquestionable character.

Neither is it to be understood that what I am about to offer in this course of essays is all indubitable scientific knowledge. I mean to claim only that positive knowledge is the foundation of the whole. Though the structure may be carried up to a dizzying height, or branched out in various unfamiliar directions, yet the underwork is in the solid ground. Or, with a different simile, just as in springtime the sap absorbed by the roots of a tree must be carried into all its highest and widest branches, or else they die, so the spirit and method of Science must be carried into all that claims to be developed from it, else such outgrowth will die and fall to the ground. The radical truths of science are the roots out of which everything must grow; and whatever is not properly affiliated to them cannot be expected to live. For this reason it is intended to put forth nothing but what is believed able to hold its place, and live and grow, under these conditions.

Let us now make a short review of the unreliable species of knowledge, or rather thought, and afterward a comparison with it of the more positive or reliable kind, in order to understand how they are naturally related to each other, what is the present state and tendency of thought, and what is likely to be the final outcome from the existing conflict of influences between them. All of the work that is to follow will then possess something of the character of prediction.

To speak first of Tradition and Revelation, these are so

nearly connected, nearly all the accepted revelations are so old, so obscure, and though written are to the masses of people so much a tradition, that for my purpose it will be sufficiently correct to discuss them both under one head. To realize how truly and how much revelation is tradition let one but remember that the Christian world has for eighteen hundred years been disputing over the natural or ordinary meaning of old Hebrew writings, absurd though they are when so understood, while only in the present century has the idea got abroad that the disputed portions are allegories, having a symbolical and spiritual sense that is rational, and were probably written with no expectation of their ever being taken for anything else.

All over the world, wherever there has been any civilization, there exist old books or scriptures that are looked upon as more or less sacred. In China, India, Central and Western Asia, and Northern Africa they are still the authorities by which people are taught, and their lives to some small extent governed. In ancient Egypt, if not Chaldea, similar writings were possessed, and doubtless served the same purpose of teaching men how to live. Greece and Rome also had their sacred mysteries and oracles, and Rome at least some sacred books. Where civilization was not sufficiently advanced for records to be made there were still oral traditions, similar to those in the written volumes or scrolls. These existed in Central America, Mexico and Peru, and are found in various barbarous or half-civilized tribes, on this continent and the other. The Kings, the Vedas, the Avesta, the Dhamapada, the Book of the Dead, the Sibylline books, the Hebrew and Christian Scriptures, and the Koran, besides various other works closely related to them, and a host of commentaries and expositions, all come into this class of documents. Some records previously unknown to us have been brought to light by the researches of modern scholars; while those who profess to have penetrated into the mysteries of the ancient secret societies tell us there are still other old books hidden away in the Buddhist monasteries of Central Asia, of which we have never had any account.

Regarding these I will quote from an author known both as a religionist and a scientist,* one who has proved his christianity by his deeds—Mr. Charles L. Brace, the founder some thirty years ago of the Five Points missionary work in New York City.

"It is a grand and consoling thought," he says, "harmonious with reason and with the utterances of inspired men, that there is in human history a continuity of divine revelations. That is, that the Spirit of God has not merely manifested itself to one race in a remote corner of the world during a few years, but that it has been struggling with human souls during all ages and among all races. Certain individuals have especially received these inspirations, and have so grasped certain moral and spiritual truths, or have led such pure and unselfish lives, as to profoundly affect the humane and moral progress of whole races of men. Indeed the continuance and relative advance of great nations have often depended on the degree to which they followed the instructions and truths taught by their great religious leaders. Under this aspect God is an ever-acting force in human history, and men and women in the most widely scattered countries, and among races given up to superstition and degrading practices, have opened their souls to this divine light. The light which they in turn have given to the world has not indeed been like the pure radiance shining forth from the Son of Man in Judea, but it has contained rays of the heavenly light, and though obscured by the mists of superstition and the clouds of human ignorance, it has yet guided many a weary soul in the dark ways of the world."

"One faith has existed in India as a reform of Brahmanism, and has extended to China, Japan and other countries, which in the life of its founder and the truths he taught showed a peculiar divine inspiration that brought

---
* Author of "Gesta Christi" and "The Races of the Old World."

it in many respects very near to Christianity. Undoubtedly in the original form of this religion are seen the workings of the Divine Spirit on a most pure and exalted human soul. Indeed the truths taught by Gautama Buddha seem to be foregleams of those taught by Christ. Never has compassion been more divinely illustrated in a human life; nowhere are self-sacrifice, human brotherhood, universal benevolence and sympathy, and purity of heart and life more directly taught than in the words transmitted of Sakya-Muni. The Buddhist legends might well say that all nature budded into spring, and a thrill of joy reached every animated being, that the blind saw, and the dumb spake, that prisoners were set free and the flames of hell extinguished, and a mighty sound of music arose from heaven and earth when a human soul so pure and holy, so filled with an almost infinite compassion, began its life in the body." (Gesta Christi, pp. 445-51.)

All these old scriptures have much similarity in character, and the quotation just made is an admission that the best of them possess a comparative equality in moral or spiritual value. Indeed the slight superiority which Mr. Brace attributes to Christianity is only what the adherents of all religions are in the habit of attributing to their own, and assuming to be greater than the critic can allow; though in this case the claimant is unusually fair.

All of them contain traces of philosophy, that is, some explanation of cosmic and human origin; they all prescribe rites, sacrifices, and observances having regard to spiritual beings; and all give some kind of ordinances for influencing the conduct of men toward each other. The three subjects of philosophy, religion and morals are more or less mixed—not separated as with us of modern times —and there are various other matters of less pretension. Most of them agree in having some portion that comes through prophets and seers from a spiritual source, a misty, undefined and little-known region outside the ordinary world, and this portion is what is here meant by *revelation*. In fact, prophets, seers, mediums, and all the phenomena of Spiritualism, seem to have been as familiar to the ancients as to the present generation; and were looked upon with much more respect. It has been commonly supposed that Buddhism has no spirit world; but many scholars think, on the contrary, that the Nirwana of that doctrine is not a state of extinction for the entire consciousness, but only of the supposed baser, material part. The Chinese doctrines appear to have a greater share of philosophy and less of spiritual teaching.

No society of any kind can exist without morality; and none considerably civilized, like those of the ancient world, without morality of a corresponding degree. Hence all the sacred books contain moral instruction. There is a variety in their injunctions; for what may be thought good morality in one country, or one state of society, may not in another. Yet there are certain great principles, such as regard for life, for property, for the family, for justice in a general sense, which are found in all systems and doctrines, as being essentials to any social existence.

This sort of moral teaching—mostly upon spiritual authority or the word of the prophet—is the only moral teaching that Asia, Africa and Eastern Europe have ever had; indeed even Western Europe and America can hardly yet be said to possess any other.

Of the political morality of these old authorities it is necessary to say only that they knew nothing of liberty or democracy; theocracy or despotism was all. Of their religion and philosophy it may be well to speak a little further.

At the time the Asiatic and Egyptian civilizations were flourishing the greater part of their knowledge was held by the priesthood or professional caste, the military, trading and laboring classes being supposed to have known little beyond what was required in the performance of their functions. It is commonly assumed that the priests kept it within their own order for the purpose of thereby securing their own power and importance, though it is possible to believe that along with this they had another and less selfish motive, as will soon appear.

According to the evidences now being discovered by scholars in ancient lore, certain secret societies, either within or above the priesthoods, and superior to all others in their mystical knowledge, existed over nearly all the civilized parts of Asia and Africa. After their decrease and loss of influence by the decay of these old nations, the lingering remnants of their membership were scattered over Europe during the Middle Ages, and some few societies yet remain, still attempting to preserve the old knowledge and teaching in its purity. Some portion of their symbolism, probably with the less vital part of its meaning, has also come down to us under the guise of Free-Masonry. The Theosophical movement of the last few years is an effort by some present thinkers to get acquainted with their ancient doctrines and mysteries.

Among the leading ideas of the religious philosophy taught by them was that of a great spiritual Source or Origin of all things, having a name of such peculiar sacredness as to be in some localities ineffable to ordinary men and known only to the few, while in other parts its utterance was supposed to give a sanctifying virtue. Creation was by emanation from this source; and it is to the credit of the old thinkers that creation from nothing was never thought of till the time of the Christian Fathers. There was a division of all the emanations into two great worlds, one of goodness and light, the spiritual; the other material, dark and evil. There was a three-fold distribution of man into body, soul and spirit, the body being further of two kinds, the familiar material one, and one of a finer substance imperceptible to ordinary sensation. The development of the soul was accomplished by its transmigration through various bodies and lives, till its final attainment of the spirit, and absorption into its parent source, the Absolute All.

Egypt and India were the centers of this philosophy, which was almost wholly speculative and spiritualistic. It is believed to underlie Brahmanism, Buddhism, and the Hermetic "wisdom of the Egyptians." It was probably known to the Persian Magi, and to the wiser part of the priesthood of the Jews. Apparently it is the fount and origin of all the rational spirituality of all the world's great religions. Prophets, seers and poets have added to it their contributions; and priests have represented it to the populace in symbols, images and ceremonial rites, which have gradually lost all proper meaning and finally become mere idol worship or dead formality.

Materialism, as a philosophy, though it must have existed latently, was scarcely known to the Eastern world except to a slight extent in India at a comparatively late period.

How ancient the secret brotherhoods may have been no one knows. How they came by their mysteries and allegories is explained only by the supposition that under the moral progress of a growing civilization they had come to experience *certain exalted states of mind*, which only a few persons unusually favored by nature could realize, and which to the masses therefore were wholly inconceivable. These, and the conceptions belonging to them, which to themselves were sacred, they embodied in allegories, and transferred to them some of the old symbols of the primitive sun-earth-and-sky worship, with a new and higher meaning, in order to preserve the knowledge of them, or some hints of it at least, to a later and more favorable time.

A considerable share of the mass of Eastern traditions, allegories, and religious dogmas became incorporated in Christianity; some of it coming from Egypt, some from the Persian Magism, some from the Hebrews, some from the Gnostics, and some from the Greek philosophy of Pythagoras and Plato. Thus it has influenced all Christendom down to the present time.

But Christianity as it now is, and ever since it became an established religion, is far from being a true child of its ancient parentage, or anything but a poor representative of the ideas taught by the old brotherhood of prophets and thinkers. The archaic doctrines may have been adulterated and debased before Christianity obtained them, but if so she still further diluted, confused and corrupted them, till they became scarce recognizable, and turned the old allegories into extravagant relations of actual fact, with a literal meaning to every word; thus compelling the mind to stultify itself by a blind, senseless belief, or else skeptically to reject them, with all the associated teachings of the Church. To those who care to know how much truth there can be in this paragraph I commend the reading of a single book, written by two students of the ancient wisdom, and called "The Perfect Way, or The Finding of Christ." Christianity has a virtue of its own in its power to arouse enthusiasm; but in rationality it falls far behind the olden type.

As already stated, the wisdom of the ancients was largely an esoteric wisdom. The best part of it was never given to the public except in symbolical dress, nor even to the lower grades of the instructed. Only the few who had reached the highest degree of merit, through their own elevated character and intelligence, could know the whole. If transferred to the populace the most sacred truths would be misunderstood, doubted, despised and profaned; while its teachers, becoming objects of suspicion and dislike, would lose whatever influence for good they possessed. This is the natural result of placing before men knowledge of what is beyond their experience, and hence beyond their ability to apprehend or believe, according to the well-understood law that all knowledge must come through some kind of sensation or experience. That truth of a high order was possessed by some of these teachers will be readily admitted by all enquirers who through their own experience come to understand what it was ; for it was the kernel truth of all religion.

Here is an obvious reason why it is that we discover in the old civilizations the traces of an elaborate philosophy, a monotheistic religion, and a high standard of moral excellence, existing at the same time and place with the lowest forms of polytheism, idolatry, and sensuality; the former for the happy few who could attain to it, the latter for the great mass who could conceive of nothing better. With no means for the ready and general diffusion of intelligence, the mental condition could hardly have been different.

In our own times, and our own religion, we still see something of the same kind—at one extreme an educated, thoughtful and moralized class, at the other a more numerous body, still worshipping charms, images, and a plurality of gods little better than demons, with elaborate ritual ceremony, while possessing no higher moral ambition than is accordant with sensual gratification and vain display. The difference between our time and the past is that we have a large intermediate class, partially educated, and to some extent thoughtful. But even the esoteric feature is not absent. Many intelligent persons believe esoterically what they find it inexpedient to utter publicly. They find that when a truth transcending the experience of any group or class of persons is offered them by one more advanced it is immediately misconcieved, likened to something base, and the author suspected, maligned, or hated, for no fault except that of having too much faith in humanity. The private conviction, and public expression will continue to be at variance in some degree until the advanced thought and the common opinion are more nearly alike than they have ever yet been.

In regard to all this there is but one special point that needs to be emphasized. A part of the old sacred books claims to have come through revelation; and the whole religious, philosophic, and moral movement belonging to their influence, and that of the sages referred to, is predominantly spiritualistic. Admitting a world of spiritual existences, there would then seem to have been a time when that world readily gave revelations to this, through prophets and seers, with a design of teaching the morality necessary to social life and individual development; and to enforce it by such religious considerations as would be effective among selfish and superstitious races of men. Certain revelations have come, and they seem adapted to the nature of those who have received them. Possibly they were the only kind of teaching that would have been accepted at all. Though differing at different times and places, they all appear to have had the purpose of making men better, more moral, more unselfish. They have operated through hope and through fear, and the sacrifices of selfish interest that hopes and fears have induced. It seems to me probable that some good result has been thus accomplished. Whether a large amount or not may be questioned; but the more appropriate question is whether any good effect at all could have been produced by a teaching that did not act upon men's fears through their superstitions, and by raising false hopes equal to their fears. Strong motives only could move the coarse, simple, indolent, brutal, nature of the primitive man. Taking this view, the instruction was suited to a weak, ignorant, selfish, and in all respects *childish* or immature condition of humanity—a childishness not so much that of the civilized child as that of the child barbarian.

In modern Europe and America we still have seers, prophets and revelations. But they are not distinguished like the old ones, no such reverence attaches to them, and being new and well known they are not traditions. The bringers of them do not cultivate any special secrecy, and their teachings are in plain language designed for all. What they tell us professes to be more rational than the ancient deliverances, more scientific, more correctly descriptive of the spirit world and of what goes on there. The doctrines taught are not yet authoritative, but the process of making them so has commenced, and but for the competition of newer ones, only time would be needed for the older ones to be endowed with that character. They are intermediate between tradition and science, showing the effect of scientific influence, and illustrating the fact that progress or improvement characterizes even this strange process of revelation. Their influence is not yet great, but they seem entitled to mention in connection with the two great extremes that constitute our subject. In Europe the most notable of these have been given by Emanuel Swedenborg, in America by A. J. Davis.

Dogma and Speculative Philosophy, like Tradition and Revelation, have a close relationship. We have religious dogmas, like that of the Fatherhood of God and the Brotherhood of Man, and less important ones thought out by the speculative founders of churches, creeds and sects; we have political ones, such as the Divine Right of Kings, or the claim that All Men are born Free and Equal; we have moral ones, such as Freedom of the Will, or the right to Freedom of Conscience and Opinion; and we have economic ones, like the right of Freedom in Trade. Most of them have a similarity in being the result of deductive speculation, in which a part of the premises is always left out, and unreal assumptions put in. When submitted to verification by being put in practice, or by testing their origins, they all alike fail, either wholly or in part. The results of criticism or of practice never justify the expectations. When we look around us we see no indication that God, more than the devil, is the father of all men; neither is there a brotherhood, in race or in sentimental feeling. Modern Physiology and Psychology do not prove the freedom of the will, nor is the ignorant and vicious person morally entitled to freedom of conscience and opinion. However much it ought to be true that we are all born free and with equal rights, there is no such equality. And in these times, when every one thinks and talks of the Labor question, it is not difficult to perceive that competition is never free, and that the outcome of it as it really is, does not prove the rightfulness of greater freedom any more than it does the opposite, if as much. Thus all such doctrines have a common faultiness, unlike the truth of Science, by means of which we can predict with certainty, and accomplish what we set out to realize.

It is but just, however, to admit that many dogmas belong to that order of truth called Theoretical, which would be true if the materials dealt with were perfect, and will be practical in proportion as we attain to the final perfection of all things. They are therefore truths when rightly apprehended; but taken as they are commonly understood, to be applicable now, or as right under all circumstances, they are only false, delusive and disappointing. The requirements of absolute morality, as well as some of the dogmas above named, are of this nature.

Deductive or Speculative Philosophy is as old as civilization, and flourishes still. It reached almost as high a development in ancient India as it has in modern Europe. One system has followed another all through the history of human thought, the last being as purely speculative as the first. Of the old philosophers Plato is the only one that is now much read. Of the modern movement, largely Transcendental, no one theory continues to hold much influence except that Scotch-English one called Common Sense, which asserts the external world as a reality, and the testimony of the senses as reliable. The Pessimism contained in the writings of Schopenhauer and Hartmann attracts some attention, and the Agnosticism of Comte, Huxley and Spencer has a degree of popularity; but neither of these is sufficiently near the final truth to long satisfy the human mind, and the prediction is here ventured that both of them will give way to a scientific Ontology more perfect than that of the Evolution philosophy as represented by Herbert Spencer.

In this country, where many speculative works are published, no one takes any strong hold upon the public mind. Of the latest development in Europe, the doctrine of Herman Lotze, I know nothing, but anticipate that it will share the fate of all the rest. Thus from the great amount of mental activity spent in this manner but little effect now remains. The Positivists have said and written much upon this failure of their opponents; but Positivism itself, so far as it is Comtism, is something of a speculation, and its own failure is about equal to that of others. Something, it is true, has been gained, out of the whole philosophic movement, but not enough to secure a basis for the organization of thought, to bring the satisfaction of enlightenment, or in any manner accomplish any great good. Like the old mixture of tradition, thought, and revelation, this kind of teaching belongs to the unreliable class. As the old was suited to a childish age, and produced by it, so speculation may be said to belong to the boyhood or early maturity of the race, analogous to that time in the life of the individual when the reasoning faculty begins to assert itself, when logic appears to be infallible, and the youth has not yet learned that what *must be* does not always agree with what *is*.

I come now to speak of Science, or the class of ideas that is most positive and reliable. By this is meant *modern* science, which though as old as the race in one sense, is yet so largely modern there is no impropriety in so defining it; which began its investigations in the material world, and as there now seems reason for thinking, is not going to end them till it has reached and explored the spiritual. It is the antithesis of both tradition and philosophy (deductive) in teaching nothing upon the authority of seers, prophets, or other revelators; nothing because it is ancient, time-honored, and respectable; nothing as dogma or the outcome of speculation. Custom, law, precedent and convention are of no account to it, except as facts in themselves, or as indicating a certain amount of probability. It acknowledges nothing as beyond candid criticism; it has nothing sacred but the truth. It investigates every part of the universe and of man with equal impartiality, save that the most easily examined is the first to be made known. It has no mysteries but are free to any one who chooses to learn them. It depends only on observed facts and generalized laws, and these are what it recognizes as the only final authority. Religion, myths, morals, politics it examines as it does any other phenomena, and reports what it can learn. Whichever system of either may best endure the test of time and criticism is to it a matter of indifference. It is confident that the one best adapted to the present wants of human nature will take the lead. It has, or should have, no preferences for anything. Its only proper object is to ascertain truth. Individual scientists may have preferences, for no one is entirely free from that species of imperfection we call bigotry; but the general aim, aspiration, spirit and intent of the scientific body is nearly such as that just described.

Science however, is not an extreme or antagonistic opposite of all former knowledge and opinion, as might be misunderstood from its being here set over against everything else. But it is a more complete, thorough and systematic knowledge, of the same kind as any imperfect knowledge, preceding it, that has a real basis of fact. It is the knowledge or assertion that has a predominance of certainty instead of uncertainty. It is subject to the law of Evolution, and advances from the indefinite and incomplete to its more perfect stage. Hence it has been already said that portions of truth capable of entering into definite and positive science exist among those notions that have here been defined as the Unreliable, and put under the head of Nescience.

Science begins with those phenomena most familiar to us. The bodies, materials, and motions upon the earth's surface; the orbs of space, and their movements in time; the crust of our own planet, and the life that is developed upon it; have successively come under its prying scrutiny. Mind, a more recondite and difficult subject, has been studied considerably, but investigators have learned that they need all the knowledge they can obtain from the forms of life below man in order to study successfully the mental organism. Psychology or mental science is therefore less advanced than the purely physical, or the lower biological branches of knowledge. Sociology, another and very large department of science, is quite new. It embraces History, or the origin, growth and development of the social organism; Government, Law, and Political Economy, which deal with its structure and functions; Morals and Education, which instruct regarding the duties of society to the individual, and of individuals to each other and to society as a whole. All these large subjects, besides Public Sanitation and Hygiene, Charities, War, and Criminal Reform, belong to Sociology. Something regarding them has been known, of course, ever since the beginning of society; but how little may be inferred when we look over the world's history, and see what poor success has attended social efforts; how all the ancient civilized communities have gone down to ruin and death so utterly that only wrecks and monuments remain of all their greatness; how the whole of Asia and Africa is in a state of moral and physical decay, ready to fall in pieces at every touch of the strong hand of Modern Europe; how all over Europe itself millions of men are kept under arms to prevent its neighboring nations from conquering and robbing each other; while scores, if not hundreds, of thousands of other men, in secret bands, are pledged to destroy the whole social fabric completely, and start anew from a state of anarchy to build up one better adapted to human happiness. Even in our own country, with the best and happiest society ever yet evolved, let one think of the horrors in all our great cities; of the gambling and speculation of all sorts, from the most honorable down to the meanest; of the hells of prostitution and pre-natal infanticide; the dens of robbery and theft; the filth, disease, degradation, poverty and misery of every description; let him think of the same crimes and miseries scattered all over our country districts, like heads of rust in a field of grain; and besides all this *continuous* evil, let him consider the occasional misfortunes of war, pestilence, floods, fires, railroad massacres, and a thousand avoidable accidents; and he will be ready to conclude that we know but little yet of social science, and are but poorly qualified for social life.

Sociology, however, like all the other Sciences, has been making progress. It, like Psychology, could only advance slowly till knowledge had been gained in the lower departments of life to be applied in the study of society—till society itself was seen to be an organism, subject to the laws governing other organisms; till its origin was studied in the life of savage races, and history scrutinized to trace its evolution to the present stage.

Of late years this science has been going forward rapidly through the labors of many distinguished men in Europe, and a smaller number in America. There is much diversity yet in the utterances of those who represent it; but it professes to have something to say concerning politics, morals, economy, and education. The best minds are looking to it for a help they can get from no other source, and it is probable they will not be disappointed; though considerable time must elapse before there can be general agreement.

Sociology, in the large sense given to it, is the last and highest of the sciences, but one field of research, both physical and mental, yet remains, that is almost new. I have said that Science would not cease its work till it had investigated the spiritual as well as the material. It has already turned its attention toward this domain, as evidenced by a number of "societies for psychical research," with their collections of facts, in addition to what individual Spiritualists and others have done before them. There are so-called spiritual sensations almost as intense and vivid as a blow upon the head or a flash of light. There is a spiritual experience, so-called, which to those who pass through it is as real as anything in their whole lives, and makes an impression that is never obliterated. To suppose that these are always to be ignored by scientific men is to assume that people will continue to be as bigoted and foolish as at present; which is contrary to Evolution and to all intellectual progress. On the contrary, all the great mass of strange fact and feeling, formerly put aside as unworthy of notice, but now beginning to be recognized, is yet to become an organized and systematic body of psychologic and spiritual science.

The Unreliable and the Reliable are now seen to be of very different character. What is their proper relation to each other? Are they totally opposed, or are they complements, one adapted to one stage of mental growth and one to another? Is one to absorb the other, and if so which? Or is one to destroy the other and take its place? These are the questions that agitate the minds of the present generation more than anything else. Some believe that the two things are totally opposed and hostile; that as Science grows Tradition with all its connected religious notions must decline till it finally becomes extinct, like all superstitions and delusions; for they see in it nothing else. A much larger party believe that traditional religion cannot be destroyed; that it has a field and will occupy it, one that Science cannot enter; that religious feelings and experiences are a reality which no science can convert into superstition; that Science indeed cannot reach their level, or know much about them, because they are discerned only through the Spirit. Another, and smaller party hold that religion is to make a final conquest of Science by absorbing it all into itself, without serious conflict or contradiction, yet retaining its own peculiar province as something beyond all science. Still another small party, who acknowledge a natural religious sentiment, and of whom Herbert Spencer is a prominent representative, believe that Science will ultimately destroy all traditional or revealed religion except the idea of an absolute and infinite Being, of which nothing can be known save its infinity and absoluteness; and this is ever to remain as the final object of all religious contemplation.

Finally, there is one other position that may be taken, which is that Science is ultimately to embrace and swallow up all of traditional and philosophic religion that is of any value, dissipating all its dross and superstition in the process, and bringing it all into its own field, partly as moral or social science, and partly as spiritual science. In other words, science is to extend itself so widely as to include everything that can be known to experience by any kind of sensation or emotion, the religious and spiritual no less than the material. However mystical and indescribable some of those experiences may be as yet, they are sometime to be analyzed, classified, and explained; though not in such a manner that all can fully understand them; for it is a law of mind that no one can conceive the nature of an experience beyond what he has himself realized. Nor is this to be done immediately. But by the slow and sure method Science always takes it will in time come to the work and carry it through.

Philosophy and Dogma are likely to have a similar fate. The domain of the former will finally be taken in by science, and a scientific philosophy replace the speculative; as in fact it already does except in the department of Ontology, that science which deals with the elements of the Universe—the conditions and materials that exist before the process of evolution begins. Dogmas, so far as they are theoretical or absolute truths, will be understood as such and taken as standards to be continually approximated, after which they become science by virtue of being known as they really are, and estimated at their true value. Though much will be saved much will also be cast away, and the process as a whole will amount to a revolution in the whole world of thought.

It is in agreement with this view that one of the two great classes of ideas is adapted to a childish or immature stage of mental growth, the other to a more advanced one. The work proposed to be done is similar to what is already being performed by every individual.

When the child becomes a man, and through better education and experience gains a knowledge superior to that of his parents, he revises the ideas taught him in his infancy, discarding some as entirely erroneous, modifying and improving others, confirming all that are sound and useful. Tradition, dogma and speculation, no matter what the subject of them, are what the *race* is taught in its childhood and youth; science is what it afterward learns, and uses to correct the former. There is a criticism of traditional *art*, now going on among artists, which may be taken as one illustration of the process. And I shall endeavor to show, farther along, that the more advanced part of the *race* is approaching a point in its development corresponding to that period when the individual passes from childhood into maturity.

If in these papers, therefore, I occupy such a position as just described, in which Science becomes the superior and critic of everything else, I trust that no one will in advance suspect me of endeavoring to destroy aught of good that has been taught us by Religion or Philosophy. Criticism, by clearing away what is false or unworthy will only leave what remains more beautiful and attractive to rational minds. And for all that is destroyed or cast away something better is likely to be substituted.

Let us next consider what motive there is for an attempt to harmonize the Unreliable and the Reliable—the Traditional, the Revealed, the Speculative and the Scientific—more truly and thoroughly than has ever yet been accomplished. Forty years ago Auguste Comte called the state of thought existing in Europe an "intellectual anarchy." It was an anarchy extending to everything, religion, morals, politics, philosophy. The teachers upon all subjects were divided into parties, sects, factions and schools, with perpetual clash and disorder, but with no harmonious, connected and permanent body of truths coming forth as the result of conflict. Since then the anarchy, except in one department, has steadily become worse. Science alone has manifested any power to strengthen and make certain its ideas, and unite its adherents. Outside of it additional sects, parties and schools have sprung up. The disorganizing tendency has not only broken one branch of the church into small fragments, but in many minds has destroyed the belief of any reality whatever in religion itself. In politics, though the old conservative and progressive parties still remain, several new parties of Socialists have arisen, some of them with aims not very definite, but one, as radical as the atheistic in the religious world, proposing to abolish the state entirely and all legalized government. Philosophy has put forth new branches, but the futility of all of them has become so apparent to many that the popular skepticism called Agnosticism has largely taken the place of philosophy and faith.

Like the egg of an animal organism, which when impregnated by the male principle proceeds to divide itself, and continues to divide and redivide its parts till they are reduced to a mass, of fine cells, preparatory to being organized, so the European church, when once the vitality of free scientific thought entered it, as it did before the Protestant Reformation, began to divide, and has continued the process of redivision till a considerable portion of it is now reduced to that chaotic, individualized condition in which it knows nothing satisfactory, has no attractions toward any existing center, and is ready to be organized anew whenever some indisputable scientific truth or system of truths can be presented as a fit nucleus around which individuals may gather and take on the functions of a vital, growing, developing body. The state is not yet disorganized to the same extent as the church, but as the elements of an equally radical change exist in it there is only a question of time *when* it will reach the same condition.

Comte made an heroic effort to unite all science into one connected and positive system; and through that to organize a new church, a new state, and a new industrial order. But his conceptions proved too limited and too unprogressive for success; and so Positivism became, and still remains, little more than a name. Herbert Spencer, with a broader view and a more catholic and liberal disposition, has made a second effort to organize science, with an accompanying aspiration to improve the present state of thought regarding politics, religion and morals. He has gathered to his standard a much larger number of adherents, but he too has limitations, and his scheme is not final. To say nothing of his metaphysics, will a system that ignores all spiritual and religious experience as delusion ever be taken as complete by the majority of intelligent people? To suppose it will may be a delusion equal to any of the opposite sort.

An attempt to accomplish the same work through speculation has been made in this country, but apparently with very little result. The anarchy of thought continues, and in the industrial and political worlds, where its results are worst, it is accompanied by fearful deeds that threaten to bring on a physical anarchy equal to the confusion of thought in the general mind. The serious danger of a long period of disorder, turbulence and crime, if the present tendency goes on blindly to its termination, furnishes sufficient motive for the best exertions of any thinker, and sufficient excuse for his efforts, even though they involve some unusual pretensions, as every such effort necessarily does.

Hitherto, as before said, nearly all teaching upon moral and social subjects has been from tradition, revelation and dogma, or the less reliable side of human thought. The generality of people, including many of the educated, have no idea of looking to Science for any authoritative and practical moral truth. To them Science is still physical, and is liable to step out of its proper sphere if it aspires to anything higher. Yet it is becoming animated by this ambition more and more, and the higher kind of teaching is likely to be one of its principal applications in the future. For instance, few suppose the law of Natural Selection or survival of the fittest has any connection with morality, or that the sociologist can make it aid him in understanding society. But already certain thinkers have shown it to have a bearing upon society, and others are anxious to use it as a justification for all existing social evils. Hence the moralist will be compelled to take it into account. Various other scientific truths have relation to social welfare; and the exposition of some of these special relations is to be the principal work of the succeeding essays.

Many persons are already engaged in the commendable labor of popularizing science, and it is not my purpose to intrude seriously into their field; but to go farther and enter a new one; to carry the application of science into the more unusual themes and subjects, some of them the most important of all. Though treating them from the standpoint of science, a close agreement with representative scientific men is not always to be expected. I anticipate using scientific data, to draw from them whatever conclusions my own thought will enable me to do, in order to obtain from science all that is possible for my purposes. And the endeavor will be to make every idea and statement so plain that persons of fair intelligence will have little difficulty in getting a clear apprehension of what is advanced.

In the first of the succeeding essays an attempt will

be made to explain how the moral or altruistic feeling originates, and to trace its evolution through various forms into a final stage of complete unselfishness. This last stage has never yet been reached, except possibly in very few and rare instances; while my desire is to show that it *can* be attained by a considerable number, and to make as plain as may be the way of such attainment. To do so it is manifest that I must point out causes of failure that have remained unnoticed by preachers and moralists; that new views must be opened out, that new inducements to moral effort must be brought forward, and better means of accomplishing the proposed result exhibited. Lessons in science and scientific theory are to be given, in order to bring out the truth that bears upon ethical feeling and conduct. Better conceptions of the essential nature of religion and art, and the true purposes of both will have to be presented. Socialism needs to be seen in a clearer light, and a more scientific character given to all its developments. Not least of all must be shown the necessity of discussion in an unselfish spirit, with sincere respect for opposed thought, and a willingness to learn equal to the desire to teach; of which I shall myself be held obligated to furnish an example. The ultimate purpose of the whole investigation is, through the achievement of the Unselfish Condition, to prepare the beginning of that Ideal Society which, as I shall hereafter show, is alike the object of the religionist and the secularist.

Of course this labor is very far from being an easy task for any one; the program is too large to be fully carried out in a short time, or with any proper completeness in a first attempt. Everything begins in the imperfect and advances toward the perfect. Some allowance for this necessary imperfection must be made by the reader in order to avoid disappointment. And as the same language probably means something slightly different to every different person, so long as words have to be used in different senses, it is well that this also should be taken into account.

Religion and Philosophy, Christian and other kinds alike, have continually failed to create and establish a condition of mind and of society like that here suggested. The same failure has attended the socialistic efforts of those who have depended only on a speculative or imperfect secular wisdom. And as both Religion and Speculation are losing instead of increasing their guiding power over mind, it becomes reasonable to expect that if such a mental and social state is ever to be reached, it will be through the aid of a more advanced and more comprehensive science.

I have said that either with or without a philosophy scientific truth would make progress, and that Ontology itself, like all other departments of knowledge, would probably in time take on a demonstrable and positive character. In reality a philosophy somewhat answering to this conception exists latent under the peculiar character of this book, and all its most original positions. It is a philosophy of oppositeness, but not in the main of antagonism; and has in it an unselfish quality that operates toward the harmonization of apparently antagonistic ideas. An illustration will aid in giving some conception of what is meant.

If we suppose an ignorant Arab from the torrid zone, and an equally ignorant Siberian from near the Arctic Circle to be taught a common language and brought together midway between their homes, in a place where they cannot see the outside world for reference, and these two should then set out to enlighten each other on points of astronomy and natural history, their statements would necessarily vary to the utmost extent; while as each knows of nothing beyond his own horizon, and can conceive of nothing beyond his own experience, there would be occasion for constant disputes. The Arab would tell how the sun rises suddenly out of the darkness, directly in the east, passes up directly overhead, and goes down directly in the west, when after a few minutes of twilight the day is succeeded by a night of nearly the same length as its own—twelve hours. The Siberian with astonishment asserts that he knows nothing of such days and nights, and cannot believe the story; on the contrary that the sun instead of passing up into the sky, goes round and round the horizon from left to right, a little above it in summer, and far below in winter; that the days in summer and nights in winter may be fifteen, twenty, or even twenty-four hours long, one after another; and that the twilight in spring and fall lasts nearly all night. He proceeds to tell of all the changes of the seasons, which to the other mean nothing, and when he speaks of the water frozen into hard ice which he travels upon or cuts up into blocks to build a hut with, this is altogether past belief and makes the man of the tropics lose all faith in his arctic brother. He too may talk of his tall palms, his camels, lions, and elephants, and the stranger birds that come to him in the coldest part of the year to go away in the warmer; while the arctic man will doubt the possibility of such trees and animals, and knowing that his strange birds come to him in warm weather to go away as it gets colder, he will naturally suspect his high-nosed friend to be a liar and fraud. The longer they talk the more fiercely they will assert and deny, ending with a very poor opinion of each other if not downright hatred; though each asserts only what he has seen, and has no intention of being dishonest at all.

To the scientist, who knows all the phenomena of both regions, and the additional fact, unknown to both disputants, that to every one alike, whether he stands at the equator or the pole, his head seems to be up and his feet down, when in reality the bodily axes at those points are perpendicular to each other—to him there is no occasion for dispute; the wholeness of knowledge renders everything consistent and harmonious. He further knows that the continually varying position of the earth in its orbit, along with the fixed direction of its axis, causes all the variation of appearances in the regions toward the poles, and the uniformity of season at the tropics. He sees a quality of oppositeness in the causes that produce, in the resulting physical effects, and in the men themselves, as well as in their views of the world. He could enable them to understand each other and be friends if they would acquire his knowledge, and enough experience of climates to appreciate the effects of heat and cold. Yet if he should say this to them they, in their ignorance, would be very likely to treat him also as a pretender, full of ignorant conceit. And as I should be liable to a similar suspicion were I to assert that all real disputes, as well as this imaginary one, can be settled and harmonized by sufficient experience and a wholeness of knowledge in those who differ, I shall refrain from such assertion, and go no farther than to state that a similar philosophy is behind a large part of what is put forth in the chapters that follow.

The general subject of the whole series will appropriately be *The Kingdom of The Unselfish*. And as the unselfish state is no less a wise one, the same domain is also *The Empire of The Wise*. It may not be amiss to say further that these productions have no connection with any existing sect, party or ism, any society or organization whatever, except that universal social organism into which every one is born, and from which no one naturally wishes to become entirely isolated. They are addressed, as all scientific truth should be, to every one alike, regardless of external name or condition, who has the ability and willingness to think and learn.

CHAPTER II.

THE EVOLUTION OF MORALITY.

IN what I have to say upon the general subject of this book I prefer to use the old and common English words *selfish* and *unselfish* to distinguish two great classes of actions and motives, in preference to the Latin ones *egoism* and *altruism*, often used by late writers, or *natural* and *spiritual* as used by the religious world. There is little difference in the meaning of the three sets of terms; but the last is not fully understood by all, while egoism and altruism are still less familiar. *Moral* and *immoral* are hardly comprehensive enough even if the religious and irreligious understood them alike. *Social* and *unsocial* might answer if confined to their highest significance; while *consciencious* and *unconsciencious*, as describing conduct or feeling dictated by the highest conceptions of right or duty, and that which is not, would be still more allowable; for one of these would include consciencious selfishness, and the other unconsciencious, that is, blind, impulsive, inconsiderate benevolence. At times I may have to use any or all of these; but the first pair will convey my meaning most clearly to the generality of minds.

Selfish and *unselfish* are however to be enlarged, or broadened out so as to include under one or the other every kind of human conduct; for though there is action or inaction that is justifiably selfish, there is scarcely any that is entirely indifferent.

These terms are applied to human feelings as well as conduct; and it must first be pointed out which feelings are to be called selfish and which unselfish. Moreover, some of them are unselfish when compared with those below them in grade, while selfish relating to those of higher or later development.

The phrenologists have given us a map of the skull on which they locate all the different feelings and faculties, and this is well adapted for my purpose. Though I do not attach any great value to Phrenology as science, yet there is a connection between the base of the brain and the animal instincts, and a similar connection of the top of the head with the moral and the higher intellectual capacities—capacities only however, not actual dispositions or attainments. These two facts, and the additional one that everybody knows something of the nomenclature, render the system convenient for illustration.

Beginning now at the base of the head, we find the instinctive love of life, the appetite for food and drink, the propagating instinct, the propensity to combat and destroy, and the desire to accumulate; all these being purely selfish. Conscienciousness, benevolence, magnanimity, aspiration, at the top-head, are in their nature equally unselfish. Then, between these in their location on the chart, are a number that are intermediate also in character. Here first are the domestic or family feelings, the affection for husband or wife, for children, relatives and friends. The regard for these is unselfish as compared with the solitary individual's regard for himself alone; and some thinkers have held the possession of a family to be the first thing necessary toward making a person unselfish in his whole character. But when we compare a woman's regard for her own *children* with her consideration for those of another woman, we see, in ordinary cases, that the feeling is still partially selfish. It is her own whom she not only loves best, which is entirely natural and proper, but to whom she gives the preference in every respect, and by whom her judgment is warped, and her conduct biased into partiality, contrary to the dictates of pure conscience, whenever any antagonism arises between these and others. There is a higher feeling, however, which loves *justice*, and would consider the rights of a stranger child as much as those of her own; and compared to this the natural love of offspring is selfish. So with the affection for relatives or other friends. The person who has friends and can sacrifice something for them is unselfish in contrast with a person who has none, and no willingness to deny self any convenience, comfort, or pleasure for the sake of another. But when the friend and the stranger have conflicting interests the friendly feeling prompts to prefer that of the friend, whether his claim be just or unjust. Contrasted with that strict regard for the rights and interests of the stranger which a love of *justice* demands, the friendly feeling is yet a selfish one. We sometimes hear a family or set of relatives called *clannish*, as a term of reproach, because all their sympathies are confined to themselves; which shows that most people recognize the distinction here made.

The same thing is true concerning *patriotism*. The love of country is an unselfish impulse beside that of the family, and still more so beside the clannishness of relatives, or the regard for friends. Most Americans who have reached middle age have realized the truth of this. But there is a *cosmopolitan* feeling, a consideration for the well-being of other nations; a willingness to see a possible friend in the foreigner; a disposition to discover the good qualities of all races of men; an ability to see when our own country is in the wrong, and to restrain it at the sacrifice of patriotic pride. This higher sentiment comes from love of justice and humanity. In comparison with it we must say that the patriotic impulse, like the others mentioned, is still selfish to a degree.

Let no one understand me to say that these intermediate feelings are not virtues, or that the lowest and primary ones are not. In their natural functions, guided by sufficient intelligence, and controlled by a wise conscience, every one of them is a virtue and entitled to profound respect. It is only when they are blind, unguided, unrestrained, and discordant that they are anything else. To those already named we may add Approbativeness, or love of fame, rank and popularity; Ambition, the desire for official place and power; and Independence or love of liberty, without which scarcely any virtue at all is possible. All of these are selfish, yet all may be so directed as to operate wholly toward social well-being; and in the complete human development this becomes their only action. In other words they all finally become unselfish.

But considering them as they now are, and to complete the definition of my terms, I must say that all crime, vice, and immorality are selfish or the result of selfishness. Also the blunders of ignorance or carelessness, in effect equal to crimes; and the degrading benevolence, the persecutions and uncharitableness of zealous but unwise goodness; for with a slight exception of unavoidable accident, all such *undesigned* offences come from a state of mind which is too lazy, thoughtless, or indifferent to learn what it needs to know, or too obstinately conceited and self-righteous to be willing to see any fault in itself; both of which feelings are of the purely selfish class. And to all the rest must be added that *apparent* morality or goodness that is prompted only by a selfish motive.

In the opposite category are included all the higher

OF MORALITY

virtues in feeling and action; all that is just, benevolent, and generous; all high aspiration or religiosity; all genuine morality; all true politeness; all consciencious self-criticism; all faithfulness to duty and to high ideals; everything that is pure and holy; last but not least, all candid, faithful, earnest thought and sincere willingness to learn. In all these there is the one common characteristic of a regard for the happiness of others.

It will be observed that I attach importance to that vice and that virtue which is connected with the intellect. Indeed there is good reason for believing it no less important than that which concerns the feelings.

There is a doctrine which claims all unselfishness to be selfish; but if true it brings a new meaning into the word, and breaks up all present conceptions of the nature of the things represented. I pay no attention to it at present because for my purpose it is better to use language in its ordinary sense as much as possible.

I will now ask attention to some thoughts upon the *origin* of moral or unselfish feeling.

Society of some kind and in some degree has existed as long as man has existed—nay, longer, much longer than that. Every ant-hill, beehive, and hornets-nest is an instance of society. Every school of fishes, every flock of birds, every burrow of prairie dogs, every herd of wild cattle, is drawn together by the gregarious instinct or social tendency; and even if without any organization, it still exhibits the first stage of the organizing process—the gathering of the materials, out of which different parts, having different social functions, are ultimately, in higher races, to be formed. Every pair that mate and bring up their young in the seclusion of a single family yet manifest more or less of the gregarious feeling. In fact the only way this feeling can be suppressed is by the individual's living entirely alone, like a spider in its den or a solitary hermit in his cave.

Society then is very old, has been very long in process of evolution, and yet its highest form is far from perfection; though many facts indicate that the more advanced part of it will before long step across that boundary line which separates the present imperfect from the beginning of the perfect stage.

But let us inquire what is implied by living in society; that is, what desires or considerations must exist in order to create and continue the social existence. These are of two classes; first, there is the gregarious instinct or love of company, the original motive that impels to society, and entirely selfish in its character. In addition there are various *advantages*, both material and mental, coming to the individual from the exchange of services and products, and the interchange of thought and feeling. These are also selfish considerations. On the other hand there must be some regard for the rights, welfare, or pleasure of the parties exchanged with, and this is the unselfish or moral consideration. Without this moral consideration trade becomes robbery, through deception, fraud, or extortion from the unfortunate; love becomes licentious; friendship treacherous; the communication of ideas untruthful. The lowest clan of savages finds it necessary that something of individual preference should be given up for the benefit of the rest, or the safety of all. When there is a common danger each must fight or suffer for and with the others. In building the common house each family must be respected and allowed its separate apartment. The individual gives up some of his wishes for the sake of the family or tribe; the family or tribe in return gives him a certain amount of assistance or protection. Each and all gain something by the coöperation.

So with animals. The herd of wild horses combine to

protect their weaker members from the common enemy; wolves go in packs to attack their common prey. Even with only two there is still combined effort; one must guard the home while the other hunts their food, each doing its share and respecting the rights of the other.

With both animals and man the unsocial or immoral individual—the one who fails to do his duty—is cast out or exterminated. Ants and bees expel the one who will not work, larger animals kick the offender to death or tear him in pieces. Monkeys cuff and scold their young ones as unmercifully as though they were fully human, for their childish offences. Men resort to vigilance committees, lynch law, exile, imprisonment and execution. If the offence is serious the offender is killed; if light he may escape with a more moderate punishment. Animals and savages have little regard for a due *proportion* between the crime and the retribution; civilized societies attempt by law to make them more nearly equal.

We can now begin to see that morality or consideration for others is the social quality *par excellence*; that which makes society possible; that without which it could not subsist. With outward circumstances that favor or compel the development of it a society grows and prospers— becomes strong, flourishing and happy. With circumstances that favor or compel immorality—a regard for self only—the society becomes weak, poor, corrupt, and unhappy, the victim of discord, anarchy, strife and crime, till completely destroyed. All the large civilized societies of antiquity weakened and were destroyed for want of morality. All of the old societies of the East, except one, are now in a dying condition for the same reason. Morality is to the social body what vital force is to the animal system; it is its life, its very heart's blood. It is that which enables it to resist unwholesome influences and continue its existence. The analogy of the two things is complete; whatever is true of one is true of the other. Morality and unselfishness will also as we proceed be more plainly seen to be one.

To understand further the progress of society and the evolution of its moral life-power, we must remember that the human child, whether savage or civilized, is born with a nature wholly selfish, having the instincts that prompt it to feed and take care of itself, like any other young animal; but with none that prompt unselfish action, and no power of thought to see the necessity of it. All the unselfishness he ever acquires he must gain as his intellect unfolds, as his parents, teachers, or books instruct him, and as the moral ability strengthens by the unfaltering habit of doing unselfish things under this tutelage. He may, it is true, inherit a better *capacity* for acquiring moral strength than his ancestors were born with, as he may a similar intellectual capacity; but this is only a superior structure of brain, not an endowment of actual feeling or thought. And teaching alone, that is, teaching of the dogmatic and didactic style has no effect. He may be told what is right or wrong because God says so, in the usual Sunday-school manner, a thousand times a year and it amounts to nothing. He might as well be sprinkled three times a day with cold water. He needs to understand the *reason* for every moral requirement—*why* it is right or wrong, through its good or bad effects upon human happiness. He needs to see these effects all traced out in plain relief, in every direction. He needs to see the beauty of holiness in his mind's eye, not merely to hear it spoken of. He should know something of the nature of society and of his own nature, with the effect of feeling and conduct upon the soul. And with all the superior excellence of the moral standard in his *reason* as well as memory, he must at the same time be encouraged, urged, induced into the habitual *practice* of unselfish conduct, to enable him to realize its excellence in his own experience, and make the habit more and more easy as he goes on in his life course. Thus he gains a moral character of which by nature he had not even a germ,—only a capability.

Now, the savage man when full grown is still only the selfish child in intellect, with the stronger passions belonging to a man's body. He must go through the same course of intellectual and moral outgrowth the civilized child does, before he is capable of living in orderly society. In one lifetime he gets but very little of it; and a hundred generations are required to give him the moral endowment possessed by the child of civilization at maturity. This will help to explain why the savage or barbarous man, like the child, forms weak social ties; why his combinations with his fellows are small and do not last long; why he quarrels and fights on slight provocation; why his selfish nature, with little of the unselfish to counteract it, is suspicious, jealous, petulant, fickle, treacherous, tyrannical, arrogant, insolent, cruel, revengeful, and when highly excited, murderous. When undisturbed he is happy, careless, friendly and playful. All these characteristics are present in greater or less degree, in the untrained child and half-grown boy. We can see them any day, if not in our own children certainly in others. And if we will try to imagine what kind of society a clan of ten-year-old children in a wilderness would form, what troubles and difficulties they would have in organizing it, in keeping it from falling to pieces, and in protecting it from childish enemies all around them, we shall get some idea of what the savage and barbarous man has had to meet and overcome in all parts of the world. We shall understand why dissensions and wars have broken up and destroyed all he could accomplish, time after time; and what an infinite amount of human suffering it has cost to obtain any society such as we would now consider worth having at all.

Bearing in mind then that man at first is wholly selfish, let us endeavor to trace out some of the steps by which during his long career he became less and less selfish, and more and more positively unselfish, moral, or social. If we follow these successfully up to the present time, we shall probably be able to obtain a fair view of what the future society is to be, and what its moral requirements. In succeeding chapters attention will be given to this; at present I will only try to show how the savage and selfish man has arrived at such a moral growth that he can organize and continue the existing grade of civilized society.

Let it be carefully observed at the outset that moral capacity, the ability to be moral or unselfish, has two causes, one of an intellectual character, the other the habit of self-sacrifice. The intellect perceives the necessity or advantage of moral action, the greater happiness to be secured by it, the rightfulness or propriety of it for that purpose; while the habit of *giving up* minor and temporary personal desires or preferences comes at length to make such sacrifice easy. The inheritance of an improved brain-structure is an aid. Finally the intellectual element reaches and includes that high conception of right and duty which requires an apparent total forgetfulness of self, in entire devotion to the noblest ideal of unselfish feeling and conduct. How it does so will appear more plainly in the next chapter. Here, briefly, the statement is that one moral element is habit, the other a perception of high ideals.

The first form of organized human society we know is the gens or clan, having for its head a woman, and consisting of her female descendants with their husbands and small children, to a number as large as can find food within a convenient distance. When it becomes too numerous it separates into two or more clans taking different names or totems.

This clan lives by hunting and fishing, with perhaps a little agriculture, as do the lower tribes of American Indians. The members find it necessary to live in groups to protect themselves against wild animals. Here is one class of enemies already existing around them; and for each one to preserve his own life he must think of the others, and help them in order to obtain their help for himself. Instead of each one's taking to his legs when danger appears, two or more must stand together against the common enemy. The blind selfish impulse to seek safety in flight is controlled and subordinated to a more far-sighted purpose of killing the enemy, by which others are benefitted as well as self.

Here at the beginning we have a true type of the whole process of moral evolution. Every virtue, of whatever name, has its genesis in a similar manner, and from the influence of the same considerations. In every case there is a larger view of the benefits to be ultimately gained, and for which present selfish impulses are controlled and selfish purposes sacrificed. Habit and heredity finally make the moral feeling strong enough to act without thought; but primarily the intellect must present the inducement. We shall see it illustrated as we proceed.

The members of the gens find it necessary further, to do for each other a *variety* of services. If one can chip out a flint hatchet more perfectly than the rest, *they* will do his share of hunting in order that he may work for them. It is the same with the one who can make the best spears, arrows, baskets, or pottery; and this is a beginning in the division of labor and the development of trades. Each one gradually finds out what part of the family's work he can do best, and does it while others work for him. But this exchange of services or products gives rise to friendly feelings. Having found profit in one kind of exchange we are inclined to another. If there is no unusual cause for repugnance, we feel well-disposed toward one with whom we exchange services, goods, or ideas; and this leads to a liking for his company. The feeling grows with the continued habit of exchanging with, or doing for, each other, and with the importance of that which is given or received. Old soldiers who have braved the dangers of battle together, and helped each other through perilous situations, seem never to forget their friendship. So with sailors, hunters, and explorers, who together have met the dangers of the sea or the wilderness.

Friendship, or the disposition to be friendly, which the savage man thus develops, must certainly be classed as one of the virtues. It sweetens all the intercourse of life, thus adding a great deal to human happiness. In every way it tends to make society more successful and more perfect. A due regard for the welfare of all around us will decide that it ought to be cultivated as a moral quality, and a stepping stone toward those of higher grade.

But the tie of *kinship*, the natural tie between parent and child, brother and sister—is it not this, some may enquire, that makes the clan friendly and well-disposed, rather than the exchange of services? On the contrary, the position I shall have to take is that exchange of service is what has made the feeling of kinship itself. The primitive gens is made up of only one half the natural descendants, all the males having married into, and been adopted by, other and comparatively stranger gentes. And although of the same original blood, and similar degrees of kinship, the feeling between them is not the same as between the members of the same gens, as is proved by the fact that feuds spring up between them, and may make them enemies. Besides, we see among ourselves that brothers and sisters separated in childhood, and growing up in different localities or circumstances, have little of the sympathy that unites those who have grown up happily together; and would probably feel none at all but for the idea always impressed upon them that they must—that it is natural they should. Even when separated after maturity, if they have no communication—no exchange of services, ideas, or feelings—for years, the family feeling dies out to a great degree, they become virtually strangers; only with the same vague impression on their minds that some natural reason exists for their being friends. In the animal world the mother's love for offspring disappears as soon as the young are able to take care of themselves. Although humanity has always had this idea of something sacred about kinship, the only reason that appears for it is the fact that everywhere society has begun with some kind of family—some group having the same ancestors. Their friendliness has been ascribed to blood, when in reality it is due to the coöperation and mutual service compelled by circumstances.

Out of the primitive barter, and its resulting friendliness, has come the sentiment of gratitude. From perceiving the necessity of giving one thing or service for another, and expecting it, it is an easy step for one to perceive the *propriety* of so doing, and to feel conscious that it ought to be the rule—that if another has done more for him than was previously paid for *he* ought to do something more in return. This is the beginning of both gratitude and justice.

But some may question if the savage man is capable of feeling gratitude. I reply without hesitation that he is. I doubt if there is any one so low or unprogressed that he cannot intellectually perceive that a favor done him gives the doer a right to expect an equal favor from him, and feel disposed to make the return. The wildest of the American Indians have proved this many a time, and so have others in all stages of savagery and barbarism. To understand that such feeling does not imply civilization or high development, we need only to look at half-civilized Christian Europe in the Middle Ages, and down to the seventeenth century. A feeling of religious gratitude made men intensely pious, but did not prevent their being comparatively unsympathetic; reckless, and immoral in their treatment of each other; utterly cruel to heretics and victims of delusion; and fiendish toward the heathens of Africa and America. If we look for anything more inhuman among savages we shall fail to find it; yet gratitude in some degree was one of the commonest feelings they possessed.

The family or clan however, though disposed to be friendly, will unavoidably have its quarrels. As it has already learned the advantage of living together, the group must be preserved, and this necessitates having some kind of arbitration to settle the difficulties. To submit to it requires that each contestant give up something of his selfish preference, and so the spirit of *compromise* begins to be learned. The old man, woman, or council that judges the case must likewise learn a moral lesson; for to make a decision acceptable and permanent there must be some elements of justice in it; and this the judge or arbitrator must not only perceive, but must put aside any personal preference for a contestant that stands in the way of a just decision. Thus, in another way, the idea of justice or impartiality gets a foothold in the general mind of the primitive society.

When the increase of population in the related groups compels them to crowd upon the domain of some other tribe, or another tribe upon theirs, then there must be a *union* of the clans, their little feuds must be adjusted or suppressed, and a war-chief or leader agreed upon, in spite of conflicting ambitions and claims. If they succeed in inducing or compelling the various antagonists to sacrifice their personal aspirations or revenges they can probably hold their ground or conquer a new one. Possibly they accomplish their purposes nearly as well as trades unions, political rings, or Irish combinations do theirs in our own times. Sometimes they unite and maintain their union, sometimes they fail. If they live in a location where subsistence is difficult to obtain, where their wits have been sharpened in the effort to get it, where they have been compelled to make sacrifices habitually, and help each other in all ways in order to live at all, then the probability is that they will be able to maintain their union and become conquerors. If their home is a locality where game and fish are abundant and agriculture easy, where less sacrifice of selfishness is required, then the selfish impulses are likely to be too strong for successful union, and they become the prey of the party having the strongest moral feeling, that is, the most *faithfulness* to each other. Subordination and fidelity in this case are *moral*, insubordination the worst immorality.

What has been stated regarding the gens or clan is substantially true in regard to the *patriarchal* family, of nomadic or roving tribes in the barbaric stage. The superior position which the father holds over his own family is by a natural tendency extended over those of his children and grand-children till his death, or till the the group becomes too large. The patriarch becomes teacher, leader, governor and judge. Deference and subordination to him is by the intellect found necessary or most advisable in carrying out the family's mode of life; and so *filial piety* comes to be demanded, encouraged, and praised as the prime virtue. Whatever selfishness is opposed to the patriarch's authority has to be sacrificed, as an habitual practice; while the influences favoring the filial sentiment gradually develop *it* into strength. And the mild despotism of the patriarch is so well adapted to his people and their life that after his death he often becomes an object of worship.

Later on in the process of social evolution comes the organization of clans or families into a tribe, or of tribes into a confederacy or government; which will be more or less republican if the tribes retain their original liberty, more or less despotic if continual war has kept them under control of chiefs. Progress in agriculture, and the partial development of trades favor the building of a *city*, which shall be the central home of the confederacy or tribe. Now comes into existence the new virtue of *patriotism*. Without this the city and the permanent location cannot be maintained against enemies, always ready to conquer and rob if possible. The necessity for public spirit is readily perceived, and causes popular opinion to require it. To satisfy public sentiment, and secure his own self-respect, for he has by this time become conscious of the nobility of unselfish action, the individual gives up some of his personal rights, property and comfort, and risks his life to defend the common home of his people. Habit, inheritance, and the ideal of duty held up to the young, tend to strengthen the sentiment in succeeding generations. The Latin tribes seem to have possessed more of this virtue than any other of the ancients known to us, and their superior morality in this respect did much to give Rome the dominion of the world.

In more modern times, when the settled monarchies of Europe came to take place of the anarchy caused by the perpetual wars and robberies of feudal chiefs and rival cities, another virtue springs up, that of *loyalty* to the king, and to his family or dynasty. The king now represents peace, order, safety, law, prosperity and civilization. Loyalty to him is demanded by the intellect, which sees the necessity of it to preserve the new and better state of things. Necessity produces it as necessity produced patriotism. In addition to his intellect, all the better feelings the man has already acquired prompt him to make temporary sacrifices, and risk his life for his king. The loyalty of the Scotch people to the Stuarts two hundred and fifty years ago is still sung by their descendants, and still awakens admiration for "all the noble martyrs who died for loyaltie."

King and country—loyalty and patriotism—sometimes came to be associated together; and thus a double inducement or pressure was brought upon a man to cause a sacrifice of selfish interests for his fatherland. Looking over the history of the race, it is easy to see where nations have conquered and lived by virtue of their patriotism, or loyalty, or both, while others for lack of such qualities have succumbed to the stronger and died. The fittest have survived in the general struggle, because for purposes of society it is the moral quality that gives fitness and strength.

In the near future is to arise that still higher or more unselfish sentiment of *Cosmopolitanism* already referred to, which takes the world for its country, and has been well called "the patriotism of humanity." It will not antagonize the welfare of one's native country, ours for instance, because the more a nation has of it the better it will be loved by all other countries, the more secure its peace, prosperity and honor; as surely so as that an unselfish person is more sure of being loved, honored, trusted, blessed, than a greedy, grasping, selfish one. Contrast the present hatred of all the Eastern world, Africa, India, China, Japan, toward England and France, with their feeling toward America, and one can easily see what it means. Not that we need be self-righteous. In our old brutal slavery days we murdered the Indian tribes, and we robbed Mexico. Yet within the next few years the new, regenerated America will be likely to make Mexico and all the Central and South

American states our firm friends. And the feeling that aspires to do this is Cosmopolitanism.*

We will now go back to the starting-point, and see what other influences are acting upon man to develop unselfish feeling. That which we have been considering is the action of the social body—the gens, family, tribe, or nation—upon the individual. Besides this there is the effect wrought by religion. Religion, so far as scientists have agreed to any definition of it, is the belief in spiritual beings and action in reference to such beings. Primarily it is regard for the spirit of some ancestor or chief; and the only sacrifice it requires is that of a few articles of personal property put in his grave, and some little attention in the way of food and drink afterward. As the chief or patriarch becomes a more important personage his horse, dog, arms, and everything needed for his life in the spirit world is given up by his relatives. These being the most valuable things a barbarian has, we may suppose it requires some little conquest of selfish interest at first to relinquish them. In the case of every private man there is somewhat of the same surrender of property, and supply of food for a considerable time. Even the man's hut is with some tribes given up to his ghost, and scarcely anything of his property is left to be inherited. In other cases when chiefs die women and slaves are put to death to bear them company; but as woman is a slave, and slaves are of little greater value than animals, the loss is of the same kind mainly, not a loss to the affections. It is only when a human

---

* The above was written previous to the last presidential election canvass, during which a bill for the exclusion of the Chinese from this country was with brutal haste pushed through a Democratic House of Representatives, and allowed to become law by the cowardice of a Republican Senate, a law which however right in its design to exclude Chinese coolies, was passed in such an insolent manner as to almost certainly turn the good will of China into hatred. And the votes for which this brutality was exhibited, and this cowardice, were those of the very lowest class of the voting population.

victim from the ruling race is demanded to appease the anger of some mighty god that the loss is severely felt. Then the victim is given up as a necessity, with the same motive and purpose with which thousands of American families and neighborhoods gave up a son, brother, or neighbor to the necessities of war twenty-five years ago. The common good, the safety of the nation or tribe, seems to require that some individual lose everything. A greater danger, or more angry deity might call for the lives of a score or a hecatomb instead of one.

It will be very natural here for some one to inquire, "Can such savage religion as this have anything to do with morality? Is any sense of justice, mercy, or good will cultivated by such sacrifices?" No, nothing of justice, mercy, or kindness, but of duty and *generosity*. Is any moral feeling involved in the sacrifices demanded by war? No mercy, no justice, no benevolence, but the generosity or unselfishness of putting aside our individual good for the good of the whole. Or, it might be called an unselfish *endurance*. I can see no difference in the situations, nor in the feelings called out by the action. To the barbarian his religion is a most real thing. *He* never loses faith in the existence of his deity; and he has no better way of accounting for misfortune than to suppose his god sends it, in punishment for his lack of duty, in not making previous sacrifices for the god's benefit or pleasure. The ignorant Christian religionist of to-day has the same view and the same feeling. What is claimed is that the effort made in reconciling ones-self to the sacrifice is a *moral* effort; that every such effort, when successful, renders a succeeding effort less difficult, till the giving up of selfish impulses may become habitual and easy. Then by heredity the following generation is endowed with a brain better adapted to an unselfish course of life. Through these moral efforts the individual comes more into harmony with his deity and his fellows, is conscious of their sympathy and good will, and further, is sensible of having reached a higher grade of development, where moral action of any kind is easier to him than before. This is moral growth—growth toward social harmony and fitness for society. The spiritual view of things is used as the inducement or pressure, instead of the material, but the result is the same.

To make the process more familiar let us observe what takes place among ourselves, under Christian religion of the highest form. Here the church, cathedral, or chapel is built, furnished and supported by the contributions of the sect; and it often involves a painful subjugation of the love of property. In some cases it takes from the poorest class of our population a large proportion of their spare earnings. And I have seen the tears come into a poor man's eyes, when called upon to pay five dollars toward the support of a little Protestant church in a country village. The money sacrifice is not often as great as this, but it is of the same kind; and the moral power gained by the habit of making it is the power of doing one's duty, not only to the church, but to the state and to his neighbor. I am far from saying, however, that there is any morality in making large demands for this kind of sacrifice.

There are many things in the line of self-denial that religion has required or encouraged, most of them favoring morality, no doubt, but many others of which it can only be said that if they develop morality the morality itself is of a merely negative kind, and of little value. Of this latter sort is the whole class of practices known as asceticism—all attempts to escape the influence of the selfish instincts by oppressing and mortifying the body; or by hiding away from temptation in deserts, caves, and monasteries. There is moral effort in asceticism; probably all the individual is capable of making; but taken together this class of actions have the appearance of being cowardly, of being efforts to evade the conflict with selfishness and evil, or to fight a part of the battle and escape the rest. Yet some of those who have taken the ascetic method have been heroes. It was, and still is, really a misdirected struggle. It is like a man's killing his unruly horse because he doesn't know how to conquer and train him to make him useful. Asceticism tries, by abusing the body, or depriving the natural impulses of their natural gratification, to starve them to death, and thus avoid all further trouble of fighting them. It is a policy of ignorance, and so far as successful creates only negative goodness by removing temptation, through partial destruction of the lower half of man's nature. It adds but little positive strength to his higher part.

Religion is still ascetic to some extent, and must continue to be so as long as the natural man is looked upon as necessarily antagonistic to the spiritual. To the ordinary churchman his selfish animal nature is still like the ignorant man's unruly horse; as yet he has scarcely conceived the possibility of its acting the part of the well-trained, well-used animal, giving loyal and willing service in return for gentle treatment and loving care.

The best type of the moral conflict is the physical warfare of the soldier, and his gain of courage by successive victories. The successful fight gives him additional strength and confidence for the next, and this makes the superiority of the veteran. Successive defeats are said to *de*moralize him, that is to lessen or take away his soldierly virtues of courage and determination. Moral strength and courage are gained or lost in precisely the same manner; not by shunning the world and its temptations, but by meeting and manfully overcoming them. In analogy with the soldier's warfare too, there must be prudence, watchfulness, tact, strategy, and combinations of forces, along with determination and confidence, in order to secure victory. The rashness of over-confidence, the belittling of the enemy, and the attempt to do a strong man's work with a child's power, will defeat, demoralize, and degrade. As an illustration, see how difficult it is for a drunkard to keep his pledge of abstinence after he has broken it once. Each succeeding time he gives way easier and sooner, till at last all hope, courage and strength are gone.

The ceremonials and liturgies of religion have a certain use in keeping up a slight habitual religious feeling, but do not add to the moral strength. Such efforts may appeal to the moral power already possessed, and perhaps call it all out if necessary; but as no new conflict is required, there is no exercise of moral force beyond what is habitual. It is like giving the muscular system a certain amount of moderate exercise at regular intervals to keep it in its usual condition—nothing more.

There is, however, in the later forms of Protestantism a method of rousing the whole moral power to fight a new battle with certain forms of sins and selfishness. I refer to what goes on in revivals. In these religion brings into use all its influence, and performs its greatest work toward the moralization of humanity. It acts upon the individual to draw out whatever good impulses he may possess, in struggling for a purpose acknowledged by him to be the highest he knows. It sets before his intellect the strongest inducement it can offer, in the promise of future happiness if he succeeds, and the strongest impulsion also in the threat of eternal misery if he fails. It thus seeks to inspire the greatest moral effort he can make. In some cases this is so successful that the more prominent forms of selfishness or sin the person is conscious of are conquered; and he then takes the largest step toward a moralized life that religion can aid him to take. From this highest result there are all degrees of improvement down to that which can hardly be observed, and is of no permanence. The effort may result in failure as often as in success; for the revivalist leader calls upon every one to make it, the feeble as well as the strong, those who by youth, thoughtlessness and inexperience, or poor hereditary endowment are totally incapable, as well as those who by previous culture have arrived at sufficient moral growth to balance their selfish tendencies. Spite of errors in the management, however, it is certain that in many cases the effort stimulated by revivals accomplishes a new and decided advance in the soul's upward progress.

Here I shall have to make some statements dogmatically, asking attention to them nevertheless, as they will be made or implied a number of times hereafter; but leaving the reader to decide what amount of credit they ought to receive.

When, under favorable conditions and wise direction, the moral development goes on in a natural way—when each victory over self gives increased strength and courage for another conflict—the moral power gets control of one after another of the selfish impulses, habits and propensities, till at last it comes to a trial with the strongest one of all, the easily-besetting sin, the incorrigible habit, the ruling passion of the natural man, which Swedenborg well calls his "life." If defeated now the moral force retires, perhaps temporarily, perhaps for a long, sad rest and recuperation, perhaps so far that it loses nearly all and must go again through its minor conflicts. But if successful, then the final, decisive victory is won; the stronghold of the whole selfish nature is subdued; there remain only short and easy battles with the remnants of the hostile force; and then sets in a final and lasting peace, a peace that can never again be seriously disturbed, a holy calm, a solemn but joyful rest, a never-ceasing satisfaction in the achievement of the grandest work possible to a human life; and from the assurance, felt to be perfect beyond all possibility of doubt or suspicion, that the soul is saved, that no serious sin or immorality can ever again touch it for harm, that its happiness is secure for all its future conscious existence.

Now, does any form of religion ever effect this result? To some the question may seem a strange one. But in reality does the Christian ever get *permanently* where he can *never doubt* his salvation? While conversion is new he may have no doubts; and some persons believe in the possible attainment of what they call "perfection," through the constant aid of an outside spiritual influence. Even if these few be confident I am free to say they cannot be *sure*, for this to me very good reason, that they do not know *all* that is required of them in order to be fully freed from sin. I venture to say to them that they still adhere to forms of selfishness of which they are unconscious, and some, quite possibly, that it will take a harder struggle to cast out than they have ever yet made; but which struggle they must sometime pass through, before they become fit for a perfect society, either on earth or in the skies. No one can know positively that he has reached that point which is the turning point in his whole career, till in obedience to duty he has sacrificed that which is dearer to him than all else except continued existence. Nor even then can he be sure he does not mistake his feelings till he has learned the full extent of the final demand to be made upon him, a demand such as the church has not put forth in modern times if ever. Therefore I repeat that no Christian has attained that degree of moral perfection, that stage of self-conquest which ensures his everlasting safety, which fits him for an angelic society, and enables him to inaugurate a Kingdom of God on earth. Having it he would already have done this very thing. The fact that neither the regenerate nor the unregenerate, so called,—neither the religious nor the unreligious—have ever been able to achieve any high state of happiness, anything comparable to the ideal Kingdom of Heaven on Earth, is sufficient proof that the point in view has never been gained.

That it may be apprehended more clearly, and comprehended more fully, what this point is, what the state of mind consequent on reaching it, and the character of a society resulting from the union of persons in that state, some aspect of the whole compound thing will be explained and illustrated as each different subject is taken up in the chapters to follow.

CHAPTER III.

THE EVOLUTION OF MORALITY

Continued.

IT was described in the previous chapter how mutual service generated *friendship*. *Kindness* has the same origin. It is toward those with whom we have had some pleasant association, or in whom we discover some good or pleasant quality, mental or physical—something capable of giving us pleasure or service—that primarily we are disposed to have good will. It is toward such persons the natural man, the barbarian, or the child, feels disposed to be kind, and willing to do something that will confer pleasure or benefit. It is the opposite class, the repulsive ones, those from whom we can expect nothing of pleasure or advantage, that naturally we consider objects of malevolence, dislike, or at least indifference. Unconsciously the mind reasons that in one case kindness will attract what we desire, or aid us to obtain it; in the other case that unkindness will repel what we dislike or fear.

It is toward persons of the first class that the feeling of *sympathy* first arises; we feel regret at their pain, and pleasure in their happiness. The child shows sympathy with its mother, and a few others who care for it, long before it manifests any for those outside the family. Indeed some persons grow up before they get beyond this primary stage. So a merchant, if he hears of a flood, fire, or other misfortune outside his own locality, and remembers that some of the sufferers are his customers, his sympathies are aroused more strongly than if they be entire strangers. So likewise in the street-car politeness, about which we see frequent jokes in the newspapers. A man may offer his seat to a woman of his own race, color, or condition, from sympathy, not gallantry, when he would not to one of a different race or class; because the first he is familiar with, by exchange of courtesies and ideas, if not property, every day; whereas with the stranger class he does nothing or very little of this kind. There is something of friendship mixed with kindness in many of these cases, but the noticeable point is that there is a *selfishness* connected with the kindly feeling; that it manifests only toward those from whom we are in the habit of *receiving* something for our own benefit or pleasure, that is, trade, care, friendship or courtesy. But now, as acquaintance widens, as trade becomes extended, as rapid and easy travel enables us to see more of the world; and more especially as knowledge makes us familiar with the modes of life and character of foreign peoples; in short, as we get *acquainted* to some extent with all humanity, the kindly feeling takes in other families, communities, and classes than those we knew at first. Intellectually we come to perceive that all these are human, like those we know familiarly; all are alike capable of suffering or enjoyment; and though we have no exchange with them except as an imagined possibility, sympathy gradually and unconsciously extends till it becomes an *unselfish* quality, feeling for the welfare of those from whom we receive nothing, as well as for those who give to and take from us, occasionally or all the time.

In this manner, as I conceive, has arisen a sympathy, a kindness, a benevolence which, unlike its first manifestations, is at last wholly unselfish in purpose; giving to those who can make no return; doing service to those who will not respond even with thanks; laboring for the child, the stranger, the poor, the insane, idiotic or criminal, the abused horse, dog or wild animal, and the unborn generations of the future. There is an additional cause however, for these higher exhibitions of the feeling, to be explained farther on.

This is one of the highest of the unselfish feelings; a second one is the love of *justice*. Now, the sense of justice is one of the very first of the moral sentiments to be evolved. Scarcely anything can be done, even in the simplest kinds of coöperation without suggesting the idea of it, and making a demand for it in practice. *Justice* means *equality*, except when applied to vindictiveness; and even here it implies something like an equality of suffering—a punishment proportional to the offense committed, or a satisfaction to the injured person in taking his revenge, as a compensation for the wrong suffered. In all other cases the idea is without question that of equality. An equality of rights in all that belongs to the family or clan, an equal share in the game caught or killed by united effort, an equal claim to be protected by the chief, patriarch or governor,—these are ideas so simple hardly any savage brain could fail to evolve them. A personal claim to his weapons, tools, or whatever he can make for himself, or conquer from his enemy by his own efforts, is a like simple conception no one can be obtuse enough to deny. The same reasoning that justifies his title to the cattle he has raised gives him a claim to own the *children* he has fed and cared for, or the *wife* he has bought from her parents, or stolen from a stranger tribe. When he comes to be an agriculturist the land occupied by the gens is assumed to belong to every man equally, that is, the use of it; while no one supposes he can acquire a title to it absolutely. The right of the next generation to use it is considered just as good as that of the present,—a conception altogether too just for *our* age of monopoly and free-appropriation to ever think of seriously. Though the stranger is looked upon as an enemy and a lawful prey, there is no thought of robbing each other within the clan; therefore the tillable ground is staked off to each family in proportion to its number, and that outside is a pasturage in common. The *mir* or village commune in Russia, not yet broken up, still represents the primitive equality in the use of land.

Thus we can see that justice enters into the daily life of the savage and barbarian as truly as into ours. His right to property, to his family, to protection, and to a share in the common soil are all based upon it. Without it he could not get along at all. The love of it grows with the habit of doing it, and from the conception of it being held before the mind as the beneficial, the fit, proper, desirable and every way superior thing to be realized in practice; including as not least of all, the *necessity* of it in order to a peaceful and harmonious way of living. Of these two elements in the love of justice the latter—the conception of its value—is given by the intellect, and is strong in proportion as the reasoning faculty is strong and clear; the former, depending on habit, is strong in proportion as the habit of sacrificing selfishness to justice is unvarying and long continued.

In all grades of society there is a call for justice; in all conditions of the race, in all the manifold relations created by domestic, industrial, and political life there is more or less demand for its manifestation. More than any other moral quality it is the condition of happiness in society.

A barbarian community may possess a good share of

the sentiment in proportion to what is demanded for a simple form of social life; or a civilized state may have too little of it, and find itself in constant turmoil for the lack. The poor, the uneducated, the unpolished may have it strong in regard to certain matters; the pampered child of wealth, luxury and superficial culture may have so little that only his ability to buy service and toleration with money renders him endurable.

Generosity and *magnanimity*, two more of the higher virtues, depend on riches; the first on riches in goods, the second on wealth of character—mental or spiritual riches. We know how easy it is to be generous with superfluous wealth, or even without when we can easily acquire more. But if we work hard and suffer much in getting it, we hold to it closely; parting with it only for its full value. If we have enough but no means for getting more it is the same. So if we have much or can readily obtain it we can give much, if little we give but little, even by making a great sacrifice of the acquisitive feeling. Jesus said the poor widow with her two mites had given more than all before her, because, being all that she had, the giving implied a greater sacrifice. Unusual conditions and motives may induce a man to share his last crust or last penny with a friend, or even give him the whole of both; but if he had a great deal more he would with the same effort give a great deal more. So we can understand that in barbarian societies, always poor, though in individual cases there may be much actual sacrifice, there will be no great gifts, nor institutions of charity. These come with peace, industry, and wealth, though the moral effort may be no greater. The less we have the harder it is to give.

With charity of feeling or magnanimity there must likewise be wealth, a wealth of moral character or goodness. The person who is struggling with all his might against the evils and falsities of his lower nature, and just beginning to rise in the moral world, is like the one who is working hard for a poor living. He cannot afford to tolerate any lack of virtue in his neighbors, or any influence from them that is going to make his own struggle more difficult. He can neither allow himself to have pity for faults, or toleration for errors, or slight to his dignity or reputation. But when he becomes stronger in goodness, wiser in intellect, higher in position, and better in reputation he becomes more generous in feeling. He is like the man rich in physical things, who can go about in his old clothes, fearing no disrespect, having no need to keep up appearances, able to give generously. He is now conscious of being so strong morally that it will not hurt his virtue, or his reputation, to speak kindly to the degraded sinner or tramp, and get acquainted with him to help him reform; he is less bigoted toward what he formerly considered heresy; more disposed to be generous to his enemies, and to meet them half way in steps to a reconciliation. He can do all these things because he is strong enough spiritually not to be in danger from the temptation or the heresy; and as soon as he is so all considerations unite in prompting him to generosity of action.

This is one of the latest developed of the virtues, one of the highest, most useful, most happifying of them all.

Two other moral qualities, equally high, and like the last two, late in development, are *modesty* and *humility*. Both are simply the product of advanced growth. Presumption and self-righteousness are the unfailing indications of a mere beginning in the intellectual and the moral life. The first steps in an upward direction bring such a change of experience, the contrast is so decided, so fresh and striking that, as with every first experience, the degree or amount of change is overestimated; the more so as the person affected can have no conception of the larger growth before him, to which he is still a stranger. With progress comes a diminution of conceit in both forms; modesty and humility as steadily taking their place. And this process will continue till the person has achieved the complete conquest of all obstinacy, bigotry, arrogance, and every kind of pride.

Truthfulness I class among the more elevated virtues; for though it is found necessary to some extent everywhere and always, so that "Honor among thieves," has become a proverb, yet it never reaches its completeness except among a very few of the best of the race, those only whose ability to think deeply and far enables them to see the superiority of it to deception, for all justifiable purposes, and in all conditions or circumstances, save those in which any kind of absolute morality becomes unjust to self, and deception is the only means of defence. Ignorance often makes deception appear necessary, when better knowledge, greater moral courage, or more faith in human nature would prove truthfulness to be feasible, and far superior in its results. It grows with the growth of intelligence, and *thoughtfulness* is its twin relative.

Self-Control, another high virtue, is gained, as we all know, through thoughtfulness, and the habitual training of our impulses to follow the direction, or wait the command, of the cool, honest judgment. Some minor qualities might be spoken of; but so far as it is necessary to consider their genesis I prefer to do so incidentally on future occasions. But there is one other of the higher sentiments, one whose origin is much disputed, and something should be said to decide concerning it if possible. What I refer to is the consciousness of *duty*; the feeling that we *ought* to do or not do, feel or not feel, think or not think; the sense of *right*, so called; the *conscientious* impulse; the conscious acknowledgment that right is superior to wrong.

One school of moralists teach that it comes only from

God and revelation; another that it is an innate or inherent feeling, a moral instinct, similar to those intellectual instincts called intuitions, by which we know a self-evident truth as soon as uttered. No one, so far as I know, has tried to account for it as the result of natural causes only, though all true scientists must believe a natural explanation to be possible.

Now, it is the natural effect of the *superstition* remaining in every mind, that all unthinking persons prefer to believe some theory that has *mystery* in it. An explanation that is too profound or too obscure to be readily apprehended, will get credit with them much sooner than one that is simple, natural, and easily understood. Every scientific explanation has to contend with this superstitious preference for the incomprehensible. Yet all generalized truth is really simple, and so is a natural explanation of duty.

Man's object in all he does is happiness. If any one wishes to contradict this he will say that sometimes man acts because he admires the inherent nobleness of a good action; because he perceives its fitness and propriety to a noble character; because of respect for the nobler part of himself; because it is godlike, and he wishes to be in some degree godlike too.

To put this all into different language, it means that man, through his intellect, has come to form a high ideal or standard, a godlike ideal if you choose—what seems to him a perfect standard of human action. Because of its *perfection* he admires it. All his experience, as well as all the teaching of the past, has convinced him that the *perfect* thing is connected with more happiness than the imperfect. No matter how small or unimportant the action, he never doubts that the perfect way of doing it gives the best results; and so whatever he knows how to do well, unless contrary motives interfere, he tries to do well, and to have others do well. In matters of industry, trade, and other affairs of everyday life he may be so anxious to realize his ideal that he will suffer loss rather than accept of poor performance; he will throw away the badly made article, or go through a long and tedious process the second time. He feels that it *ought* to be done right, and is disgusted or indignant with the wrong. His consciousness of *ought* or *duty* in the small affair is precisely the same *feeling* as his consciousness of ought or duty in regard to *moral* action. In both cases alike the performance ought to be up to the standard; it is botchwork, it is a fraud, it is disgusting, or hateful, or discouraging, in short, it is *wrong* if it is not. Every good *mechanic* can understand how an *artist*, or a genuine *moralist*, feels over good or bad, right or wrong performance in his particular line of action. This idea will not be acceptable to all; it may seem degrading to morality; it may touch the feeling of *pride*, like the question of human ancestry; but if no difference can be discerned in the *feeling* of *duty* as applied in the cases mentioned, then let us honestly admit that it is the same.

But though there is no difference in the nature of the feeling, there is an immense difference in the importance of the things compared. To the conscientious person moral right is right above everything else. It has a pre-eminence over all other considerations because of its importance; because of the vast amount of happiness or misery that may result from right or wrong procedure; because the happiness of one individual even is immensely superior in importance to matters of industry, art or business. This is the real point of difference, and accounts for the superior reverence given to moral right, and the intense hatred of moral wrong.

To illustrate. One person's life may depend upon another person's benevolence, or that of half a dozen children upon his charity. We remember the gifts of money, goods, and credit poured out upon the people of Chicago a few years ago, the help given to the yellow-fever-stricken people of Tennesee, and to the sufferers from forest fires in Michigan. Such results impress us strongly with the beauty and glory of benevolence. A single measure of *political justice* would make the whole population of Ireland rejoice, and twice as many more in other parts of the world. *Patriotism* may save the life, liberties, and future welfare of a great *nation* for unknown generations, as in our own country twenty-odd years ago. *Truth* and *fidelity* are vitally important in all close associations and partnerships. *Financial dishonesty* may keep the people of a city or state poor for many years, or *honesty* give it credit and prosperity. Even a few *words* at the right or wrong time or place will cause a person to feel happy or miserable for a whole day. Contrasted with such *moral* results as these, the effects of good or bad workmanship, of true or false art in ordinary subjects, are of little account. Human welfare is so much more affected by moral or immoral conduct, that moral right or wrong comes to be looked upon as entirely different in essential character, when the real difference is only in degree of importance.

If now we analyze the moral standard, we shall find that everything required by it aids human happiness through unselfish conduct; and this is what makes it admirable. Nothing but its happifying influence on humanity could make the godlike character godlike; nothing else could make it noble; nothing else render it worthy of a God; nothing else enable the aspirant to respect himself for imitating it; nothing else make it perfect. This is the original but now unconscious reason for loving the perfect, and aspiring to imitate or realize it in thought, feeling, and action.

All the higher moral sentiments have now been briefly

noticed, and a natural origin for them traced out. But before summing up the results, and advancing to new ground, let me say a word of justice for another kind of influence acting upon man to fit him for a more perfect society. It is the effect of opinion and custom not embodied in law, or in religion; but coming, in some degree, from every individual to every other, and bearing upon almost everything that is said or done. It relates to the customs, usages and conventionalities of *politeness* or *good breeding*. In savage and barbarous life custom is equal to law in the civilized. It is perhaps even more effective; for a custom once established, the savage scarcely ever thinks of varying from it. In civilized communities the more important of these customs get recognized in law; but the less important remain as the requirements of politeness. Now politeness demands many little self-abnegations, even some of greater magnitude, and at times a strong self-control.; all of which is moralizing to the character, and becoming habitual makes greater self-denials possible, when higher duties are to be fulfilled. To this cause may be attributed a great amount of good. It is doubtful, indeed, if politeness as an aid to good character, has ever been duly appreciated. The young, it is evident, must begin their moral training in little things. Good manners are good morals of the minor kind; and so far as they have no moral point, they are or should be matters of entire indifference. A child's moral sense ought not to be confused by making indifferent actions right or wrong, and those which *are* right or wrong indifferent. As the beginning of a moral development that is to end in complete unselfishness, politeness can hardly be overvalued. Its oneness with morality, and the connection of both with society, are easily seen. To the man who lives entirely alone good manners and good morals mean nothing; they are of no account; he has no occasion for either. It is only when he comes to associate with others that he needs politeness or morality.

Let us now see how far we have come on the road of development, and what is yet before us.

While unorganized society demands of us politeness, or morality in little things, the state, the principal form or organized society, requires of us justice to our fellows, subordination, loyalty to the government, and patriotism. It manifests its own morality in return by attempting to preserve order, to protect the rights of the individual, to furnish him some little education, and in various ways to advance his welfare. Patriotism is the most unselfish sentiment it has evolved, while cosmopolitanism is in germ.

Religion brings us up to the idea of forgiveness, which is a form of magnanimity, a complete setting aside of the selfish vindictive impulse. But religion—the highest form of it—does still more. It holds up to us the conception of a forgiveness, a generosity, a benevolence conferred before it is asked, bestowed on those not conscious of needing it, who do not appreciate the gift or thank the donor till long after they have received its benefit. This high ideal of unselfishness, though not peculiar to the Christian system, is, perhaps, presented by it more conspicuously than by any other religion.

The efforts of parents for their children are to some extent of this character. So in occasional instances are the efforts of estranged friends toward renewal of their former friendship; yet in both these parties there is some expectation of additional happiness to be realized by themselves as a result of the unselfish action. There are other manifestations of benevolence however, in which the expectation of any return to self, even that of seeing the recipient of bounty enjoy it, is very slight; and in some there is only the imagination of what will be enjoyed by the stranger man, woman, or child after the benefactor's death. Of such manifestations are hospitals, asylums, and other institutions for the victims of misfortune, together with libraries, and provisions for educating the orphan children of the future. We cannot credit any one motive for producing all of them, for every person is moved by impulses more or less different; but as the predominant one, we must say that these come from fidelity to high ideals of *duty* and *humanity*; which at the same time is fidelity to high ideals of human needs and rights, is devotion to that sense of *ought* before referred to, as coming from an intellectual perception of what *should* be in order to a more complete or perfect happiness.

There is yet one other manifestation of benevolence, which is if possible still more unselfish than any of those mentioned. I mean benevolence to animals. Any one may be kind to his own horse or dog; there is a tinge of friendship in it; and the most cruel of men can be kind to those he loves. But when this sentiment interferes to save from cruelty an old mule belonging to another person, where no return is possible, except the owner's hatred; or when it feeds a starved, mean-looking, strange dog to save its life, while the same dog would not be allowed in sight if it had any one to care for it; then we see kindness in its purest form, free as possible from mixture with any selfish feeling. Such acts come from devotion to a high and pure standard, contemplated and loved for its own excellence till the tendency to realize it has become instinctive, yet not so strong but it must sometimes be reënforced by a consciousness of duty—a conscious perception that even a dog or a mule *ought* to have some means of happiness. Still, however, with what seems a strange blindness, humane people yet fail to see that harmless *wild* animals have the same natural right to life and freedom that man himself possesses, so long as they do not through excess of numbers intrude upon the domain, or limit the welfare of some superior race. The proposition is a self-evident one. And though the barbarous man naturally takes delight in his power to kill anything and everything, the civilized one should long before this have become tired of such fiendishness as sportsmen practice; and the only apparent reason he has not is that a false teaching has justified brutality of this kind.

Such are the highest developments of the unselfish spirit. A proper question now is, how much of it do we possess? If we look around we discover persons who exhibit it in all degrees, some capable of its best manifestations as above described. Many of us know such individuals, who fairly wear out their lives in labor for others—for the sick, the family of helpless children, the unfortunate in various ways, the heathen, so-called, whose souls they hope to save. I have heard a lady say she always spoke to a dog when she met one, because it always seemed to make a dog feel happy to be spoken to. I have seen another take up under her handkerchief a handful of half-frozen wasps and drop them outside the window, so that, where unlikely to do harm, they might have a chance to continue their lives a while longer. Not long ago I read of a man who deliberately placed himself where in all rational probability his life would be sacrificed to a horrible disease, in order to preach the gospel to a colony of outcast lepers. And lately the newspaper told us of a coal-miner, a poor, rude, ignorant Pole, who in spite of warning rushed into danger and saved his friend's life at the loss of his own. Similar instances of moral heroism occur frequently. They are all around us, and are reported by the press every few days. And when we see how many are capable of doing them, and estimate how much unselfishness there is in the world, we are moved to inquire why it is that the condition of humanity is no better. What is it that yet remains before the general happiness of the true society can be realized? Are the difficulties in the environment—the material conditions that surround us? Are they in the depravity of human nature? or are they in our lack of intellectual growth? Is it not because our way is dark, and we see not how to proceed faster, that our moral progress is so slow, and our miseries still so great? The hindrance is not physical, for physical progress has improved everything about us, and with our physical means we could tear down the mountains or bridge the oceans, almost, if we desired. There has been a great deal of philanthropic effort, but it has effected little good. There is much of education in childhood, and still more of teaching in sermons and books in later life. Religion, romance, poetry, music, art, all appeal to our better sentiments more than to our baser ones, and yet we scarcely advance. How much better are we than a hundred years ago? Somewhat certainly, but only a little. How much happier? Some of us enjoy more, and some of us suffer more keenly than any did then; the proportion of happiness to misery may not be very much increased.

The traditional explanation of the fact is *natural depravity*. The scientific view answering to natural depravity is that the aboriginal man, or the civilized child, is born with his animal, selfish instincts predominant, and his higher ones, which fit him for society, only in germ. The process of adapting himself to society is the process of developing his moral sentiments. He is still in the transition state between savagery and complete civilization. His moral feelings are in all stages of growth, in different individuals and races, from the most childish to the most mature. All around us we see the various grades, from the savage to the civilized, from the brute almost to the angel. Such differences are necessary results of evolution. But selfish motives are still predominant in all but the few. Man's intelligence has not yet sufficiently advanced to show him the superior happiness of the life controlled by social feelings; it has not enabled him to harmonize the conflicting impulses in his brain; nor taught him how to so instruct his children that along with their physical maturity they shall grow into moral strength, and fitness for close association. In short, moral and social science have not kept pace with material. The material naturally gains its development before the higher kinds, just as do the faculties that take interest in material things. As before explained, Physics and Chemistry must be known before we can fully understand living things, and Biology before we can fully comprehend society. Thus it happens that while physical science is well on toward its full growth, a large part of the social and moral is yet to be learned.

But here will come up the objection, "Have we not already the Ten Commandments, the Sermon on the Mount, all the ancient wisdom summed up in the writings of Solomon, all the choice selections from the sacred books of the old religions, all the moral speculations of the philosophers, with all the modern teachings of liberty and democracy; and all these exhibited in a thousand lights and aspects, by moralist, preacher, poet, novelist; and do you mean to tell us that we do not yet know all our rights and duties, or that we could not make ourselves and others happy if we only did as well as we know?"

Yes, what I mean is that notwithstanding all that, something still remains to be taught and learned; and that something is a word to come from Science. Whatever we know, or whatever we might do if we would, no one's life is ever fully up to his own standard—his own conception of what he ought to do. But the more we know the more perfect our standard will be, the more we shall be inspired by its beauty and stimulated to make it real, the more easily we can surmount our difficulties. Therefore, the more we know the better we shall do.

It is because it lacks the knowledge science is yet to give that religion has no greater moral influence. The church has no hope of a Kingdom of God in this world; or at any rate, not till after some hundreds or thousands of years more of extremely slow improvement; or else till it is purified by fire and reinhabited by a race of saints. Neither Christian teaching, nor any other, has ever been able to fit more than a very few persons, if any at all, for such a social state as the Kingdom of Heaven is supposed to be. Nearly all Christians expect to be purified and prepared by some miraculous process after getting out of this world before going into the society of the angels. Very few believe they can attain to a sufficient degree of perfection here to save them from consciously committing sin. And even with these few the source of strength is not within themselves, but in the spiritual power outside, on which they depend for grace in every trial.

Is there then no possibility of human nature's becoming so moralized, or spiritualized, or progressed, that the individual can *stand alone* in his goodness; incapable of consciously doing a wrong to any living creature, or of failing to right an undesigned one; and beyond the liability of falling away from his union with God and all good souls? Here on the material earth, in this material organism, full of its natural desires and impulses; here where all is now discord and conflict and sin and sorrow; here where the human tree has its natural roots, and where already it has attained partial growth, can it not continue to grow, to develop its buds and blossoms, its beauty and fragrance, its full-grown ripened fruit in all perfection? It is my duty to assert that it can; that its destiny is to do this and nothing less; that this is the human destiny indicated by science. Science teaches us to expect an age of perfect men and perfect institutions at some period in the future. It will be the inevitable result of evolution. Evolution means nothing if it does not imply a progression from the imperfect to the perfect. Even if our present civilization should go down to ruin, another one must sometime arise; and improving upon ours as ours has improved upon previous ones, it would at length realize the perfect social condition. The only question involved is of the time *when*. Herbert Spencer is generally recognized as the best representative of scientific doctrine; and this is one of his statements: "Thus from the persistence of force we finally draw a warrant for the belief that evolution can end only in the establishment of the greatest perfection and the most complete happiness." A similar idea is expressed or implied by him more than once, and moreover, I think it to be the general opinion of scientists, especially of all those who accept Evolution as a philosophy. From a number of thinkers expressions of the same belief could be quoted.

Then, if so many scientists have faith in a coming age of perfection, what is the difference between their view and mine? They, like the few religionists who admit its possibility, put the time of it far off in the future, both the culmination and the beginning of it. They have no expectation that the beginning of such a period may be near at hand. They do not see any preparation for it already nearly or quite accomplished. On the contrary, in my view, while the general prevalence of such a state is still some distance away, the commencement of it, among the most advanced portions of the race, may occur at any time; and will do so as soon as any two persons standing on unselfish ground, and looking through scientific eyes, shall discern the manner of its coming.' That beginning may be perceptible in twenty-five years, or ten, or five, or even one. There are children (I see such every day) which might be so trained by education as to qualify them for the perfect society by the time they become men and women. At least that is my very strong belief. There are mature men and women in every community who, so far as I can judge, need only the proper enlightenment of the intellect to be morally capable of anything required. It is the highest kind of intelligence that our best people now lack, more than they do moral feeling. The latter has long been cultivated in such poor way as it could be without acknowledging the need of intellect or of science; henceforth the intellect is to do its part, and it is likely that better results will not be long in coming forth.

The work now before me is to show what yet remains to be learned and done, before the better part of humanity can reach the unselfish stage of their development. Of this better part some are in the church, and some outside of it. Of those within it some have already, through conversion, achieved the conquest of a part of the selfish nature, while a part remains—how much or little need not be here considered. A few have progressed so far as to have given up all selfishness of which they are aware; hence they feel conscious of being saved; they know that through grace as they suppose, they have conquered and put under their feet all that they knew of as standing in their way. When they can be enabled to see what yet remains it is not unreasonable to believe some of these few will triumph over that also, and know through both reason and feeling at the same time, that their salvation is made final and sure. Others, without passing through the process of conversion, have inherited much, and in a quiet, gradual way have added to their inheritance, thus reaching a condition of good promise.

Of those outside the church the more advanced have inherited much nobility of character, which in many cases has increased by a faithful adherence to conscience, and especially by intellectual culture of the more ennobling kind. These, too, have their unknown forms of selfishness, yet to be contended with when plainly seen. From the less cultivated, but honest and thoughtful persons of this class I anticipate that many will be found able and willing, when properly enlightened, to come well up toward the high demand of the perfect standard.

Neither the party within, nor that without the church, knows the moral condition of the other. The churchman may be conscious of a spiritual experience to which the outsider is yet a stranger; and the secularist, while looking upon such experience as delusion, knows that in his intellectual view he has gained upon the other. Both may yet come to the same view and the same experience; and thus become conscious of their real brotherhood. Both have unexplored corners of their brains in which lurk unknown demons of selfishness, and especially that easily-hidden devil of the *intellect* known as Bigotry. The exploration of these dark corners, and the dragging into light of the still untamed monsters, is the task to be attempted in future discussions.

In the full growth of the moral sentiment it will constantly and permanently dominate all the other feelings of the man. All that is selfish will become unselfish. He will not only be incapable of voluntarily doing wrong, but he *will* be capable of voluntarily righting a wrong done through his error; though he have to sacrifice his property or his reputation, his pride, his affections, or his opinions. He will act from the unselfish feeling, and think from the unselfish point of view. He will acknowledge the claims of another as readily as he asserts his own or sooner. He will see clearly that the rights and happiness of two persons, other things equal, are more important than those of one. He will be able to criticise himself habitually, to put himself in the place of others, to see his own mistakes and faults as quickly as theirs, to learn that his sufferings are the result of his own imperfections as much as those of any one else, or of the world he lives in. He will desire to learn what is right in order to do it, and will be willing to accept truth, without prejudice or reserve, from any person or source whatever.

Moreover, with such a willingness to learn there will be an *ability to discover* scattered grains of truth from all quarters, and a complex wholeness of truth, now totally unknown, which will enable him not only to completely reconcile all his desires and impulses of every kind, but to perceive means and modes of happiness of which he has now no conception. There is no wildness of either fancy or reason in saying that all this is simply the natural and inevitable result of the unselfish development—that full outgrowth and perpetual dominance of the moral sentiment, which by analogy is the blossoming and fruiting of the human plant, or by a still better analogy, is that mental state answering to the physical condition of puberty—a mature *intellectual and moral manhood and womanhood*—which is to fit humanity for that perfect and happy society here called the Kingdom of the Unselfish. It will be the manhood and womanhood of the *race*. And this condition of mind once attained, it can no more be lost or receded from than a man can again become a child, or a tree reinvolve its fruit, flowers and buds, and grow downward into a little plant. It will have become an organic part of his mental constitution. Though spiritual influences, in some sense, may aid him to reach it, when finally and fully reached it will not be dependent on the grace of God, or any spiritual power, any more than the use of his legs after he has learned to stand alone and walk. It will remain with him a permanent possession, and be his normal state of mind as long as consciousness endures. The childish, ignorant, selfish, unsocial, savage animal of the past, will have evolved into the mature, wise, unselfish, divine man and woman, capable of evolving a society that shall also be worthy to be called divine.

CHAPTER IV.

INDEPENDENCE.

BEFORE commencing on any further work it may be well to repeat, in more definite manner, what has been already said concisely, that the causes operating to produce morality are two-fold in character, consisting on the one hand of an inducement or compulsion perceptible to the intellect—something to be desired or feared; and on the other hand the habit of self-abnegation, self-denial, or self-sacrifice, through which moral action becomes easy. Now the part belonging to habit is, except in the case of children, what every one must do for himself mainly, with such help as friends can give by making favorable circumstances, or by encouragement and sympathy. My business here is to set forth the first part, the inducements that appeal to the intellect, these being still two-fold, the attractive good to be desired or hoped for, and the repulsive evil to be dreaded or feared. To the undeveloped man, or in the beginning of *the moral life, the *necessity* of a moral course—the fear of consequences to follow if he does not take it—is the principal influence. The attractive part—the benefits of such a course—he does not yet know, or if at all but slightly. With the more developed person, who has already learned something of the su-

INDEPENDENCE. 79

perior happiness conferred by unselfish conduct, there is less need of appealing to the fears; the excellence of a high morality is conceivable to him; the more perfect the standard the greater its attractive power, and this alone may be sufficient. When both hopes and fears can be appealed to there is the greatest effect; as for instance, when some great danger that cannot be avoided makes even the timid desperately brave.

We hear it said sometimes that every man makes his own god, to suit himself. This means that God is an ideal embodiment of his standard of morality or goodness. He has formed a conception of God, or more probably has accepted one already formed, which is best adapted to his own nature—that of a being superior to himself, an ideal character to be imitated and approached, yet not one possessing qualities different from his own, for of such he cannot conceive at all. It is a more perfect being of his own stamp. The more unselfish he himself becomes the more unselfish becomes his conception of the deity; and thus his idea of God comes to be a good indication of his own grade of moral advancement. The improvement of his own character allows and enables him to take a higher view of the character of Deity. This higher view of Deity is then a new and more perfect ideal, stimulating him to still better conduct and still greater improvement.

From such considerations as these then, it is obvious that if I endeavor to convince men of the possibility of a higher moral life,*I must do so by holding up a more perfect and attractive ideal of moral excellence, by pointing out greater or more real dangers from immorality, or else by showing an easier path, through better conditions, toward realizing whatever ideals we have. Perhaps all of these may be to some extent combined.

Another point needs a word of explanation. War, famine, pestilence, accident, have been mentioned as occasions that bring out moral feeling and action. They do or do not, according to the character already acquired. A healthy boy is made robust by exposure to cold, dampness, storms, and all kinds of rough outdoor life. But a feebler boy might be injured by the same conditions, unless first exposed to milder ones, and afterward gradually accustomed to those more severe. The exposure must be tempered to the degree of vitality that is to resist the bad influences. A community that would flee before the presence of Asiatic cholera might be able to face a mild type of yellow fever without disgrace. In the first case they would prove cowardly and heartless; in the second they might show much bravery, tenderness and generosity. Those compelled to brave the dangers and miseries of the lesser disease would by so doing probably acquire enough of the nobler moral quality to endure those of the cholera, if called upon to do so afterward; when without such milder exposure first they would fail, and be demoralized instead.

I will now go on with the subject of Independence, as the groundwork and necessary condition of a moral or unselfish character.

It was well said long ago, "The day that makes a man a slave takes half his worth away." It does worse than that, for it takes away his moral worth entirely. He is not only unaccountable, in the ordinary sense, but he becomes an instrument for evil in other hands. He is placed where for the sake of his physical life he gives up all moral vitality. He is like a plant which when all its higher development is taken away lives only in its roots, till conditions become suitable for a new upward growth at some future time. But if no such time comes, if the new shoots are cut off as fast as they sprout, the root also finally dies. To all appearance it is the same with the human being. If the feeble moral efforts and ambitions put forth by the slave or dependent, continue to be opposed, discouraged, blighted by the circumstances of his life, and the human influence that affects him, he finally loses all aspiration or desire to grow, becoming totally selfish—gloomy, indolent, mean, sensual, cowardly, treacherous, bitter, cruel and unprincipled—morally dead.

But if complete slavery does all this a partial slavery has the same blighting effect in proportion to its degree. In this country, it is commonly supposed, no one individual is a slave to another; but however that may be in law, many are *virtually* slaves to persons and to circumstances combined, and some are the slaves of persons or circumstances alone. A lack of training in practical worldly wisdom makes many an educated person in some degree a slave to circumstances, and to any individual of superior wealth or influence. Having no power to take hold of the world and compel it to give them an honest support, they of necessity are dependent on some stronger person, and must give up their wills to his; their hopes and aspirations must be put down to suit his convenience; their lives must be more or less controlled and guided, their characters suppressed and stunted, or warped, twisted and deformed, by subserviency to the necessities or pleasure of the stronger one. The dependent becomes servile unavoidably. His very life and physical comfort are secure only by his doing so. He cannot afford to risk the displeasure of one who is his only means of support. Cowardice, deception, meanness of every kind, may finally become so habitual as to be a second nature. His moral prostitution is at last complete; he will sell his conscience, and every good quality to obtain the satisfaction of his merely animal wants. He is utterly degraded, though he may never commit outrageous crime, unless in some way that is comparatively safe; for he has become too cowardly to take any risk.

The class most liable to become dependent takes in a large proportion of educated young men. The professions are so crowded that an education for them is little better than none at all. An industrial or mercantile education is better, but still it must be of the most thorough and efficient kind, one that will enable its possessor to take a place at the top, or crowd an ordinary man from one already occupied; else it gives him no surety of obtaining a support without degradation. A rich man may leave his son a fortune, but unless he can confer on him the business tact to keep it well invested, and that higher wisdom that will prevent his spending it for selfish pleasures, the legacy will take wings and leave the inheritor a helpless wreck.

The young man educated by wealthy parents is already handicapped in his life race by notions of respectability, which make him feel himself above the vocation of a mechanic or farmer, and incline him to that of the merchant or transporter. His pride is an influence which goes toward making him a slave. By it he is obliged to take up an occupation already crowded with workers and aspirants. Unless having unusual talents or influential friends he must struggle for even a low position, and must work long and faithfully before reaching a place that will give him what he considers a respectable support. He must put up with more or less of degrading submission, he cannot afford to marry, and he is tempted to steal.

Instead of being burdened with this false pride, he should be taught that any occupation in which he can make use of his knowledge and brain-power, thereby gaining an average income, or a decent livelihood with something over for the future, is sufficiently reputable. Anything better than this is either very good fortune, or else in some manner or some degree immoral. There is fairly a difference in the respectability of what are called honest avocations; and one is conscious of this when permanently engaged in work that a person of inferior ability could do just as well. But if it is one into which he can carry his intelligence, the only other consideration necessary is that of natural attraction or peculiar fitness. Selecting such a one among those trades or professions that make use of applied science, and making himself an artist in it, as he should aim to do, he is likely to become independent in both property and character, with a fair prospect of adding to this all the other virtues.

Tilling the soil is in these days equally a trade involving skill and applied science; and the ideal farmer is not only a man of brains, but may be an artist also if he will.

If we go into the mill, the factory, or the shop of the mechanic we find in every case that it is the best workman who is the independent man, who has the most courage, who is most prompt to resist the tyranny of bosses and sub-bosses when necessary, who is most good-natured, frank and generous to his fellows. The poor workman, who knows he will be the first one discharged, is inclined to be cowardly and mean, to submit to indignities from everybody, to buy favors of overseers by presents or obsequiousness, to turn traitor to his fellows when there is disagreement between them and the employer, to deceive and take underhanded means for retaining his own position. Deception is the only sort of defence the weak person has, and when once compelled to resort to that, other and worse meannesses are liable to follow.

So in the mercantile world; while the strong man, able to manage his business well and successfully may be honest, fair and truthful if so disposed, it is the weak or unskillful one who resorts to dishonorable methods and mean practices; who cannot afford to be fair when he has an advantage, still less to be generous or magnanimous; who knowingly does a losing business till compelled to fail, and cheats all who have trusted him; repeating the process again and again as long as he can deceive any one into the folly of giving him credit. Finally, bankrupt and disgraced, he is forced to degrade himself, outwardly, still lower, and take up any kind of mean service that will enable him to live. To expect any moral character, any unselfish behavior, any high aspirations from him is futile. He thinks only that the world owes him a living somehow, and will get it any way he can, regardless of others. The "degraded savage" we sometimes hear about is less unfortunate morally than he.

True it is, at the same time, that the greed for wealth has now become so all-engrossing scarcely any business man can entirely avoid degradation. The accomplished and successful will rob and crush his weaker competitors to pile up his gains still higher and higher, as if he could never be satisfied. The same process that makes a slave makes a tyrant, and that which makes a thief has already made, in some way, a robber; so that while the weaker is being demoralized in one direction the stronger is demoralized in an opposite one. Yet the superior talents of the stronger, by assuring him a competence, and thus making him independent, enable his better impulses to come into action sometimes under proper incitement; whereas in the weak, unskilled, and unlucky there is no chance; such a one is compelled to be base, and to live by base methods, in order to live at all. No moral structure can arise without the corner stone of an independent spirit; and this must have a foundation of material wealth or some sure means of securing a livelihood.

The large class of those who grow up to maturity without any industrial or business education includes a great many women. The natural aversion of mankind to hard or monotonous labor, with the increasing dislike and disgrace of it generated by wealth, idleness, and an education mainly ornamental, form an influence which operates toward increasing the number and proportion of such women. At the same time the necessities and incidents of industrial competition are constantly throwing a larger and larger number of such women into the ranks of those who labor for wages. The competition of women against women in all occupations now open to them is already severe; and with the whole tendency of the industrial world operating to render it still more so, is it matter of wonder that they are induced or compelled to sell their virtue along with their work or in lieu of it; and that nearly all over the area of modern civilization honorable marriage decreases, while degrading alliances and all kinds of crimes against woman are on the increase, in some localities very rapidly.* How can it be different till women are fitted for an independent life by an education and training that will enable them to obtain it, as far as is possible under existing industrial arrangements?

Even those women who are supposed to be fortunate in securing a home and maintenance by marriage to men of property,—is it at all certain that their condition is improved?. The testimony brought out in divorce cases indicates that many of these marriages are still only relations of tyrant and slave, and anything but favorable to moral growth.

With the married poor there is the same liability to misery from the same fault. A poor and uneducated woman, without taste or technical ability, has no resource outside of marriage except to do menial work for a household, which is degrading in two ways; first by being dirty or menial in itself, and second, by the de-

---

* For confirmation of this statement see an article by Henry Hayman giving results from Von Oettingen's *Moralstatistik*, in the Fortnightly Review for September or October, 1886.

grading treatment she receives as an inferior person, and the perpetual consciousness of being so considered. And, by the way, it is one of the most hopeful indications of moral life that ignorant servant girls become capable of rebellion against the spirit of caste, which insults them by every word and look, and which cannot do otherwise so long as the superior party is willing to have an inferior in the house and make no effort to raise her to an equality, but on the contrary, looks upon her as always to remain inferior. There can be no satisfactory domestic service till the superior has acquired enough of the social spirit to try whatever means may be available to elevate the less fortunate, to consider her entitled in every respect to polite treatment, and still further, to be willing to learn that degrading work cannot be paid for in money alone; that there must be in it something of that willing service that friend gives to friend or child to parent, and something in the spirit and manner of the employer to draw out such service. Then there will be little complaint of unwilling, dishonest, or troublesome servant girls, and until then the more rebellious and troublesome they are the better; for thus they show enough of the spirit of liberty to resist their degradation.

But the poor, ignorant and incapable woman, tired and indignant from her service as an inferior, takes to marriage in hope of a better condition. She is still however just as helpless; she cannot command the respect of her husband, who is selfish and low in his instincts, and becomes drunken and brutal. She can be nothing but a slave. Submission to rough treatment, to coarse animalism, to hard work and excessive child-bearing, robs her of health, strength and hope, till finally, as I have myself seen, she can submit to be sworn at by her half-drunken husband as they go along the street, making no resistance, but a whining apology instead. How much worse fate does any woman ever reach than that?

Again it is unfortunate that women, while needing useful scientific knowledge equally with men, especially all that has a bearing upon their natural function as mothers, or their traditional occupation as housekeepers, they are yet taught to regard the more ornamental sort of education or accomplishment as the more important. All the old hereditary opinion of their own sex and the other tends to confirm this view, and render them indifferent to their greatest need. They have made some progress of late years in discovering what they lack, and have done something toward supplying it; but the amount of this latter effort is but a small part of what is necessary for their safety and moral well-being.

I do not forget that certain teachers have always told them they were already the most moral or unselfish half of the human family. But they will do well not to believe too strongly in this grateful delusion. Their virtues are mostly negative ones, that may go with weakness and a subordinate position, not the positive ones that indicate strength. Their unselfishness, omitting exceptions, is the sacrifice of weak desires, feeble hopes, and small ambitions, not that of great or strong ones; and though the superficial appearance may be the same, their goodness is more that of natural innocence than that achieved by temptations met and overcome.

A false pride regarding manual labor has been mentioned as slavery to an idea. Slavery to circumstances may be when a man has a family he can barely support, when unfortunate relatives need all he can spare, when employment fails, or when ill health or accident has so crippled his powers he can make his way only by closest economy, and with a harder prospect before him as he grows old. This man however is not in so bad a moral position as some others. If qualified for his occupation he may show no bad spirit from fear of losing it. If the hardship of his perpetual struggle is liable to drive him into some dishonesty, his having a family will in most cases aid the growth of unselfish feeling, as a counterbalance to the unfavorable condition. His poverty however, prevents cultivation of the intellect, and unless having done so beforehand, he and his family have but small chance to get acquainted with high ideals, so as to appreciate their excellence and beauty. The most they will obtain of any kind is likely to be from the cheap newspaper.

That lack of surplus wealth which compels one to do work for a living is conducive to morality, if the work done is useful. But when poverty is grinding, when it uses up all the energies in labor, allowing one no leisure time to think or to enjoy, then it is anything but favorable. There is nothing with which to be generous, no animal spirits with which to be cheerful or friendly, no wealth of knowledge and thought to make one strong, magnanimous, liberal, charitable or just.

Many of the professional class are but little better off in this respect than the poor laborer. The politician, the clergyman, the teacher, who has no other occupation to fall back upon, and whose abilities are not of the first order, must be something of a coward and slave. The politician does not dare to offend many of his constituents by exposing corrupt practices or antagonizing any purpose of his party; the clergyman must not condemn his wealthy and influential parishioners, no matter what their offence; the teacher cannot venture to teach anything that is not religiously and socially orthodox to his employers, whatever he believes to be the honest truth. All these are mere representatives of the average mass, or of the most influential party; they can learn nothing, say nothing, do nothing any better than the majority are

INDEPENDENCE

ready to accept. For physical needs and comforts they sell their consciences and become degraded—less truthful, courageous, and conscientious than they would be if not dependent on somebody for the means of living. The few who become moral heroes or great thinkers, and lead people up to a higher moral grade, are made independent by superior talents, or by simple tastes and habits, if not by possession of property.

To all this complaint the answer may be returned that nobody who gives service for hire can be so independent that he will not at times be required by the necessities of his situation to sacrifice something of what he considers truth or justice, or let himself down a trifle from the high standard set up by his own interior self-respect. He must do that or be liable to do something worse. The difficulty is one common to all sorts of positions and employments.

This statement is also true, for the reason that society is organized on a selfish basis, at least in its industrial part, and the spirit of this dominates in all religion, law, and education, so that everything works in a manner to cultivate selfishness. Yet there is a difference in situations nevertheless. A man may be so circumstanced that he will have to degrade himself continually; or again so that in his independence he will rarely be required to violate conscience or self-respect, and then only in some very small matter. One position is to be avoided, the other sought.

Independence we must have—the consciousness of liberty, the love of it, the determination to keep and use it. Without it no one can do unselfish deeds, even if disposed; for the fear of circumstances or of persons is liable to repress every good impulse before it is carried into act. To have it we must have material strength, that is, power to command the means of living and maintaining our individuality. It may be had without property if a person already has the knowledge that can preserve health, and the skill that secures employment. Such a one is in fact more independent than if owning property, but lacking knowledge and skill. Even the farmer cultivating his own land, who has always been taken as the type of a free and independent man, may through ignorance lose his health, and through sickness lose his farm to die a pauper. The intelligent man has after all the surest prospect of maintaining his independence.

There is no need of commending industry and frugality as secondary means of attaining to a state of freedom. Every one admits the propriety of practicing these virtues while they *must;* though very many by their conduct prove that they consider them virtues only so long as they are indispensable. Very few perceive any virtue in simple tastes, habits and surroundings of themselves; those who do being the few who think most, or who have become familiar with the thought of great minds. The struggling poor, who most need to practice frugality, are continually kept down by a weak ambition to keep up the appearance of greater wealth than they possess. This fact is a discouraging one; for although it shows a desire for equality, and is really a sign of life, yet it betrays a lack of knowledge and thought which allows all better purposes to be defeated.

Apparently there is no way to change this state of things except by some kind of education that will make the poor wiser than the rich now are. The rich, with all their wealth, have no culture, save in rare instances, that renders them wise enough to set a good example. The poorer class and the intermediate, equally blind, imitate the foolishness of the rich; both alike wasting their money and time in senseless efforts for pretentious vain show, and in seeking by all sorts of delusive ways to enjoy a contemptible kind of happiness. Unless some great changes in social administration are to take place, it is difficult to see any better prospect for the poor, the weak, the uncultivated many for some time to come. For it may be relied upon that nothing less than serious, earnest thinking, over actual positive knowledge, and the contemplation of true, noble standards of character and living, with the reasons for all their excellence clearly seen, will enable the masses to discover a possibility of greater happiness, and induce them to attempt its realization. The people must be acted upon in a more effective manner than church or state has ever tried. These have done and are doing what they may according to their wisdom; but the good result is very small. The upward progress is so very slow, while the opposing influences are still so very strong, that some persons of good intelligence doubt that society will ever be any better—doubt if it will not on the contrary become so corrupt as to sink into final ruin, and an age of darkness equal to that which followed the decay of the Greeko-Roman civilization.

But what shall we say of the present duty of the rich— the idle, the extravagant, the luxurious rich, those who now spend their time in trying to enjoy life, with scarcely a thought of giving enjoyment to others, except by throwing away the money that cost them little or nothing. Is it entirely in vain to ask them to set a better example—an example of plainness, of modesty, of temperance, of learning some useful knowledge, and doing some useful work in the world? Does the pleasure they obtain overbalance what they suffer from ennui in their idle hours, from the repression of their better impulses, from the consciousness of living a comparatively ignoble and useless life, from the suspicion that no one of high character and true nobility has any respect for them, nor even others any more than the outward show of it due to the power of money. Spite of the idea, taught them by almost everybody, that wealth exempts from labor and prudence, they cannot justify or respect themselves. They must feel that something is wrong. They know their muscles and brains are designed to be used, and feebleness and disease torments them for neglect of Nature's requirement. They have an average share of moral sense, and must try to satisfy it with the excuse that their idleness and prodigality helps the poor. Perhaps they need to be told that their whole course of life tends to make labor disgraceful and degrading, a heavier burden to be borne by the masses who toil. Their prodigality makes all who wait upon their wishes servile, insincere and base. Their influence thus becomes morally poisonous. It generates slavery, degradation and corruption. Whatever good there may be in their mode of life *this one serious bad fact remains*. They must be as well aware of it as everybody else, and when they allow themselves to think, the conviction of its seriousness will creep in upon them, and the consciousness that they are living untrue lives,—lives untrue to themselves, and untrue to the world of humanity, whose labors in the past have placed them in their fortunate position; while the return they make is worse than nothing, a balance of evil over good.

But furthermore, wealth does not in all cases confer a feeling of independence. Among the wealthy are many —more of them women than men—who are dependent upon fathers, brothers, husbands or wives for all they have to spend. And though a son or daughter who will make some little effort to add to a parent's happiness may be freely granted all that is desired, there are great numbers of such persons who have to feel that the money or support they receive comes unwillingly, or as a disagreeable matter of course, for which no satisfactory return is ever made. Such dependence is entirely fatal to all nobility of character, all worthy motives, all earnest thought. The dependent of this kind is more degraded than a slave, more unfortunate than a pauper made so by adverse fate; for the rich dependent can scarcely have a trace of self-respect, while the pauper or slave can feel that he is not one willingly. Even when some affection goes with the money gift, the recipient must be sensible that affection ought to be paid for only in affection, and that still no proper return is made. No true love ever reaches the willing dependent; for he or she has become so wholly selfish there scarcely remains anything in the character to attract the sincere affection of anybody.

Is there any salvation for these unfortunate victims of good fortune, the most unfortunate perhaps of any except the criminal? I know of only one,—such a change of affairs as will throw them on their own resources, compelling them to learn some useful work, and acquire some useful knowledge, as the only condition of their living at all.

No one need envy this class of persons. Brought up in affluence, pampered when children, taught little or nothing of much value, encouraged to believe themselves superior to working people, allowed the gratification of all their whims and expected to make no sacrifice of any kind, they necessarily become selfish, haughty and arrogant, unfriendly, impolite and disagreeable, with no true conception of what goodness, morality, or unselfishness means. When the wealth on which they depend is thrown away or lost, as it is almost sure to be, they are left helpless and miserable, with no preparation to battle with the world, and nothing within themselves to sustain them in misfortune or bring any comfort. In their struggle they are at a continual disadvantage; their education is worse than none, and the process of unlearning is terribly severe. In many cases their lives are filled to the brim with misery, and end in reckless despair or crime.

What terrible wrong is it in society that allows such a result as this,—first the excessive accumulation of wealth, and afterward the long torture and sacrifice of its victims ?

In that bright future to which I have previously called attention, toward which we are fast hastening under the progressive influence of scientific ideas, and whose beginning will probably not long be delayed—in that condition of things there will be no rich nor poor, no free robbery under the name of competition or freedom in trade, no monopoly, no extortion, no speculation, no gambling, and what is more, no *spirit* of gambling covered up in the desire to make large profits with little labor or expense. Although labor, by itself, may never be wholly agreeable to us, the *circumstances* connected with it, the *respectability* of it, allowed by every one, and the full natural *reward* secured to it, will altogether remove the old traditional curse, and render it always pleasant. No one will be educated to avoid or dislike it, and public opinion will not only hold it honorable, but all gain acquired without it as dishonorable. No man or woman will be so ignorant as to suppose he or she can be happy without it ; no one will willingly be dependent upon a rich relative even if there were one, or consider such a position as otherwise than debasing. Every woman as well as man will be a worker, whatever she may take her work to be. The present idle class, if any of them should be so fortunate as to reach that state, will in ceasing to be idlers and spendthrifts cease to be shallow and frivolous; while those who now do nothing but work will by having less to do, and a better reward for doing that, be able to obtain some better culture for their hearts and brains. Opportunity to labor will be the acknowledged right of every one; and no one of either sex will need to fear the loss of employment for any honest freedom of speech or action. The means of independence being thus secure, the independent spirit comes in as naturally as fullness of breath in the pure, sweet air of a balmy spring morning.

When the necessary condition of morality can be secured in freedom to labor and to live, and the beginning of it becomes manifest in a spirit of independence, it is then possible for a person to have moral courage, to dare do right, and to speak the truth. Whatever his conscience may command he will be free to do if he will. He will have no excuse for failure except his own weakness. The servility, deceit, treachery, cowardice, tyranny and general baseness of a state of slavery or dependence will gradually disappear, and their places be taken by the opposite qualities of manliness, frankness, faithfulness, honesty, friendliness and general amiability. Generosity being germinated with these, it becomes possible to graft upon it successively all the higher forms of self-sacrifice; the process, if continued, terminating in the complete conquest of the selfish nature, and the permanent outgrowth and preponderance of the unselfish impulses.

Here then is the beginning of the course; here the first step to be taken toward gaining that high estate. The succeeding ones may be different to every different person and no systematic order or plan can be made out. In treating of them hereafter I shall take them up merely as it happens.

But now, let us suppose that all people were industrious—none were idle—all the rich who now live on their incomes; all the dependent women; all the genteel loafers and sports; a good share of the invalids, who would be well if they had useful work; all the gamblers and speculators; all the intemperate and lazy tramps and saloon ornaments, with nearly all the saloon keepers besides;—all doing honest work of whatever kind they could do best. What chance would then remain for the present toilers; how much employment would they have and what wages would they get for it? With society as it now is, with the same ideas concerning property and the relations of capitol and labor that now prevail, what would these workers do? With another army of workers almost as large as their own pressing into the labor market, competing for the work to be done and the money to be paid for it, what could they do but emigrate —all who were not too poor? Do you intimate that many of them would be occupied in frivolous work of decoration for the rich, who would spend more for such work than they now do? They already spend for as much of it as they can appreciate, or fashion demand, yet cannot give employ to all who want it. Remunerative new enterprises are few, and nothing would remain but emigration. And when emigrants shall have occupied all the swamps and pine barrens of New Jersey and the Atlantic coast, all the worn-out lands of the Southern states, all the inhabitable parts of the Rocky Mountains and the Alkali plains, (for the best soils of the West are already taken up) when they have spread over the frozen wilds of Northern Canada and the torrid jungles of Central America and Mexico, still the same condition of things will exist. Is the process of expatriation to be continued forever? Are the poor to be eternally crowded out into the swamps and mountains of the earth, to meet the fate of wild beasts if they can do no better? And what if after this part of our country has become thickly populated, and the best lands all occupied, these people who are thrown out of employment should refuse to be driven into the mountains and swamps? Do you say that will be a question for your children or for their children? Still that has nothing to do with the rightfulness of the matter. And is it right to leave a troublesome question to them? Is it right that the process of starvation and expatriation should be kept up till their time? Can you in any way make it out to your conscience to be a right thing at all.

If, however, this problem seems too hard, take it in an easier shape. You must admit that every one ought to have some occupation; it is necessary in order to have any independent feeling, or any moral character, or to be anything but a nearly worthless parasite, supported by somebody's industry. This is indeed too evident to be denied or fairly questioned. Yet, suppose all idle people in our country to be immediately converted to that doctrine, and turned into workers, either useful or merely ornamental, what would be the effect notwithstanding emigration? How many thousand tramps would be made, how many hundreds die of starvation, and how many thousands from fevers and the various diseases that kill off the poor, living on poor food, in unhealthy dwellings, in filthy or malarious localities? And where is the wrong in society that prevents a right thing from being done without such fearful consequences? Please, reader, take the question home to yourself, think of it whenever it has a chance to come up, ask yourself what the right to labor means to one who has no other way of living, yet is thrown out of work for a long time. Put yourself in his place, and perhaps some thoughts will come into your brain that never were there before.

"The curse of the poor is their poverty" said the wise old Solomon; and I must add that it is the great obstacle to their gaining a spirit of independence, and an advance in moral growth. The old problem—how to remove it—is still unsolved, though later efforts are more hopeful than previous ones. Whatever I can do toward the final solution will be offered in another essay when

I come to discuss the industrial philosophy and policy of a society as it will be when approaching the Unselfish Stage.

In all that has been here advanced it is not forgotten that there are other causes or conditions of immorality than poverty or dependence; nor that instances of moral heroism are frequently found among the poor. A poor man may be courageous and independent because he has learned to endure discomfort and semi-starvation, or in his ignorance become reconciled to poverty as his unavoidable fate. In either case he has ceased to have wants, and by going backward to nothing has acquired a certain independence—the independence of the savage. In other instances an unselfish bravery or generosity may be exhibited because the manifestor's life has been ruined by some mistake or other misfortune, and being of little value he or she does not hesitate to risk it for some good purpose. But the virtue in such case comes through degradation, not through development, and may contain as much of recklessness as of generosity.

CHAPTER V.

VANITY AND PRIDE.

IN taking up different forms of selfishness without regard to order I begin with Vanity and Pride, two weaknesses not generally considered very serious, but which in reality are two very great hindrances to the full growth of the unselfish nature. Both of these are virtues at the beginning of the moral career; both are aids, inducements, and encouragements at the time when moral impulse is feeble, when popularity and position help one to be worthy of what is professed, of what is credited by reputation, or of what belongs to the position held. The love of approbation stimulates to attempt praiseworthy conduct; and when a higher position is thereby gained pride helps to retain it permanently; and to a certain extent protects against temptation. But like the shell of an egg to the young bird, their protection finally ceases to be needed, and then they obstruct the further development of that which they protected. Like the egg-shell also they have to be broken, to let the enclosed life out into the free, air and sunshine, naked of all false clothing, stripped of everything that does not belong to it. After a mighty struggle, perhaps, with the enclosing shell of pride, the growing human soul at length steps out, weak and exhausted it may be, but rejoicing in its new-found liberty.

By Vanity is meant the feeling of approbativeness, the desire of praise, of popularity, of being well-spoken of. *Pride* is of various species—pride of success, dignity or pride of position, pride of self-will or obstinacy, pride of opinion, pride of learning, pride of goodness or self-righteousness, pride of wealth, pride of race, blood or caste. All of them agree in this that they claim something to which the person is not honestly entitled. The selfishness of pride consists in dishonesty holding on to its position; the sacrifice or mortification of it consists in a person's being compelled to step down or fall to the place where one rightfully belongs. Apparently there is an exception to this when the bad conduct of a single person disgraces or degrades a whole family or society, in the public estimation; but really in such case the disgrace comes from erroneous opinion—there is no true *judgment;* for every individual is entitled to stand or fall upon his own merits only, regardless of any other, and according to this rule the previous statement is true, and the sacrifice of pride is a step toward honesty.

In its essential nature, then, Pride, as the time arrives for a higher outgrowth, becomes a fraud, a thief or a cheat, a robber holding what is not its own. Vanity is a beggar. Vanity might have been called a kind of pride —the pride of reputation; but there is this marked difference between it and others, that vanity belongs to weak characters, and pride to stronger ones, corresponding to the difference between the beggar and the one who takes. The one who manifests much desire for praise or popularity is ordinarily a fop, a dude, a butterfly, a braggart or a pretender—all names that imply some inferiority of intelligence. Persons of much stronger minds may indeed have it, but they possess pride in a stronger degree. The one who has most pride is generally the one who cares least what people think or say of him. Every one has somewhat of both feelings, the proportion varying to any extent.

In saying that pride, like the bird's egg-shell, is to be broken, shed, and left behind, let me not be misunderstood. There is sometimes a breaking of a man's pride which breaks the whole spirit of the man; but that is not the kind of break that is required. That is a break, caused by circumstances; one which crushes the man's self-respect and degrades him, *because no unselfish feeling is concerned in it.* But when he surrenders his pride in obedience to duty, his conscience, the most interior part of him, obtains a deep satisfaction, and his *inward self-respect is greater than before.* He is not crushed, except outwardly, and instead of being weak and hopeless he is stronger, more hopeful, better prepared for all the honest and useful work of life. In the true and natural process the surrender of pride is a sacrifice of selfish feeling at the behest of the moral or unselfish, because it stands in the way of some good that needs to be done. Then every result of the operation is good, and good only for all concerned.

Let us see first how the process works with Vanity or Approbativeness. To those who have not yet come to desire a higher life—a moral condition beyond the ordinary—I can say nothing except that they must combine as much wisdom as possible with their love of admiration. I am speaking mainly to those more advanced, who are conscious of having aspirations.

Any person who attains a moral development superior to that of his neighbors is liable at any time to be suspected, disliked, and reprobated, simply because he will sometimes do things with the best of motives, things which with those motives are entirely right and proper to all who understand them, but which to those not actuated by such motives appear to be prompted by unworthy or suspicious ones. These people, for a reason previously given, are unable to conceive of any better moral state than they have themselves reached. Being obliged to account for the better person's action by their own motives only, they attribute to him or her the same purposes they would themselves have in doing what seems to them to be the same thing; consequently it is an inferior motive, and he or she suffers an unjust loss of reputation. It is a natural result, one that cannot be helped, a thing to be expected and prepared for as far as possible. No condemnation is to be given to those who misunderstand, no contempt or unfriendliness.

Any one, therefore, who sets out to reach the Kingdom of the Unselfish will suffer more or less from this loss of good repute. Besides this, the candidate for the Unselfish degree must be prepared to do unselfish work wherever it needs to be done, and in some cases it may need to be done among those who are low and vile. Whenever any one shows indication of willingness to take a step forward every true man or woman should be willing to offer a helping hand. But any association with the degraded and disreputable may, for a time at least, entail more or less disgrace upon the respectable person so associated. The reproaches cast upon Jesus two thousand years ago will be repeated almost as quick and as much now as then. This too, must be discounted in advance. The praiseworthy conduct will receive its due appreciation at last, but it may be necessary to give humanity a long credit before it is ready to pay.

There are persons who, having lived all their lives in society, have talents and accomplishments fitting them to win admiration and praise from people who consider themselves less fortunate. While many of these lack the qualities that give stability and solid worth of character, their social education teaching them to be selfish, there are others who possess good impulses and are capable of making much moral progress. But though accomplishment makes all intercourse with our fellows easier, and is thus useful for a good purpose, all expectation of popularity or admiration from it for its own sake must be given up. The life that aims at pleasing people must be thoroughly subordinated to that which aims at cultivation of the nobler feelings. The praise of the many may have to be exchanged for that of the few, the very few perhaps, and these few themselves not popular. Everything that is bright, pleasant, graceful and beautiful, will after these qualities have become unselfish, be appreciated as heartily by the earnest workers in this new realm as by any outside of it; but none the less the present sacrifice must be made, the unselfish sentiment must come to completely dominate the selfish, before the latter can secure its natural and proper satisfaction.

Let us suppose that in all these ways the ordinary love of approbation is crucified in an earnest effort to reach a higher state. What return is there for this loss of admiration from the many? There is the more hearfelt admiration of the few who can sympathize with the soul's moral struggle, and who will bestow a genuine and just praise upon every effort to cast away vanity or pride, as a step taken toward that happier condition. Being just in their criticism they will give all the commendation that is deserved; no one will fail to get what is due. Though less in quantity it will be better in quality. Moreover, it will reach some who never expected it, and who never do receive the credit they deserve from the thoughtless and morally indifferent men and women of the world. The *desert* of it and the *bestowal* of it will both have become unselfish. No thought of treachery or pretense, no lurking sting of envy, will remain to adulterate or poison the happiness of either party. It will be deep, sincere, spontaneous, natural, free, just and happifying. The commendation of the good is reënforced by that of one's own conscience, and thus becomes worth far more than that previously received.

Somewhat akin to vanity is that sort of pride which refuses to submit to unfavorable criticism, and becomes very touchy at the least apperance of faultfinding. Those who have it most strongly are sometimes described as being very *sensitive*; which means that their selfishness sticks out all over them like a porcupine's bristles, so thickly one can hardly touch them anywhere without hitting one of these selfish points and getting pricked. It is a form of selfishness very difficult to get along with, and those who have it suffer from it nearly as much as those whom it affects.

This kind of pride is universal. Everybody has a share of it, and justifies himself in having it, or rather never blames himself for it, because he has never been seriously taught that it is a vice. The church it is true, tells him that if a brother has cause of offence against him he must settle the matter privately, which implies an acceptance of some degree of blame. And the Roman church further requires that his sins be submitted to his confessor for reproof and punishment. In the family too, and among intimate friends there is more or less faultfinding; while children are taught that they *must* submit to it, not that they ought to. In none of these proceedings, except possibly in the confessional, is the right view of the matter taken. No one ever gets the idea that he or she is *morally bound* to accept adverse criticism, from whoever is sufficiently concerned to offer it, and without getting angry in return. Here is the proof and illustration. Every one condemns that criticism exhibited in gossip, tattling, backbiting, slander. Partly because more harm than good comes from it, but more because no one is willing to submit to it, or acknowledges any duty to do so, or any right of others to canvass his faults. "They are nobody's business," is the common expression, and the common opinion. Those who speak of them are considered greater sinners than those who are guilty.

This common sentiment in regard to criticism, public or private, is what needs to be entirely reversed. Instead of no one's having a right to talk, every one has such a right. Instead of getting angry at it, and feeling justified in so doing, every one should be expected to submit to it without anger, or any sense of insult or injustice; and if it be true to correct himself or herself accordingly. Instead of being nobody's business, one's conduct is the concern of everybody who knows of it. Nearly every one has a moral sense that is hurt and offended by any outrage or injustice, whoever may be the author, or the victim of it. So every one has an intellectual sense that is disgusted by silliness or folly, and has a right to put it down by criticism. Every one too has an artistic sense that is pained by whatever is rude, slovenly, awkward or ill-mannered. There is an injustice suffered by all whose feelings are hurt, and justice allows them to speak of the offense and the offender. And instead of having this criticism whispered around privately, for fear somebody's selfish pride will be damaged, it ought to be done openly and frankly, with no thought of apology or excuse. The culprit is not the one who talks, but the one who complains of talk. "Mind your own business" commonly implies the existence of something that will not bear the light. The proper return for gossip and criticism is to surprise it by frankly admitting one's error, making it right as far as possible, and letting one's repentance and good conduct be canvassed as freely and far as was the bad. As long as the present assumption is maintained that nobody has a right to criticise except the one or the few most seriously affected, so long will gossip flourish and slander be complained of. But if people could once understand that a certain person submits habitually to correction from others, they would have much less disposition to discuss such a one's affairs. The greatest wrong in the whole matter is the assumption of a privilege to do wrong and escape all punishment.

Let me not, however, be understood to approve of the ordinary faultfinding and gossip, as the *best means* of correction. On the contrary it is crude, harsh and every way imperfect; often so unjust and slanderous that the subject of it is well entitled to criticise the critics in turn. The more correct method, for those ready to accept it is, whenever applicable, a private one. The proper critic is some friend well acquainted with the offender, and who can apply criticism with no motive except to benefit; just as the disinterested physician administers harsh medicine, or the surgeon cuts out a foreign growth. Rightly viewed, there is no more occasion for bitterness of feeling in one case than in the other, nor by either party. It is simply moral medicine and surgery; the two things being as near alike as two analogous things can be. And if people could be rightly educated concerning this matter there is reason to believe certain ones would become so expert in this kind of treatment that their services would be sought for and rewarded, as readily as we now pay an expert for curing a fever, or setting broken bones.

In the future society this result is certain. In the first place because the advanced intellects ready for that society will see its wisdom—will see a great benefit to be derived from it; and secondly, they will be morally ready to give up their pride as a matter of duty to others. For in every refusal to submit there is involved some loss, some injury, some undeserved suffering to another person or more than one. The proud feeling is purely selfish in this case; the willingness to submit is unselfish. No honest and true feeling can be hurt by submission; for not only will every one afterward have more genuine respect for one's self, but will receive more respect from all whose good esteem is best worth having. There will be no bitterness nor contempt in gossip, no slander, no treachery to friends, no concealment, no confidential tattling; for all occasion, all excuse, all desire for it will be taken away. Yet individuals will be talked about still, talked about just as is a sick person in a conference of his friends. All the spiritual symptoms, the diagnosis, and the best method of treatment. But this supposes all these friends to know that the patient has the same desire to become morally well that he has to be physically well; and the same tendency to improve under treatment,—a state of mind which among the class in view will be certain to exist. Still more, *every* one will be a friend.

Acceptance then of unfavorable criticism, whether given in kindness or in anger, without resentment, but instead with a *calm, candid self-examination*, to see if the accusation be true—this is to be acknowledged as a duty, as a requirement of simple justice. The way is then open for a reconciliation of estranged friends, and the settlement of all kinds of quarrels and difficulties. The parties concerned are now kept apart by a pride of the same stamp as that which resents criticism. It is looked upon as a humiliation for one to approach the other. Neither can afford to do it. If the view which one party takes of the cause of offense be correct there is no reason for making an advance; that is for the other to do, who is so plainly in the wrong. When he or she does it will be time enough to forgive.

Now this reasoning somehow always produces bad results. The differences are never settled, the parties never reconciled, the forgiveness never asked or granted, except rarely, when mutual friends arrange a *com-*

promise, and persuade the opponents to be at peace. But a compromise is only a lesser evil, it is never satisfactory, the right feeling is never restored by it. There is no sacrifice of a false pride, as there ought to be; while there may be a sacrifice of independence, which ought not to be. With or without compromise the bad effects remain, and this is sufficient to show that in some way the ordinary reasoning is defective.

The trouble is that each one is reasoning from the selfish point of view; all the time thinking of how much injury he or she has suffered from the other, never of how much the other has suffered from him or her; always thinking of the good things one's self has done, never of what has been done by the other; always of the provocation received, never of the provocation given; always considering self to be well-disposed and honest, never allowing the other to be so; never putting self in the other's place to see with that other's eyes or feel as the other may feel; never criticising self except to justify, always criticising the other to condemn.

This is the selfish reasoning; it is also the selfish feeling. There is no generosity, no magnanimity, no pity, no justice in it. It needs to be entirely reversed. First, by admitting that you (the reader, perhaps) are selfish in it; second, by remembering that the other party is, like yourself, feeling selfish and thinking from the selfish standpoint. With a different feeling and different view there will be different action. How is it to be brought about? Selfishness in one confirms selfishness in the other; generosity brings out generosity. Try the opposite policy all through. Admit that your enemy may have some sense of honor if not of justice —some little disposition to do what seems to him or her the right thing. Then take the unselfish point of view by putting yourself in the other's place. Instead of thinking what provocation you have had think of what you have given. Think, besides all the harm you have done, of all the good you have failed to do. See if you can find where you have been unjust. It will be easy to see where you have been unkind or uncharitable. Think of what may have been misunderstood. Be candid enough to admit that you may have misunderstood something yourself; for selfishness is always suspicious. Think how *everything* must appear to the opposite party. Think of what there may be in that person's character or circumstances that disposes to wrong doing, or that may palliate it. Finally, make an effort to be generous. And whether any one else is so or not, determine that you will at least be *just*, and do all that can be asked of you. Whether at fault much or little, even if but a tenth part of the blame belongs to you, confess your guilt as far as you see it, and more when you discover more. Don't enquire what the other one will do. Leave that *for* the other. If you are the first to know the right way be the first to take it. Acknowledge the most mortifying things of all; the greater the sacrifice of pride the greater the moral work done, and the better the effect. And believe me, such an effort will seldom be in vain. Your willingness to learn your own fault and to make it right will incite the same disposition on the part of another, and bring out only good in return. The gloomy, hateful, obstinate, and unhappy proud feeling is but a poor thing compared to the unselfish one that will be developed by the unselfish course here indicated.

But never attempt a reconciliation with a purpose to prove yourself better than another—to show that you can do right—without caring whether a good return is produced or not; for this is only the same old pride in another form—the form called self-righteousness, which taints and spoils a great many efforts designed to be good. Be unselfish enough to desire a good effect on the other party, for the other's sake. If the return is less than you think it should be, still be generous enough to remember that he or she may not be able to see his or her faults as readily as you do yours, and feel and act accordingly; not perhaps with as much of the old friendship (if it be a friend) but with more of charity. There may never be as good a result as you hope for, but there will be good feeling, what there is; and you will be sure of increased moral self-respect, and satisfaction of conscience; not only for obeying the mandate of duty, but in the thought that you are helping along some other soul in its progress toward the unselfish state.

In that unselfish condition there will be no pride to prevent reconciliation, nor even to make difficulties. A misunderstanding will need only the asking of a question to bring out an explanation of all that seems wrong. Confidence will be so strong it cannot be seriously weakened. The apparent or suspected misdoings will be so many occasions for renewing and strengthening it; for every such occasion will develop a new proof of faithfulness, and of the moral quality that cannot be false, or consciously do another an injury. Self-criticism will be a habit stronger and more common than that of criticising others; so thorough indeed there will be little need of the other kind; but the right of others to criticise being acknowledged, there can be no quarrel. The very beginning of it will be its end. If arising through haste or thoughtlessness, the impulse to it is already mastered as soon as one has time to think, and the pride also that might support it. If a quarrel or difficulty *could* exist that fact would be conclusive proof that two persons at least had failed to reach the unselfish condition they supposed themselves to be in.

Friendship will find itself in a new world; a world where all is faithfulness instead of treachery; where all is frankness in place of deception; where all fear of disappointment is gone; where every one is interested in every other, and the sentiment is free to flourish, expand and grow, and rejoice in its own unbounded satisfaction.

But criticism of the kind now in view may have a much larger field of usefulness. All varieties of defects and misdemeanors—habits, looks, dress, carriage, manners—all the little things now spoken of to everybody except the right one, can all be treated openly and fairly, with a rational plan for effecting the improvement of every fault, when once the right state of feeling has been gained. When the criticised as well as the critic has a desire for improvement, and both are actuated by a good motive there is a very different prospect of results from what has ever been known under the old methods and spirit. All the false habits of thought and speech, as well as feeling, can then be reached and corrected. The whole man or woman, though rough and irregular as a wild apple-tree in an old pasture, can be trimmed, smoothed, balanced, grafted, straightened up, trained to grow into a beautiful form, and to produce beautiful and wholesome fruit in good deeds, clear thought, and graceful behavior. The very circumstances and personnel which will constitute the social environment, will furnish a new stimulation to the moral soil, a new moral atmosphere, and a moral climate like that of perpetual spring.

One of the earliest and most common forms of pride is *obstinacy* or self-will—the determination to maintain a position because change would imply a confession of error and be humiliating. It, like the sensitiveness mentioned, is the virtue of the slave made free—of one just beginning to acquire manliness and self-respect, and who cannot therefore afford to risk the loss of any reputation or dignity. To such a one it may be useful, but it will be outgrown long before a person reaches the Unselfish Stage.

The self-estimation on account of *wealth* seems inexpressibly foolish to any high view of life or destiny. One may rightfully rejoice in the possession of a moderate amount of property; but nothing more. It makes no one better except by the advantages given for self-improvement; and one disposed so to use it soon casts off all the pride. It is the ignorant rich who manifest such pride offensively. If wealth is inherited it is only a piece of good fortune. If the owner has gained it by his talents and energy, these also are inherited, and the case is altered only by inheriting the means of getting instead of the thing itself. If he has acquired it by cultivating a smaller inherited power still the activity of mind which disposed him to do this is likewise an inheritance, a piece of mental good fortune which enables him to obtain the material one. He has what his ancestry and his circumstances have conferred upon him—nothing more; the poor person has the same. Circumstances may take the wealth away, and it is then as foolish to feel degraded by the loss as to feel elevated by the possession.

What makes the pride of wealth still more senseless and disgusting if possible is the fact, known to almost everybody except the ignorant rich themselves, that there are higher grades of talent than the talent for accumulating money, and higher aspirations than the desire to be rich. The student, the thinker, the artist, the investigator, all have a higher order of talent and skill; and because they have higher aspirations they subordinate money-getting to a nobler purpose and remain poor —too poor in many cases to carry out their better purposes. Their better talent however is still an inherited one and confers no right to despise another.

What the man himself, independent of causes acting on him, can do is nothing.

The assumption that material wealth gives superiority, or ought to give distinction, will never gain admission to the Kingdom of the Unselfish. One must be far beyond the stupidity of believing it, or the dishonesty that would allow himself to pass on such an assumption if he could.

Still less will the pretense that idleness indicates superiority find any favor. The Kingdom of Heaven, wrote Swedenborg, is a kingdom of uses; in which every one finds some occupation of his time that will be of use to others by conferring happiness, directly or indirectly, and is never idle. He reports a great number of industries and services as organized for making human energy useful and happifying.

Well, whether this may be correct or not regarding the spirit world, it will certainly be true sometime of this world. An unselfish person can have no wish to be idle, cannot possibly be content unless his abilities are put to some unselfish use, some effort tending to produce happiness, either directly and immediately, or remotely by fitting himself for greater usefulness in future. Purely selfish enjoyment or amusement for its own sake can have no place among such persons. For rest, for recreation, for satisfying the bodily and mental needs, for every useful end there will no doubt be a full sufficiency of it; never for any such motive as now animates the selfish classes in their enjoyment of idleness. Idleness dissipates every good quality of the human mind or body; is in every way degrading; and one of the very last conditions of which a person should ever be proud.

The pride of position or *dignity*, the haughtiness of race and caste, the aristocratic spirit, however exhibited, is not a feeling of very exalted nature. The purely aristocratic disposition is best seen in some of the least advanced people, in fact next the very lowest. Most persons have seen, and have despised or ridiculed it, in the lower grade white man or black. In all such people it is a relative virtue, aiding them to retain a position superior to what they formerly had. As their superiority is but little they must make the most of it, and cannot afford any appearance of letting down. With those of higher position or higher caste the case is the same. With all who exhibit the feeling there is a lack of magnanimity. Like the poor man who puts on the appearance of being rich, one must claim all he has a right to claim and more. As he gets higher or better he is less afraid of being let down, and becomes magnanimous. Finally he can lay aside dignity, and all affectation of worth, knowing well that he cannot lose the reality.

There is another reason why the pride of aristocracy (not the aristocrats themselves) should be despised by all who have reached a true high-mindedness. The inferior in order of *development* are the superior in *importance;* they are like the base on which a superstructure is reared, or the root from which grows the more highly developed stem of the plant. In the life of the individual or the race it is the latest development that can best be spared when that or the lower must go. The mental education can wait upon the *physical.* The *foundation* being saved a new upbuilding may be accomplished. From the *root* of the plant a new stem may grow. From the *lowest* industrial class in society the higher ones may arise. But take away the fundamental part and no higher development can ever exist. Thus while one part or one class has a superior evolution the other has a superiority in importance—in inherent value. Where then is the sense in one's despising the other?

The inferior in development have their species of pride no less; a pride not of superiority but of equality. Agreeably to the law that nothing can be known except through experience, they naturally have no consciousness of the superiority of others; and can learn the fact consciously only through their own growth. The coarse body and brain, the awkwardness that goes with poorly developed or poorly controlled muscles, the imperfect vocal organs and pronunciation, the want of humane sensibility, and the slow apprehension of ideas, are all indications of inferior development; and if the subjects of them could learn this much it would help them vastly toward the attainment of something better. They can be taught to see a difference between themselves and others, and will be aided by any kind of teaching that points out in detail what it is that constitutes that difference. They have not reached the point where they can throw off their pride quickly after being instructed regarding the nature of it, but whatever enables them to realize their inferiority of development in some one or more respects helps enable them to believe in the possibility of it regarding other things; and thus by arousing a desire for improvement facilitates their moral progress. For, the love of equality—the desire to obtain an equal development and an equal happiness with that of the best—is one of the very strongest desires in human nature, and gives hope for the elevation of every one who can be convinced that he or she does not already possess it.

There is a real and indisputable superiority of blood and of race; but here also the superior has probably been produced from the inferior, and contempt is very much like despising one's parents after they have created and furnished the means by which the child has gained a superiority.

One more species of pride remains, the very last to be given up. It is the feeling that self is entitled to credit for *something;* that it is an individual separate from all others, and can do something independently of all else. The Christian religionist meets this claim in a partial way by telling the individual he is nothing; that his salvation is wholly the work of a mediator; that every good act or impulse is the work of the Holy Spirit and comes from above; that in him is no merit; that he can do or be nothing of himself but accept the truth and submit to be nothing. The scientist can reach him only by showing that all his commendable thoughts, feelings, words and actions originate in causes beyond his individuality and his control; that his imagined freedom and hence merit, is a delusion; that he is more completely nothing in the hands of Fate than he is said to be in the hands of God; for he cannot even be free in choosing to be nothing. This I may endeavor to show in another essay. Assuming it to be possible, or assuming the religious doctrine to be true, this pride of individuality and freedom is just as truly a fraud as any of the rest. When it is at last surrendered there comes the outgrowth of true humility or modesty, a virtue worth more to human happiness than a thousand kinds of pride.

The pride of the intellect—conceit, bigotry, pride of learning or knowledge—and the pride of goodness, or self righteousness, are purposely omitted here, and reserved for separate chapters, in which they can have treatment more at length.

All kinds of pride, we can now see, are arrogant and pretentious frauds. Not that proud people are conscious of such a quality in the thing, but it is none the less true. As long as the false claim is unquestioned pride flourishes. When vanity is hurt it is because a false reputation is shown to be false and then shame takes its place. When dignity is mortified it is because an individual has been holding a position higher than he or she is entitled to. When the aristocratic spirit is humbled it is because the possessor of it shown to be so little above the despised ones that pretence of superiority is ridiculous. The exception is only when a mistake creates a wrong impression, and then the fall is not likely to be permanent. The very consciousness of pride (aside from satisfaction in a good thing) is itself the proof of a moral condition far from superior. The desire, the claim, the enjoyment of superiority—of being better, happier, more fortunate, more honored, more praised than another—for its own sake, is purely selfish, a desire for something others cannot have, and a wish to prevent their having it; for certainly all are not expected to have it at once. Exclusiveness is all that gives it a value. The very thought of ambition is thus corrupted with injustice. A moralized ambition can seek position or desire superiority only for its usefulness—for the ability it confers of increasing human happiness. A higher position, a greater honor, can be honestly, conscientiously, unselfishly taken only when conferred unsought, and used for the benefit of all. Real superiority is willing to be shared.

In the Kingdom of The Unselfish there will be no pride. Every one will try to help his fellow realize the greatest *usefulness* his peculiar talents can achieve, as the means of giving him the most honor and the highest position, as well as most happiness in other ways. Emulation, rivalry, competition will be dead; and their place be taken by higher motives—aspiration, desire to perfect others—the artistic impulse, with humanity as the material of art. Distinction can be won only by discarding the desire for it, and substituting a desire for the elevation of the lower, and the promotion of the most worthy The highest will be that one who, in addition to all other fitness, shall be able to take the lowest position and do most gracefully any menial service needing to be done. The ability to do this is the best evidence of that *moral* ability required at the head; because the opposite disposition, which seeks position for its own sake, is immoral and selfish in desiring to take it away from others. Jesus expressed it clearly when he said, "Let him who would be greatest among you be your servant." The effort will be to realize equality instead of inequality. Inequality will not then stand in the way of friendship. "The ignorant," said some old Hindu sage, "are not the friends of the wise, the man who has no cart is not the friend of him who has a cart. Friendship is the daughter of equality; it is never born of inequality." When, however, there is no pride to prevent the more developed from offering help to the less fortunate there will be no pride to prevent the acceptance of help; and so with free service and free acceptance there will be friendship and good will from this cause alone, in addition to all others.

Here too, the modest and sensitive will find their opportunity. The cold haughtiness of wealth and position will not freeze them into silence and quiet as now; poverty and lack of outside finish will not hinder the appreciation of the inner qualities; external accomplishments will be quickly put on under the encouragement of the unselfish friendly spirit, and with the impelling power of aspiration.

As the unselfish spirit will give no offence by pride, neither will it by slight or disrespect. Respect will be so deep and sincere there will be little need to think of the external forms by which it is now expressed. The utmost freedom and approachability will exist without impoliteness ever being intended or suspected.

Now contrast this spirit and these anticipated results with the present effects of false pride—the caste feeling, the effort to keep up appearances, the disgrace of poverty, the success of brass and pretension, the suffering from loss of wealth and social standing, the suicides from sudden ill fortune, the envyings of the unfortunate, the heartburnings and bitterness of defeated ambition—then believe if you can that all these evils are to last for thousands of years. But be assured of my strong faith that some of the better part of the race will begin very soon to put them away, and take on feelings of an opposite quality, in preparation for such a superior state as we are contemplating.

What then is it that is to take the place of this false, hateful, selfish pride? It is a true and honest self-respect, a consciencious self-respect, a self-respect that can be humble and rejoice in the strength of humility, depising arrogance, pretension, and aristocracy as unworthy a full-grown human soul; a self-respect that will take pleasure in moral perfection, whose aspiration will be to be perfect as the ideal Father in Heaven is perfect; which will strive to make the soul pure and true, and strong and brave, and clear and bright and beautiful with every quality that can add to human happiness; and which, while rejoicing in every such acquirement, will do so without any particle of that pride that can be unpleasant to another.

CHAPTER VI.
INTELLECTUAL IMMORALITY.

BY this phrase I do not mean a depravity or immorality of the intellect itself, which may be said to always do as well as it can; but an immorality of the feelings, *regarding* the intellect, warping, twisting, perverting, repressing, confusing, and stultifying its operations. Bigotry, prejudice, sophistry, illiberality, and inhospitality are some of the names by which it is known. There is still another, one not so well known, but it describes a fault altogether too common; this is mental *indolence*, a sheer laziness of the brain. It afflicts all orders and conditions of people, even some who with their muscles are very industrious. Some have it when young and outgrow it mostly as they become older; others are as incapable of mental labor at sixty as they were at six. It indicates lack of development, and is one of the most difficult and hopeless to deal with of any of the mental faults. All of them are hard to overcome. They are perversities, evils, sins, even crimes; equal in importance to the moral defects, and equally heinous in character—equally evil, villainous, and misery-producing in their *effects*. All too are selfish—disgustingly selfish, in their spirit, when clearly understood. Yet few condemn them as vices, though every one despises them in others while allowing them in himself. Very little is said or written against the moral quality of them by preachers and moralists, though their wickedness is visible at all times and places, and though the subject might be preached or written upon for months without overdoing. It is high time this species of immorality was dealt with according to its true character.

To call these things evils or immoralities is alone equivalent to calling them selfish ; but to see more plainly that all of them are born from the selfish nature let us observe how closely bigotry is connected with conceit. "My knowledge is so great, so correct, or so minute as to be sufficient; and my judgment is infallible; your knowledge and judgment are inferior, false and worthless." This is the true feeling of bigotry, and whoever will examine his or her own consciousness when the foolish or offensive notions of others are contemplated, will find some of that feeling. "Others are not as worthy or capable to form a correct opinion as I am; their views are not entitled to as much respect as mine; I will not give up mine to anybody. I can teach them something; and if they were only honest and candid they would see as I do." This is the real spirit that almost everybody has, and like other forms of pride it is full of arrogance and contempt.

"But isn't anyone entitled to feel that his opinion is best?" That depends upon how he has come by it. If the opposite view has been taken in the first place as equally probable, or if other conflicting notions have been considered as equally worthy till proved inferior; if one and all have been looked at candidly and thoroughly, with a sincere determination, made in advance, to give up all preconceived ideas if necessary, and with the mind fully reconciled to that possibility, then the opinion arrived at is conscientious, and is justifiable till further evidence changes it. Otherwise it is not justifiable, nor is the claim of superior knowledge.

But how many people take this course in forming

their judgments? Not one in ten thousand. Do they ever contemplate a reversal of their present ideas as possible, and reconcile themselves to such a possibility in advance as if it were already actual? Do they consider the opposite view as equal to theirs, or the holders of it as equally worthy of respect with themselves? Not at all. They constantly hope and strive to find their present opinions confirmed; and delude themselves with a promise that they will believe otherwise when the evidence comes. Their own side must have the benefit of every doubt, and not be affected by aught that can possibly be turned aside or mitigated. Their minds are like a court in which the accused is condemned before trial, and every effort made to convict him right or wrong. There is no more justice in one case than in the other. The opposing view is entitled to every allowance claimed for ours. When we are capable of giving it, and of thinking of what belongs to that as quickly as we think of what belongs to our favorite idea, then we are capable of thinking honestly—not before. All the pride and the favoritism we naturally connect with our own view must be given up before the examination begins. The same self-renunciation required in any other sacrifice of pride, conceit, or arrogance is required in this; and it cannot be too complete.

Most people are familiar with the effects of *religious* bigotry in the form of persecution. I mention it less to accuse any particular religion than to remind ourselves of the vast amount of it that has come alike from most of the great religions; the peaceful Buddhism, which appears to have never resorted to it, being one exception; and Parseeism, perhaps too sincere in its moral warfare against wrong to take up a physical battle against belief, being probably another. Both these were religions having a dominant moral motive. Brahmanism, Judaism,

Paganism (Roman), Christianity and Mohammedism have tortured and slain millions of human victims, causing an unspeakable amount of agony to the race, yet scarcely can a solitary good be mentioned as resulting from it all, or associated with it. Even the lesson of its uselessness has been learned by only a few; the danger of future persecution, and of religious strife, is not yet removed from Europe or America, so long as Jews are liable to loss of life from mobs, and freethinkers of all kinds are looked upon as immoral and dangerous. What a commentary this upon the natural selfishness, and stupidity of human beings! Certainly it is no wonder the Christian world is confirmed in its belief of original sin and natural depravity.

This is the worst of the great sins of bigotry. But there are plenty of smaller ones. Conceit, self-righteousness, ambition, or other vices have been more or less connected with them, but the main factor in the complex cause has been bigotry—the spirit that would not learn or listen. How much of the horrors of the French revolution might have been avoided had not the human masses in conflict been utterly possessed by this vile disposition. To come down to our own time and country, there need be no hesitation in asserting that our nation was for twenty-five years prior to 1860 governed by the worst elements in its population; that they disgraced its history for all time, and sacrificed thousands of innocent lives by the unjust conquest of Mexico, the allowance of slave smuggling, and the extension and encouragement of slavery till the end came in a great civil war, mainly through the blind, obstinate bigotry of decent and respectable Northern men, who would not believe or listen to anything that reflected upon their ignorant pride or partisan prejudices. I do not mean that their opponents were *not* bigoted, but that such results came from the bigotry of one party, and might have been prevented by the candor and honesty of even a small proportion of the voters responsible for them. Why should not the feeling that induces such conduct, or rather which prevents better conduct, be hated and disgraced equally with the disposition to murder, or slander, or steal? The results are no better; why should the cause be ignored or excused?

See our political campaign for the last choice of a president (1884). Think of the immense expenditure of time and money, and breath and brain, in the effort to convert the small percentage of voters needed to turn the political scales. Yet how many were changed? Only a few Irishmen and a few Independents, nearly all of whom would probably have changed without any effort at all. How senseless such a contest! Partisan bigotry prevents any good from all this vast labor, except that perhaps the rising generation have learned a little something they might not have learned otherwise —a mere trifle many of them will forget before the next campaign.

Look too, at the Christian world, or that part of it which has most life, divided up into numberless little sects, all alike spending their energies in defending or propagating their peculiar doctrines, and all incapable till lately of uniting in any good work, and now only partially, because of the estrangement resulting from bigotry in regard to these doctrines—doctrines as utterly empty and worthless for all practical purposes as chestnut burrs of last year's growth. Even the heretical and socialistic sects and parties, that have been produced by the Protestant tendency, continue to despise and hate each other, with the same old bitterness of their progenitors.

See how even in almost every little dispute or debate each of the contestants comes out with a firmer adherence to his own opinion than he had before; while both parties have more or less ill-feeling, wounded pride, or positive hatred, instead of a closer approach to the actual truth that possibly lies somewhere between them.

Think still further of the thousand and one petty difficulties arising every day between husbands and wives, parents and children, relatives, friends, playmates, workmates, neighbors—associates of every kind, because everybody has this disgusting conceit and unwillingness to learn of another—a contemptible pride that is nothing but pretension, claiming knowledge it does not possess, and an ability to form correct opinions when it has no such ability. Why should not every person who desires to be decently honest despise such a miserable fraud, and cast it utterly out of the mind?

Narrowness, illiberality, and prejudice are simply other forms and names of the same selfish pride and ignorant conceit which is the essence of bigotry. One special manifestation of it requires a few words. It is that which takes the form of *inhospitality* to new thoughts, discoveries, or inventions. To be inhospitable to a friend, or one in need of physical comfort, is acknowledged to be mean and reprehensible. But refusal to entertain thought or discovery, that may be of immense good to humanity, is not considered any offence; it is stupid, of course, a long time afterward, when the new thing has gained a recognition, but nothing worse; nobody condemns the immorality of it; though the effect is the same as if every one knowing of the new comer in the world of thought had deliberately conspired to destroy it, intending to prevent the world's receiving its benefits. The devilish character of such a design, and the devilishness of a blind, stupid, bigoted rejection of new truth are in effect precisely the same. The crime and the blunder are one, and it is the same mean spirit of perverse selfishness which permits one as much as the other. In that same spirit some of you who read may say that this is new doctrine and you have a right to reject it. New, or at least unfamiliar, it may be; but such a reason for rejecting it is to an *honest* thinker no excuse at all.

The history of great inventions, of scientific discoveries, of advancing thought in philosophy, shows how difficult and terribly slow has been the work of gaining hospitality for such new developments. Long years of patient waiting and suffering to the lone thinker in many cases, obloquy and contempt in others, final defeat and death before recognition in some, success and triumph in a few—these are the rewards that come to the highest human talent devoted to its highest work. This is what some are pleased to call the overruling of a divine wisdom; to any one who is willing to think honestly it means human selfishness in the form of bigotry. It is one of those great curses of ill-fortune that stand in the way of all development.

Selfishness will even defeat its own interest for fear a wiser policy might be of benefit to some one else. This is not to be thought of; and any measure, policy, or suggestion that may appear favorable to others will be refused all fair consideration. Persons are sometimes said to bite off their own noses out of spite; and here out of envy or jealousy they refuse to learn what will be to their own advantage. It is a common stupidity, and can be easily seen in both small affairs and great ones.

The unwisdom of the good is scarcely less than that of the selfish and mean. Some of the most careful thinkers believe that the efforts of reformers and philanthropists produce more harm than benefit. Certainly there is much evil mixed with the good they accomplish. And universally their minds are one-sided. They assume their views and projects to be wholly good; those opposed to them to be wholly false and evil. They overestimate the importance of their various reforms and hobbies, and thus become jesuitical in advancing them, setting them so high that unjust or doubtful means are considered justifiable in accomplishing a purpose. Their one idea is looked upon as the one great cause or cure of social or individual miseries, and no other is believed to be of any value. And thus nearly all reformers, some of whom think themselves to be progressive, come to be as bigoted as any of those whose bigotry they condemn.

Some of the very best people, morally, persons who are sincerely conscientious so far as they know the right, and who if equally wise would be prepared for a higher life, do by the rigid confinement of their thought within certain limits, shut out the very light that might lead them far toward a real heaven in place of the imaginary one for which they seek and hope. They have been taught bigotry from their childhood; and any opening of the mind to new truth now is infidelity and sacrilege. The very claim that such limitation of thought is necessary is itself suspicious and an evidence of weakness; yet it comes to be made by all religions, as the result of their being based on the authority of some revelation. *In this way religion at length serves to defeat the moral progress that should be its one supreme end.* The religious moralist becomes unprincipled in his thought, notwithstanding his desire to be moral. The founders of religions and sects do not teach men to learn from others. They are themselves not free from bigotry. "Learn from us only" is what they say or mean. All of which is the opposite of the final teaching, which will be, Learn from all—from any source whatever.

These bigoted good persons are not the self-righteous in the ordinary meaning. The self-righteous are mostly those who are merely beginning in an upward course, and to whom goodness is so new, strange, and striking that it causes itself to be relatively overestimated. The state of mind is not favorable to learning; but in that stage of growth it may not be so advisable to stimulate new thought as to encourage the new feeling that has arisen. There is however, another phase of moral development, commonly called Phariseeism, a more advanced stage, in which the person is truly moral and aspirational, and because he is so despises, and separates himself from, all below him, becoming a sort of moral aristocrat. Even this style of goodness has yet something to learn from the very class it despises and shuns; and whom, by avoiding or putting far away, it helps to still further discourage and degrade. The pharisee must yet carry to these debased ones the acknowledgment that they have suffered wrong as well as done wrong; and the assurance that they are not to be forever deserted, or neglected, but assisted and taken along in company with the more fortunate into a better social state destined for all. And when met in such a spirit as this they will at least prove themselves to be more human than was supposed.

One of the worst of all the forms of intellectual immorality is the self-conceit springing from superficial knowledge. Like self-righteousness in the moral department, a little knowledge at the beginning of the intellectual career makes a powerful impression on the before ignorant mind, by its constrast with the previous vacancy. Like all new experiences, it leads the person to overestimate its value and importance; and judging by self, as all men do till experience has taught them better, he takes others to be like his own previous self, and assumes a present superiority. The feeling may be general, or may regard only some special kind of knowledge. Persons naturally modest will exhibit this consciousness of superior wisdom when they come to learn some new thing. And though they may continue to advance in the narrow path they are now going, it is almost impossible for them to learn anything outside of it. So far as intellectual progress generally is concerned they are stuck in a slough of conceit more difficult to get through than the Slough of Despond of old Bunyan's Christian. Indeed they have no desire to get beyond it. Believing themselves wise, and contented with a first installment of knowledge, how can they be otherwise than bigoted toward everything not in harmony with their own limited possession?

In young people we must expect this and be patient with it. If they keep on in their first narrow path they will ere long come to another and may pursue that also. But many persons of fifty or sixty years are still nothing but boys and girls in this respect, and in their case the fault becomes disgraceful and demoralizing. They harden themselves into a set of notions that can only be changed by the most severe experience. They hinder the improvement of all around them, and keep back the advance of all knowledge and goodness. Their state of mind is as selfish and mean as that of the robber or thief. Not of course that they see it in that light, but that is the way they may see it perhaps, at a later stage of their progress.

To illustrate, pious people will learn nothing outside their church and sacred book, or even their special branch of the church. Respectable ones will take nothing unless it comes from inside their respectable clique; and learned ones must first ascertain whether a person offering an idea is educated, and in what particular school. Having got as far as they have they feel completely sated with wisdom, and anything more would make them sick. Some good observer has said that when a doctor of divinity has written a book, and put his ideas on record, it is time for him to die; for he will never learn anything further. And though not true always, it is true generally, and true of many others besides doctors of divinity.

An obstinate and contemptuous skepticism of any kind is a pretty sure indication of superficical knowledge, no matter if the victim of it professes science; he has not yet acquired the true scientific spirit.

Conceit, pride and intellectual stubbornness are not however to be condemned absolutely. In small and weak minds they are probably necessary to some extent, being like the silica which the grass or wheat plant deposits in its outside layer, to stiffen it so it can stand alone, and grow up into the sunshine. When the mind becomes, through knowledge and practice, *capable* of standing alone, it no longer needs the protection of bigotry, or the defence of conceit and self-assertion. It is safe, and not afraid to venture out of its old home, or its old familiar path of thought. Some will say its fear was needless. Of this I am not sure; it may need considerable time to digest, appropriate, and get strength from, what it finds in one place, before taking new materials from new sources. I am only sure that all these inferior qualities must be outgrown and cast off, before the mind can reach that state of complete unselfishness belonging to the new and higher condition of the man and of society. It behooves every one to at least put himself in the way of making an advance.

There yet remains the serious fault of mental indolence, which as here referred to is a laziness of the mind in its thinking department. It may observe and memorize perhaps, but will not take the trouble to think. Dreaming, talking, sentimentalizing, is all easy enough; reasoning alone is hard work. Multitudes of men and women drift into whatever religion or politics, medicine, society, or occupation may happen to be before them; never troubling their heads; living to eat, drink, and be merry; and expecting to drift into heaven when they die; for no other virtue than their stupid indifference.

The biggest truth in the universe might be offered them, but would have no interest; it would not tempt them into thought. They might be threatened with every kind of misfortune and ruin; yet they would rather take the risk than learn to use their brains.

The fault is common enough with men, but still more so with women. It is their great mental weakness. More than anything else it allows them to make mistakes, to be confused, deceived, cheated and robbed. It is a misfortune to which they are born and from which few of them escape. They are often credited with a faculty called Intuition, assumed to be superior to the reasoning faculty, and able to make up for all deficiencies. But this, so far as it is normal, and not some kind of mediumistic power, is in reality only a quick command of all the mental resources, obtained through memory and observation. The business man, the hunter, the savage—any one accustomed to quick decision and action—has the same readiness of intuition. The abnormal species of intuition may sometimes be of use to women, but it is exceptional, and not always sure to be correct.

Not to do women any injustice however, it must be admitted that a majority of the other sex exhibit the same immaturity of brain. They blunder along through a thoughtless life, some lucky enough to get through comfortably, others the cheap victims of knavery, accident, and general misfortune. But I wish to impress upon women more especially the necessity of improvement here, because I believe they will find this fault their great impediment in attempting to reach that high goal that is set before them. Their pride, their ambition, their enmity, their luxury, their vanity even, they can overcome with less effort than men; but their mental inertness, especially in middle life, with a weakened nerve system, will be a mountain of difficulty. Yet it is not at all insurmountable. The difficulty is one that will lessen with every effort, while with every successful effort additional strength and energy will be gained. The mastery of one truth gives strength to the mind for the contest with one more obstinate. The contemplation of great subjects drives out small ones; the habit of such thinking creates interest in such subjects, and taste for stronger thought, nobler work, and higher aspirations. There is no woman of good natural ability but can master if she will the grandest thought of the greatest men who have done great thinking. Women could not originate it—at least never have done so—but when once invented or discovered, a great truth, like a great invention in machinery, can be made comprehensible to any mind of good capacity. There is nothing to discourage women from undertaking anything they need to learn— nothing, that is, except their own present weak energies, or indisposition.

In addition to all the blunders and generally vicious results of *willfully refusing* to think, there are those of thoughtlessness and careless ignorance, no less deplorable. Being just as bad in their effects as the bad effects of design, why should they have less reprobation? If a presidential election is lost by carelessness a vast number of people are ready to blame the offender without mercy. But when a railroad accident occurs, or a score or two of men are suffocated in a coal mine, or killed in a hundred other ways through somebody's careless failure to think, scarcely any one seems to consider it a very serious matter. The loss of another person's life is of little account compared to the defeat of one's own selfish personal opinion,—is about the way it stands in the ordinary mind. This, it seems to me, is an entirely wrong view, and a wrong feeling. A blunder is equivalent to a crime, and the failure to think as reprehensible as the failure to will. One is as properly punishable as the other. The results to society or to the individual are the same, and both are therefore equally *un*social or *im*moral. A more enlightened opinion will, I believe, hold them to be so, and a truly uuselfish person will no more cling to his intellectual faults than to those now called moral; will no sooner excuse himself for the selfishness of conceit, ignorance, mental laziness, or bigotry than for the selfishness of desiring to rob, kill, or steal. Selfishness of disposition will be considered selfish without any exception, and the consequences of it vice or crime.

Nature's mode of dealing with all the weaknesses of the intellect is very simple, and is well known. It is given in that old proverb—"Experience is a dear school, but fools will not learn in any other." The same idea has been expressed poetically:

"Great truths are dearly bought, not found by chance,
   Nor borne upon the wings of summer dream;
But grasped in the great struggle of the soul,
   Hard buffeting with adverse wind and stream."

All truth—all wisdom—is the product of experience; what has come to us without our own experience has come from the experience of some one else. Part we obtain by experience in reality, part by experience in imagination. And lucky is the one who can learn from the experience of others, instead of going through it himself. This however refers to experience of evil or suffering. Truth is equally learned by experience of good or happiness. The mind must be acted upon in some way —either drawn or driven—it will not move of itself. If not attracted by the ideal picture of a higher happiness, it will be forced by the reality of a deeper suffering. Thus far in human history it has mainly had to be driven by suffering. It now remains to be seen if there are yet any who can be sufficiently attracted by the beauty and glory of a higher ideal. If not, then the old experience of misery must still go on.

There is yet however, one other mental weakness; one that is common to minds of all grades, the educated and the ignorant, the feeble and the mighty, differing only in amount or degree among them all. What I mean now is the *superstitious* feeling or tendency—the disposition to discover superior truth or value in what is strange, mysterious, or incomprehensible—to imagine deep thought in some wonderfully complex sentence that nobody can understand; to regard the stranger as superior to one who is well known; to find something sacred, precious, or beautiful in an old book whose origin is hid in oblivion, or in some dark allegory no two can interpret alike; and to reverence the ancient or "time-honored" institution and custom.

Of course the most fully developed and thoughtful mind has the least of this disposition; but still there are very few who will not, other things equal, think better of the ancient or customary thing than of the new one; and perhaps nobody but will have more respect for the stranger than for one equally worthy who has always been known.

There is no need of condemning this strange propensity; every one, probably, will admit the foolishness of it, and yet no one attempts to cast it wholly out of the mind. This however, is one of the things that must be done before the highest truths can be learned, or the fullest moral advancement reached. The stranger must not be taken for a wise man, nor the prophet in his own country for a fool. Incomprehensibility is not to be taken for deep thought, nor pseud-ideas for solid truth, however wonderful or fascinating the language that sets them forth. Truth, and nobility of sentiment must be taken for just what they are, no matter how plain, simple, or humble their origin or expression. In no other way can truth have justice done to it, or man become able to learn all things.

But moreover, there is a natural cause for intellectual perversity, aside from conceit, pride, stubbornness or inertness. There are opposite truths, opposite aspects of things, and opposite tendencies in the human mind. The opposite phases of all movement have become recognized in scientific philosophy under the name of the Rhythm of Motion, (see Spencer's First Principles) or more familiarly as universal Action and Reaction. The same character of oppositeness or polarity may extend to objects as well as movements. Day and night, summer and winter, are produced by the rhythm of the earth's motions. But the ice of the poles, and the heat of the tropics, are results, not of the earth's movement, but of its form and the stationary direction of its axis; they belong to the thing itself. For aught we can yet say there may be a similar oppositeness in all the qualities of things whether in motion or at rest. The mind, too, has many qualities that are antithetical, besides opposing views and judgments. Some individual mind is always ready to take the opposite side. Unfortunately the contrasting views are taken by different persons. With very few exceptions, the individual mind has never become so polarized within itself that it could willingly, and for truth's sake, look calmly at the side opposite that where its gaze is first fixed. The first view is likely to be an exclusive one; that one is considered wholly true, the antagonistic one is wholly false. Being a pure assumption, as this notion is, it is amazing how the great majority of people will obstinately ignore all evidence favoring a contrary opinion; closing their eyes to plain facts, and denying testimony that, but for their prejudice, would be entirely reliable. Notice how frequently when a statement of opinion is made an opposition to it immediately springs up; and how earnestly a dispute about nothing will be carried on till bad feeling is arrived at, but rarely an agreement. Many persons will be even impolite in their undue haste to oppose something they hear said. Others would oppose but for some reason of prudence. A few are inclined to admit some truth on the part of their opponents; but the general tendency is so clearly a disputatious one that it might serve for a good proof of natural depravity, as it is in fact a good illustration of the native selfishness.

To say that this disposition is morally wrong because of its quarrelsome spirit, is only a truism. But to see how it is intellectually wrong, after admitting that a universal polarity in thought and things is possible, may not be so easy. The trouble is that the *individual* mind is not polarized in its *thinking*, so that it can look in opposite directions of its own motion, without the aid or compulsion of other minds. It needs to learn that because one doctrine or set of ideas is true, the other is not always necessarily false, evil, or hostile. There are truths and theories which are complimentary to each other, each necessary to the whole truth, and both in harmony when the whole truth is known. Scientific men are already somewhat disposed to learn this. Mr. Spencer especially, is inclined to see reconciliations; while all men of wide information come to discover the possibility of them, and are therefore less exclusively attached to one idea. This sort of liberality is likely to increase with increasing knowledge, and likewise the number of complementary truths, till finally we reach a complete harmony; the really contradictory, erroneous or delusive notions being of course eradicated.

The feeling then, which prompts to the present quarrelsomeness ought to be put aside, squelched, extinguished; and in place of it should be acquired a willingness to learn, and to accept a possible harmonious truth in the idea which at first seems so antagonistic to our own. Still more than this we should do; we should try voluntarily to make acquaintance with that which is opposed to us, to find if there be in it a truth that can be made accordant with ours. To be willing to accept it when forced upon us is not enough; we should seek for it ourselves before it is pressed upon our attention.

And this is precisely the spirit that will characterize all the mental operations in that new world of the Unselfish, that Empire of the Wise, now about to make its appearance, and like the little stone in the prophet's vision, to grow, till in the coming centuries, it fills the whole earth. There can be no complete heavenly condition till there is a scientific philosophy at the bottom of all thought, which will command universal acceptance, from which all can reason, and by which all can be persuaded and led. However angelic persons may be in their feelings, however well-disposed toward contrasting views, unless there is a common intellectual groundwork there will be lack of entire sympathy, there will be some shadow of estrangement, while their agreement in moral purposes will cause a perpetual sadness of some degree concerning the intellectual disagreement. Moral goodness alone, in the ordinary sense, cannot suffice; there must be an intellectual guidance capable of laying foundations on which all can unite, and by means of which an agreement in minor truths and details can be secured. Having this the unselfish development will gradually induce all thought as well as feeling into a complete unity.

Fortunately I can say, with fullest confidence of being correct, that the carrying of the unselfish feeling into all the thought, as here insisted upon, will bring forth that universal basis as surely as daybreak brings the sunrise. The *moralized* intellect will discover the *highest* truth.

If it shall prove to have that polaric quality that has here been assumed as probable, then there will be a remarkable confirmation of such a philosophy in the fact that it leads towards peace, conciliation and friendship, where the old assumptions and methods tend to discord, hatred and strife; one producing a *moral* result, in place of the *immoral* result perpetually wrought by the other.

In the new intellectual Empire mental indolence will be unknown. Every person will be animated by a sublime curiosity to know all the great secrets of the universe, and an intense desire to become acquainted with all the myriad forms of activity, life and use upon the surface of the earth, and within and around it. Every accomplishment and grace that can add attractiveness to the individual, and give pleasure to others will be undertaken and learned with an ardor such as we rarely see, stimulated by conscientious and noble purposes. Every one will stand ready to assist the weaker, the less fortunate, the less advanced, the least attractive, to bring them up to an equality of development with the more favored. The sensitive, the unassuming, the neglected, if they only possess the moral quality, will there find a home, and will realize a bond of union which no difference of worldly conditions, of education or accomplishment can break. In the spiritual sunshine of its atmosphere they will put on brightness, beauty and grace like chilled and stunted plants transferred to the rich, warm soil of the sheltered garden. No lack of sympathy from kindred minds will there sadden and blight the soul hungering and thirsting for knowledge, goodness and beauty; for there all will be aspiring after every kind of perfection, and determined to achieve it. They will have reached that stage of human evolution when such motives and purposes have become the dominant ones of their lives. And though an absolute perfection can never be attained, they will be pressing forward at a rapid pace, and all the great essentials of a perfect character will be acquired much sooner, perhaps, than any one can now believe. No one will have any idle time, there will be no ennui, no repression, no lack of opportunity or field for exertion; for every one will find his or her natural place, and in getting into it will have the assistance of every one else.

In that new world of thought and feeling there will be no willful blindness, no pride of opinion, no ignorant conceit, because there will be no selfishness. But there will be independence; and no doctrine, law, custom or sentiment will escape criticism, or be of any validity without good reason behind it. Yet with this, again, will be no pride of originality, or ownership in ideas; no claim of any credit for thought, which comes as the result or product of all previous thought. Looked upon as the effect of causes, there will be no lack of charity for immature and inconsistent thinking; neither will there be any effort to force ideas upon an unwilling mind, or urge it beyond its natural rate of growth, through the arrogance of superior knowledge or new-found wisdom, not yet sufficiently wise or moralized. The advice Buddha is said to have given his disciples is expressed in the true unselfish tone.

"Take heed that no one, being 'scaped from bonds,
Vexeth bound souls with boasts of liberty;
Free are ye rather if your freedom spread
By patient winning and sweet wisdom's skill."

There, instead of disputes over words and quibbles, will be found persons of previously antagonistic views striving candidly to learn from each other, and to find the cause of their old disagreements, that it may be removed by a completer knowledge. There, instead of people ever ready to talk and anxious to display, will be seen those more ready to listen than to talk, and unpretentious enough to take a hint from any child. A novel sight truly, this will be, the desire to talk, to dispute, to teach, all gone; swallowed up in the new and stronger desire to learn, to think, to grow; drowned and forever extinguished in sober meditation and the calm, steady earnestness of an honest intellectual purpose.

But, let me again repeat, before one gets as far as this, and in order to reach, accept and take in that central or fundamental truth that is to be associated with it, or indeed any important truth short of that, the mind must be qualified to do some noble work. It must think great thoughts, and become to a good degree capable of thinking clearly, critically, exactly, and above all justly. The weakness of the lazy brain is to be outgrown; carelessness to be corrected by earnest thoroughness; prejudice and bigotry to be put under foot forever; the pride that refuses to acknowledge ignorance or mistake to be discarded for manly honesty; and the shallowness of conceit displaced by wider knowledge. Actual opinions and doctrines are to be treated as facts having reasons or causes to be investigated and understood. The most repulsive of them is to be looked at squarely in the face, with a sincere desire to discover whatever of truth or beauty may appear in it to other minds, and with a firm determination in advance to accept all that may be found worthy. The conservative has to learn from the progressive and vice versa; the scientist from the religionist, and the religionist from science; the socialist from the individualist, and assuredly the friends of the present order must not long hesitate to learn something from the socialist. No matter how dreadful the ideas of either one of these may be, there is no escape from them except through honest, unselfish thought. And whatever the subject, of any sort, that may come before the mind, the timidity that dares not trust the reason fully must be forever displaced by that strength and confidence of judgment that will follow, and abide by, the conclusions of the reason to the utmost limit they can be drawn.

Scientific knowledge and teaching is to take the first place instead of traditional. The body of science we already possess is the foundation work of all that is to be added to it; and if the view of this book is correct it is the elementary part of all our future intellectual possessions. A careful and earnest study of it is the necessary first step toward the formation of reliable judgments, toward the moralization of intellect, and toward the acquisition of that culture which is indispensable to the new moral and intellectual condition we are contemplating. Without such an acquaintance with science one is sadly unprepared for the brain work of even the present time. The coming century, more truly than any other, is to be an age of revolutions; of revolutions in thought and in manner of thinking, as well as in many other things besides. In these days of swift communication the intellectual world is advancing so rapidly that few know how far it has already gone toward the opposite point from which it started—away from the traditions and speculations in which its movement began. Most of us get little information concerning the thinkers in the advance of this movement, who are planting the seed thoughts out of which new evolutions and revolutions are to come. Only one who searches out, and becomes familiar with, this most advanced thought can judge from the signs of the times, understand new facts and events, or adapt himself to coming changes.

To all those who dread to think of some outrageous set of ideas, repulsive to all their present feelings, whether prejudices or convictions, I wish to commend one little story or fable of the medieval times, and to assure them that as a parable it is true, that it is scarcely extravagant, that the mental operation suggested by it has an outcome but little less joyful to the courageous thinker than that of the story to its courageous knight. It is the subject of one of the poems of Paul H. Hayne.

"The poem takes us back in imagination to the time when the Normans ruled in Sicily. A goodly ship sailed from Cos to Smyrna in the loveliest season of the year, and, passing many palm-covered islands, whose odors were wafted on the soft breezes to those on the ship, they became intoxicated with enjoyment, and sank into a delicious, dreamy repose, while the vessel drifted on whither she would, as the currents caught her. Among the passengers was *Avolio*, a gentleman well skilled in arms as well as learned in the arts and sciences. He persuaded his companions to land on the perfumed isles and explore their mysteries. They went ashore, and strayed about, passing from one delight to another. Suddenly they saw before them an elevated piece of ground, covered with dark and dismal trees. Everything around grew hideous and gloomy. The companions of *Avolio* fled in terror from the dreadful spot, while he, spell-bound, could not fly, but was impelled to move onward. On, on, he was urged, until he found himself before a towering gateway, where stood a dismal mansion, buried in gloomy ivy. From this house issued an immense serpent

"Which showed its fiery fangs, and hissed in the gleam
  Its own fell eyeballs kindled."

The monster quickly disappeared, and again appeared, having the same shape, but changed in aspect. *Avolio* demanded in the name of God what it was and why it came in such "questionable shape;" when

"A voice, thin and low,
Broke like a mudded rill: 'Bethink thee well!
This isle is Cos, of which old legends tell

Such marvels.   Has thou never heard of me—
The island's fated queen? . . . .
Foul as I am, there *was* a time, Oh! youth!
When these fierce eyes were fonts of love and truth;
There *was* a time when woman's blooming grace
Glowed through the flush of roses in my face;
When,—but I sinned a deep and damning sin,—
I cursed the great Diana! I defied
The night's immaculate goddess, argent-eyed,
And holiest of immortals! I denied
The eternal night which looks so cold and calm—
Therefore, O, stranger! am I what I am!'"

She went on to tell *Avolio* that she must remain a serpent forever, unless she should meet some man, braver than Ajax, who would kiss her on the mouth, and thus break the spell and restore her to her former shape. *Avolio* was touched by her story, and after receiving a solemn assurance that he should not become the victim of a plan arranged for his destruction,

"He signed the monster nearer, closed his eyes,
And with some natural shudderings, some deep sighs,
Gave up his pallid lips to the foul kiss.
What followed then?—a traitorous serpent hiss,
Sharper for triumph? O! not so, he felt
A warm, rich, clinging mouth approach and melt
In languid, loving sweetness on his own,
And two fond arms caressingly were thrown
About his neck. . . . .
He raised his eyes, released from brief despair—
They rested on a maiden tall and fair—
Fair as the tropic morn when morn is new;
And her sweet glances smote him through and
    through."

The *Queen of Cos* became *Avolio's* bride, and the bold lover had no cause to regret his courage."

This horrid monster is what every sectarian and partisan sees in his opponents—what every religionist beholds with terror in the infidel, and the freethinker looks upon with hate in the religionist; what opposing politicians imagine each other to be; what the conservative sees in the radical and the radical in the conservative; whose very ugliest features appear in the socialist as he is viewed by the man of wealth, position, and power, while to him the man of wealth and power is scarcely less repulsive. There is no way to destroy the hideous thing, and nothing remains but to face it fairly and squarely, look it full in the eyes, and come in contact with it where it appears the worst. While you look every feature will gradually soften and change; before long you begin to see beauty where before was ugliness; and at last the repulsive features have so far disappeared that you are surprised at the beauty of what remain. The transformation will not in all cases be as great as that in the poet's dream; but it will be enough to make you rejoice that you took the courageous course. For one I can testify that the choicest truths I have ever learned have been acquired in this manner, and that to me the fearful monster has become a creature of beauty and joy that will remain with me forever.

For all young people who have reached the age when they begin to think, to reason, to criticise, the lesson is especially suitable; and is not amiss for older ones who have not yet by mental slavishness stultified their brains, and become ready to fly at the first appearance of danger. Whatever the doctrine of any body of men, whose character is above the level of downright crime, no one need fear to investigate it, if he is conscious of being honest in his own soul.

CHAPTER VII.

CONCEIT AND SELF-RIGHTEOUSNESS.

THROUGH all modern time, and how far back I cannot say, moralists, and especially religious moralists, have held the idea and taught it to the common people, that all moral or immoral conduct implied what they called freedom of the will. The person must be a "free moral agent," capable of doing one thing as easily as another, or at least as truly capable of doing either, else he is not properly punishable or rewardable for conduct. This doctrine has become the generally accepted standard of Christendom, by which nearly everybody condemns or excuses an offender. It has also happened at the same time that certain fatalistic religious doctrines required man not to have a complete freedom of choice, and hence millions of pages have been printed, and millions of brains tortured, to settle the question of the absolute freedom of the individual mind. Scientists, as well as religionists, have taken a hand in the discussion. The greater part of the religious world have argued for freedom, because it was thought necessary in order to justify the ways of God to man. The believers in science have more generally taken the opposite view, and in the physiology and pathology of the brain have found more evidence against the notion than for it. The latest book on one side claims that man is a creative first cause like the original creator; the latest scientific works show more plainly than ever before that the human brain, like everything else in the universe, is the subject of cause, and in its operations manifests law.

Now, as there is some confusion in the common mind regarding these matters, if we can go back to the beginning, and trace the growth of ideas, we shall get a better understanding of where we are, and perhaps of where we ought to be.

I have previously shown that originally *justice* consists of two ideas, one the conception of *equality*, the other of revenge; though revenge also implies equality of a certain kind, that is, the satisfaction of making another person suffer as much as we have suffered from him. When punishment of crimes by law began it was to take revenge out of the hands of the individual sufferer, who had always taken satisfaction himself, or if killed had been revenged by his relatives (very much as some of the people in Kentucky and the southern states still do) in order that the state and the law might more effectively and surely revenge and protect the weak against the strong. Revenge is still the main object of the law's punishment; that is, while it aims to protect society, it does so by a punishment that will deter the offender from further crime, just as the individual himself would do by his own revenge. The popular feeling that *demands* punishment is also a revengeful one. Except with boys and girls to some extent, the state makes very little effort to reform the criminal by educating him, or in any way changing his nature. If he is deterred by suffering that is considered enough, though at heart he may be as criminal as before. And here mark the point, that it is because men are conscious of having no justification for taking revenge on the criminal unless he is a free agent, that they insist on his being free. If not free, but compelled to do wrong, no one wishes to be revenged. If not free they are uncertain what to do with him (unless he be insane) for they have not yet become generous enough to think of shutting him away from society for the sake of educating and reforming him. Neither do they know they could afford to do such a thing. The religionist too, especially the one who has a perpetual hell ready to catch the criminal after death, feels awkward when called upon to justify it, if man is not as free to do good as evil, and capable of doing either. So the churchman, as well as the jurist, has an object in insisting upon freedom of choice.

But there is a reason stronger yet why both these parties, and all the rest of us, are disposed to believe in the free-will doctrine; and that is that it justifies our own self-righteousness. If we are not all free, what right have we to feel supercillious toward all the poor wretches we call depraved and vile? Are we not better than they because we *chose* to be better, of our own free will, when we might have chosen otherwise? Oh, Yes, that is a very pleasant notion, and allows us to feel sanctimonious; it gives us a right to despise the criminal, and all the unfortunate, to shun them or hold ourselves aloof when they need help, encouragement, sympathy or instruction. What if they do keep going down lower and lower all the time, and becoming more and more unhappy? Didn't they choose to go down hill while we chose to go up? And so haven't we a right to feel our superiority because we got it ourselves; and a right to despise them for not choosing to have it; and a right to leave them alone in their wickedness and misery?

Yes, that is very flattering; but cannot any one see that it has the spirit of hell; that if every one had always possessed that spirit no charity would ever have blessed the world; that no steps would ever have been taken to relieve present suffering or prevent any for the future; or if done done with the I-am-holier-than-thou feeling, and produced no effect; that Jesus never would have associated with publicans and sinners; that no Magdalens would have been saved; no drunkard, no criminal would ever have been offered the hand of sympathy, and aided to recover his lost place in society? On the contrary, what sort of spirit is it that *does* such things as these? It is one born of the consciousness that we ourselves may be liable to stumble and fall, or that we have done so already, like the unfortunate ones we are trying to help; that we are not so much better than they; that circumstances do decide us to act better or worse in spite of all our power of will and self-control.

Here then, are the governmental influence, the religious influence, and the promptings of our own conceit, all united to maintain this old doctrine of a free will against any contrary view brought forward by a more scientific age. It seems to me plain that it belongs to the selfish side of human nature; that selfishness clings to it as a justification for selfishness; as a good reason for refusing charity; as an excuse for hard-heartedness, brutality and cruelty; as an apology for leaving the poor in their poverty, and the criminal in his crime. The moralist, it is true, claims it to be necessary in order to hold men to their duty, and that therefore his motive is not selfish; yet at the same time it is made to justify punishment, and the desertion of the offender. Therefore it is selfish; for the unselfish disposition does not desert the offender in his sins; it clings to him till the last hope of reformation is gone. So, even in the best case the motives are mixed; and I must still repeat that the doctrine is one adapted to please all the selfish instincts—those of revenge or punishment, indifference and indolence, conceit and self-righteousness.

Before bringing considerations against this dogma, it is well to state that it is not now held with the rigidity of former times. So far as can be learned from condensed statements, its friends do not exclude motives as causes, or try to get beyond cause; but in some way there is a substantial freedom claimed in spite of motives or causes. Even the author of "Man a Creative First Cause" does not try to ignore science, or deny the effect of motives. But this is only to say that these people have learned from science, and their former views have been thereby modified; in other words, there has been progress.

Still, however, so far as actual freedom is claimed at all, it must be as something uncaused. If one can make a choice without any predominating motive to influence him in either direction, then that choice is an effect without cause, a result that is not produced. Of course the words are absurd, but so is the idea. However much the liberty may be refined away, and however much may be allowed as the effect of motives, yet if anything at all is done or decided in pure freedom it is without any cause; it is a choice without any motive, or with no one motive stronger than another. From one of these conditions it must spring forth, either from a perfect balance of motives, or from no motive at all; otherwise it is not a free choice. Nobody can conceive how a decision or action can came forth from no motive, nor any more can one conceive of its coming forth from a perfect balance of motives. Both are equally impossible. What then remains? Only to admit that when we seem to ourselves to be conscious of ability to decide in either one of two or more ways, then the motives impelling us are nearly equal in strength. When they are various and confused, neither one strong enough to determine us against the rest, then we hesitate, and think, and think, and think, till finally appears some new motive, or new knowledge, that is a reason for deciding, and we make a choice; we are determined by that new influence at last. If the motives are all or nearly all on one side then we are determined instantly when occasion arises, or even decided in advance.

To those who are already determined to talk or think about what a man can do if he *will*, it can only be said that that has nothing to do with the question. It is not what he can do after he wills but before he wills. If he wills, or has a mind to, he can do almost anything, if he doesn't break his neck in doing it, or meet with some other bad luck before it is accomplished.

But *before* one wills or makes up his mind every one else practically acknowledges that a choice will be determined by motives as causes. Therefore they bring various inducements to bear in one way or another, never doubting that if they can bring one sufficiently powerful the determination will be as they wish. The motives may be bad or good, and in either case they estimate how strong the opposing ones are likely to be, and act accordingly. If a small temptation will decide a choice they do not offer a large one. If they know a person is liable to be tempted, but wish him to stand firm, they bring inducements to strengthen him as he is. Everybody without exception, from the little child to the oldest man or woman, acts in every-day life upon the assumption that man is no more free in his choice than a dog or a horse. Whatever they believe, when they come to *act* they act upon the theory that man is subject to cause and effect, and his choice the result of a combination of forces called motives, feelings, reasons, inducements, influences, views, education, etc. That is the way common sense gets the better of one's belief or speculation.

It is only when the propensity to blame, to punish, or to destroy comes into action, and we wish to justify that, that we resort to the free-will notion. We then use it as an excuse for selfish action toward others. But on the contrary, when we are blamed or punished ourselves, we always manage to find extenuating circumstances. It is others, not ourselves, who might have done right as easily as not.

A doctrine put to bad uses becomes suspicious. And in this ordinary use of it to justify selfish action toward others we may see the true character of the Free Will dogma. It is selfish and born of selfishness. To condemn or punish for revenge it furnishes an excellent excuse. To justify the fiendish vindictiveness of an eternal hell it was necessary to the old theologian. But when we blame or punish for the reformation of the offender there is no need of any free will theory to justify our action.

The whole make-up of the human organism is against this old doctrine, to prove which I will present an argument from the anatomy and physiology of the nervous system. As all well-informed people in these days know, the nerves of sensation from the surface of the body, below the head, and from the internal parts also, pass from their origin to the spinal cord, thus forming one side of the cord or spinal marrow, and all together at the top pass into the brain. Those from the head and face join the same bundle after it gets inside the skull. The sympathetic or vegetative system, which carries on the nutrition of the body, likewise sends some of its fibers to unite with the same great bundle. After receiving all that come from every part, and being joined by the optic and olfactory in front, and by the auditory behind, the whole together pass through two small bodies at the base of the brain called the *optic thalami*, and from these the fibers spread out again, and radiate to every part of the outside of the brain. The outside or grey matter of the brain is a thin mass of nerve cells, and in the outside layers of these cells the sensitive fibers appear to terminate. All these brain cells, which are supposed to be somewhat like minute electrical battery cups, have their own minute fibers, passing off from the outside to connect them with others in every direction, and uniting the whole mass of grey matter in one complex solidarity. From the *lowest* or *inmost* layers of cells there go fibers that radiate or converge from the whole outside of the brain back again to two small bodies at the base called the *striated* bodies, situated close to the optic thalami, through which the bundle of *sensitive* nerves passed before radiating to the surface. These fibers however, that have converged back from near the outside of the brain to near the same local center at the base, are not sensitive but *motor* nerves, by which the muscles are made to act. Being all brought together here in the striated bodies, they then pass out of the skull into the spinal cord, and form another part of it through its entire length. Fibers are sent off to the face from inside the skull, and from some thirty different centers along the spine at the points where sensitive ones came in, all of them going to muscles in the same locality where the corresponding sensitive ones took rise. I speak of their taking rise, passing to the brain and back, and ending in the muscles, not because that indicates the present manner of their growth, but because the currents of nerve motion that pass over them take that course. Otherwise stated, the two sets of fibers run side by side from all parts of the body to the optic thalami and corpora striata at the base of the brain, and after being separated there we find them again in parallel radiations to the grey matter at the outside.

This is the simplest outline of the system. There is really some slight indirectness in following out the plan, and there are cross connections between the hemispheres and various other parts of the brain, besides some fibers that have not yet perhaps been fully traced, or their exact functions ascertained.

The cerebellum or back brain is substantially like the front brain in its arrangement. Part of the sensitive fibers leave the main bundle soon after entering the cranium, and from this point they radiate or are distributed to all the outside parts or grey matter of the cerebellum. From the same gray matter the motor fibers converge to a center and join the main bundle of motor cords passing down into the spine. It is thus a smaller brain, connected probably with the cerebrum, but able to perform its functions independently.

A sensation then, as a general fact, travels from the surface where it occurs, through the sensitive fibers to the cord, up the cord to the optic thalami, and from there to some part of the outside matter of the brain, where it may spend itself as feeling, with no other result; or it may start an impulse backward in the motor nerves that will cause muscular motion in the part where the sensation came from; or result in any one of a thousand possible movements, external or internal.

But I will quote from the physiologist a more detailed and definite description. It is from Letourneau's "Biology."

"We can thus follow" he says "along its whole anatomical career, and in all its physiological metamorphoses, the impression received by the terminal extremity of a sensitive nervous fiber. If, for example, a hard body strikes violently any part of the cutaneous envelopment, the molecules of the nervous fibers, harshly touched, enter from point to point into vibration; the shock communicates itself first of all to the cells of the spinal marrow, then to those of the optical layers, then to the cells of the cerebral convolutions. * * On reaching the superficial cells of the convolutions the shock, the vibration, the molecular movement, whatever may be the form thereof, awakens in these cells an altogether special phenomenon of consciousness or sensation. But we are only yet at the half of the circuit. The sensitive cells which have incurred the shock communicate it in their turn to the subjacent cellular strata. These last cells, a little larger than the superficial or sensitive cells, a little smaller than the deep or motory cells, are probably the thinking cells. In these the molecular shock is transformed into ideas. The ensemble of these thinking cells constitutes the soul of the organism. They take account of the causes of pain, combine the means of preventing its return, and their decision communicated to the deepest cortical layers is there metamorphosed into volitions. In effect the deep cells of the cortical layers are motory or rather volitive. They ordain the muscular movements necessary to prevent the return of the painful shock and to ward off danger. The command is transmitted along the convergent central fibers, then through the cells of the striated bodies, and of the spinal marrow. Finally from the motory cells of the peripheric nervous cords this command arrives at the muscles charged to execute it. The cycle is then complete, and the mechanical stimulation of the extremities of some sensitive nervous fibers has, like a succession of gun-discharges, determined a sensation, a ratiocination, a volition, and movement." (Am. ed. pp. 386-7.)

But not always does the reactive or motor impulse wait for a command to come from the brain. There are gray cells all through the spinal cord, and centers in it where the telegram seems to be taken off the wire, and a motor dispatch sent back before the brain has time to accomplish it. If your fingers get pricked you pull them away before having time to choose or will anything about it. And so of many similar things. This involuntary action is what is called the *reflex action* of the cord. In the sympathetic system there is still less dependence on the brain; nearly everything is done without any choice or even consciousness regarding it. The nerve centers or ganglia return the motor impulses that are needed, and report to the brain through another nerve when they get ready, if there is need of doing so at all.

The reflex action, which is simply an action and a reaction within a nerve circuit, is shown most plainly in animals that have had the brain removed. There is no conscious interference from the brain, and the reflex action is prompt and decided. Any animal or human that may have the nerves of its limbs irritated immediately after will move them as quickly as ever before. The frog, because it dies slowly, is an animal commonly used, and after its decapitation has been known to use one foot after the other to remove something from its thigh. An electric irritation of the chest stimulates a movement of both arms in the headless human subject to remove the cause. And so of any number of similar experiments. The sensation goes only to the spinal cord, and the motor impulse returns from there to effect the movement.

The movements made by the living human body exhibit reflex action in all its grades from the most simple to the most complex, or from the purely reflex and involuntary to that most completely under voluntary control. The twitch of the leg which a child makes when its foot is tickled, or the start that a strong man shows when a thunderbolt comes crashing down close by him, is an instance of what is purely reflex or involuntary. The movements we make in sleep are reflex, coming from a sensation of discomfort slowly making itself felt, and at length accumulating sufficient force of reaction to cause us to turn over or take some easier position. Sometimes a dim consciousness is associated with it, as when the sensation is one of cold or heat, which *may* secure the reactive movement for more or less covering, or *may fail*, even after the brain is aroused sufficiently to know what is wanted. To make the statement correct we must say that some of these movements affect that part of the cord, or great bundle of nerves, which is inside the skull, though they do not fairly reach the voluntary consciousness.

To make the statement correct we must also say that breathing, coughing, swallowing, sneezing, are examples of reflex action, which may take place simply as such, or may be modified more or less by volition. We may breathe or cough, or check the impulse for a while and refrain. The balance of the two kinds of action is very close. If one gets a piece of tough beefsteak in his mouth and chews on it a while, yet does not dare to swallow, he will find such a struggle going on between the involuntary tendency to swallow and the voluntary one against swallowing, that he may think he is destined to be choked in spite of all his will power.

In addition to such mixed impulses we have certain motions that are at first voluntary, but afterward become involuntary or reflex; though, unlike the ones just mentioned, we can resume the whole control when we choose. Most of our walking is of this kind. The more common movements of the fingers in playing musical instruments, in knitting, and in various kinds of labor, are the same. After sufficient frequency and continuance of habit, the volitional control is given up, the hands and feet being left to the control of the spinal cord.

All the instincts and appetites of the body are so many tendencies to reflex action, controlled more or less by the will. A moderate appetite for food is easily enough controlled; that of a man who has involuntarily fasted for three days gives much more difficulty. So of the drinker's appetite for liquor; controlled for a time, it after a certain period. demands a spree so imperiously that he gives way to it. Any one can think of similar illustrations.

Now comes in the special point of all this preparation.

What is the difference between the involuntary and the voluntary action? It is simply a difference of degree in the *complexity* of the reflex action. The simple reflex is very simple action and reaction. The higher forms are *indirect* reflex action, having the circuit divided, and connection made by an additional nerve, or more than one. The most complete thought, judgment and action of the human mind in regard to any matter is an exceedingly complex reflex action, having many connections and transfers, like a telegram sent to various offices, and consuming much time, before it finally brings a response.

The reflex action, already complex, becomes still further compounded by causing a first reaction in some one mind, which through muscular action communicates itself to the senses of some other mind, and from that second one, by a similar reaction, to a third, fourth, or any number of minds. This last might be called the *social* reflex action, the different individuals representing the separate cortical cells of a single brain. All the various forms of nerve function are thus essentially the same; and it is only through the varying degrees of complexity that the lowest and highest—instinct and reason—have come to seem like things of different nature.

In the experiment of the headless frog, before referred to, we have the first and simplest form of *complex* reflex action. The irritating substance being placed on the thigh of one leg, the foot of that leg is by the direct and simple reflex action raised to remove it; but failing to reach it, the continued irritation passes across the spinal cord, and stimulates the motor nerve of the opposite leg, till the foot of that leg is raised, and pushes off the caustic substance. Now, if the frog had its head on one might think it reasoned about the matter, inferring that when it could not succeed with one foot it must try the other. The result however is the same through a complex reflex action. Why did not the second leg move its foot toward its own thigh instead of the opposite? Apparently because the impulse did not come through the same nerve that it did in the other—the ordinary sensitive nerve of the leg—but through a cross connection from the opposite side; the impulse through each nerve leading to its own proper or habitual result. But the action is just as intelligent as if the frog had had its head, and reasoned upon it for half an hour.

Let us next notice the difference between the nerve system of an animal like this and that of man; and it will help us to understand how thinking may be a reflex action. I quote again from the biologist Letourneau.

"The more voluminous the nervous cords are the more developed will be the nuclei of the optic layers, the stronger the current of sensations and impressions, and the more vigorously agitated will be the cortical perceptive centres, (or convolutions) those nervous elements that have consciousness of sensations, which weigh them, compare them, register them; consequently the more difficult will be their ponderatory labor. If at the same time these cortical layers have *little* surface and depth, in other terms, if the cerebral hemispheres are little developed, the animal or man will be peculiarly instinctive—will blindly obey the actual impression. If, on the contrary, the perceptive centers or convolutions dominate then the being will be intelligent, reflective, master of itself. It is by virtue of this law that the inferior vertebrates, in which the nervous intercranian vesicles, olfactory, optical, &c. are as voluminous as the cerebral vesicles (or convolutions) have but a rudimentary intelligence.

"It is easy enough to explain why a particular man having otherwise little intelligence, is nevertheless endowed with this or that sensitive aptitude. It is enough that the external ear be well shaped, the nucleus of the optic layer that corresponds with it voluminous, and the portion of cortical substance in relation with this nucleus rich in cells, in order that the individual, though otherwise ill endowed, should have musical aptitudes. We thus comprehend singular facts that have seemed abnormal to many observers; for example that many idiots have shown a taste and even an aptitude for music." (Biology, pp. 44, 142.)

In the half-idiotic musician there is a certain part of the outside brain that is well developed. When the whole outside brain is well developed there is ability for all kinds of thought or mental performance. There is a larger mass, and a greater number of cells of the grey matter. These cells being all connected with each by minute fibers, an impression carried to the outside of the cerebrum at one point may, if strong enough, be carried all over the brain in every direction, and be deflected and reflected in a great number of ways, before it finally excites a motor nerve to carry out some movement of the body. The reflection of a sensational impulse through these hundreds of minor connections between the brain cells, forth and back in every direction, before it reaches its final reflection into a motor nerve, is what is meant by complex reflex action. In the frog experiment mentioned there was only one; in the human brain there may be a thousand or any indefinite number. They correspond to the process of thinking. Certain physiologists believe the process of thinking does take place in these cells of grey matter at the outside of the brain. The manner of their location, and the way they are connected with the sensory and motor fibers, is a strong evidence that thought is their real function. The sensory fibres from all parts of the body, passing between the cells of the more interior layers, terminate in the extreme outer ones. The motor fibers begin at the extreme lower or most internal layer, and between these outermost and innermost layers are a number of layers of intermediate cells, through which the sensory impulse has to pass to reach the motor fibers, when it thus terminates. But it does not always reach far enough for that. It may be turned back in its various travels over the minute fibers till it exhausts itself in bitter or pleasant feeling, or shows itself outside the brain only by a blush, a smile, a billious spell or a heartache. We know that in well developed brains, after impressions are experienced through sight, hearing or feeling, there is usually some interval of time given to thought before anything is said or done in response. It may be a minute or an hour, a month or half a lifetime. There is apparently no part of the brain where this intermediate thought, between feeling and action, can go on except in these intermediate layers of cells, between those where sensation terminates, and those where motion begins. Assuming this to be their function its operation becomes more conceivable than formerly. Where there is but little grey matter in the cerebrum, as in most animals, reflex action is but slightly complex, and sensations quickly result in some kind of movement. In men of inferior brains, where there is more however of the cell matter than in most animals, we find impulsiveness of disposition, and hasty or premature action, just as in the animal or the child, with its partially developed brain. In those persons whose brains are fully grown, the convolutions numerous and the grey matter deep, will be found the most thought before action, and as a consequence the more complete control under excitement; because the impulse from sensation passes through a great number of cells before reaching the motor fibers. If by counteracting reflections it is prevented from reaching the motor fibers, it may finally come to rest in some cell or group of cells, and six months or a year afterward another impulse from sensation may strike that cell or group of cells, discharging the store of force that was laid up by the last motion within them, renewing the thoughts of the former time, and continuing the new compound impulse till it results in action. Or it may again disappear in the cells, and have to be reëxcited a third or a fourth time, before the feeling is sufficiently strong to end in words or deeds.

These cells having somewhat of the character of battery cups or minute Leyden jars, those in which motion ends accumulate a store of nerve force, and when this is discharged by another impulse of thought or feeling it may again accumulate force, much as the cells of a muscle, after its natural exercise, acquire new force for subsequent action. And being connected with each other, as those of the muscle are not, a very faint impression on the senses—a mere whisper it may be—can rouse to action a great number of them, and so generate an excitement that will end only in the most extravagant movements. Their connection with the central consciousness ceases at length, and they again recuperate their communicating power, ready to be impressed and discharged by the next movement from sensation. They wear out by excessive use and new ones take the places of the old, as in any other tissue of the body. And when a part of them become exhausted, without being replaced, the thought and memory become feeble, slow, and imperfect, deranged or senseless, just as any other function becomes weak and imperfect when its organ loses strength and perfection.

Well, what has all this long description of nerve function to do with freedom of the will, and with conceit and self-righteousness? I answer that a belief in free will depends very much on ignorance of the nature of the brain. Because man cannot see the whole round of the cycle of cause and effect in his mental operations, he imagines that he creates a beginning point in it somewhere himself. Whatever phenomena men are ignorant about they assume to have some personal cause, acting like a free will, and called a god. In primitive times there are many of these—one for every kind of power manifested in Nature—and they are made to account for all phenomena. But at length, by increasing knowledge, they become reduced to two, one for the universe as a whole, and one for man himself. These two are supposed to be the ultimate causes producing everything that cannot be brought into the domain of positive knowledge and law. Just as fast as we gain knowledge of a new department and introduce science into it, the god gives up his control, and moves back to a position behind all phenomena, where science is not quite ready to follow, and where many believe it cannot advance. So this thing called a will, and by one writer called a "Creative First Cause," to primitive men, and to ignorant civilized ones, is responsible for everything the man is and does; even for all his religious and political beliefs, his insanity and melancholy, including suicidal mania, for which laws in some of our states are still idiotic enough to attempt punishment, just as did the blind religionists of three hundred years ago. All the bitterness of the old political strifes contained an implication that men could believe one thing as easily as another, and therefore ought to be blamed and hated if they did not believe aright. Still more rigidly was religious belief held to be a matter of choice, and all heresy involved moral turpitude in refusing to accept the old doctrines, which any one, it was believed, could see to be true if he would. Hence punishment for it was considered right; and every heretical sect down to the latest has suffered punishment for its own heresy, and then just as promptly turned upon the heretics that went out from itself, and tried in some way to punish them,—by contempt and depreciation if nothing worse.

As, through increasing knowledge, we have come to learn that beliefs are the consequences of character, of habits, of personal interest, and especially of education, we have come to have more humane feelings toward the erring, more charity for offences we cannot quite understand, more friendliness for those of different political, religious or social views, less confidence in our own righteousness, less of the conceited, arrogant and bigoted spirit which engenders bitterness, hatred, and strife. And here is the core of the whole matter. When this conceit of our own *somethingness* is finally cast out of our brains, by the knowledge that every operation going on within them is subject to law, like all else we know; that cause and effect rule to the utmost in every thought, feeling, and imagination; that nothing ever originates in the mind as self-caused or without cause; that all our apparent freedom, when most free or self-controlled, is still traceable to some cause, provided we understand the brain's action, and with honest willingness to learn and unlearn, try to find the back-lying antecedents of what seems so spontaneous—when we have this knowledge, and this candor, then the last vestiges of self-conceit and self-righteousness have lost their rootage, and must also be thrown out. Though we may feel capable of controlling ourselves under all possible circumstances, of choosing such lines of conduct as we shall never condemn or regret, of determining our destiny for all future time, yet we shall know that we are still subjects of causation, as truly and completely as the atom of sand by the roadside, or the stick that floats on the waters. We shall realize that there is nothing in us as independent beings beyond all others; nothing outside of the great universal domain over which law rules with perfect authority; nothing except a capacity for superior development, and its accompanying power; which capacity has itself been acquired through that same great process of evolution which has developed all things to their present state.

The Christian world has been striving for two thousand

years to be charitable and humble, but could not for want of a true philosophy, and a scientific knowledge of the human organism. The church, instead of being able to lift up the fallen and depraved, finds itself growing self-righteous as soon as it begins to be prosperous; and then, separating itself from the unfortunate, it pushes them farther away, and sinks them still lower in misery and despair. The religion of the rich and cultured becomes only a sentimental fraud.

Self-conceit is the root of that constant assumption that whatever is not *our* truth is a falsehood to be antagonized, a stranger, an alien, a spiritual barbarian, to be despised, and refused all hospitality. It makes us blind to all the beauty and glory seen by others, shuts us up in a little narrow world of our own, and blights all intellectual growth.

Both these mean dispositions unite in creating discord and disfellowship among those who should be bound together as with iron bands in every noble cause. They are the first prompters to envy, jealousy, and all hateful selfish feelings. Under their malign influence reform organizations, labor unions, and patriotic brotherhoods go to pieces like rotten wood, or lose all cohesive power and all effective energy for their own good purposes.

Conceit and self-righteousness are the two great unseen but most powerful enemies of unselfishness—that charity which "suffereth long and is kind, which envieth not, vaunteth not itself, is not puffed up, doth not behave itself unseemly, seeketh not its own, is not provoked, taketh not account of evil, rejoiceth not in unrighteousness, but rejoiceth in the truth, which beareth all things, believeth all things, hopeth all things, endureth all things, and never faileth." Like other kinds of pride too they are frauds, making pretension to something we do not really possess.

And the false idea of freedom, which underlies conceit

and self-righteousness, thus affects us in all the innumerable thoughts, feelings, and acts of our daily life—in our homes, our business, our amusements, our religion, our everything. I wish however, to show more especially its connection with two subjects,—our treatment of criminals, and our matrimonial life.

The treatment of criminals has never till of late years been anything but vindictive, brutal and cruel. How could it be otherwise when the guilty one was considered guilty only because he might have been good as easily as evil; that he was as free to choose one course as another? The natural impulse to vengeance would have been sufficiently cruel anyway, but the belief in the criminal's freedom made it more so. It justified men in imposing any extreme of punishment. If an offender was as free to do right as wrong, yet chose the wrong, why should he not receive all the punishment any one was disposed to give, even to killing for a small offence? And that is the way men did reason and feel. Many a time I have heard them say of some offender, "He might have done differently, or, he knew he was doing wrong; now let him suffer:" "He has made his own bed; now let him lie in it."

It is only since modern science has given us some idea of a cause for all events, including all human action, that a more humane feeling has taken the place of the old cruelty, and the prison been looked upon as a reform institution, with efforts to make it such in reality. As Science becomes able to show us still more of the criminal's nature, and the motives that impel him to crime; how he comes to possess bad tendencies; how a selfish competitive society leaves him to grow up without education, or any useful knowledge by which to get a living; how when hard times in the business world come on he is thrown out of such poor employment as he could get; how intoxicating liquors are thrust before him at every turn; how loneliness and depression drive him to drink, to dissipate for a time his unhappy feelings; how, if he has any brains at all he must realize the injustice of social inequality, and feel that he has been badly treated in being shut out from wealth and comfort; how he will instinctively believe he has some right to live, along with the rest; how the indifference to his fate which he sees in nearly every one around him provokes him to turn his hand against all alike, rendering him desperate and reckless as to what he may do; how in such a condition he is ready to quarrel and fight, to plot burglary and theft, and when he is successful enjoy the consciousness of his ability to rob, glory in his shame, and so continue his evil course; while his children, inheriting all the father's depraved tendencies, are still further cut off from good associations, still easier led or driven into the criminal mode of life; till at length every kind of horrible fiendishness becomes developed; —when we come to see the rationale of all this we shall become yet more humane, and be willing to put the criminal into a reform institution, where instead of being tyrannized over by ignorant and brutal officials, he will be taught his duty to his fellows, and the reason for it, and how he can learn to live a true life. Then charitable juries and other persons will not aid the guilty to escape the law, knowing it best for himself as well as for society that he should be caught and convicted. His length of sentence will not depend on the vindictiveness or clemency of a judge, but on the wisdom of his teachers; who will decide when he is a safe man to be at large, and never release him until he is. When that time comes we shall not be so unprincipled as to drive away our bad characters, to inflict their deviltry upon other communities, nor so ungenerous as to leave their children to grow up under the tutelage of the criminal class.

But we shall never make these desirable changes so long as we are ignorant and self-righteous enough to believe that we are by nature or grace superior to our fellows, or that they are by nature villains, or that any one of us is independent of laws and causes which determine our action.

When two young persons take each other for better or for worse, according to the formula their more experienced parents have made for them, it is always with an expectation to avoid the worse condition entirely. They promise eternal love in the fond belief that they have control of love, and of all their future desires and aspirations. But alas! they are the most complete ignoramuses in the whole world. They think their feelings are to remain always the same, when they will hardly be the same for even three weeks. They imagine they can chain up their thoughts to one little spot for a lifetime, when they will be sure to break loose and wander away in spite of all care and watchfulness. They never seem to discover that love is exclusive and devoted to one person while it is temporarily satisfied with that one, yet ever ready after a time, of uncertain duration, to be dissatisfied with that one, and equally exclusive and devoted to some other. They are so unaware of the nature of their passion that they take the uncertain element of it to be lasting, and ignore the more certain part as of no reality. They are blind to the fact that when they promise they are in their most favorable moral condition, and are assuming that to be permanent, when it is going to change rapidly and surely for the worse. They forget or ignore a thousand unfavorable influences that will operate to bring alienation and discord between them as soon as they come in contact with the world. And so with but small prospect of an ability to keep their word, they promise one of the most difficult things human nature can undertake. No wonder that in most cases love is a failure and a disappointment; that a husband or wife is a necessary evil; that marriage is a continual misery; and that infanticide, murder and suicide are frequent developments of it; besides a large unknown quantity of unfaithfulness, resulting in diseases that curse the innocent, as well as the guilty, for a lifetime, and for an unknown number of generations.

Exceptional instances there are, it is true, in which love and marriage results happily, and the parties are able to keep their promises with sufficient fidelity. They are the few fortunate ones who possess spiritual sympathies—unity of thought and feeling upon the most important matters of life. They are the most highly developed characters, possessing the greatest moral power, and the largest stock of reliable knowledge, along with some peculiar adaptations to each other. They come in contact with so few who can compete with them for a person's affections that they are able to hold each other, and allow of the promises being fulfilled. Even they, however, do not know how much longer they can do so; the future is still invisible, notwithstanding they may have much confidence in their own ability.

But there are few, I imagine, who do not feel in their own consciousness how foolish is the pretence of freedom or self-control in matters of affection. They know they have never had it—that in their hearts, if not outwardly, they have failed to keep the engagements they made with such unhesitating confidence. And yet this pretence of freedom is made the excuse and justification for all jealousy, all the reproach and bitterness that married parties bestow on each other, all open abuse and cruelty, all the revenges, quarrels, fights, murders, and suicides that occur by the thousand every year in every country, and bring incalculable blight and ruin upon great numbers of people. An immense self-righteousness lies back of the jealousy, contempt and revengefulness thus manifested; and the belief of a free will in the offender is the root out of which it has grown. Were it not for this false idea of freedom—of an ability to control the affections, which does not and never did exist, there could be no reason, no justification, no excuse for all this marital crime. The course of action that now terminates in such horrors would arouse no impulse of revenge, no disposition to be cruel. Sorrow, mourning there might be, but no murder nor suicide in addition. If the natural instability of love, in precisely the same sense that all other desires are liable to instability in the pursuit of their objects, were known and acknowledged, there would be no more disposition to punish for a change in the affections than there now is to punish one for a change of appetite for food, a change of ambitious projects, a change of intellectual studies, or a change in the methods of obtaining wealth. What the true character of love is cannot be exhibited any further here, though it is a subject that needs light thrown upon it more perhaps than any other. The point to be observed is, how completely in regard to it the profession of freedom proves itself a fraud, how easily nature, working after its own laws, defeats all efforts to thwart its operation, and what an infinite amount of wickedness and suffering is caused by the teaching and acceptance of this one old false, fetishistic notion, born of the ignorance natural to the undeveloped, selfish man, and continued in our time because men are still too indolent to use their brains, or too timid to trust their reason when it acts.

We never can finish up and perfect our own lives, speaking in the comparative sense, till we accept ourselves as we are, all of us imperfect, varying only in degree, some very low and some very high perhaps, but all united in one common bond of imperfection, which is as true of our self-control as of all our other qualities; all of us having the same origin and the same destiny; all in different stages of growth; some advancing rapidly, some slowly or not at all; some starved and stunted into slow decay, some blasted by misfortune, and withered till apparently dead.

Man is only an atom, floated and tossed about by continual storms on the great life ocean, till by evolution resulting from existing forces and conditions, he at length acquires power to partially control his surroundings and himself. No one can know that he is self-centred beyond the chance of temporarily losing his balance; for though he may believe he is or will be under any circumstances he can imagine, he can never know what temptations may yet sometime assail him. As he can never become absolutely perfect in any other respect, so he cannot in this. If he is wise he will acknowledge his liability to error and sin, and while rejoicing in his own goodness if he has attained any, be willing to lift up any less fortunate one he is able to reach, no matter how low that one may be.

We never shall arrive at the Kingdom of The Unselfish until we have this knowledge of ourselves, and this willingness to accept our nature as it is, with the desire to make it as perfect as possible. The ambition to claim a high origin for our souls is as foolish and vain as the pretence of nobility from our ancestors. Whatever of good we inherit was stored up for us in our ancestors by that universal process of selection by which Nature, in an imperfect way, secures the preservation of the fittest individuals and qualities. *They* were driven by circumstances to develop whatever talents and excellencies *we* now possess. When by this process we become sufficiently wise to understand the purpose to be accomplished, and use the power we have gained to assist

Nature in its accomplishment, we shall soon attain to that moral condition where, if we cannot escape the occasional liability to sin, we *shall* possess the *unfailing ability to repent*, and an *organic* desire and determination to repair the wrongs we may do without deliberate purpose.

Then all the little discords of life will be resolvable into harmonies. Then old quarrels can be settled because we shall be willing to admit, and able to discover, good qualities and purposes in others, while confessing our own imperfections. Then old misunderstandings, can be talked over and explained, because we shall have more confidence in the offender, and less in ourselves. Then we shall be capable of true charity, because we shall know there is a cause for every crime, every sin, every little meanness, every bad habit and propensity, every fault of conduct or constitution, no matter what. Then we shall not expect too much from others, nor promise too much for ourselves.

The sad thought in this connection is that the selfish, the young, the inexperienced and unwise must suffer before they will be ready to learn. We may pity them but cannot help, till they have tried their own way and failed; in most cases probably not till every effort and every resource for *selfish* happiness has been exhausted. When all their exertions have ended in utter misery and hopelessness they may be induced to surrender the last strong-hold of selfishness, the pretence that they have some superior righteousness, or some capability of their own, independent of natural law, and cause, and evolution. Then they may give up their pride, may submit to criticism, may be willing to take position on the lowest round of the ladder if necessary, in order that they may find their true place, and be helped into making their best progress. In the Christian's way of viewing it, they must be disciplined by trials and tribulations till they become broken and humiliated to the point of acknowledging that they have no worthiness in their own character to plead as a merit for salvation. Though this is not the true object of humility, the state of mind produced is an approach toward the correct one. It is liable however to turn into a new kind of self-righteousness, the feeling that they have become the Lord's chosen; and by virtue of that have some title to look down upon the sinners and reprobates, who have not done so well as they, by their own free will and choice, *have* done.

The genuine humility I am speaking of cannot return into any such state as this. It comes from a settled conviction or knowledge of what the man really is as the product of evolution. The subject of it sees himself and his moral condition as the resultant of all the natural forces that have acted on him from the beginning, not only of his own life but that of his ancestors. He rationally knows himself to be produced and developed by natural causes, including the influence of other human beings as a part of those causes, in precisely the same sense that a stick or a stone, a mountain or lake, a plant or an animal, is the result of such causes. He knows that from their influence he never does nor can escape. He sees his less developed fellow men as the subjects of less effective causes, or less favorable conditions, and knows that some change in the tide of fortune may yet carry them beyond himself; while in the worst case they are only later plants growing in the same great human garden, where the earliest ones may not be the best. This view gives him a fellowship with all human, all animal, even all vegetable creatures. He and they have all travelled the same highway; and if he is now near the head of the procession he will rejoice in his good fortune, and be glad to assist those who are struggling up behind him toward the same mountains of Beulah that he already has in view.

With such a conviction as this we can have no lasting ill will toward any living thing. The way is open to reconciliation with all former enemies, with all unfriendly ones who are not still in the class referred to, of those who are blindly and haughtily determined to have their own way and suffer. Even these, criminal though they may be, will receive from us only good will. Their very offences will be made the occasion for assisting them by necessary teaching, while they are suffering the punishment that is to convince them impressively of the wrongfulness of their course.

In conclusion let us ask ourselves if this spirit of humility, of modesty, of charity, of universal fellowship—if this is not the sanctifying quality that will unable us to reach the final Kingdom of All Good; to build up a society such as the world has dreamed of for a score of centuries, and hopeless of realizing here, has imagined to exist in a far away heaven of less material beings and things. When we shall have acquired humility we shall be able to acquire whatever else we need; the last root of the selfish fungus will be dead, all its obstructive power will be gone, and all its evil effects will be quickly cast out of the regenerated mind, vitalized anew by a moral influence superior to any heretofore known. All good qualities will germinate and flourish in the new conditions with a vigor unprecedented.

"Man in the sunshine of the world's new spring
   Shall walk triumphant like some holy thing."
The prophecy, false, delusive and disappointing though it has always been. will nevertheless prove itself gloriously true.

It is no impossibility that I have in mind. Useless to tell me it is something too far in advance for any of the present generation to reach. It is the true life of the future now beginning to announce its coming in definite, scientific, practical thought and statement, as it has before announced it in the dreams of poets, the visions of seers, and the abortive attempts of speculative socialism. The imperfectly fertilized fruit-blossom falls useless to the ground, or the young fruit withers and decays when partially grown; but a later germ on the same stem, receiving its full fertilization, develops and matures a fine specimen of its fruit. So will it be in the human world. Religion, morality, or the social spirit, vitalized and staminated by science, will produce a splendid fruitage, equal to all that even poets and seers have conceived to be possible. If I did not know the possibility of such realization in a way that none of these have ever known it, I should not be making this effort to have others understand what it is, and to represent to them some of the glories this earth of ours may take on when a number of minds, imbued with the sympathy of a like attainment, shall attempt, as they certainly will, to bring forth its full effects in human life. It depends upon every individual reader how soon the beginnings of this happy change are to appear.

CHAPTER VIII.

NATURAL AND SOCIAL SELECTION.

EVERY one is supposed to have some idea of that great truth called Natural Selection, which has immortalized the name of Charles Darwin. But if all know something of it, not all understand it clearly, and few perhaps, even of the intelligent, take in its full comprehensiveness. The object here is to show its relation to Social Selection, and what is the outcome of both combined in operation.

Mr. Darwin, in studying the problem of the origin of species, and in connection with it the variation of animals and plants under domestication, was led to give special attention to a process of nature somewhat similar to man's own selection, by which some of the varying animals and plants came to be naturally preserved, so as to become the progenitors of new varieties and species. The process is sufficiently simple,—those which varied in such a manner as to give them a better chance of getting food, or escaping their enemies, were preserved, and their race perpetuated, while their fellows were destroyed. Their new characteristic, whatever it was, enabled them better to live and flourish in their environment, their surroundings, or circumstances, than their ancestors could. They became better adapted to it, or were able to find a new and better environment. Or if their predecessors had been driven out of a good habitat they became better adapted to the poor one. Any new quality that enabled them to preserve life better, was perpetuated and increased; because those that did not have it were more easily destroyed, and left fewer progeny, while those that had it saved their lives, and left more descendants. The variation may have been something that assisted them to endure heat or cold; to hide themselves, or make themselves seen; to fight or to escape; to swim, fly or run; to climb trees or dig holes in the ground; to conceal their eggs, or carry their young with them. A small difference made a variety in a species; but as this variety varied again, and the second one varied into a third the difference became great enough to make a species or a genus. The same process, continued for a long time, made differences or variations great enough to constitute orders, families, classes, and all the distinctions we know among plants and animals. That is, all these differences were preserved by the selection of Nature, in allowing all that did not possess them to be destroyed in the struggle for life, against enemies and the hardships of the environment, leaving only those best adapted to the situation. In this manner such immense changes have occurred, through long time and many generations, as to transform reptiles into birds, and four-footed land animals into whales, porpoises and sea cows, to say nothing about the descendants of an ape-like animal becoming men.

But selection is only one half the process. The other half is the anatomical and physiological adaptation caused by the action of the surrounding influences upon the plant or animal. A change in the environment or circumstances compels some change in the living thing affected by it, and this is a variation,—a good or bad one as may happen. Some causes we do not know may produce such differences. They must be produced by the circumstances and conditions of the habitat, before they can be selected by the destruction of the unchanged and less fit individuals.

As a general thing this combined process has resulted in producing superior races from the inferior, and the result is what we call high development. But in exceptional cases it has preserved the inferior for inferior habitats, where the superior could not live, and degraded the superior to fit them for the bad conditions; as we may see in the case of the whales, seals and other water mammals, in the negro man of the low, hot coasts of Africa, and in the dangerous classes of white men who inhabit our swamps and mountains, or the dirty and dismal back streets of our large cities.

Now let us take note of a very important new influence, by which the process of selection becomes changed. After it has produced a race of men having sufficient intelligence, man interferes with Nature's work, and selects what is best for himself. Even animals are said to do this, by the females selecting the males. But man does it more conspicuously, and beyond any doubt. The farmer finds a bed of sorrel creeping into his grass-field, or a bunch of Canada thistles, either one of which is better able to live than grass, and would thrive in spite of it if left alone; but he immediately kills them out, thus selecting the grass to be saved. So he kills off his inferior animals, though they could live where better ones could not, in order to breed from those that fatten the easiest, or give the most milk, or travel the fastest. In this way he has preserved those that suit him best, till he has produced very fast horses and powerful ones, very fat pigs, and cows that give a large quantity of rich milk. So the poor laborer, not able to keep a cow, has changed the habits of the goat till it can live on weeds and refuse, yet produce milk enough for a small family.

Nature would not produce either one of these. In fact if left to Nature's influences they would all lose the superior qualities that make them so useful to man.

Man thus interferes with all kinds of plants and animals, to select those best suited to his own life and happiness, regardless of theirs. Natural Selection first made him capable of doing this, and then he proceeds to improve upon the process that gave him his intelligence. Still further, after Nature had adapted him to the best environment she could give him, he begins to react upon his *habitat;* and changes it in various ways, usually to his advantage, but sometimes making it worse. He cuts down the forest, or plants a new one, to improve the climate; drains the swamp to make the air and water more pure; protects himself from cold and heat by his dwellings; destroys all poisonous plants and hostile animals, while favoring those that furnish him food, drink, medicine or clothing. Finally, he exchanges with his fellows whatever he does not need, to obtain what he cannot secure within his own environment.

Here are the two most important methods of man's interference with Nature,—one the interference with natural *selection*, the other the interference with his *surroundings*. Let them be noticed and remembered, as they will be referred to again. Society, as well as the individual man, attempts to do a little in this line, but not enough yet by either mode to indicate very much progress.

Natural Selection operates upon *societies* as freely and powerfully as upon animals or plants. From the very beginning of social organization it has been operating to destroy those groups, tribes and nations least fit to endure. With them, as with the animal world, there is a perpetual struggle against physical forces, against climate, and against enemies of their own species ever ready to prey upon the weak. The more robust, the more intelligent, the more moral in certain qualities, survive; the inferior go down, after a time more or less prolonged. It may be a good while first in some cases, but eventually the crowding of population, and emigration of large numbers, brings a stronger race in contact with the weaker, and the latter falls a prey. For instance, the strongest of the half-civilized nations of this continent preserved themselves and their civilization for hundreds of years; but at last came the white man, as unscrupulous as a wild tiger, and robbed and destroyed them with as little mercy. It was what they had done in a less severe manner during their own career. The civilized American still crowds, oppresses, robs and kills the red man—or did but a few years ago. The land, the game, the forests, and streams are finally destined for the superior race, and the superior part of the inferior. All over the world the process of taking away goes on. Nothing can arrest it till the stronger race has become sufficiently intellectual and humane to accomplish by innocent or merciful means the same result now produced through slaughter, starvation and disease.

It is easy to understand how Natural Selection acts among the savage and barbarous tribes of men,—how those with the strongest bodies, best weapons, best ability to stand by each other, most skill and courage, will press upon the territories of the weaker, fight and exterminate them, occupy their lands, and leave a numerous progeny of the same hardy, warlike people to hold what they have gained. No pretence or excuse is needed; for they acknowledge no right but that of the strongest. Indeed, sometimes it is a matter of death by starvation themselves, or conquest and death to somebody else. Nature in this operation knows nothing of any right but that of the superior, or more strictly, that of the fittest. Instances of such movements are furnished by all those migrating hordes which at different times left Asia and wandered into Europe, conquering and settling wherever they could; and at a later period by those Tartar tribes which overflowed from the Siberian region into India, Persia and Asia Minor, till finally stopped in Europe on the banks of the Danube.

In this manner have grown up centres of civilization all over the earth, wherever a stronger race got possession of a better country than its neighbors, thickly populated it, and in consequence adopted agriculture as the means of living, and cultivated the arts and industries of peace as well as war.

But with these strong and civilized communities the work of selection still goes on. They pursue wars of conquest whenever and wherever any advantage is to be gained, becoming larger and still more powerful, up to the limit where their organizing and integrating capacity begins to fail. The Roman empire was the completest illustration of such growth; though all the great empires that preceded it went through the same process. All of them however, lacked the vitality that could enable them to live. That vitality, as I have before said, is the moral feeling. In none of these civilizations had morality become sufficiently developed to hold the masses of people together against their outside enemies, or prevent internal dissensions. For lack of this they became internally corrupt through wealth, luxury, and sensual indulgence, till pride, servility, selfishness, meanness, jealousy, faction and cowardice took the place of patriotism and union. In this weakened state, corresponding to the old age or sickness of an individual, they fell victims to a younger and more vital race, who are to go through a similar course of national life, with such better fortune as additional moral progress may qualify them to obtain.

The Norse-Gothic-Teutonic race, which finally conquered the Roman Empire of the West, and overran nearly all Europe, is now taking its turn as the dominant factor in building up the leading civilization of the world; and its ability to create one that shall sustain and perpetuate itself is perhaps to be tested right here in our own country within the next twenty-five years. If it succeeds the future is bright with hope for the whole human family; if it fails the darkness and anarchy of the middle ages may be again upon the world for an indefinite period. A hopeful person may have faith that it will meet the occasion triumphantly, and that this nation will take the leadership of the world's affairs for centuries of the immediate future, if not for all coming time.

At present the stronger nations of Europe are preying upon the old, worn-out, feeble ones of the East, and the barbarous tribes of Africa and the Pacific Islands. Only one of the old nations seems to have much life; that one, Japan, may absorb enough of Western vitality to continue its existence. All the rest appear to be doomed. There is only the question of how many years before they will all be dominated and used for the benefit of the white civilizees of Europe. In these days, however, the robbery is not so direct and unconcealed as formerly. There must be some excuse for making war, some little pretence of justice, or some claim to improve the condition of the conquered masses. Neither is the manner of robbery so directly by the strong hand as once; it is now accomplished partially by means of trade. The opportunity for trade is the great advantage the conqueror gains. This is the main purpose of all that is going on in Africa and Asia to-day.

Such is the way Selection operates among groups, tribes and nations. Next, let us trace its operation among individuals. We shall find it working out the same result with them as with the social organizations composed of them.

Referring first to the vegetal and animal kingdoms for comparison, we find that wherever there is room or opportunity for any form of life to get a foothold there it is sure to appear, and compete with all the rest for an existence. However dreary, wet, cold, dry or barren the soil something will live on it. Vines will find a place among the thickest trees and bushes. Parasites and mosses cling to every old tree and stump, and lichens to the rocks. Then, every form of vegetation is fed upon by some kind of animal life. To find a perfect leaf upon a tree you must take it when young, while many are begun upon even in the bud. Besides this every animal, including man himself, has its enemies. Every little creature in the air or water, on the ground or under it, has some larger one waiting to rob it of its life in order to sustain its own. In the vegetal world there is a universal competition for sustenance, the fortunate ones getting it first, while those that fail starve and die out, as does the undergrowth in a forest. In the animal world all that do not live upon the vegetal prey upon the weaker forms of animals. Every contrivance and method the most ingenious human being could have devised for snaring, decoying, catching, holding and killing, is employed by animals against each other; and as many equally cunning devices for safety or escape. One continual robbery and slaughter has been going on for millions of years—ever since life had its first existence— and will continue for an unknown period to come. Whether more happiness or suffering has yet resulted from it no one can say, and to Nature herself (supposing it personified) it makes no difference. By means of it she has compelled every species and order of life to perfect itself as far as its constitution and circumstances would allow, and out of the best of these she has produced still superior ones, as a general result, till the process has ultimated in man; and in man one race has become superior to all the others in strength, courage, intelligence, and capacity for complete moral development. By this stock of men, it seems probable, the whole earth is ultimately to be peopled, to the extinction of the rest, and of all animals and plants detrimental to man's happiness. Then Nature's long and cruel process of Selection will have accomplished its main purpose, and what remains to be done will be done by man himself.

Now, in the world of human society we find everything I have just described as existing in the animal and vegetal. Wherever there is room and opportunity for a human being to find sustenance there is one crowded in, competing with his fellows for all he needs or can get. Competition is the rule and practice so universally that few ever think of it as otherwise than entirely right and proper. It extends through all occupations, from the scavengers of our city streets to our teachers, statesmen, authors, and all the professional class; to all indeed except a few who have already acquired more than they can use. Here too, it is just as merciless as in the lower world. With occasional exceptions, every one who cannot sustain himself suffers and finally goes to the wall. The strongest, or more correctly, those best fitted for the social conditions of the time, survive, flourish, and leave their progeny. The selective process is not so clearly seen, but is equally effective. The weaker person, or one less fortunate through circumstances, is first crowded out of one position into another less advantageous, then out of that into one still inferior, and becoming demoralized by his ill luck is more easily pushed still lower down, till he gets so low he is unable to sustain himself in a state of health. All the while he is going downward he may be pushing some other one less able or less fortunate than himself out of one place after another, while this one may repeat the process on one still inferior, till the weakest one fails to obtain sufficient wholesome food, is poorly sheltered from cold, heat and dampness, is compelled to live in filthy surroundings, till disease, despair, and dissipation make him an easy prey, leaving his children to grow up as they can, sickly, ignorant and depraved, to fall more easily under the crushing out process than did the parent. Some go down quickly, others more slowly; but rank after rank they are continually going down and out of sight, each robbing and pressing down the one beneath him, as steadily and surely as the large trees of the forest by their growth deprive the small ones of nutriment and sunshine till they die. All this is simply the effect of competition.

The human enemies, too, that prey upon humanity are as numerous and varied as those that prey upon animals and plants. When one by industry and frugality has obtained more than his necessities require, if he is generous enough to allow it, some sickly, or inefficient friend, relative, or co-religionist will fasten upon him, like a parasitic plant to a tree, or a flea to a dog's back, to live at his expense. Indeed, the parasite class is a large one, and likely to become more numerous as human nature becomes milder, till men are wise enough to prevent its increase by propagation, and limit it to the accidental victims of misfortune.

Every one who is feeble or undeveloped in any particular finds some enemy prompt to take advantage of the weakness, and thrive at his cost of suffering. Every one ignorant of the extent of human meanness and villainy is astonished to discover some thief, swindler, or murderer anxious to rob him of property or life. Human spiders, of unspeakable malignity, set their traps, and lie in wait for every unsuspecting creature who can be lured into the net, and held till his last drop of blood has been sucked. Human wolves, some of them in sheep's clothing, stand ready to seize, ruin, and devour every unwise and defenceless woman that deceit or accident may bring within their reach, and with a heartlessness no canine wolf can equal. Human crocodiles, with tears more hypocritical than those the reptiles are fabled to shed, swallow up the substance of their nearest relatives, or dearest friends if once they get it within reach. Human prostitutes both female and male, like leopards and dogs that hunt other animals for the favor of their master, are ready to sell their bodies and souls to catch the unwary, and rob them to the utmost for a share of what they obtain. And of all venomous snakes the vilest and most venomous are those human ones who sneak about some one who may have provoked their wholly selfish and brutal natures, till they can safely strike at reputation or life, or what may be dearer than life itself. Still further, there are human vampires that fasten upon their victims, and drain them of all vitality, till they sink into the grave, murdered without any sign of guilt or violence.

And these are not all. There are all possible kinds of these enemies, with all degrees of power to injure, from the ruthless fiend who murders the innocent in cold blood, to the little-souled pests and torments, that buzz and sting, and peck and bite, and against whom there is no defense. Every device and means that ingenuity stimulated by want can invent is made use of to effect their purposes. Every natural appetite is tempted, every amiable sentiment is flattered and cajoled, every fear or sensitiveness is bullied and threatened, every ambition is encouraged, even every sacred feeling and aspiration is imposed upon, to bring the victim where he or she can be cheated and robbed, or used as a tool to rob others. Every trap, treachery, pretence, lie, swindle, I might almost say every vice and crime, is an effort in some way to take something from another—to gain at his expense

—or else to resist such robbery. In trade, in government, in church, in society,—everywhere the great game of robbery, in some shape, goes on against all who are not prepared to detect and resist it. It has thus gone on unceasingly since social life began, and on some parts of the earth may continue for centuries yet to come.

The human race suffers in one especial manner in which animals do not. Their intellect is not sufficient to overcome their instincts, and so they do not become depraved. Man, with his stronger intellect, has discovered unnatural gratifications for his appetites, and has practiced these in opposition to his instincts. Every species of intemperance, luxury and sensuality he has indulged in, because he possessed reason sufficient to discover means of doing so, but not enough to perceive the full consequences of his action. He has fallen a victim to his own weakness of thought and of self-control. Rich or poor, fortunate or unfortunate in other respects, if he is weak enough to be tempted some one stands ready to draw him aside, and rob him of property, character, health and life. Millions of the weaker part of humanity go down from this cause every year; they have always been doing so; and yet the gain of intelligence and character, to the wiser and better part that remain, is comparatively little; the weak ones are destroyed almost as fast as ever before; so small an improvement is made by Nature in a long time, and at such a vast, such a horrible expense of suffering.

Even yet there remains still another method of operating against the less fortunate. As in the contests of nations or peoples the superior combined to conquer, and exterminate or enslave the weaker, so within the nation or people one group or class is united against a weaker class or an individual, to take still more the benefit of their superiority. In olden times the priestly class did this, and has not yet forgotten how to do it; the political

SOCIAL SELECTION

or governing class has always flourished at the cost of the governed; the professional and mercantile classes still make their big salaries and profits at the expense of those who do inferior kinds of service.

Some persons in this country make an outcry lately because the transporting interest takes advantage of its monopoly to increase its gains more rapidly than it ought. But reprehensible as this action may be, it is no worse than that of other classes and individuals. All the great merchants, all the eminent lawyers, physicians and preachers, all who hold high positions, take advantage of their ability and opportunities to gain all they can; and indirectly, but no less surely, it is all at the expense, finally, of that humblest class which, though sinking itself, supports all those above it. The tillers of the soil, the diggers in the mine, the mechanics who convert raw material into things of use and beauty —the workers with muscle instead of brain—these are the ones who by giving more labor than they receive in exchange, furnish subsistence to all the more fortunate classes.

From man downward to the lowest grade of animal life one order lives upon another, the stronger upon the weaker; finally it is the vegetable world sustains the whole.

But here we come to another feature of the Selection process, one worthy of special attention. I mean *fortune*, chance, the good or bad luck of individuals, species, races, or nations. Besides the influences acting constantly on an organism, there are occasional and extraordinary ones. If a seed happens to be carried by the wind, or by some bird or beast, to a favorable locality, and dropped there at the right time, it may germinate and produce a tree superior to its parent. Every other seed may fall where it grew, and if it springs up at all may have no chance to become a tree. So if a pair of animals wander out of their usual habitat into a better one, through fright or in search of water, the result may be an improved variety, and later an improved genus or order. On the other hand the misfortune of eating some poisonous plant may kill off the superior members of a species, who have discovered a new habitat, and but for the poison would have made an improvement. No one can estimate how much the evolution of living things has been helped or hindered by such chance influences. Nature can do nothing to favor her work, nor to avoid misfortune. All she can do is to take advantage of an opportunity when chance brings it. And chance is as likely to bring what will check the process as what will help it on. A thousand seeds may be wasted before one reaches a spot where it can live; and though the purpose or end of all this movement is to produce more perfect things, yet generation after generation lives and dies without improvement, till at length some chance gives a favoring circumstance, and an advance—a very slight advance—is made. A great many attempts consume a vast amount of force, but are fruitless toward accomplishing the object; and whether the animal life that continues all this time is worth living to the animal is far from certain. Let us hope that it is; for otherwise Nature is a sad blunderer. It has been common to speak of Nature's works as perfect; and as regards the best of them that may be true in a relative sense. But we now know that everything has reached its present state by evolution from a very imperfect one; and that in the process an immense amount of time and energy have been consumed without effect. It is only after intelligent humanity has been evolved that effects begin to be produced with the idea of reaching perfect adaptation through the least waste of time, means, and suffering.

In society the effects of good or ill fortune are no less conspicuous than among the lower orders of existence. Among primitive societies, if one by having a better opportunity became more advanced, and consequently more prosperous than the rest, yet happened to be shut in by limited territory, its neighbors found excuse for fighting and robbing it. Only when such a society had a location where it could communicate its intelligence, and its moral as well as physical improvement to others, and so gradually build up a larger and continually increasing tribe or confederacy, that it had any chance to live. Any little quarrel may produce war between a small tribe and its neighbors; and though the equal of any surrounding it, the small one may be blotted out, and all its progress lost. The Erie tribe of Indians were thus exterminated by their Iroquois brethren. The Polish nation was thus killed, and its people checked and put back from the position they had gained. Whole communities in southern France were thus slaughtered for attaining to a superior religious and moral development. A similar fate overtakes whole civilizations. All the progress made by the Indians of Mexico, Yucatan and Peru was thrown away by the Spanish conquerors. They and the surrounding peoples gained so little from it we may with sufficient truth say it was lost to the world. So of the old Eastern civilizations, the Egyptian, Assyrian, Persian, Phoenician, Greek and Roman; though their attainments were not wholly lost, most of them were destroyed. The Alexandrian library and museum, though perhaps over-valued, was certainly worth saving to the world. These are a few conspicuous examples of Humanity's ill fortunes. Smaller ones could be pointed out by the historian.

Every one knows how a similar good or bad fate attends individuals in present society. If one by good luck finds opportunity to acquire sufficient property for comfort, but not enough to tempt him into luxury and dissipation, he makes progress, and leaves an improved progeny behind him. Where a majority of individuals are of this type a prosperous community grows up. Another individual may be born with qualities equally well adapted to his time and society, but if he fails to inherit property or to find an opportunity of acquiring it he fails to advance, and his children may deteriorate. The third generation, inheriting less of the social qualities demanded, goes down to a still lower grade, and may become paupers or outcasts. If one of these again finds encouragement to strive for a better lot, and by small success gains a new stock of hopefulness and energy, these qualities transmitted to his offspring may enable some of them to again acquire wealth and all the means of progress.

Here, too, we find the unfortunate individual who makes too much of an advance. He attains fitness for a social environment better than exists. His qualities are those of the future, and as much out of place as those required by the past. His neighbors fail to understand him, he becomes an object of neglect, and when the difference is great of suspicion and dislike. He wishes to go faster than those around him, and to induce them to keep up with him. In short he is some kind of reformer. If unable to communicate his spirit to the community in which he lives, he must discard or repress his own peculiar thought and feeling, and be content with that of the community. If he wanders on alone his isolation from others is death to him sooner or later. Persecution may or may not take his life directly, but neglect, misrepresentation, suspicion, loneliness, and every kind of discouragement, finally drive him to invalidism and a premature death, suffering for the sins or moral deficiency of others, and leaving few or no children to inherit his untimely goodness or wisdom. Jesus, Socrates, Gallileo, and all the prominent reformers, are examples of this type. Their unfitness for the society of their time may be as great as that of the criminal, whose qualities adapt him only to a very low social condition; and thus by what seems to many a strange regulation of things, the reformer and the criminal meet with a similar fate. Each attempts to force the ideas belonging to a few upon the whole body, and encounters its resistance. Too little development and too much are equally undesirable to the social mass, hence equally unadapted to the social conditions. Nature, we may say, insists on having the whole mass go along nearly together; one who is much ahead or behind—superior or inferior—is the unfortunate one to be selected out or exterminated. On the contrary one who, in all respects equal to the mass, can take a very small step in advance, becomes at once the admired leader of the whole, and insures his own greatest good along with that of the entire social body he leads.

Of the two unfortunate classes, the memory of the criminal remains in disgrace; that of the reformer, after some scores or hundreds of years, when the general advance of his people has nearly reached his own, becomes respectable, grand, glorious, even that of a god. During life the criminal may by education and discipline acquire some imperfect adaptation to social surroundings; the reformer, if earnest, can live only by discovering or making a new habitat,—that is, by developing a new religion or a new social state.

I have said that Nature's purpose in all this was ultimately to produce perfection. But while she produces new varieties, some of which are able to find new sources of food or a new habitat, she at the same time adapts the old species more perfectly to its surroundings, which may be quite unfit for a superior race; and thus many of the inferior forms of life are able to continue their existence. So of the inferior races of men, and the inferior forms of society. They still hold their ground, and will as long as the superior ones do not need to encroach upon them. They do not improve in any way; they aim only to so adapt themselves to circumstances that they can live. Of such the Chinese furnish a good example. European peoples have come to perceive that they can not only adapt themselves to their conditions, but can improve the environment and themselves also. This perception makes the difference between the progressive condition of Europe and America, and the stationary condition of Asia and Africa. As yet however the idea has but little influence. Very little, compared to what might be, has ever been done by society toward its own improvement, or to give the individual a fair opportunity to perfect himself. That is to come in the future, after society shall have attained to a knowledge of itself and its power,—when, like the individual, it has gained its consciousness of comparative freedom, and superiority to circumstance. At present the individual, except in rare cases, can only adjust himself to the social environment as it is, without expecting to make much progress. Sometime, society, with its power a million times greater than that of any individual, may be wise enough to use that power for the preservation of its highest class, now equally unfortunate with the criminal; and instead of preserving and perpetuating its criminal and parasite classes, will by education on one hand and supression on the other, eliminate them entirely. Society as yet has no idea of doing as much for its members, in comparative effect, as an ignorant farmer does for his flock of sheep.

Meantime the old process of selection by blind natural means must still go on, killing out by slow tortures the weakest and least fit members of the social body; those also who, though fit and qualified by nature, are born into unfavorable circumstances; and those who by advancing too fast have become fitted for a better social condition. Cruel and wasteful the method is—horribly cruel and wasteful—but no other is possible till society has gained intelligence sufficient to become superior to it, and to accomplish an equal or greater progress by humane instrumentalities. Suffering tends to develop intelligence, and we may reasonably hope that the needed wisdom and humanity of sentiment will sometime be attained.

We must not however be unjust to Natural Selection. Its method, though tedious and cruel, is better than none. If there were no causes operating to destroy the weak and unworthy this human world would probably be crowded with idiots, lunatics, cripples and invalids, with reckless, unprincipled and criminal wretches, who althogether would make life a burden too grievous to be borne by even the most fortunate. Part of the evil has been taken away from us by Selection; and through its aid we shall ourselves at last be able to throw off the greater part of what remains.

It is the development and selection of intelligence and morality, in other words, the adaptation of man to society, that will finally enable society to take selection out of the hands of its mother Nature, and to do the same work more efficiently as well as humanely. What moral progress is yet made acts more in opposition to Natural Selection than in coöperation with it. It is the humane sentiment that gives the criminal the benefit of every doubt, and virtually encourages him in crime, besides leaving him at liberty to generate a dozen other criminals, to succeed himself when finally killed by some one of his own class. It is the sympathy and tenderness fostered by society that cares for all our invalids, lunatics, idiots and beggars, keeping them alive, and enabling them to add still other invalids, lunatics, paupers and idiots to the next generation. It might be fairly questioned if every physician is not more of a curse than a blessing to society, provided he really accomplishes much in the saving of life. Regarding lawyers the question would be still more allowable. In these and similar ways, prompted by goodness, but without sufficient wisdom, the race helps to retard its own progress. But in the future this, like all other drawbacks, will be overcome by a further increase of intelligence and of the social spirit, till the blind and cruel method of Nature shall be superseded by a wiser and gentler one of man. Let no one suppose, however, that I would abridge the life or comfort of any one now living; I would only prevent the transmission of their miseries to others.

To Nature pain, wounds, disease, death are nothing. A million lives may be lost, or a hundred generations live and die without improvement; but when the opportunity appears she avails herself of it and makes a step in advance. The counteracting influences, the loss of previous attainments, the waste of power, may be great, yet some little advantage is gained. A civilization may go down, but in place of it there is a new race capable of greater advancement. The sick, infirm, deformed and vicious may be saved against her intent, but an additional fitness for society is at the same time acquired. Unwise Religion may persecute and millions die for heresy, but at last the idea of total self-conquest becomes understood. And so, in spite of all hindrances, something is accomplished toward the evolution of a perfect race, which shall ultimately, through gentle means, take the place of all inferior ones, occupy the whole earth, and bring forth the perfect society.

What now, is the moral lesson that Natural Selection

teaches to the individual? There is one, and one of no little importance. It is this,—that while one factor in the complex cause of all he suffers is chance or misfortune, the other factor is his own shortcoming. This, too, is misfortune in the larger sense, but it is that over which he has some control. The proportion of one to the other may vary indefinitely, but both of them are present. Aside from what Fortune does, Nature or Natural Selection gives him what he deserves. A certain part of his unhappiness is because he has not adjusted himself to the persons and things around him, or not sought for a more congenial environment. If he complains his complaint lies, in the average of cases, as much against himself as against his ill luck, whether that comes from inanimate causes, or from the influence of other persons. The lesson then is one of self-criticism. If he possesses but little of what he desires, let him set aside the effects due to bad luck, and see if his own deserts entitle him to anything more than what remains. Let him separate the part of Fortune from his own part, and if he criticises himself as thoroughly and severely as he is disposed to criticise everything else, an improvement will be likely to result.

To give this some illustration, we may say that one who makes health an object of sufficient thought and care will, as a general thing, possess health; while one who cares little, thinks less, and learns nothing about it, deserves to lose what he may chance to have, and is sure to do so sooner or later. It goes to, or remains with, the one who best appreciates and uses it, on whom it confers most happiness, and who is therefore best fit to have it. In regard to property, one who has the quality of mind that loves money, and the self-control to retain it, with energy to make proper effort, will, in a majority of cases, secure more or less of it; whereas, if poverty is his lot, he is probably lacking in these qualities, in a majority of cases, and sets his desires more upon something else. It appropriately belongs, within certain limits as to amount, where it can be best appreciated, and preserved. If position is the object, the one who has the ambition to climb, and the kind of talent to secure it, is for both these reasons the best fitted to have it. And so when knowledge is the object sought, the matter is so plain every one will admit that the one who can best appreciate and use is the one who will obtain it; for the talent that enables him to desire, appreciate and use is the talent that will enable him to acquire; while the one who fails is the one to whom knowledge would be less useful if possessed.

It is now easy to see, too, that if the element of good or ill fortune can be removed by social action, so that competition for either of the things mentioned will be equal and fair to all, the effect of Selection will be to push every one into that situation or employment for which he is best fitted, and where he can be most useful to himself and to society,

Self-criticism is thus not only necessary for the individual's own good, but is due to those around him; for by taking blame to himself he avoids putting it upon others. Moreover, by refraining from injustice to them, he will more easily secure their good will and assistance, in his battle against whatever ill fortune may be in his lot.

Wherein he finds himself successful and happy, it will likewise be well for him to discount the good fortune, and discover how much is due to his own good qualities only. The practice may save him from getting light-headed, and enable him to avoid some disappointment. In the part that is owing to chance he may find the influence of certain persons toward whom he should feel grateful or at least considerate. In every way the criticism will prove to be a most excellent discipline, both for his own benefit and that of all with whom he associates.

There is one special consideration the unfortunate should remember,—one that has never received sufficient attention. Every form of weakness, ignorance, carelessness, inability to protect oneself, and every submission to injustice, is a direct temptation to the selfishness of human nature. We habitually blame others for what may seem an unprovoked attack upon us, when our own feebleness is an encouragement to imposition, insult, robbery, or whatever the offence may be; and when if we were strong in all respects no attempt to abuse us would be made. It may or may not be correct to say that one who offers temptation is equally to blame with the one who offends; but there is at least some fault in the victim. Nature allows no excuse for the weakness, and it is punished by some one ever ready to take advantage of it for selfish purposes. Only when the Unselfish Stage of human evolution shall be reached will this be different.

We have not yet considered Fortune itself. How will the man of scientific thought feel regarding that? Precisely as he now feels regarding what he knows to be the inevitable. So far as the causes of it may be changeable in future, though he could not previously have anticipated or guarded against them, he will exert himself to make the future better. So far as he can learn a lesson from good luck also he will do it, and thus put himself in the way of further good luck. But in a matter entirely beyond his power to change he will view it just as an animal appears to do; having no one to praise or blame for it, no need of being either grateful or complaining, for one or the other. If good he rejoices over it; if bad he escapes as quickly as possible, and makes the best of what remains to him. Regret, sorrow, agony it may produce in him, but no *bitterness* of feeling. The causes of it are or were beyond the control, or the anticipation, of any person. The temporary indignation that would destroy a material thing to prevent any possible future harm, may exist for the moment, but soon passes away. The life still before him may be looked upon as a new life, into which he is just born, with whatever abilities, defects, and chances may yet be his; and if worth living he will set about living it in the best manner possible, putting behind him regrets and thoughts of what might have been—if—knowing well there was no if. There is a great difference between getting reconciled to what is known to have been the inevitable, and becoming so reconciled to what is not known to have been such, but is believed to have been susceptible of change. Having this knowledge the man of scientific thought is the best prepared of any to meet whatever fate may be in store.

The conviction that while the past has been inevitable, the future depends largely upon our knowledge and character, is an inspiration to effort; while honest self-criticism discloses our true situation, and prepares for wiser action. With it we come into a favorable condition for learning whatever may be necessary. Nature insists upon complete fitness for everything before she lets up on our pains and penalties. Nothing less than fully developed intellect, and full-grown moral character, will enable us to escape from her clutch, and from the liability to suffering and premature death. She watches for every defect in our constitution or conduct through which we can be made to suffer. Every weak place where we can be broken or bent; every sore point that can be irritated; every species of ignorance through which we can be waylaid; every moral inability by which our fellows can be turned against us; every imperfect development in our mental or physical nature; and every lack of a warning experience; all will be seized upon and used against us, till at last, through much tribulation, we are driven into that wise condition where we know what she requires of us for our own good, and are willing to comply with all her demands. Then the time of our release has come, and with it our certainty of happiness.

CHAPTER IX.

NATURAL AND SOCIAL SELECTION.

Continued.

THE same competition or rivalry that goes on in the lower world, and is called the struggle for life, is going on in every part and function of organized society,—as it always has gone on, and to some extent, or in a modified way, probably always will. The whole work and activity of society is an exchange of service of one kind or another, or of the products of service; the worker receiving something for what he gives or does which enables him to live, and satisfy his own wants. All who do not give service, or products of labor in some way, are exceptions to the general rule, such as children and invalids, dependent on the individual, and the pauper, and criminal classes, living at the expense of the social body.

There is no need of saying what competition means in regard to trade and manufacture. Every laborer for hire knows too well what competition for employment means. Competition between nations has been so much discussed in this country during late presidential elections that every voter, at least, ought to understand something of what is meant by that. Every politician is supposed to know about competition for office, and for governmental favors. In the same way every trade and profession has within itself a certain amount of competition for the profits and rewards of that occupation. In all these cases it is the individual struggling for his own benefit directly or indirectly.

Man is originally unsocial; that is, selfish, working only for himself individually, or the few most nearly connected with him. Before political society began, Natural Selection wrought only for the individual's benefit. It made him the strongest, giving him success in proportion to strength, shrewdness, and selfish determination. These qualities enabled him to obtain the best arms, the most property, the highest position, the best home, the most beautiful woman; and to leave children, who, at the start, could have a better chance than their competitors in the universal struggle for life.

This natural selfish and reckless competition ends in all sorts of inequality. The strong hand, and the unscrupulous disposition, come to decide every contest, and to appropriate what is most desirable. It is so at the beginning of society, and in a less extreme way it is so still. Whenever present society becomes partially disorganized, by political revolution, by pestilence, famine, or any disorder, the tendency to go back to this primitive state of things is plainly apparent. Man has been compelled by necessity to become *partially* social, to be *less* selfish, to pay *some* regard to justice. The tendency of organized society is directly in opposition to the unrestrained selfishness of the primitive man; and its principal work, as will be more apparent farther on, is to convert his natural selfishness into unselfishness. Yet in spite of this, in every civilized community the conditions of the people still grow more and more unequal with every advance of knowledge, and its application to art and industry. The nearest approach to equality is in the state of barbarism. Everywhere above that stage we find extremes of riches and poverty, of education and ignorance, of nobleness and meanness, of respectability and degradation. In the great cities of civilization where is the greatest wealth, luxury, and culture, there is the extremest poverty, the lowest degradation, the most fiendish crime.

In the numberless wars of conquest in which stronger and weaker tribes and nations have struggled for the better parts of the earth's surface, its soil, timber, minerals, and all natural resources,—which by simple justice belong equally to the whole population, and to every new generation as much as to the last,—these have been distributed among the powerful leaders of victorious armies; and thus all over Europe the greater part of the soil comes to be held by a few princes, nobles, aristocrats of various names, and their favorites, who are thus immensely rich, while a large proportion of the people remain poor for want of their natural inheritance. In England and Wales, for instance, there is more land lying idle in the parks and game-grounds of the aristocracy than is contained in the whole kingdom of Belgium, which supports six millions of people. In Asia, which has been conquered over and over so many times, the rulers, who control the soil, live in luxury on the heavy taxes drawn from the miserably poor who cultivate it. A large part of the Western world has been given or sold in large tracts to the favorites of the conquerors, or of the politicians who govern. And even in our own country, where professedly some consideration is given to the rights of the masses, their wild land is sold for a song, or donated for premature railroads, in tracts large enough for counties and kingdoms, to native and foreign depredators and speculating corporations, utterly regardless of those who will need to occupy it in future, and of the present class of small farmers, who are threatened with perpetual poverty by the competition of such large landowners. In the same manner the governing politicians have at various times sold or given away mines, forests, fisheries, and water-powers, all over the country, and the fortunate possessors of them have accumulated wealth, and founded rich families, on what was thus acquired from the common stock. Nature has given all this advantage to the strongest, the most crafty, the most unscrupulous, as well as most enterprising, in spite of whatever efforts are made to prevent, just as she gives the best wild fruit on a tree to the strongest, quickest, most enterprising ape in the African forest.

These are the effects that appear in taking one view of the general result of inequality produced by Natural Selection. Let us see further how it works in trade and industry.

All are sufficiently familiar with the ordinary operations of trade and manufacture, and with the tricks, traps, frauds, and brazen-faced falsehood by which traders deceive their customers, and try to get the best of their competitors. Leaving out of account the few honest dealers, who are compelled to defend themselves by all fair efforts to secure trade, the spirit of the commercial world is the same as that of the animal world, which uses every kind of artifice to catch its prey, and to elude its stronger enemies. The gambler, who by his deceptive methods takes something for nothing, is perhaps the most extreme representative of it; the small storekeeper, who aims to get a profit beyond pay for time and labor, shows its most moderate form. It is the desire to get something for nothing, or much for little, by whatever means may be available and necessary. The poorest have it as well as all the more fortunate;

and with few exceptions would be glad of any chance to get rich by the ordinary methods.

The trade competition has for its good result the production of the capable and systematic business man, who in most cases performs useful service in distributing products, without any very excessive reward for his exertions. In a less number of instances it is now well known that the strong, the greedy, the unscrupulous gain advantages over the rest, and build up fortunes at the cost of their unsuccessful rivals, as well as of all who are their customers. The small merchant and the small manufacturer are constantly being driven out of business, and their trade absorbed, by those who have big capitals and established custom. The city dealer takes trade from the one in the country. The small farmer is becoming extinct in some parts of Europe; and though still holding on among ourselves, his time will come. Even the small preacher and the small editor have their business taken away by the big ones in the large cities. And the poor laborer who is not tough enough to live cheerfully on poor diet, with a miserable shelter, loses the chance to sell his labor, and gives place to one who can. The poor, the weak, the unfortunate are constantly being displaced, and their trade or opportunities appropriated by those more capable or more unscrupulous as the case may be.

The element of chance has been all the time present, and taking advantage of this, Nature has produced men of big properties, just as she takes advantage of favoring circumstances to produce big trees. You may say if you choose that the man himself takes his opportunity to collect a great mass of wealth; but the tree may be said to do the same, and both act for themselves according to natural methods, and by means of natural forces, under natural promptings to action.

We now see that the result through trade and industry

is the same as the result from war, and spoliation by force. The spirit of both are similar; in both it is the same as that of the animal. The difference is that force and violence being forbidden under the industrial regime, the trader accomplishes his ends by friendship, deception, and fraud.*

But it is not yet fully understood how the great landholding, mercantile, manufacturing, and transporting princes come to be all alike monopolists, and spoliators of the less fortunate. This it is necessary to make plain.

As before stated, whatever natural resources exist upon the surface of the globe belong naturally and rightfully to each generation of men that successively occupy it. The soil, waters, minerals, timber, wild game, fish and fruits, are in this category of natural resources. The doctrine is a very old one, once so self-evident that nobody questioned it; and is still acknowledged true by a number of the political economists, besides being specially asserted by Mr. Henry George and others, who of late have made it so familiar to the American people.† The ownership of land in fee simple grew out of the European feudal system, as an improvement upon that robber scheme, by which the strong chiefs of conquering armies had become possessors of nearly all Western Europe. Fee-simple ownership has disposed of the largest part of the American continent, has converted land, mines, water-powers, lakes, timber and oil into commodities, and made them objects of trade like everything else. Whoever obtains a tract of land where a young city or village can grow up has a piece of good

---

*Those who have never learned that trade is largely a modified form of war may find it well illustrated in an article in the Popular Science Monthly for Jan., 1888, by David A. Wells, showing how all the commercial nations take measures to protect their own trade from the damaging influence of aggressive traders in other countries.

†One of the strongest statements of it was made nearly forty years ago, by Herbert Spencer in his "Social Statics," chap. 9.

fortune that enables him to gather wealth, not through his own labor, but that of others, in return for which he gives back to them this land, that was theirs at first, and should have remained in their possession. If another by the same good fortune gets possession of land on which oil is found, or any valuable mineral or timber, he has the same opportunity to make money out of what should be the property of the whole community. He obtains a monopoly of a certain commodity or privilege, of greater value than his labor could pay for, and by having it becomes rich. No other one is allowed any *opportunity* to obtain it, or to share in it, as all might have done had it remained in the original common ownership. All opportunity for a share being taken away from the many, and given to the single one, constitutes a gross violation of natural justice.*

The fact that land, with its contents, is limited in quantity, and like products, can be divided up and got possession of, gives no justification for making it property, nor can render such property legitimate. Neither can labor spent in its cultivation. The original soil given by Nature, *however poor in fertility*, is, like air, water, and sunshine, an *indispensable condition* of all animal and vegetable life—one of the four things without which no life can exist; and it is for this reason, *and because it is capable of being made productive*, that it belongs to the whole race. It is the universal storehouse from which every living thing that occupies it, directly or indirectly draws its food-supply. By exclusion from it man can be deprived of life as truly as by exclusion from air or water, or the plant by exclusion from the sunlight through which it is enabled to grow. Neither if it were all cultivated, and all its produce exchanged, would those

---

* Mr. George, in reasserting the right of the whole people to the land, with all it contains, and especially to that increase of value given it by the building up of towns, has done society an excellent service, and is entitled to much credit for his earnestness, whatever may be the fate of his scheme to recover the rent value of land to the state, by a tax upon land property only.

facts constitute an excuse for monopolistic ownership, unless every adult person was assured the opportunity to exchange an equal amount of labor for its produce; and then there would be no object in possessing. The occupant who, by cultivation, has made it better than nature gave it has the best claim to the use of that particular spot he has improved. And, by the same reasoning, one who has impoverished it can rightfully be compelled to live on his deteriorated soil till he dies, or till he brings it up to its natural quality.

Though the other natural resources—those contained in, or belonging to, the land and waters—are not indispensable to life, as is the soil, they are indispensable to comfort and progress; and being equally the bounty of Nature, it is self-evident that no one can make any better claim to them than another, or obtain any title that will be valid for more than one generation.

Now, in what way does the class of persons who monopolize these natural resources differ from the *merchant* monopolist, who claims to be no monopolist at all, but trades freely and fairly with whoever comes to him, allowing everyone else the same chance? Yet he has a large trade, by whose profits he has become much richer than the average of men, while by having a large capital he can keep his trade, and destroy the business of any less wealthy man who attempts to compete with him. He *is* thus a monopolist, but of what? Not of the metals, coal, oil, or timber on the earth's surface, nor even its wild animals; but of the *trade* from a considerable number of its human inhabitants. Having their trade the result to him is the same as if he had their service for a certain time as slaves. They each give him a small percentage (very small perhaps) more than they receive from him in his services, and this, which is his profit, is sufficient to make him wealthy. He then uses his wealth to retain that trade or increase it—to prevent any one else from getting any share of it—till he has accumulated a fortune far beyond the average. As long as he retains his opportunity certain others have *no* opportunity. The opportunities that *would* exist if he had only a small business, sufficient to give him a competence merely in return for his labor, are taken away from others, and retained by him as his monopoly of trade. Legally any one is free to compete with him, but practically no one can do so without a capital as large as his own; all poorer men, unless they can combine their strength, are shut out from the game.

Most persons will say this man found or made his opportunity by hard work, prudence, careful study, and enterprise; and therefore deserves all he can gain because he did better than his fellows. That he deserves greater success than one who makes less effort is true. And he who by his thought, skill, boldness and energy opens a new source of employment and wealth, is entitled to all the credit and good will he receives, besides something more than the ordinary in his material reward. But the successful man did not make his *customers*, nor make their *necessities*. Both of these existed on the soil beforehand. *Population* and *its wants* constitute a natural source of wealth as truly as any of those before named. Those wants create the demand for every kind of labor, in both production and distribution, to supply them. They are what every one must depend upon to give him opportunity and pay for his labor, unless he goes back to barbarism, and clothes himself in skins. Population and its wants are what every one finds when he comes into the world, as naturally produced as soil, water, or mines. To the merchant,—and no less to the manufacturer, or transporter, who also supplies the wants of population,—they are natural resources of a different kind, which he works upon, and draws wealth from, as truly as does the miner from his lode. He uses his brains to find, and take advantage of, the opportunity they furnish, just as another man uses his brains and energy to utilize the timber on his land, or turn the soil into wheat, or kill the wild bison for his skin. He does not make use of his fellow men as directly as does a slaveholder, but indirectly he induces them to give him a profit from the results of their labor—something more than the mere average pay for his services. If he secures a large custom, and holds it long enough to get rich, he becomes a monopolist of trade, and of other men's natural opportunities, precisely like one who monopolizes land, or the wild pine forest that grows on it. He thus deprives others of their natural share, and their natural opportunity for employment.

It is not the intention here to condemn the great merchants, manufacturers or transporters, or the corporations, trusts, and syndicates they form, as being *extortionate* beyond others in the *prices* demanded for their products or service. On the contrary, the economies of the large scale have enabled them to reduce such prices; and competition, or some one motive or another has influenced them to do so as a general thing. They exert a downward pressure upon wages, as do smaller operators; and by their use of improved machinery and processes, they throw men out of employment faster, probably, than would their small competitors in doing the same amount of business; in this respect being worse only by doing things in a larger way. Their real crime, like that of all the rest, consists in appropriating a part of the just reward of labor, by taking higher prices, or paying lower wages, than would be necessary under a different system; and in monopolizing the opportunities of other men, by throwing some out of employment, and keeping out others, thus depriving them of their natural right to labor, one of the first and most important of all rights, and which, as proved by the hundreds of suicides occurring every year from want of work, is truly their *right to live*.* In doing this however, they are no worse than the system that produces them,—no worse than the popular sentiment that honors a millionaire for his wealth, and thus encourages him to accumulate vast amounts of it for the sake of distinction.

To make the nature of the case evident in another way, let us resort to a few figures. In this country at the last

---

* One specimen of these cases is given below, as found in a N. Y. daily paper, February 15th of the present year. The heartlessness developed by the conditions and methods of business enables people to read of such instances day after day with a hardened indifference, that never takes the trouble to inquire if there is any injustice in society, or if there will ever be any less number of suicides.

"On the top floor of the tenement 316 West Thirty-ninth street, shortly before noon yesterday, George Wick, 20 years old, a painter, cut his throat from ear to ear after failing in an attempt upon the life of his wife. He lived in two small rooms with his wife, Amelia, and their 3 months' old baby boy. Wick had been out of work for fourteen weeks. Though he is said to have tried hard, he failed to secure employment, even at odd jobs, and became despondent.

"Members of the West Thirty-fifth street Presbyterian Church, where he attended services, heard of his condition, and knowing his case to be a worthy one, helped to pay the rent of his rooms. Wick's parents, and those of his wife, who are all poor people, also helped the unfortunate couple as much as their own slender means would allow. Wick went out to look for work yesterday morning, and returned more than ever disheartened. Calling his wife into their bedroom he exhibited a bottle of laudanum, and said sadly that they would both be better off dead.

"He spoke kindly and didn't act like a crazy person," said his wife to a *Press* reporter last night. "He had talked to me once before in the same strain, and I had persuaded him to change his mind, saying that we would struggle along somehow, and that everything would come right in the end. I talked cheerfully to him yesterday, too, but he said there was no hope for us. Then he put the bottle to his lips. I snatched it away, and in the struggle most of the poison was spilled. Then he seemed to become frantic. His razor lay on the washstand and he grabbed that. I tried to take it from him and he caught me by the throat. There were tears in his eyes then.

"'You must come, too,' he told me. 'I can't leave you behind to suffer alone.' As he pushed the razor up against my throat I screamed, and, tearing away from him, ran out of the room. Some of the tenants heard my cry and ran into the hall. I remembered my baby lying in the rocker, and thought if George killed him he might just as well kill me, too, so I started back. Just as I entered the room George staggered out of the bedroom covered with blood. He looked at me a moment and I saw two big tears roll down his cheeks. Then he put his hands up to his temples and fell down dead before I could reach him."

"During this recital, Mrs. Wick, who is a slender blonde, sobbed bitterly. Her husband, she said, had always treated her kindly, and the neat appearance of their rooms evidenced the fact that she was a tidy housewife. Ugly scratches on her throat tell of her struggle for life. Wicks was insured for enough to give him a decent burial. His remains will be taken to the Lutheran Cemetary to-morrow.

"Philip Wick, the dead man's father, said his son had called on him that morning and had seemed cheerful. There was nothing in his appearance or his conduct to suggest what was evidently in his mind at the time.

"Mrs. Wick's mother, Mrs. Amelia Ott of 354 West Fortieth street, called at the suicide's apartments and induced the heartbroken widow to go home with her. As she took her baby from a sympathetic neighbor, Mrs. Wick burst into tears and moaned: 'Poor baby! Thank heaven you can't realize what has happened.'"

The same paper of a later date makes the statement that "in the city of New York alone *seventy-eight* people committed suicide because they 'could not get work,' during the past year," (1888.) *Press*, March 13, '89.

census there were not far from fifty millions of people, and their total wealth not far from forty billions of dollars; while the increase of wealth is at nearly the same rate as the increase of population. Divide the forty billions among the fifty millions, and it gives eight hundred dollars to each person as the average possession of property. If the whole property could pass into the hands of millionaires, then to every million that went into the hands of the rich there would be twelve hundred and fifty (1250) persons who would have nothing. But as it is still far from being so unequally divided, there is a much smaller number of the poor to one who has a single million, besides many who have a little more or less than eight hundred. With competition tending constantly toward inequality, however, those who have little are continually at the risk of losing it, and of increasing the number of the poor, as their property increases the wealth of the rich.

The millionaire does not, as a general thing, take directly from those who have little, but from those who also have wealth, some of them rivals, who compete with him in speculative enterprises at a loss. The less wealthy in turn draw from any who may not be able to resist, and these last from still others, till finally, a certain number must die with nothing, in order that certain others may have a great amount.

A considerable proportion of the poor are of those born such, and who never make any suitable exertion to be otherwise. Another portion is of the sickly and feeble, and another of those who are careless, wasteful, extravagant, or morally defective. Still another part, how large or small there is no means of knowing, consists of those who, notwithstanding industrious habits, good character, and proper effort, yet fail to obtain their share, and end by accumulating nothing. Who are they? They are respectable men and women, constantly coming into the industrial world, but being without powerful friends, capital, or a brazen cheek, never find a fair opportunity, —never have sufficient employment to enable them to make any gain, their chance being monopolized by some one who gets rich. To make a suppositious estimate of their number, and leaving aside all the poor by their own fault, let us say that where one man obtains a hundred thousand dollars,—the average shares of over a hundred persons—there are five of those who will be poor in spite of willingness to labor and to save. If the rich one acquires a million there will be fifty of such deserving poor. When his million has increased to twenty millions there will be a thousand of the poor, who with their children, fifteen hundred more, are enough to make up the population of a good-sized village. Let this man of twenty millions still increase his wealth till it amounts to a hundred millions, as some of our richest men have done, and there will be the population of a small city, twelve thousand five hundred (12,500) persons, who can never have anything beyond their daily necessities, in order that this one may have his hundred millions. All the while the big fortune is being rolled up they are coming into the business world—the larger part of them—but never finding the chance they seek; while a smaller part are dropping down out of the ranks of trade and labor, because their opportunities are taken away by an unscrupulous competition from capital in trade, and from an excess of labor in every kind of service.

The estimated number here supposed may be too large or too small to agree with the actual. But even if there be only one worthy poor man or woman where there is assumed to be five, there are still far too many for the fact to be reconciled with justice.

The competition from which they suffer is one which instead of bringing to the top the moral man, the one best fitted for a happy society, favors the one who is most willing to be degraded. In labor it is the Chinaman, the Negro, the inferior white man of all nationalities, the one who can best live on poor food, in a shanty for a home, in woods, rocks, swamps, and all filthy and malarious localities, who quickest finds opportunity to work. The cheap, inferior, unsafe man comes to fill positions of trust and responsibility. In occupations requiring more intelligence it is the one who can be most servile. In trade it is the capitalist who with least regard for his conscience or his fellow men, uses his power to drive, or to keep, out of business all the men of small capitals, compelling these to crowd upon others less fortunate than themselves, that is most sure to succeed. The honest merchant, and the self-respecting workingman, both suffer that the one man may keep the opportunities that rightfully belong to a dozen, a hundred, or a thousand. For, the world's opportunities, let it be remembered, are what exist in its natural resources, including population; and these belong to the whole people alike. The wants of population give all the possible opportunities for every kind of labor and exchange. No one has any moral right to shut out others from a fair and equal chance to labor and live. No one in a civilized society should ever be able to get the power of doing so. Every natural means of getting a living belongs to all men and women equally, and trade is one of these. Every person who obtains much more than the average family share of wealth robs one or more of his fellows as truly, though not often as consciously, as if he took it out of their pockets. He does it through their ignorant willingness to give him profits that are not paid for in equal work, or else by monopolizing their natural opportunities for labor and trade. We can easily imagine how different it would be if every one could have a chance to take his turn in monopolizing either trade or high-salaried labor, for a limited time.

If any one wishes additional figures to bring out the results of monopoly, let him calculate how many must remain poor in his own village or city in order that the rich may acquire, not their millions only, but their hundred thousands, their fifty thousands, their twenty-five thousands; making sure to count out all the lazy and thriftless, the children, invalids, and disabled. In a new country, where openings are ready for all, these classes may perhaps include all the poor there is; but in this Eastern part of our country there will be plenty of others. If in looking around he sees only comfortable houses, and respectably dressed people, let him ascertain how many of those houses are rented by clerks, mechanics, and professional men who never have one of their own, and how many others are covered by mortgages that will never be redeemed. Those he finds who inherit their wealth are simply the representatives of a past generation, of whom substantially the same things may be said as of this; and several generations of poor men may have aided in the accumulation of what they now possess.*

Here, then, we have the main secret of the great dispute between Capital and Labor, between Wealth and Poverty; and here is the key to a final solution of the problem involved. It is in this monopoly of labor and trade, of which every one is guilty who holds on to his present advantage, to gather up a large fortune. Every one sees how the great landholder and the transporter are guilty; but hardly any one suspects the great merchant of being equally guilty. As now made plain, all the rich, however their wealth has been gained, can see what their crime against society is; a crime not in many cases by deliberate intent, but by inheritance, by cus-

---

* It is scarcely necessary to point out how much this distribution of property resembles the lottery or gift enterprise which, in one form or another, is so common a feature of the business life.

tom, by false moral education; a crime which all, rich and poor alike, stand ready to commit, waiting only for a favorable chance. And until this view of the situation is generally known and accepted, no considerable advance can be made toward a reconciliation of Labor and Capital, or a better distribution of wealth.

Take another consideration to confirm the general truth of what has been said. In the carrying out of the present unscrupulous competition a large part of man's natural fortune in the earth's resources is wasted. In our country much of the once fertile soil has been made barren by reckless cropping till exhausted. The former wheat lands of New England, and the tobacco fields of the South were so treated, and are now comparatively worthless. The waste of timber is going on in the same way. "Before him man finds the sweet wilderness, behind him he leaves the desert," is the poetical way of expressing it, and in the old world this is literally true. Now, it is indisputable that one generation of the earth's inhabitants are as well entitled, morally, to the use of its surface as another. But the generations succeeding us will find themselves heirs to worn-out lands, stripped of their fertility and natural wealth, because the selfish, reckless men of this and former times have puffed it away in tobacco smoke, burned it up in careless fires, poured it into the sea in sewage, or built great needless piles of wood and stone for ostentatious distinction.* And all this criminal waste and huge in-

---

*The immense waste of sewage and garbage in cities and villages, which pollutes our streams and offends the eye in unoccupied places, every pound of which contains elements that make possible a pound of food at some future time, could probably be saved (although previous attempts have been mostly failures) by a system of private alleys between streets, and a partial return to nature through the use of earth closets, in convenient ways that can be devised when the demand for them shall come. Yet hitherto man's efforts to utilize his animal and vegetal refuse have succeeded but poorly; he has returned it to the soil in filthy, undecomposed manures, compelling his cultivated plants to feed on them, till his fruits and vegetables have become almost as full of disease as himself and his domestic animals; ready to rot, blight, and mildew at every unfavorable change in the soil or the weather. And still he calls himself civilized!

justice is a part of that evil fortune which is constantly thwarting Nature's purpose, until the time when she, in spite of it, shall have developed mind of sufficient power to understand her ways, and assist her in her efforts toward human happiness through human perfection.

To restate all this, with some variation, unlimited rivalry or free competition in society results in success of the strongest, the craftiest, the most unscrupulous, as well as most active and enterprising, just as in the animal world. Whatever advantage one of these strong ones may gain he uses to gain more and still more. What he cannot accomplish alone he is shrewd enough to achieve by combining with others of the same sort, and in this manner the joint stock company, the big corporation, the political ring, are able to do almost whatever they desire. Thus we see that free competition ends in monopolies, and monopolies prevent any further free competition; the process ends by suppressing itself. There comes a time when only the corporations, the big factories, the merchant princes, the great landowners can do any successful business; and in place of a general and free competition we have a commercial and industrial feudalism, with its great captains of industry and transportation, and its great lords of trade. As long as the industrial barons compete with each other, trade, as ordinarily conducted, remains a species of war and robbery, carried on with less murderous weapons, and in a gentler manner, by which the life of the victim is shortened to a less extent. The workman or assistant under them is somewhat better off than the serf of former times, as long as he is able to work; but he is still to a considerable degree a slave, and as a general thing must be content with what the employer allows him in wages or privileges. Servility is often demanded of him, and the most servile is the most fortunate.*

Although trade has superseded war as a means of living, it is not wholly separated from it. In former times whole cities and their populations were destroyed to obtain trade, and the privilege of taxation, for the competing victor; and in later ones force, along with fraud and diplomacy, has been resorted to when necessary, to make the customer submit. I have already mentioned India, China, and Africa as countries in which this operation is now going on. Always it is the stronger, the wealthier nation which robs the weaker, or one less developed in its industry. It is with the same indifference to another's welfare that the big manufactory robs its smaller competitors of their trade, till they are compelled to retire from the contest, or retreat to new fields of custom. The large merchants crush out the smaller ones, and not content with taking away the opportunities of those in their own line of trade, they assail those in other lines and ruin still more. The huge bazars set up a dozen different departments, and by cheapening the goods in some attract custom and break up the trade of weaker dealers in all those lines.† Some of the more fortunate victims of this war are taken into the employ of the victors, much as in the old-time wars a man who was down was allowed to live on condition of becoming a slave. The less fortunate, reduced to poverty, and becoming worse and worse in their circumstances, are finally killed by want, depression, anxiety,

---

* *Capitalism*, the name given by the socialist to the industrial system of the time, does not seem to me its truest name, though that describes one of its most prominent features, especially in the period since the disappearance of the old or military Feudalism. Its deepest or most fundamental character is individual selfishness in purpose, demanding free competition as the proper condition of its activity. This individualism has always characterized the world of trade, ancient as well as modern, and its competition has been that of the animal and the savage.

† The big manufactory, the big railroad, and the big corporation of any kind, acts in so similar a manner that the devil-fish comparison, and the "octopus" name, have become familiar as applied to all of them.

starvation, disease and suicide; their death never being attributed to the original and true cause.

This picture may to some seem overdrawn, but is it so in reality? In all the great centers of population in Western Europe and Eastern America this state of things already exists. The Industrial Feudalism predicted sixty years ago by a distinguished socialist* is now here, and needs only time to make itself universal. The only way of escape from it has been through emigration to the free opportunities of a new country; but emigration will not be available always. Those who suffer from it make, with few exceptions, no complaint against the cause of their misery; they have been taught the doctrine of free competition so long and so thoroughly they never think of doubting its propriety. And this condition of mind precisely suits those who prosper. Competition has enabled them to monopolize; and conscious of their present advantage they protest against any interference with the freedom of trade in general, and of their own kind in particular. Every one who has a chance to profit wishes to be undisturbed in making the most of it. So the American slaveholder used to cry out to be "let alone." He wanted freedom to use, buy and sell slaves, and to extend the commerce in them over new territory. A great nation, when it had acquired the ability to manufacture and sell more cheaply than its neighbors, began to preach the Free Trade doctrine to the world, and has sent its literature here by the ton to convert its best customer and most effective opponent. The liquor-seller, aware of having the slaves of alcohol in his power, wishes a free chance to sell, and fights with his money and his vote against all interference. And for a similar reason certain men believe in Free Love.† "Let

---

*Charles Fourier.

† The following sneer at woman's virtue comes from a Boston organ of extreme Individualism.

" Not content with getting the "age of consent" raised from ten to thirteen, a

alone" thus becomes the cry of the tyrant and the robber as readily as it does that of the oppressed.

It is not necessary to accuse all these classes of people of deliberate wrong doing; for, as a rule, men find a way to make their beliefs or their consciences agree with their selfish interests. And there is a proportion of genuine honest men among the upholders of all these kinds of freedom. There are theorists who sincerely believe in unlimited free trade of every sort, and teach it as the sum of all social wisdom.* They mean that unrestrained freedom to compete which ends in monopoly and slavery,—the freedom of the natural, selfish, unsocial individual man, as against the right of society to take any measures toward its own improvement. To the unfortunate weaker party going down in the conflict they offer the insulting advice that a poor man should bring no children into the world till he is sure of being able to support and educate them; a doctrine that has no applicability to the rich. The quality of the children is of no account in either case; those of the poor man may be bright, healthy, and beautiful, those of the rich man idiotic, sickly and depraved, or vice versa, and it matters not. The only question is, can the parent support them till they are grown up? To me this seems, without exception, the most utterly selfish, heartless, and in every way *base* idea that ever was openly published to the world. The poor, it is not denied, are many of them reckless and brutal in their indifference to the prospective fate of their children; but they have no

---

bevy of impertinent and prudish women went up to the Massachusetts State House the other day and asked that it be raised again,—this time to eighteen. When a member of the legislative committee suggested that the age be placed at thirty-five, since the offence aimed at was as much a crime at thirty-five as eighteen, the petitioners did not seem to be terrified by his logic. Evidently these ladies are not afraid that their consent will ever be asked at all." Liberty, Feb. 11, 1888.

*A pamphlet has been published in London which advocates the most unqualified freedom of the trade in alcoholic liquors, as the most effective means of securing general temperance.

ideas so unhumanly unjust as this one, born of English culture.

These teachers, professors in colleges, editors of great newspapers, preachers of that gospel which Jesus brought to the common people and the humble, suffering poor, they go yet farther, and say to the still more unfortunate victims of industrial warfare—those who are left with neither means nor employment—say to them in the words of Malthus, "a man who is born into a world already occupied, his family unable to support him, and society not requiring his labor, such a man has not the least right to claim any nourishment whatever; he is really one too many on the earth. At the great banquet of Nature there is no plate laid for him. Nature commands him to take himself away, and she will not be slow to put her order into execution."* At present this man can be aided to emigrate; but when emigration becomes too expensive or too difficult he is allowed no right to live, and has nothing to do but commit suicide, taking care to drown himself, with a heavy weight about his neck, to save other people the expense of his burial.

To crown all, these teachers of economy, morals and politics, frankly tell us there is no hope of any material change in this condition of things. Mill, Spencer, and all the English economists, with their disciples on this side the water, are agreed that natural selection must continue to operate in the manner it has always done and is now doing; generation after generation of the unfortunate must suffer and die in their poverty and degradation; the rich will continue to monopolize wealth, culture and luxury; the man without capital or wealthy friends must be content, in this country as well as in Europe, to work

---

*" Man neither does nor can possess a right to subsistence when his labor will not fairly purchase it." "Society in furnishing employment and food to those who cannot get them in the regular market attempts to reverse the laws of nature." "He who ceases to have the power to subsist ceases to have the right."
These are further quotations from Malthus,—*Essay on Population, Book, IV. Chap. VI.*

for smaller and smaller wages, and finally be reduced to a bare subsistence, with a prospect of his employment being diminished by frequent periods of hard times, by additional labor-saving machinery, by lessening demand for products on the part of the unemployed, and by increasing difficulty of emigration; pauperism and crime are to be struggled with as now; till at last, in the course of centuries of misery, a better race shall be produced, and in some unknown way a better industrial condition be reached. *

This is the truest representation of them that I can make; for in all candor and honesty, I cannot see that they mean anything different. This is the program they submit to us, with all the confidence of men who feel sure their knowledge is correct, and that what they predict is unavoidable. It is fair to enquire if there could be, in the wildest anarchy anything very much worse.

But let us open our eyes a little wider yet. By what to most people seemed an unfortunate coincidence, the free-love element took a share in the presidential election of 1884, along with free-liquor, and free-trade in general. This, however, was no coincidence. That element belonged in the company it took; it must show itself there sooner or later; for its character is, like that of the others, a selfish regard for the interests of the strong, and indifference to those of the weak. I do not mean to intimate that the candidate of one party was more reprehensible than thousands of those who opposed him—the difference in parties is not any too great

---

* "Take, for instance, Prof. Sumner of Yale College. Can he be anything else than an agnostic? His lectures to the students—for some reason or other frequently reported in the newspapers—are directly at variance with the theories of theology and the whole spirit of Christianity, for he teaches flatly and with cruel emphasis that the scientific doctrine of the survival of the fittest should be applied to human society with all its logical consequences. The weakest must go to the wall, says Prof. Sumner, and the strongest must succeed among men as among beasts. The sentimental view of social questions he laughs at asunworthy of sensible and educated men, who, according to his notion. should watch without a quiver the progress of the struggle which is 'hurrying on the survival of the fittest.'" (*N. Y. Sun*,—article on "Atheism among College Students." 1886.)

—but never before in this country were similar tendencies strong enough to enable any party, by its toleration, excuse, justification or advocacy of its candidate, to make all three of these "freedoms" together, a test of the doctrine and policy to be voted for and established by the American people. This is precisely what was done in effect at that time, though the endorsement was not a strong one. That the former slaveholder and his children would sustain the party was to be expected; while the votes that turned the scale came from the half-Americanized city of New York, and from the neighboring towns, largely inhabited by a similar population. That a large part of the voters could not see what the real issue was only again shows how easily the ignorant and thoughtless masses of men and women can be misled through their prejudices, and induced to aid in their own degradation.

The result, therefore, of that election indicated more plainly than anything before it, that, unless the prevailing tendency shall be strongly checked, this country is to be Europeanized; that the industrial masses are to be crowded steadily downward till they are no better than serfs; that tyranny, servility, and moral corruption are to become the general condition; till the excesses of such a state finally provoke a reaction of general tumult, riot and revolution.

Since then another presidential election has, by a slight reaction, put the opposite party in power; but the change in the popular vote is so small that it indicates little real change in popular sentiment. And though the Protective policy voted for may continue to be maintained, its effect, especially as partly counteracted by immigration, can be only a slight retardation of the competitive movement; the outcome, a few years or decades later, will be substantially the same.

Of course it will be said that this is the view of a pessimist, seeing only the black and horrible side of things. No, I see whatever bright side there is; but the black side of competitive industry, the fiendishness hidden in its purely selfish doctrine and policy, has never been fully exhibited to the world. It is a system that compels men to develop not only every legitimate talent and energy, but every illegitimate and reprehensible one also. Every trick, fraud, swindle, and gambling operation that can bring money; every device to rob inexperienced women and young persons compelled to venture into the business world; every grab-game by which something can be stolen from the common resources of the people (for this is only a competition to see who can get it first); every knavish, lying and mean deception to get custom away from another, or a profitable situation under an employer; every prostitution of talent to vile uses for gain; is the direct product and outcome of the competitive system. The struggle for existence under it at length becomes so intense and fearful that every possible kind of service is sold for money; every favor, almost, must be returned in some way that will be of money value. By the inequality of wealth generated, wealth becomes a means of distinction, a badge of superiority, and a title to respect. To secure these, officials betray their trusts, for something that in some direct or indirect manner brings money. Professional service of every kind is tainted more or less with this moral prostitution. Humble service, likewise, must have its little "tips," or it is not fairly given. The mechanic, for no bribe but his wages, assists in whatever cheat his employer may design. The essential character of the system, therefore, does not consist in doing better service for the same money, or the same service for less, as is commonly supposed, but in taking whatever method will bring it the easiest, quickest, surest, or the most of it. To some persons the easiest method is a fraudulent one. Others will take an honest and straight-forward course, by natural preference, as long as it remains practicable. Some will be honest for the same reason that others will be dishonest, namely, because they think that will be the best way to obtain the money. It may be asserted in reply that such is not the design of theoretical free competition,—that its friends do not justify dishonesty,—which may be true enough; but the fact is that free competition is not fair competition; that fraud succeeds in gaining wealth, and the wealth dishonestly gained brings distinction, respectability, position and influence. Or, if in some cases there is a protest against allowing all these to dishonest wealth, it can at least command the means of luxury. There is thus held out a continual temptation to fraud and legal villainy. As long as this is true (and no one can say when, in civilized societies, it was ever otherwise) the system must be judged by such results as here charged.

It is not denied that there are faithful officials, honest business men, conscientious professional men and mechanics. But their morality is mostly the product of outside influences; while the tendency of competition is to make their number less and less. A certain degree of mercantile honor, or faithfulness to contracts and trusts, has always been considered a necessity in doing business; but it may be questioned if even this is not being assailed and weakened, and likely to be destroyed by the prevailing tendency.

Take notice of a few more facts, to show where the drift of things is carrying us in these days of supposed enlightenment, liberty, and progress. The Malthusian doctrine that the poor man has no moral right to have a child, and if without employment is commanded by Nature to take himself out of the world, was set forth by a minister of the gospel of the meek and lowly Jesus, who had not where to lay his head,—and was advocated with a good motive only. The hopeless prospect of the future for the workingman has been believed by such men as John Stuart Mill, Herbert Spencer, and Professor Cairnes, three of the most tender-hearted men in England. Why have they been so ready to accept such utterly heartless and cruel ideas? Because the reverence for property, taught them by the Competition doctrine, makes the robber gains of the millionaire appear to them more sacred than human happiness—yes, even more sacred than human life.

In London, the center of the modern industrial and commercial world, and of Free Competition propagandism, where dwell the richest of the rich and the most degraded poor on the face of the globe, where everything holy and unholy is converted into money,—there is where little girls, from ten to thirteen years old, are sold by their parents into a life of shame and ruin, to gratify the peculiarly dainty sensuality of certain rich villains, some of them believed to be lords, princes, lawmakers, and judges.* It is entirely right and proper, a very romance of consistency, that London should be the spot where vice of this kind is carried to the last extreme; because it is the center and home of the teaching and practice that would naturally end in the vilest of all commercial transactions. Other great cities may be nearly as bad, but according to all reason, propriety and justice London ought to be the worst.

Let us look also at a point on our own continent. In the state of California, having a gold-producing region and a virgin soil, where nature could be robbed of its resources with the greatest ease, an unrestrained grab-

---

* See the Pall Mall Gazette articles on "The Maiden Tribute of the Modern Babylon," July 1886. It is a remarkable fact, though in keeping with all the rest, that the editor who exposed this diabolism was sent to prison three months for a merely technical offence committed during his investigations, while the real criminals, whose money tempted the half-starved poor, escaped all prosecution.

Since then a human fiend in the Whitechapel district has been allowed to commit free murder, and the most horrible mutilation, on a half-score of female victims, without as yet (Dec. '88) being captured by the police.

game has been going on for thirty-five years, with gold, metallic or representative, for the principal currency, and Chinese labor, cheaper than the white man was able to furnish it. In all these respects the situation has been favorable to what is called "free competition;" and the outcome of its operation is,—great wealth, numerous millionaires, land held in immense ranches, hard times for poor white men, and a mass of social rottenness in the chief city, where twelve-year-old boys catch vile diseases from degraded Chinese women, openly imported for purposes of prostitution.* The result is but little different from what it is in London; in both localities man, woman, the whole human being, happiness, hope, conscience, decency, is inhumanly sacrificed to the almighty god of money.

Other localities are as yet behind these centers of operation, but are approximating the same condition, and need only sufficient time to reach it. Well and appropriately has it been said,—"The worst of all barbarisms is the barbarism of the civilizee."

---

*See report of a Congressional committee appointed some ten or twelve years since to investigate the condition of the Chinese in California.

Also the following requoted from the N. Y. *Sun* of Oct. 18, 1887.

"The San Francisco *Examiner* says that the steamship City of Sydney, which recently arrived in that port brought $60,000 worth of Chinese girls to replenish the slave quarters of that city. Though such importation is against the Chinese Restriction act, against the Contract Labor act, and against the still older law prohibiting the immigration of women brought for immoral purposes, their owners will find no serious difficulty in landing these costly chattels. A few dollars for witnesses, something more for a lawyer, and $17.50 apiece for court fees will settle the matter."

Still further, the following from the N. Y. *Press* of July 25, '88.

"San Francisco, July 24.—The Grand Jury, after a session of seven weeks, has made its report It declared that in the city crime is organized for offense and defense; that elections are controlled by 1,200 or 1,500 criminals, leagued together and rendering 'quid pro quo;' that the leaders have a pull on men in authority; that matters have reached such a pass that to offend the criminal element means political ostracism, and that a reciprocity exists between criminals, gamblers, prostitutes, bosses and policemen.

"A great deal of attention was given to the Chinese quarter. The report speaks of the place with horror and loathing, and says it is a haunt where crime flourishes, despite the police."

CHAPTER X.

NATURAL AND SOCIAL SELECTION.

Continued.

THE last chapter exhibited some of the worst features and results of the industrial system called Free Competition, under which the commercial world has always lived, which ends in *freedom* only for the strong, and in *competition* that is seldom fair. Let us now look at society from an opposite direction to discover what there may be to relieve the fearful prospect given from the first point of view.

When individual men first begin to form society, in order to accomplish by coöperation what they could not as individuals, that society comes to have a purpose of its own, which the individual separately had not. With society as with the separate individual the object is human happiness. With the individual it was his own personal benefit, regardless of his fellows; with society it is the happiness of the whole, or at least of the greatest number. To society then, that man or that institution, that law, custom, habit or industry that can add most to the social happiness—the good of the whole—is the one best fitted, or most fit to survive.

Then it is that justice becomes a standard by which

to judge of what is fit. It is not that which is best for one or for a few, but that which is best for all equally, that is now demanded. It is the justice of equality which makes every one contented with his situation, and attaches him in unity with all, thereby rendering the social body powerful for its purposes. Inequality, on the contrary, weakens the social organism by provoking discontent and disunion. Why should one suffer and die while another enjoys and lives? Why one be born with disease and deformity, another healthy and beautiful? Why one dwell in a shanty, another in a palace? Why one grow up ignorant, and another be well educated? Why one do disgraceful work for small return, while another has a sinecure place, good salary, and honor besides? Why one go with shabby dress, horny hands, and body begrimed with dirt, till he can have no pleasure in touching anything, or comfort in seeing himself at all, while another is clean, comfortable, and able to contemplate himself with satisfaction? Why one forever unfortunate and miserable, while another is comparatively fortunate and happy? These are the questions the poor and miserable have always asked, which the worker and the socialist are continually asking; but no one has ever given them an answer. No, and of all the wonderfully wise men, philosophical and clerical, who teach the unfortunate to accept their present evils, to reconcile themselves to hard work and small wages, to live on bread and water and be content with nothing but their "fodder" for comfort, till some thousands of years of blind natural selection has made an improvement, not one of them *can* give any answer. It is almost a pity the modern sphynx could not bite off their heads; for of all enemies of the suffering poor these teachers of falsehood, who justify perpetual wrong in the name of science and culture, are the very worst.

This prime distinction, between the purpose of the

natural, selfish individual man and the purpose of society, has been recognized more or less clearly from the earliest times. Old Hesiod, one of the first Greek poets, is credited with saying, "Let fishes and wild birds and beasts devour each other, but our law is justice;" that is, equality—the right of every one to live, and not be devoured by the rich and strong. Justice, Equality. Morality, Unselfishness—this has been the burden of all religious teaching, the pretense of all law, the inspiration of all the best poetry and romance, from the dawn of civilization to the present day. During all that time a contest has been kept up between the unsocial individual and his fellows. Society has ever insisted upon bringing him into harmony with them—into a condition where he would do them no wrong. It has always been inculcating the morality of justice, of liberty, of fraternity; the equal value of every human soul; the duty of elevating the degraded, and of aiding in every way those who need help. The state through law, and the church through religion, have continually made efforts, feeble and unwise perhaps, and often counteracted by their own immorality—yet still efforts, to attract or force him into his true relations. In short, the principal object of civilization during all the past has been to accomplish the feat of bringing this wild, selfish, unsocial man from the condition of savage individualism into adjustment with his fellows in a state of society. That social influence is the "power that makes for righteousness," and this conflict is, in large part, what the eternal warfare of good and evil means.

In the effort to do this, society, as does the individual man with his plants and animals, interferes with the process of Nature, and, in a very imperfect manner as yet, selects for itself that which is best for the social good—that which favors justice or equality, or is for the interest of the greatest number. It attempts to select out its worst criminals, and in certain cases of necessity the weakly born and least useful have been so treated in earlier times. Regarding institutions, customs, industries, trade, it is the same. Through the government it brings its power to bear upon slavery, monopoly, polygamy, the saloon, the brothel, the gambling house, the school, the church, the museum, the library, the almshouse; selecting one to be destroyed, and another to be preserved. It has often done this in a blind and selfish way; for society, like the average individual, has always been more or less blind and selfish, the teacher but little better than the taught. It will continue this process with increasing skill and effectiveness, till it has attained institutions fitted to develop social or moralized men and women, at the same time selecting out with more thoroughness all those persons who cannot be so fitted for society.

All political, ecclesiastical, marital, judicial, and charitable institutions, with their changes and modifications, are interferences with natural selection, which society has already made. So is the legal regulation of inheritance, of property or office. And the execution of criminals is its vindictive and cruel method of selecting out a few of those least fitted for social life.

In a similar manner society must hereafter come to deal with the element of fortune. The present selfish doctrine is that no one shall be happy except those who have good fortune; all who have bad luck must suffer without help, other than what a few benevolent persons may extend as a slight mitigation. And if the state at present gives to its paupers the bare means of dragging out a miserable existence, or builds a hospital for the blind or insane, the maimed or orphaned, it is done from a feeling of benevolence, or as a duty owing to religion, not from any consideration of justice to those unfortunates. It would scout the idea that they had the right to claim anything on the ground of justice. But this very claim I make bold to present on their behalf. The natural and moral right of all to an equally good fortune, on the ground of a natural capacity to enjoy, is what determines the duty of one to help another in time of need or distress. There is no other rational ground for such charity as most people acknowledge it their duty to bestow on the unfortunate. It is on the same ground only that the weak are entitled to protection, or that the child may claim an education. And by precisely the same reasoning the child is entitled to an education as nearly equal to that of any others as its capacity will enable it to receive. The inferior in capacity have still a right to the means of culture and moral improvement so far as their abilities allow; while the indolent and careless are no less entitled to that education or discipline that will teach them at least not to be a burden, if they cannot be really useful to their fellows. Further, to deny that society is justly under obligation to remove or prevent some of those inequalities of fortune that exist so numerously in the financial world, is no less unreasonable than to deny any of the other claims here set forth. It is the equal capacity to enjoy, or to learn to enjoy, that gives the right in any case, and it matters not what the kind of misfortune is. Justice, equality, and the social good are all one thing; and by favoring equality in opposition to fortune society can probably benefit itself quite as effectively as in any other way.

Among ourselves every one now believes the best man ought to succeed; but now, observe, it is not the one who is best for himself, but the one who is best for society and for social ends. Nature may give wealth to the miser, who hoards it, or when he dies leaves his millions to those who have no need of them; but it is not such a one we say deserves wealth most; it is one who will use it well for himself and others. The unprincipled politician may, in the existing state of things, be most sure of obtaining office; but the one we say ought to succeed is he who will be most conscientious and faithful. To repeat, it is the one best fitted for good society,—the one who can promote the social happiness. We now live in a social environment, and the individual best adapted to that is the one we wish to be successful,. the one society, so far as it does anything, seeks to preserve and to favor. As society becomes wiser its work will be done more efficiently; till at last the criminal and parasite classes will be entirely suppressed; every one will be educated into fitness for social life; and Equality or Justice become the acknowledged law. Under such a law Natural Selection will act on the individual only to bring him, through honest and fair competition, into the place where he can be most useful.

Here, then, we have the parties to the long fought battles; one possessing a set of ideas favorable to the selfish individual, the other a set adapted to unselfish society. Take notice that it is not any existing society to which these latter ideas belong, so much as they do to a better one. And looking over the field, what is now the situation of the opponents, and how is the conflict likely to end?

The party of Individualism, the advocates of that selection by which Nature gives everything to the strongest— the one best able to take by force, fraud, or cunning—of that policy which in spite of all philosophy and religion, spite of all just and humane sentiment, has always prevailed in the past, and caused the ruin of all the old civilizations; that party, with its doctrine and policy, is still predominent in the state, the church and the school; its leaders include our great politicians and statesmen, our great preachers, our college professors, even our greatest philosopher. They tell us the present ideas and practices are to prevail forever; only that brute force and open fraud are no longer to win; these are to be discarded in the warfares and competitions of society; but concealed fraud, cunning, deception, demagoguery, adulation, servility, favoritism, inherited wealth or position,—these, it is not denied, are within certain respectable limits, to be allowed their usual operation, and along with industry, frugality, and a certain amount of honesty, are to be the means of success.

On the other hand, the Christian church with some degree of fidelity to the Founder's teachings, for several centuries protested against the taking of usury, as well as against other forms of wrong-doing;* but never I think has made any serious objection against monopoly, speculation, or profit-making in excess of payment for service. A few socialists only have ventured to oppose such things; while these too, in attempting to form societies on a new basis, have given an extra share of the common product to talent, skill and capital, as does the established order, and none of their efforts have been successful. New religious sects have gone back to take on the doctrine and sentiment of the primitive Christianity, and under the old inspiration have tried to realize something of its communistic feature in small associations. They also, like drops of milk in an ocean of water, become absorbed in the surrounding mass, and the latest of them have nearly disappeared, or are virtually as dead as those of earlier times. Socialism, in its most rad-

---

*Since this was written I learn that an important difference between ancient and modern usury was pointed out by Ferdinand Lasalle. In the ancient, and the later Roman times, money was loaned chiefly to relieve some necessity of the borrower; and interest was an extortion, by taking advantage of such necessity. In modern times money is borrowed mostly as capital, to be used in making more money, and interest on it becomes virtually the capitalists share in the profits of the industry his loaned capital has helped to carry on. The change of public opinion regarding it is largely owing to this change of use.

ical and desperate form of Nihilism or Anarchism, * is rapidly increasing its strength in Europe, where the extremes of social condition are most pronounced. That opposite form of it called Social Democracy or State Socialism is likewise gaining influence; while through the press the doctrines of both sects are being distributed over all civilized society, or more correctly perhaps, under its surface. Their ideas are creeping into much of the literature of the time, including popular novels, and even into orthodox pulpits of the church. It begins to appear as if the next social movement might be one of the whole body politic, not the isolated effort of a sect.

In this connection a word may be said to those people who seem to think the present society justified by science because Natural Selection reigns in it. Natural Selection reigns in it, where not interfered with by Social Selection, just as in the animal and vegetable kingdoms, subject to whatever fortune may be the result of acting causes. But the powerful animals, the lions, elephants and whales, and the big trees, have become exempt from the operation of the law. Occasionally there may be some competition between them, but comparatively at least, they have passed beyond all danger. So the rich, the established, and the fortunate, in the human domain have escaped the influence of Selection, and taking advantage of their good fortune, have used it to secure themselves and their children still further from any danger of rivalry. The law can operate only so far as all are subject to the same competition under the same conditions, which again is a state of equality. Neither does *Evolution* justify or excuse one portion of society more than another. The Nihilist believes in Evolution as much as does an English economist, and the Evolution process has produced both the anarchist and the millionaire, as

---

*The school of Anarchists, here classed as Socialists, are really Socialists in *purpose*, but Individualists in *method;* having an inconsistent mixture of ideas and apparently capable only of making discord and confusion.

well as all the other antagonistic social elements. Indeed the action of every man himself is a part of the social evolutionary process; and hence the question properly comes home to every individual capable of understanding it,—Shall the rude and cruel haphazard selection of nature, through unlimited selfish competition, be continued indefinitely; or shall society interfere more efficiently than ever before, and make a more perfect selection of its members and institutions for itself?

The weak points in the position of those wise teachers who tell us, with such an air of infallibility, that there is no help for generation after generation of the unfortunate yet to go down in their misery, are several.

First, is the assumption that they know all about society and social science; which, notwithstanding their much study on the one line of Economics, seems very like a grand pretension.

Next, they continually talk to us as if there were no good or ill fortune—as if every one had a fair chance to show his fitness for success—as if there were some real equality to start with. Everybody else knows this is not correct. The son of the poor man does not have an equal chance with the rich man's son, though in every moral or social quality he may be equal or superior. The child born to a higher social position, or a better education, has opportunities and aid that the less fortunate one does not. In the present industrial world there are conditions into which one may be born, and only the most superior native intelligence, energy, and perseverance will enable him to escape. Such conditions exist all over Europe, they exist in our backwoods country districts, and in the poorest localities of our large cities.

And one of the most egregious of all the false assumptions made by our wise economists is, that because most of the children born in these unfortunate localities are inferior to the average, all of them must be. Every one who has any knowledge of human nature can see that among these children are a large number who have qualities equal to the average, and that some of them are as bright, healthy and beautiful as any among the best. By natural justice these are entitled to a good education, and opportunity for a fair start in life's race. For want of it they remain as they grow up, ignorant, poor, helpless and degraded.

Again, the assumption is constantly made that trade is honest and just—not a state of modified war, robbery and grab-game selfishness at all; that competition in it is open, fair and equal for everybody. But while there is much trade that is fair and honest, any one who cares to observe will quickly discover that its inherent spirit and character is the opposite; and the more severe the competition, the more that spirit is manifest.

Still further, the assumption is that there is no aristocratic spirit for one to contend against who attempts to rise from the lower ranks. This, though a matter of less importance, is yet a reality that ought not to be entirely ignored.

Yet again, there is an indifference to general, or more correctly perhaps, to *universal* education, which does not indicate a keen sense of justice toward the child. This is more especially true of Mr. Spencer. If the child's parents do not educate it no one need care to, is about the impression I have taken from reading his books. I hope it is not correct, for I am the 'last one that would suspect Mr. Spencer of any *conscious* injustice or indifference to human welfare. As his brain has been continually filled with economic doctrines born of the selfish trade spirit, and true to their origin, it is scarcely surprising that these produce some bad effect on his character, in spite of the noblest intentions.

The assumption in this case is that the child will get an education somehow if it needs, or has an attraction for it, and be able to compete on an equality with his fellows.

Now, every old farmer knows that a spring snowstorm which would select out one feeble old sheep from his flock, is likely to kill off a dozen of healthy, promising young lambs; and he is wise enough to save the lambs. But the child or uneducated man is no better able to bear exposure to the selfishness of his fellows in the present society. Temptations that have no effect on the educated and well-informed will destroy thousands of the ignorant, childlike minds that have had no intellectual growth or equipment. They become morally corrupt, and society must suffer for the neglect of the child. I do not wish to be understood that such education as the state usually furnishes to the child would always, or even generally, save it; but such education as Mr. Spencer himself recommends to intelligent parents would go far in this direction. There is no more equal chance, however, for the uneducated to become *moral* than to become rich; and the society that neglects them does not do justice to all its people.

Yet once more, there is an assumption most of these teachers make which is as false as hell. It is that the man who desires to work can always find employment. In reality he may be compelled to lie idle half his time, and all he earns be barely enough to keep him alive, without decent clothing or shelter. He may have no means of acquiring information, no chance for accumulating capital to compete with others in business. There is no equal start in life's race to the workingman, and the society that does not secure it to him is not just.

In regard to all these matters and many others besides,

society, aiming at justice, will see that it has yet much to do. It is manifest there can be no complete and final end of the conflict till we reach the stage of the Unselfish Development. But a great deal can be done to hasten the approach of that condition. What we need first is a general conviction of the social sinfulness; and following on that a moral regeneration more deep, thorough, and universal than any that has ever reacted against irreligion, slavery, or political despotism,—one that will fire men's hearts with a love of justice no self-love can suppress, no money buy, no friendship turn aside, no flattery cajole, no terror scare, from doing its righteous work. With this there will be combined efforts that shall render it effective.

The measures taken, whatever they may be, must be such as will put the whole power of society on the side of Equality against Inequality,—against all those conditions, laws, customs and practices that are unequal, and in favor of whatever tends, in any just manner or degree, toward equality of condition. Society must not only select its fit members, and adapt them by education; it must also do something toward making the environment equally favorable to all. It must attempt the elimination of chance or fortune, so that Natural Selection may have its fair and proper operation. Monopoly of every kind must become a crime, as it really is—a gigantic crime, the greatest of all causes of social misery. Monopoly in ordinary trade must have no more toleration than any other; for it is the most common and far-reaching of all. Inherited wealth must not give one person an advantage over another equally worthy. And herein is the necessity for a more thorough education of that kind which will confer upon the individual a knowledge of the world he lives in, including the human part of it, in place of ancient and middle-age notions, theological or classical.

The criminal and pauper classes are to be educated and reformed so far as this is possible; those with whom it is not possible should be utterly suppressed by confinement for life, and exclusion from all opportunity of perpetuating their breed. When society becomes just to them there will be few found incapable of improvement. The same exclusion method of eliminating idiots, lunatics, and the monstrosities of inherited disease will be resorted to when sufficient intelligence has become spread among the people, through the propagation of scientific knowledge. And the means to accomplish a part of this work of education and reformation may, even under existing conditions, be found by withdrawing from the monster fortunes of millionaires, through graduated taxation, a small part of that wealth which was once the common inheritance, and has come into the hands of its possessors through good luck, favoritism, or dereliction of duty on the part of those who should have been its faithful guardians.* The millionaire himself, like the criminal and the pauper, is to become extinct.

But let us bring the conflict of ideas down to its latest phase; and by observing its most advanced points we can perhaps see better what its further stages are likely to be, and how it will terminate finally.

While the doctrines favoring the selfish spirit of individualism have attained their most complete development in England, those ideas and measures (outside of Socialism) which contemplate the restriction of competitive selfishness for the benefit of the social mass have found their strongest presentation, and greatest influence, in

---

*Some years ago I published a pamphlet advocating graduated taxation on all property, as a remedy for most of our industrial evils, by its being made severe enough to prevent great accumulations. It was afterward abandoned as being impossible to enforce, except to a moderate extent as above intimated. Even if practicable it would be but partially just, a half-way measure, like several others, and prompted by a needless fear that Social Democracy involved too much interference with personal liberty.

America.* Common Schools for universal Education, Protection to Home Industry, Homestead Exemption from process for Debt, Free Public Lands to Actual Settlers, National Paper Currency, Anti-Monopoly laws regulating Transportation—these are some of the most prominent of the latter class.† Whatever faultiness there may be about any or all of them, they are indications of the effort society is making to check the onward rush of unregarding selfishness, now threatening to overcome all opposition. They are all interferences with natural selection and *laissez faire*. All of them, however inconsistent in some respects, aim at making man superior to money, and his welfare of more importance than the interests of capital. They are the external ebullitions of that force within society which is constantly asserting the superiority of the mass to the individual; constantly struggling for the benefit of the many rather than the few; which has developed one part of the race into some sort of democratic government; and which, if not defeated, will ultimately realize the greater accomplishment of Democracy in Industry,—a condition in which all men and women will do honest work; in which all will have an equal voice in the management of the natural re-

---

*Of all American writers on economic subjects Mr. Henry C. Carey seems to have perceived most clearly the tendency of the "free competition" doctrine, and to have opposed it with most of the unselfish spirit. Though not sufficiently advanced to acknowledge the universal title to land, he commended its free division, and holding in small areas, as most favorable to the industrious poor. And whatever new developments have arisen in economic science since he wrote, the issue is still the same as he saw it—unrestricted freedom for the strong, fortunate or unscrupulous individual or nation; or on the other hand, use of the social power for protection of the commercially oppressed, and advancement of the general good.

† It will be questioned how Protection is a socialistic measure, especially after all the befogging of the subject during late presidential campaigns. The real point is that duties laid simply for defensive protection, of a weaker industry against a stronger, cause a wider distribution of industrial establishments, of the profits of the industry, and also of the benefits of employment, than there would be without such protection. Monopolistic concerns grow up under it, but there are more of them and smaller ones, and less inequality of wealth in the community, than would exist with national competition entirely free.

The system carried out by England a century ago was not protection in the proper sense, though often called so; but a grasping and monopolistic aggressive policy, by which she built up her great industries at the expense of all Europe and the American colonies, when she had no need of protection, or little if any, her own industrial development being, as a whole, not inferior to that of other countries.

sources belonging in common to the race, including production to supply the wants of population; and in which all will share in the product of their labor in proportion to what they contribute. Profit-Sharing, Coöperative Stores and Building Associations, and the scattered attempts at Coöperative Production, though themselves transitional and temporary efforts, are already the feeble signs of what is yet to come in full measure if the unselfish impulse shall be finally successful in the long battle of the ages.*

Democracy itself, without such an ulterior result, will be a failure. Indeed, it is scarcely untrue to call it such at present. What we possess of it in the government of this country may have been of some service to the masses in a moral sense by giving suffrage to the humble, and thus increasing their self-respect; but within the nation it has made commercial enterprise so free, and given it such facilities to work out its natural results, that Monopoly, Industrial Feudalism, and Plutocracy in politics, have arrived nearly as soon, probably, as they could have done in any case. These are now its foes, shouting its name perhaps, but acting in opposition to all its spirit and purpose; and it must crush them and go forward, till it becomes true Industrial Democracy as well as Political, or else wither into an abortive thing, its substance gone, and nothing but an empty shell remaining. Only as a transitional institution, a step by which to obtain the means of inaugurating a more perfect state of equality, can it be and remain a success. If it fails to do its further work, the doom of the old republics is likely to be repeated by the new.

The prevailing system of thought is well represented

---

* The first great American Socialistic measure was the establishment of common schools; and besides those mentioned above as having some tendency of the same kind, and that immense interference with the rights of individual property by which four millions of slaves were set free, it is frequently noted that the Post Office has always been, in this country, a socialistic institution. The Post Office is really more than that,—it is communistic, making the rich and populous communities pay for the accommodation of the poorer ones.

at this time by Herbert Spencer. His late writings, upon the misuse of governmental function by unwise legislation, show that he still retains the ideas of thirty years ago, and that no farther advance is to be expected of him. His exhibition of legislative failures proves plainly the lack of social science among legislators, and adds to the long history of blunders made by ignorant goodness; but in reality proves nothing against social effort wisely guided by social science. In regard to this matter a new thinker, Lester F. Ward, on our own side of the Atlantic, has taken steps in advance of Mr. Spencer or any one of the same economic school. In a work upon "Dynamic Sociology" he shows how society has been successively adding to the functions of government, as the social intellect and conscience have become developed, till it has acquired all those it now performs. He further points out a very important enlargement of the function of Education, which it must yet perform before any very great improvement in society can be effected. His thought is worthy the attention of all persons capable of taking interest in social science.*

Mr. Spencer and Mr. Ward, among accepted thinkers, may be taken as the best present representatives of the two conflicting tendencies in society,—Mr. Spencer of the *laissez faire* or let-alone policy, which would leave everything but the punishment of crime and the enforcement of contracts to the blind, selfish regime of Natural Selection; Mr. Ward of that by which society is to establish justice, encourage equality, eliminate the element of fortune, and favor human development, as the proper social work, under control of the qualified scientific intellect. Mr. Ward, however, is not yet consciously aware that the fostering of equality, and the elimination of fortune, are natural parts of the program he has

---
*Mr. Ward's book, and Mr. Spencer's "Man and The State," just referred to, are both published by D. Appleton & Co., N. Y.

adopted; and so far as I know he has made no statement concerning those two points.*

The same two tendencies appear not only in men of moderate views like Spencer and Ward, but likewise among the most radical of Socialist advocates. The two principal parties of these, both having a common motive of opposition to the present order, are yet dominated in their *thinking* by the same contrary impulsions; one, the Anarchist, or Individualist party demanding the most absolute freedom of the individual from all restraint outside himself, as the only social salvation; the other, the Social Democracy or Collectivist, advocating the extension of a common or public regulative superintendence to all industrial operations, for the sake of justice to all.

The different meanings given to the word *justice* by different persons is a curious illustration of the spirit that exists underneath all the ideas and acts of the antagonistic parties. To one it means security in the right of complete liberty to do whatever he will,—to make the most of his talents, opportunities and good fortune, regardless of any other; provided he does not infringe upon the equal right of any other to act in the same way. In short, it is justice to himself,—to himself certainly, and apparently to all others as well. He sees the logical perfection of the doctrine as it is put into words; but the spirit animating him prevents his seeing that in society, where every one is connected in a thousand ways with every one else, the words represent no actuality; that no such absolute liberty can be exercised without doing it at some one's loss, pain, or disadvantage, especially in gathering up fortunes; and that it will be possible only in an ideally perfect social condition where every one

---

*By thus distinguishing these two men I would do no injustice to Mr. Spencer, and am far from intending any disparagement of the great work he has already accomplished.

shall be unselfish enough to desire no more than an equal share of anything.

To the other kind of man justice means equal freedom, equal education, equal opportunities, equal results, equal happiness for all. And this justice for others has a greater claim upon him than his own liberty regarding the little details of industrial life in society. One idea is the justice of him whose thought is dominated by a selfish instinct, even though his better nature doubts, denies, or scorns the indictment; the other conception is the justice of the unselfish character, capable, to some extent at least, of forgetting personality in a desire for the welfare of all.

To go back from this partial digression, the Anarchist or Individualist would abolish government, and with it, as he believes, the monopoly in land, by withdrawing from it the support of law. He would carry his doctrine to its logical outcome, and leave competition absolutely unchecked. What else he would do is uncertain; but if his method of destruction should destroy any of the forms of monopoly, his plan of negation gives no security that it would not grow up again, nor that most of our present miseries of unfair competition would not be either continued or again revived, under the same let-alone policy that now allows them to exist. In short, the Individualist, though he may desire to be a socialist, desires still more an unsocial kind of freedom.

On the other hand, Social Democracy proposes to abolish the whole competitive system, by employing the functions of a democratic industrial supervision. It would establish democracy in industry, and by securing employment, as the only means of acquiring property, to all alike, it would secure a greater practical freedom to the workingman than he, or indeed any one but the rich, has ever possessed. By far the most promising of all schemes, it will doubtless have imperfections in its details when they come to be wrought out, and if these infringe upon any innocent liberty they will be modified; for there will be no need of interference with any liberty except that of the criminal and that of the monopolist; the communistic feature being only the common ownership of the natural resources, and the new governmental feature extending only to the regulation of industry. It may be taken for certain that when all the temporary plans and methods referred to have come to their failure, this, in all its substantial parts, will finally be adopted; for the human sense of justice will never be satisfied till some approach toward equality in the benefits of industry shall be realized by the whole people.

That all these other schemes are temporary and transitional is sufficiently evident from the fact that the advocates of none of them discover their true antagonist in unregulated competition itself; that they seem not aware that competition necessarily ends in monopolies and combinations; and that hence none of them proposes to strike at that earliest, most universal, and most injurious of all monopolies, the monopoly of trade, nor at the competitive method, which is the tap root of the whole tree of industrial evil. Coöperation endeavors to fight ordinary competition by another form of competition, *while the existing wealth with all its power is in the hands of its opponents.* Its schemes are for the benefit of the few only who are engaged in them, who, like the rest, are hostile to all competitors, and cannot be otherwise till coöperation becomes *universal,* which would be the Industrial Democracy above outlined. Profit-sharing gives the workingman a small bonus to render him more faithful in his employer's competition against all the rest. Neither of these injures any form of monopoly; and operatives and managers in both are animated by the old selfish desire to get all they can for themselves, regardless of what their competitors lose by their success. Mr. George's plan of taxation, aimed at land-monopoly, attempts to cut off one head of a four-headed monster, devouring the people, leaving three other heads, the mercantile, manufacturing, and transporting monopolies, to devour as fast as they may. Mr. Clark's scheme* to tax all the natural increase of wealth into the hands of the State for the benefit of the next generation, spends most of it in paying the governmental expenses of the existing population, and the rest in public improvements; allowing the new generation to come on the field with no more opportunity to employ themselves on the land, in trade, or in mechanical work than they would have at the present time. None of these plans would prohibit the accumulation of great fortunes; none of them could prevent great wealth from conferring honor and distinction; none, therefore could extinguish the ambition to be rich; nor could any or all of them abolish more than a small part of the poverty, misery and crime that go with inequality. And thus the Individualist social physicians may, (with no desire to offend) be compared to quack doctors, practicing on the symptoms of a patient, unaware that he has a poison virus in his blood, accumulating corruption and breaking out in one disease after another, which they endeavor in various ways to cure or prevent, yet leave the original active cause of all of them to operate unchecked.

The correct understanding of the two great tendencies in the political world is hindered by their complication with two great tendencies in the intellectual world,— one, the active and progressive impulse, the other the inert, stationary, or reactive inclination. The complication is increased by the fact that each one of the four, according to a law by which opposite things overlap

---

*Explained in a small work called "Man's Birthright or The Higher Law of Property," published by G. P. Putnams Sons, New York.

or intermix, possesses, along with its own peculiar character, somewhat of the character of its opposite. Still further, either one of the two last named may be associated with either one of the two former, at different times. Hitherto all advance has been accomplished through the action and reaction, mainly antagonistic, of one phase of movement against its opponent. In the future, it is to be hoped that they will become mainly harmonious and coöperative. The Individualist and Collectivist movements, being each still mostly selfish in its *personnel*, when one becomes victorious it may ignore the general welfare for the sake of some freedom to the individual; or the other may over-ride some just liberty of the individual, in its regard for its own object. Either one of them when long established in power may become inert, or stationary, and hostile to the progress demanded by justice. The progressive disposition then sides with the one that has the greater justice and enlightenment in its purposes; for though the progressive element has its share of both selfishness and weakness, its ultimate object, whether a conscious one or not, is both justice and enlightenment, and the moralization of itself as well as of its opponents. In matters of a political nature it is the true *social* sentiment *par excellence;* and though in a preponderant sense it is constructive, and may primarily be disposed to stand by the existing organization of a state or a church, it is not so necessarily and in all cases. For, the political or religious body may itself come to be only the instrument of a selfish individual tyrant, or an equally selfish oligarchy or aristocracy; and then the progressive feeling must sympathize with the oppressed majority, or with the individual deprived of a just liberty; because its own *ideal* is not a national or an ecclesiastical polity of any special sort, but *human* SOLIDARITY,—in other words, that justice or morality which secures the rights, welfare, harmony and unity of *all*, the individual included with the mass. What other social or political aim could possibly be progressive?

At the present time the abuses of liberty are becoming so enormous and so unprincipled that the progressive impulse will be on the side of Collectivism.* As an example of how a movement may change its original predominant character, it may be observed that Christianity, at its beginning the most progressive of all movements of its time, has, in its two main branches, long been the most obstructive and reactionary; the Protestant sects alone manifesting any tendency to advance. The sympathy of the Romanist body with the conservative political party in America is well known.† As Conservatism has but one principle, Inertia—to stand still or fall back—it is easy for its different forms to sympathize and act together. On the contrary, the progressive sentiment breaks up into a multitude of sects and parties, often hostile between themselves, and spending more of their power in strife with one another

---

* Liberty to trade and accumulate has been carried so far that the practical freedom to live, without beggary, is taken away from a large minority, if not a majority of the people. Every one who cannot say that, accident excepted, he is reasonably sure of always obtaining a livelihood for himself and family, is one of those who have lost the freedom to live.

† It is well exhibited in the results of the last election (1888) in the Democratic city of New York, as given in one of the daily papers.
"The Roman Catholics have taken the city.
Their hand was in the sale of the Coogan party to Hugh J. Grant.
They already have every member of the Board of Tax Commissioners.
They have for years had and still have the control of the Board of Aldermen.
They have the Mayor, the Sheriff, the Comptroller, the Counsel to the Corporation, the whole Board of Tax Assessors, the majority of the Police Justices and of the Civil Justices, the Recorder, the Commissioner of Public Works, the Superintendent of the Street Cleaning Department, the Clerk to the Board of Aldermen, the Superintendent of the Bureau of Elections, several of the Justices of the Supreme, Superior and Common Pleas Courts; the control of the Board of Estimate and Apportionment, the majority in many of the ward boards of School Trustees, a large portion of the Board of Education, the control of the Department of Charities and Correction, the majority in the police force, the control of the Fire Department, of the Board of Street Openings, the whole of the Armory Board, the Register of Deeds, the Commissioner of Jurors, one-half of the Commissioners of Accounts, Supervisor of the *City Record*, the Collector of the Port, the Sub-Treasury, majority of the Commissioners of the Sinking Fund, the majority of the delegation in Congress and in the State Senate and Assembly.
The Church of Rome is nothing if not political. It is the dominant party in this city. The majority of voters in this city belong to that party. The head and leader of this party is Archbishop Corrigan." *Mail and Express,* Nov. 7, '88.

than they use against their common antagonist. This too, it may be noted, is another of the ways in which Humanity defeats its best purposes, for want of that higher intelligence, and that truer social sentiment which would be capable of doing justice to all.

CHAPTER XI.

NATURAL AND SOCIAL SELECTION.

Continued.

THAT some system resembling that of the Social Democrat will take the place of the present order, notwithstanding the various efforts to patch and plaster up its weakest parts by a partial coöperation, and thus keep it in existence, is made sure by the self-evident character of the ideas on which the coming system will be based. These I will attempt to state systematically though it will involve some repetition of previous statements.

1. That the whole surface of the earth, with everything contained in land and water, is by natural and moral right the possession of its whole population equally, for sustenance and use, is a proposition that no one willing to think honestly can long continue to doubt. Land is the only *basis* of all food-production vegetable or animal, the *instrument* which, however infertile, can be so treated and used that food can be produced from it. The *capability* of the soil to produce food, and the *capability* of the poorest soil to be so *improved* that it *will* produce, is what renders it equally indispensable to life with the air that is breathed, the sunlight which as the source of heat is a necessity to all vegetable and animal growth,

and the water by which the internal operations of all animal and vegetable organisms are carried on. Either of them taken away, all life is destroyed. No authority, of any kind, can rightfully take away or limit this natural right of the whole population to either one of these four indispensable means of living, or give to any individual a title to any portion of either one different from that universal title inherent by natural justice in every person alike. Water, the more direct source of fish-food production—lakes, rivers and seas—is equally with land the common possession by the same natural right, which no power can justly alienate. Whatever mineral or organic substances, existing on or in the land or water, can be made useful to man—metals, stone, timber, coal, salt, petroleum, gas, clay, sand, fertilizers, gums, spices, medicines, wild fruits, fish and game (so far as man can rightfully take animal life) pearls, diamonds, gems—are all parts of those natural resources given by God or Nature to the whole race to be its common inheritance, that fortune, so to speak, with which it was endowed when the first man and woman came into existence. They, like the soil and the waters, are the perpetual property of the race. The use of land or water for highways of transportation, or of the latter for water-power force, is likewise a part of the same universal possession.

2. Every succeeding *generation* has an equal right to all the natural resources of the earth. To suppose that one could have such a right and another not would be totally absurd. It follows that there can be no absolute right of inheritance other than this by which one generation inherits the use of everything the last one possessed. When those materials which constitute the natural resources of the race are converted by labor into things of use and beauty, it is only the *use* of those things to which any person by his labor can acquire a

right. The wood, stone or metal—the organic or inorganic *material* of which they are composed—belongs alike to each generation, and no moral title to it can be acquired in any way by an individual. The *use* of articles is all that can justly be bequeathed from one person to another. And whatever material is not so abundant that all who desire can have a portion cannot be appropriated, even in its use during life, except by the common consent, obtained by paying a bonus for the common good if demanded. There can be no justifiable monopoly, even in use. No one can have any moral right or permission to *waste anything*. The fertility of the soil naturally increases with time, and our successors can claim that land, at least, ought to be in as good condition as it was received by us. The reckless waste that has been going on for ages, and is still, is utterly thoughtless and unprincipled. No one can righteously throw away a stick of wood or a bone—any vegetable or animal matter—where it will not fertilize the cultivable soil when it returns to dust; nor a tin can or piece of old iron where the metal cannot be recovered at some time in the future if needed. Every ounce of it belongs to the future men and women as much as to us; and only the use of it belongs to anybody. The material of every kind, that exists on the earth or in it, including all the natural resources above named, is the continual birthright of the generations forever.

3. The *human population* of the earth, as much the production of nature as its animal or vegetable productions, is also, by its multitudinous wants and the employment they furnish, a source of existence to three-fourths, if not nine-tenths, of the people living in civilized society,—to all in short, except the few who could live by the barbarian method of hunting and fishing, or in other words, without ever working for one another. Every person born and coming to maturity, in such society, has an

equal natural and moral right with all others then living, to a share in this universal employment by which so large a proportion of its members enable each other to live. Nobody has a right, nobody can give any one a right, to more than his or her equal share of this employment, created and furnished by civilized society, or of the rewards of it, by a monopoly of agriculture, trade, manufacture, or transportation. All the profits of the merchant, manufacturer, or transporter, beyond a certain amount sufficient to pay him good wages for his service, represents so much labor or employment blindly given to him (for want of knowing any better way to do) by those who exchange their labor or its products for what they obtain of him; the continued opportunity of receiving this constituting his monopoly. The monopolist of trade can no more acquire a moral title to his profits than the monopolist of land can to his. Each of them acquires his gains in the same way, that is by obtaining and holding opportunities of doing something for the common service, which opportunities belong to every other man as truly and as much as they do to him. In one case they are opportunities to use the soil, in the other opportunities to distribute goods to consumers; and in both cases the monopolists give back those opportunities to those who assist them for wages, but keep for themselves a part of the natural reward belonging to those opportunities. The same is true of the manufacturer and transporter.*

4. As a corollary of all this, every adult man and woman is morally entitled to an *opportunity* to invest his or her labor in agricultural, mechanical, mercantile, or transporting service for the common good, in such manner, and on such conditions, as will be most satisfactory to all concerned, and to receive the full natural reward

---
* Population, with its wants, as a resource furnished by Nature, is a necessary foundation doctrine of Collectivist Socialism. Socialism is like an animal crawling on one leg, instead of running on four, till it finds this out.

for such labor. This right is equivalent to the right to live at all, except by beggary, and can be nullified only by the most outrageous injustice. To rent the common land to the highest bidder, and use the proceeds for the public good, as Mr. Spencer once proposed, or for the same purpose to sell *licences* to manufacture, trade or transport, would not secure this right to all; for a state of things may be supposed to exist, especially a transition state from the present, in which only the wealthy could compete in bidding, and the poor would have no equal chance. There is no safety for all except in a guaranteed right of employment according to fitness.

5. As the general satisfaction must be secured, the *reward* for different kinds of labor must be so graded that all occupations will be voluntarily performed; and this requires that those most disagreeable shall have the largest pay, other things equal, and those most pleasant the least.

6. *Woman* being equally capable of enjoyment with man, and thereby equally entitled to all the means of enjoying life, is justly entitled to the *same pay or reward* for her appropriate work that man receives for his; and to an equal independence in the control, management and use of whatever property she may be able to acquire.

7. As every one can justly claim an equal share if he or she desires it, so no one can claim any more than an equal share, in that *total amount of employment* found necessary to satisfy the wants of society, whether it require ten hours labor a day or five.

8. The right of every one to have the undisturbed *possession*, use and enjoyment of whatever he or she gains by honest labor under conditions equal to all, and to the enjoyment of every *liberty* that is not necessarily injurious or annoying to another, is no less sacred than the right to labor and to live.

9. The equal right of all to the common and universal opportunity to labor, to live, and to enjoy, and the necessity imposed on all alike to obtain a subsistence only by labor, involves the right of all children equally to an *education*, such as will prepare them to fulfil the ordinary duties of life, enable them to select their proper occupations, and acquire the additional training necessary to fit them for special performance. This includes at least the ability to read, write, and speak the common language correctly, to keep accounts, to respect the ordinary requirements of good breeding, and in one sex to handle the commonly used tools of mechanical work and agriculture, in the other to do the elementary work in its own appropriate labors. Aside from all other considerations, it is the right of the child when grown to obtain an equal chance with those already in the field; and it is the duty of society, whose vocation is to secure justice, to see that every one has this necessary amount of education.

10. As every man and woman is equally interested in the good *management* of the natural resources belonging to all, and as monopolies of the various kinds, great and small, cannot with justice be allowed to carry on industrial operations after the present method, it follows that those operations can be properly carried on only by such leaders—superintendents, bosses, foremen, etc.—as a majority of the men and women who are to work under their direction may elect as the best qualified to supervise and direct.

11. As all monopolies are totally indefensible; as all large properties have arisen by some one's obtaining more than an honest share; as the present method of holding real estate has no just ground; and as no one can have a moral right to manage a part of the universal estate in a manner contrary to the general well-being and consent; therefore society has a just right to *retake*

possession of land, mines, factories, stores, railroads, etc., whenever a majority of the people may be convinced that such a measure is necessary or desirable, and on securing to the holders a certain limited amount of property, not easy to define, which each may be supposed to have honestly earned during life, or to have honestly inherited when it is not the product of monopoly.*

12. The right to share in the *political* administration of the country through suffrage is one belonging to all, irrespective of race, sex, nationality, wealth or culture; for the simple and sufficient reason that all are affected by it. Neither one of the things here named can rightfully be used to confer suffrage or to prevent its exercise, nor yet the length of time an adopted citizen has lived in the country; and even the age required of minors might be lowered a few years. But the right to perform *any* public function is limited by the ability to do it well; and the principle underlying Civil Service Reform is a proper one for suffrage as well as for all offices. The industrial chiefs referred to (par. 10) may properly be elected by a vote of all who are to be under their direction, and who are supposed to know what one among themselves is best qualified to supervise each special work they are performing. So may all officials of township, city, and county administration; whose character and fitness as individuals is the only matter to be decided. But when the highest offices of the nation are to be filled, and its legislators chosen, when *political principles* and important *national measures* are to be accepted or rejected, then the state should require of the voter some knowledge of the governmental organization, some acquaintance with its

---

*It is to be hoped that confiscation may never have to be enforced by physical power; and there is some reason to believe that it never will. The greater probability is that many holders of great properties will give them up voluntarily from conscience; and that others, when they find a strong balance of the best sentiment against them, will, like the French nobles in the time of the Revolution, make a virtue of necessity, and give up their old claims with the rest. When all do so together it will not be so very hard a thing to do.

political history, and sufficient understanding of the principles and other issues involved in political contests, to be able to vote intelligently in regard to them. Nothing less than this demand is justice to its most intelligent and capable class, whose votes, under a system allowing every one a vote on every subject and every office, are completely nullified by the votes of the incompetent, and who consequently lose their natural interest in political affairs, leaving them to be managed by those less capable and less conscientious than the average voting population. Any one who has not sufficient desire for this higher suffrage to go before a justice of the peace or some other judicial authority, and qualify himself by exhibiting a sufficient intellectual and moral capability, at least three months before any national or state election, should never be allowed to exercise it ; while under such a test the immigrant just arrived, the eighteen-year-old boy or girl, the individual of any race or either sex, who declares a sincere loyalty to the country and the government, may be made an elector. With the universal education above required and supposed, the poorest as well as the richest may obtain this vote, and those only are excluded from it who are so obviously unfit that they refuse to make the mental exertion necessary to an intelligent choice.*

Some of these basic ideas may prove too radical to be fully adopted by any sect of socialists at the present time. But when the competitive system shall have developed all its evils, and the struggle between that and

---

* If any one will take the trouble to observe the conversation of the mass of voters in this country at the present time, he will discover that one-half of them —more or less—do not know what political principle means, and are totally incapable of deciding what one is right or wrong, or of comprehending the effects of a great national measure. To give these persons the kind of suffrage last referred to, while they remain in such mental condition, seems the very extreme of political foolishness.

It will do no harm to add, though it should not be necessary, that, if there were sufficient opportunity for education in the Southern states, the application of the above principle to suffrage would solve the race question there, so far as it can be solved at all, by a method entirely just to both races.

The whole control of both suffrage and education may have to be given to the national government, even before any general socialistic movement has arisen.

this shall be well begun, whatever the conscious purpose of the contestants, the momentum of the victorious party will be likely to carry it to a completely radical outcome before the contest is finally ended. No consistent scheme of socialism can stop short of guaranteeing to the people all the human rights enumerated in the twelve propositions above. They are all really indispensables, without which any less thorough system will not be sure of complete success or of lasting continuance.

No one familiar with the truth of these ideas can doubt that such a contest in the intellectual world is coming on, nor any more can he doubt that the victory will be with the party they represent.

The elements that are to form this victorious party are yet in a very chaotic and discordant state. Socialistic parties are like half-awakened soldiers in the night, misled by false cries, and striking at each other in the dark, not knowing the signs by which to distinguish friend from foe. The leaders cry Land, Liberty, Cooperation, Anarchy, Communism, Taxation, and Combined Trades-Unionism. Labor often relies for guidance on men whose brains are saturated with English Economy, the very doctrine that is used to justify all the wrongs of the workingman, and keep him a helpless slave forever, the prey of unscrupulous competition. Social Democracy as yet scarcely appeals to any except that part of the laboring class organized into trade unions. It must necessarily begin by addressing itself to workingmen, as the greatest sufferers, and the most vitally interested in any hopeful change; but in addition, it should make its appeal to the whole people, the capitalist included, and show that all can find a greater happiness in social renovation. The socialist still has too little faith in human nature, and takes the capitalist to be an unchangeable enemy. The capitalist looks upon the socialist in the same light, neither one considering that both (that is, the persons, whatever their estate) must yet be brothers, if there is ever to be any harmonious society. The socialist leaders have thus far come from the ranks of the intelligent class, if not the wealthy, as by natural process they should if society is to take selection wholly into its own hands when sufficiently wise. A considerable part of those who labor for wages have neither sufficient intelligence to guide, nor conscience to control them; and their only power is a power to blindly destroy. Such as these can never be reformers, even of their own wrongs. And though the capitalist class will not be socialists, as a class, neither the clergy nor the professors, yet a considerable proportion of all three may become such when all persons alike shall be addressed in the right spirit, in behalf of a project designed to do justice to all.* The final question is to be, not one of *class interest*, but one directed to the MORAL SENSE; and each person will decide

---

*At the dinner of the New York Free Soil Club last Tuesday evening, Courtlandt Palmer, a millionaire land-owner and rent taker, said that in England the Socialistic Party was making great strides, because of the impoverishment of the workers. He continued:

"The same social conditions hold good in all other countries. The rich are getting richer and fewer, and the poor, poorer and more numerous. How are we to remedy this state of affairs? Through rent, interest and profit the few are gradually concentrating all wealth in their own hands. We should nationalize all monopolies. As a landlord I can't sign the declaration of principles of this club. I am a monopolist, and getting nearly all my income from rents—do not earn the money I get. The reform must be made general and must include as well as landlord monopolists like myself, railroad monopolists like Mr. Vanderbilt, and profit monopolists like Arnold, Constable & Co. When this is done I will cheerfully sign the declaration of principles." *Workmen's Advocate* June, 4, '87

See also the following from the *Christian Union* as an indication of similar feeling among the clergy.

"Whatever force or justice there may be in the proposition to increase the taxes upon land and take it off of other things—and we are inclined to think there is a measure of force and justice in this proposition—we do not believe that any readjustment of taxation whatever will solve the relations between labor and capital. Nor do we for a moment suppose that they can be solved by mere individual benefactions, whether by charity doled out to the poor, however generously, or by increase in wages, however equitable, or even by participation of profits in individual concerns here and there. * * * The employers and the employed must become partners in a common enterprise. The term 'boss' must drop from the workshop as the term king has dropped from the State. The tools and implements of industry must become property of the many, not of the few; and the proceeds of industry must come to be equitably shared. This involves nothing less than a radical revolution; but we believe that it will be wrought peacefully, not by bloodshed. * * * When all capitalists are workingmen and all workingmen are capitalists, there will no longer be a problem of relationship between capitalist and laborer to be solved. And we have gone further in America toward this consummation in this nineteenth century, though it lies still in the future, than any other country has gone in this or any other epoch."

it by his or her willingness or unwillingness to be content with a just share of the world's wealth; a share which will be comparatively equal. When this question comes fairly home it will divide socialist parties and all labor organizations, as well as the church, the politicians, the farmers, and the whole community.

How long a time will be required to bring this change no one can estimate very closely, but eyes willing to look can see that change of some kind is actually coming. There seems to be an opposition to the established order, made up from all kinds of socialistic reformers, and the various opponents of existing abuses, discordant but capable of better combination, which is arising and accumulating power throughout Europe and America—a social thunder-cloud that may grow into immense proportions, and is likely to make occasion for a vast deal of trouble if it should at last burst over the civilized world. Twice already in modern times a similar storm in the social elements has occurred; once when the War of the Peasants convulsed all Germany, and again when revolution culminated in a Reign of Terror in France. Let us hope that when the third one comes a reign of terror will not come with it; that the humanizing influences of the last hundred years have moderated the furious spirit which on those occasions drenched the earth with blood. Yet the reckless resort to dynamite already manifested, and the equally reckless and inhuman manner of suppressing the disorders of striking mobs, is not at all assuring.

That storm, should it come, will probably bring the life or death struggle of all modern civilization. It will be, in a preponderant or majority sense, one of the weak against the strong, of the poor against the rich, of the ignorant against the cultured, of the degraded and despised against the lordly and respectable; and in it the greater justice will be not with, but against, the powers that now control society. All former societies have lacked sufficient vitality to resist and destroy the immoral or unjust influences that generate commotion. Now it is to be seen if ours has become enough stronger in moral quality to go through its crisis and live.

When a thunder-cloud arises in the physical sky we relieve it of its dangerous element by gently drawing it into the earth through the lightning-rod. But justice is the only conductor that will relieve the social cloud of its lightning, and only in extraordinary measure and power will this be sufficient. If the more intelligent of the great middle class of our country, neither poor nor rich, neither cultured nor ignorant, but possessing a full average share of common sense and moral quality,—if they shall take the course that has here been indicated (first twelve paragraphs) in time, they may save this part of the world from horrors that are almost sure to fall upon Europe, and may accomplish a relatively peaceful transition from the old industrial order to the new.

In this view the little conflicts between Capital and Labor are but the picket skirmishes preceding a far greater and irrepressible conflict between similar combatants. The commercial world is rushing with its whole force toward that extreme which will bring the Social Revolution as its reactionary effect.

The skirmishing of Capital and Labor will continue, and schemes of emigration, coöperation, and profit-sharing will have some effect in delaying the ultimate contest. It may not come immediately, for the masses are slow to awaken, and years are required to get an important idea established in the ordinary brain. The logic of events however, will bring people to their senses when all other methods fail. Occasional dynamite horrors may be expected, and military murders in time of strikes; suicides and desperate crimes will be no less frequent; thefts, robberies, and frauds of every sort will be as many and as mean as they are at present. To the general mind there may be as many signs of fear as of hope; but those who have some faith in human generosity, and some further in human rationality, may indulge a quiet belief that the conflict will end in much better things instead of worse.

What the immoral condition is has always been known to the unfortunate classes, and to the Socialist thinker; but how great inequality of wealth is unjust in all cases has never before, perhaps, been clearly shown. The monopoly in ordinary mercantile operations, by which fortunes far beyond the average share are secured by some individuals, and others thereby deprived of their natural opportunities and portions, has not before been exhibited as a true monopoly. Hereafter the rich and fortunate will be able to understand the wrong. The conscientious rich man to whom these ideas may come will easily learn what is his duty. His wealth has cost far less in toil and suffering than it previously cost others to produce it, or else it is a plunder from the common storehouse of natural resources, belonging to all alike, both of present and future, and in either case is a wealth not his own beyond a certain moderate amount. All the rest of it belongs to the world; and whatever the law of present society may allow him to do with it, morally and in justice, he is bound to use it only for the good of humanity. Inheritance can give no just title to it, neither can chance opportunity; for chances, good or bad, are given by Nature, and should be shared as far as possible. Neither can the ignorance or the necessities of those who were willing to exchange for his profit. Nothing but equal labor, privation or suffering, for the labor privation or suffering of others is absolute justice, —the standard toward which we ought to strive. To repudiate this ideal, and spend for selfish indulgence, ostentation, or favoritism, will violate the conscience, degrade the soul, and forever torment the memory, as surely as the damp air of the marsh will rust the polished steel.

To the poor, the ignorant, the unfortunate I must say that with all life, vegetable, animal, and human alike, Nature's ways are the only ways possible until she has produced men sufficiently intelligent to discover her ultimate purpose, and take the work of selection out of her hands. Your misfortunes are a part of what has hitherto been the inevitable. They are the outcome of a selfishness common alike to every class of men. They result from commercial teachings as old as trade itself, and of practices the poor stand ready to adopt as quickly as the rich when the opportunities occur. Profit-making to the greatest extent possible is the aim of nearly all. Those who have succeeded and become wealthy are, with few exceptions, no more conscious of wrong-doing than those who have failed. All together have unknowingly been guilty in purpose if not in deed. Thus, with so little cause for mutual reproach or bitterness of feeling, there is little justification for violence or counter-injustice. No movement to right the wrong except an unselfish one—one both just and considerate—can finally prosper; and such a one will bring good to all classes and conditions of men.

But enlightenment of the intellect must precede all action toward improvement. All the long ages since society began are the time Nature has taken to develop a society with intellect and moral purpose to take selection in human affairs away from herself, and complete the social organization by placing a true basis under all its most important functions. That fact, instead of being an excuse for delay, is a reason for all practicable haste; but such a change in external matters involves an equal or greater revolution of thought in the general mind. The first step toward this is the promulgation of ideas in a manner that will carry them into the brains of the poor and the rich, the worker and the idler everywhere. Nothing can be done either with or against men whose consciences are educated into the belief that injustice is justice, and that the order of things in the world below man excuses all wrong in society. When the intellect is convinced motives will act upon the will; and many whose wealth, position or mode of life now places them in opposition to all change will be among its energetic friends. The motives exist so abundantly in human misery that no one can then avoid feeling their impulse. That half the poor would starve if the rich were to labor, under the present conditions, is alone sufficient proof of the existing wrong. If monopoly and the inequality of wealth were removed, and opportunity preserved for all alike, all those now poor would have wants to be supplied, and every kind of labor, except such as minister to luxury and vice, would be in regular and certain demand. All those progressive movements which aim to benefit mankind would spring up into new life and vigor; for the poverty of one class, and the selfish indulgence of another, now act as a *constant obstruction* to progress. *Inequality* is the great incubus, fastening itself on the breast of society, and rendering it more and more helpless for all good work or moral growth. Democracy, Education, Morality, every kind of improvement, will be gradually strangled, and society itself will die in the convulsions of anarchy, if it is not thrown off completely and forever.

In view, then, of the two great antagonistic tendencies that have been exhibited, and as a matter of vital moment for the present hour, it becomes the duty of every man and woman, who has obtained a partial view of the future, to take up a missionary work in the circulation of ideas that shall help awaken society to a conscious sense of its actual situation.

It will be expected that before leaving the subject I should give some intimation of how the criminal, worthless, or inferior members of the social body are to be eliminated by humane means, in place of the savage process of Natural Selection, as it exhibits itself in competitive society. The problem does not seem to me so very difficult, and perhaps might not to others if there were a more earnest desire to solve it, and especially if there were more thought of doing so through a method of justice, instead of an unjust one like Malthusianism.

It has already been said that the incorrigible or unsafe criminal should be secluded for life, and the perpetuation of his breed thus prevented. And when besides this we do justice to woman, by securing to her the opportunity of earning her own subsistence in all cases, and so make her sufficiently independent to follow the dictates of her own conscience in regard to childbearing, the problem, I believe, will very nearly solve itself. It will be one of those things that come right by natural outworking, after the great first business of life, the winning of bread, clothing and shelter, shall be settled on a true basis. When woman is able to be true to herself and live, and her education ceases to be directed toward marriage as a means of support, she, like her brother man, will naturally prefer to grow upward rather than downward, and to do a right thing sooner than a wrong one. There is no woman so stupid or perverse that she would not rather have bright, healthy, beautiful and amiable children than feeble-minded, sickly, deformed or depraved ones. If single she is not likely to marry a man who will be the father of the latter sort, nor if married will she continue to bear them one after another, to her own suffering, danger and disgrace, when she can any day turn her hand to some labor that will supply all her needs independently of such a man. When her own work will give her a home she will not sell herself to some inferior man to obtain one. With employment already assured to her, and the same pay for it that man receives for his, she is not going to marry some worthless wretch in order to get occupation for herself by keeping his house. When wealth shall be so evenly distributed that it confers no great distinction or advantage, she will not for a fine establishment throw herself away on some rich, fast-living, diseased *roue*, old or young, and help to fill the world with feeble, scrofulous imitations of humanity, a perpetual misery to her and themselves, till they fall into their premature graves.

Moreover, with woman sure of being able to realize a home through her own labor, she will be less anxious to marry, and less liable to seduction; while, if seduction still rarely happened, she would not be driven into prostitution, and her child educated into degradation or crime, by their being made social outcasts as now. So far as regards this last matter, any change will be better than the infernal teaching and sentiment than now drives betrayed women of keen sensitiveness into despair and suicide, or if capable of more endurance into a life of shame. The masses of men and women read of the instances in their newspapers every day in the year, yet with true Chinese stolidity, look upon them as a matter of course, that will never be any different. The polygyny and polyandry of the savage never produce such horrible results as do the fiendish notions of Christendom.*

---

*Francis Estrada was a young Cuban who had been tossed about the world since childhood, and early yesterday morning he swallowed a dose of Paris green and gave up the struggle to live. The only mourner who stood above his body yesterday in his room at 25 Bleecker street was a girl he had picked out of the streets, Maggie Wallace, and whom he had made his wife. She had been betrayed a few

Still further, when woman shall find that it is possible for her to have superior children, instead of being compelled to have poor ones or none, as a large proportion of women now must, she will be likely to take some interest in the question of human selection through parentage, and do whatever she is able toward producing a superior strain. Then that dream of certain enthusiastic minds called Artistic Parentage may in some cases come to be approximately realized. It is hardly possible until the woman, as well as the man, can have some freer choice about who the other parent shall be.

But now, the inferior and discarded ones, these victims of a cruel fortune, suffering for the sins or bad fate of their ancestors, many of them fine-grained and sensitive, capable of strong domestic attachments, and of making pleasant homes,—are these to go forever without love, dragging out miserable lives of loneliness, that kill by slow torture? Not at all. Let the men of this class have

---

months ago, and when he met her, was one of the thousands of the city's unfortunates.

Both had been flung out of the society of comfortable people, and so they joined their fortunes, and in her rooms on Bleecker street began life anew. They had been legally married, and everything goes to show that the woman foreswore all her evil ways on Christmas eve, when she became Estrada's wife.

His father died years ago, and when his mother married into an American family her child was sent out into the world. The day after Christmas Estrada started out to canvass for a Broadway photographer. He met with little success, although he worked hard and was assisted in his endeavors by the woman he had made his wife.

Their room was on the second floor of the house, but they passed much of their time in the room of a couple on the floor below. Day after day he spoke of his fruitless effort to make a living.

This is her story of his last night on earth: "I saw him," she said yesterday, "at 7.30, when he came home from work, and gave him some money. I had to get something to eat. I then noticed he was vomiting, but thought it was from drinking. He went out and I saw him again at 11 o'clock sitting on the sofa in Mrs. Desser's room (on the first floor). He said he was too sick to go up stairs, and I returned to my room. He went to sleep on the sofa, and I came down stairs at 6.30 a. m., and found him lying dead on the floor."

Mrs. Desser, who slept in the room in which Estrada died, said: "I saw him standing outside at 11 p. m., and he said he did not feel well. I asked him to come inside, and when he did we laid him on the sofa to sleep. He was moaning and vomiting all night, and in the morning when we awoke we found him on the floor dead."

They took the dead man off the sofa and laid him on the floor. Over his body they threw a tattered blanket and then sent for the police. His lips were firm set and his hands were clenched as though in his last agony he had made a desperate attempt to hold the thread of life. The Coroner said Estrada had poisoned himself, as every one knew quite well. The body was removed to an undertaker's for burial.

Maggie Wallace, or Mrs. Estrada, is now in the same position in life as before Estrada met her, and the people who saw her looking at the body of the man who

whatever love they can honestly win from women who are past the age of childbearing; and let the women of such age be free to accept whatever of it they can attract and hold. They have morally no right to it sooner; and if before this they attempt, by frauds against nature, to enjoy it, yet prevent its natural results, that unnatural kind of love is likely to prove far worse than none. If they must have children on which to set their affections there will probably be a sufficient number of healthy orphans to be adopted; and scores of facts go to prove that when these are *truly adopted* the parental instinct becomes as well satisfied as with children of the same flesh and blood. With these they can have families and homes; while the moral sense in all persons will approve such a course, and no misery will have to be endured as an affliction of society.

Those who are too weak-minded, reckless, diseased or intemperate to be worthy of love, home or family can only be allowed to live and die in as much comfort as

---

had befriended her and struggled in vain to support her, wondered whether all the Christian and charitable societies in the city would prove as sacrificing a friend to her as the unfortunate she met a few weeks ago. *N. Y. Press, January* 12, '89.

Here is another case from the same paper, Dec. 13, '88.

The mystery surrounding the suicide of the beautiful young woman from the ferryboat Jay Gould, plying between Jersey City and Twenty-third street, Tuesday night, remains unsolved. Her body is still in the keeping of the dark waters to which she confided it. It was a strange suicide, and it doubtless was done to hide a deep secret. For nearly an hour the young woman, who was handsomely attired, went to and fro while the boat was on her trips, irresolute and wavering. Tears welled in her large, lustrous eyes as she wandered about, apparently in sore distress.

At least 100 women must have noticed her distress, but they all pulled their dresses more closely about them, lest the hem of their garments might be touched by her as she passed up and down in her walks. A kind word might have saved her; a thoughtful inquiry into her troubles might have eased her spirit. But they came not, and during two trips the poor unfortunate stayed upon the boat, desiring to end her existence and yet hesitating. At length two men noticed her and divined her purpose. They sought to watch her, but she eluded them, and, fearing possibly that her secret might be discovered, she became suddenly resolute, jumped quickly upon the guard rail of the boat, folded her arms upon her breast, leaned over and fell into the river. So far as known she uttered no word.

The ferryboat was, of course, at once stopped and search made for her, but the river had claimed her body, and the boat kept on, while the women whispered the thousand things that have induced the unfortunate to end her life so rashly. The river is now being dragged for the body.

"Often," said Dr. Kate Bushnell, "at a meeting of the W. C. T. Union, have I tramped the streets of Chicago for days trying to find some one to take into their homes a young helpless girl who had no home, no friends—nothing but the street for a refuge, and usually it has been a fruitless search. I have returned only to place in the young mother's arms her helpless baby and turn her out into the world. Heaven only knows what became of them."

their labor, aided by the benevolent care of individuals, will enable them to obtain, under industrial conditions similar to those lately outlined, which will at least permit them to be selected out without starvation, brutality, or injustice.

No one however, will suppose that all this can be done with thoroughness till a far better degree of knowledge concerning the human body and mind shall become prevalent among the social masses. The more complete this knowledge the more complete the work.

I will close this chapter with a quotation from an orthodox Christian source, which is another testimony going to show that in the church, half dead as it seems to be, there is considerable thought upon these matters, and that such social heresies as are here presented are not without countenance from the Christian world. Like a former quotation it is from the " Gesta Christi " of Charles L. Brace, a book which Dr. Storrs of Brooklyn pronounced worthy of being circulated by the million.

"It is not to be assumed, as is done by most writers on this subject, that the modern form of the distribution of wealth is the final and perfect one, and that society as it now is is substantially what it must be in all coming ages, or what our Lord contemplated in His future Kingdom of Heaven or regenerated society of all men. A Christian writer in the early Middle Ages would have had equal right to assume that society must always be made up of landlords owning vast tracts of country, who protected their vassals, of large bodies of military followers, and of serfs bound to the soil; or that justice in regard to quarrels over property and land must always be decided by the judicial duel. Neither of these conditions was directly touched upon by the teachings of the great Reformer; yet the principles he taught must gradually undermine both. The feudal system belonged to a stage of human progress. The modern industrial and commercial system may be equally a phase in the gradual change or advance of mankind. A condition of society in which enormous masses of human beings are born to an almost inevitable lot of squalor, penury, and ignorance; and still other multitudes to incessant labor, with few alleviations or enjoyments; while another considerable class, with little or no effort of their own, have all the blessings of life and transmit them to others—in other words, an industrial system which leaves to the few who are gifted with the brains, or enjoy the fortune, to lead industrial enterprises, the power to reap the benefits of labor, while the many who toil only gain a bare pittance—a society which presents on one side enormous accumulations of wealth, while on the other it offers classes ground down by poverty and pinched with want, is certainly not the Christian ideal of society, or any approach to the 'Kingdom of God on earth.'

"The great moral progress of the future of the race will plainly be toward some form of a more equable distribution of the proceeds of labor. What form this will take it is as impossible to predict as it would have been for a citizen of the Roman empire at the time of Tacitus to predict the present condition of Europe.* * *

"If we read Christ's teachings with perfect candor, and as far removed from present habits of thought as possible, we discover a continual tendency towards exalting poverty, humbling wealth and equalizing the conditions of life.* * * There is a certain tone throughout the gospels, if not of communism, at least in favor of greater distribution of wealth than would suit modern ideas. Christ and the apostles warn incessantly against accumulation of wealth. They almost denounce the rich; they praise and commend the poor; their sympathies are strongly with the working classes; they urge continually the diffusion of property in whatever way would benefit the world; they warn those who do not scatter their acquisitions among the needy; they leave the impression everywhere that a greater equalizing of human goods, a moderate acquisition, and a raising up from poverty is what is demanded. The parable of Lazarus has been too often interpreted under modern conditions, and it may well be that some explanatory features given by Christ are omitted by the historian; but its literal interpretation plainly contains a plea against the great inequalities of fortune in this world." (Gesta Christi, pp. 93-5).

The tracing out of the details of operation, in changing from one social regime to the other, and of the administration afterward, is a task not contemplated for this book. Some of those changes may be difficult; many of them will appear so to those who have no sympathy with socialistic effort; none will prove impossible when the demand for them comes in sufficient strength. They are mostly to be inferred from the principles set forth at the beginning of this chapter. Some outlines, not supposed to be altogether certain, can be found in the "Coöperative Commonwealth," of Lawrence Gronlund, and perhaps others in other socialistic works.

CHAPTER XII.

NATURAL AND SOCIAL SELECTION.

(Continued.)

HAVING in the previous chapters exhibited the great conflict perpetually going on, and soon to reach its crisis, between the selfish spirit operating under the law of Natural Selection, by which might makes right, and the unselfish or social spirit striving for justice or the greatest amount of happiness; and having in the last one referred to some of the steps now being taken in the transforming process that must ultimately revolutionize our present industrial methods, I must now go farther and suggest how the methods of justice may be more completely carried out, in that still more advanced condition which is the Ideal held forth in this book.

The system outlined as to its fundamental principles in the last chapter will necessarily precede anything more perfect; for those principles must have recognition before there can be any truly just society. Being accepted and carried into actual operations, the minor questions of right and wrong in industry tend to decide themselves. The more important affairs of life being settled on a basis of acknowledged justice, the predominance of justice in these works itself out into all the less important till it becomes universal. As no contention, great or small, can be permanently disposed of till done righteously, this is the reason the final question will come to be with every man whether his love of justice shall enable him to be content with only what belongs to him.

When any social body of considerable size shall adopt the basic principles of such a plan it will be a most hopeful indication of an approach toward the unselfish stage of development in a considerable number of people; and a reasonably sure promise of its arrival to them within a comparatively brief period. For, the unselfish stage in regard to industry is little more than the application of justice to all its details, as justice has been defined in these papers. And when an individual shall be capable of this he will probably be capable of becoming unselfish in regard to all the conduct of life.

All the various improvements in the method of conducting industry are steps or stages toward the Kingdom of the Unselfish, in which there will be complete liberty and perfect justice—freedom of trade no less than of everything else, and industrial justice as one of the most necessary of all things. Trade can safely be free only when it is honest, when it ceases to be a means of robbery or exploitation, either of individual by individual, or of nation by nation. Then it may be as free as the southwest wind, wandering over the earth as it will, and carrying a healthful influence wherever it goes, with no one wishing to hinder its progress.

The Ideal State contemplated comes by a growth of the mind from the natural selfish into the cultivated unselfish stage of development. None of the schemes for improving the industrial condition proposes to change the selfish spirit into the unselfish through a higher enlightenment, or promises to assist that change, except in the slow and gradual way it is always being advanced under favoring circumstances. By creating such circumstances, some of them, and especially that last described, and approximately known under the name of Social Democracy, will aid largely in bringing the final outcome, by giving independence to the character of the individual, and enabling him to obtain the means of a better culture, besides taking away in some cases the means of corruption. They are called steps or stages, in an industrial sense, as an improved political or religious condition may be a step in the same direction of a different kind. The industrial steps, however, will be of a more effective character, as it seems to me, than any other that can be taken.

But, it may still be well to observe, until the Unselfish Condition is reached no complete equality will exist. Though industrial justice may do much to advance men in the direction of that state, the true equality, that commands the respect of the best, is the moral and intellectual equality that comes only after sufficient culture has been gained to allow of pride and bigotry being subdued, so that the less advanced can, with true willingness to learn, and desire to grow, be drawn or lifted up to the higher level.

And further, while the adoption of such an industrial regime might be a great help toward the complete moralization of persons and affairs, we are not dependent on it as the only means of introducing such a state among individuals. On the contrary, the more highly moralized individuals must labor to bring about the conversion of the masses to the acceptance of such a system. But either with or without it, and under the most favorable conditions of things as they now are, individuals will still be likely to advance, one by one and group by group, into the Unselfish Stage.

The main point in the industrial philosophy of Unselfishness was given to the world forty years ago, in the formulas, "Equal labor for labor," and "Cost the limit of price," by Josiah Warren, a man of whom few have ever heard, but whose name ought not to be forgotten by the generations of the future. "Cost," means labor, privation, endurance, suffering; and together, these formulas mean equality in labor, and equality in its results, between man and man. They are completely antithetical to all the doctrine and spirit of the individualistic, competitive regime, with its profit-making, speculation, gambling, and extortion; they ignore Political Economy, that pretentious and wonderful science which consists mainly in teaching freedom for whoever is able, to lay hold of whatever he or they can get, or for whoever can resist, to keep it from being taken. They are in short, the embodiment and representative of Justice, and of the greatest ultimate good in all industrial arrangements,— the extreme opposite of all that now obtains.

Mr. Warren at the same time believed in the most complete individualism in the ownership of property, and control of business affairs. He stated the dogma of the "Sovereignty of the Individual" in its most absolute form, so far as regards these subjects of its application; but strictly limited in all cases by the proviso,—"to be exercised only at his own cost." He took no position regarding the common possession of land, and of the free productions of nature, nor any concerning the right of opportunity to labor; but as his doctrine of Cost, or of Equal labor for labor, would operate to prevent all speculation, monopoly, extortion and profit-making (beyond payment for labor) the whole natural effect could be but little if any different from that of an individual management or superintendence of industrial affairs for the benefit of all, similar to what would exist under Industrial Democracy, except that the individual appoints himself instead of being elected. At any rate, his individualism in industry, subject to the Cost principle, is a very different thing from individualism on the principle of obtaining as much as possible at the *least* cost; and apparently it could do little harm. Of the experiments made by himself and by his disciples I find it difficult to say much; they were both successful and unsuccessful; and for the final failure various causes existed, aside from imperfections in the theory professedly taken as a guide. The Cost principle is the original, peculiar, predominant and vital part of his teaching; and this is a genuine contribution to the world's knowledge and thought.

Turning now from the contrast of ideas let us see society as it is under the influence of one set of them, before representing it as it will be under the dominance of the other. It is not difficult to perceive how the animus of the "let alone" doctrine has permeated all the social divisions, and is manifested about us in every-day life. It is the spirit of the natural, unprogressed man and would appear in abundant measure without encouragement; but the economic teaching does nothing to check it, and when by severe competition the struggle for the means of living becomes intense, and self-preservation the first object, religious or moral teaching has little effect, while the church itself is fettered and gagged by having accepted the same economic doctrine. We may see the generality of the population bent upon self-indulgence nearly as much as at any time in the past; the exception is only somewhat larger. In the general opinion, when a man has accumulated money he has a right to spend it for selfish ends if he chooses. He himself believes in this right more strongly than anyone else, and if remonstrated with will quickly give an answer not altogether polite. The rich therefore, with few exceptions, use their wealth for luxury, for high living, for amusements, for magnificence and ostentation. All the poor and ignorant have of course no higher motive, and so spend whatever they can spare for the luxuries of tobacco, beer, and liquors, for cheap entertainments, for pleasures of poorer quality and greater danger than those of the rich. It is true that the poor, having less of comforts, have stronger temptations to a bad use of money; but blind selfish gratification seems to be the almost universal object, and few think of questioning the right to pursue it. Women are animated by the same disposition as men, and so far as they have the means most of them take the same course, in a useless life of pleasure, just as two thousand years ago. The justification of selfishness is the same now as then, namely, the right because one has the power. All suffer for want of a higher purpose; some of the best doubtless feel keenly the need of an all-controlling, unselfish object for which to live and labor. Pleasure ends in vanity and disappointment, as the very least of its bad results.

That "life is a fraud" is a feeling so common one can meet with it almost any day, and thoughtful people gravely discuss the question, "Is life worth living," just as they might have done in the Dark Ages or the days of Roman decline, when anarchy, vice, crime and civil war were almost perpetual everywhere. Though our age is supposed to be the happiest the world has ever seen, the Pessimistic philosophy has sprung up among thinkers more strongly than ever before. Every one seems conscious of the misery caused by universal selfishness; yet every one insists that it is absolutely necessary for him or her to be selfish in order to live. "It is the competitive life," writes some one, "that crucifies humanity."

We see the selfish spirit very plainly in the prevalent indifference regarding human welfare and even human life. Every one has all he can do in looking out for himself. No one feels it his duty to pay much attention to any wrong or suffering going on about him. He may give something if asked for a contribution, but is not disposed to take any trouble. His nearest neighbor is no more to him than the most distant stranger. Railroads, explosions, accidents of every kind, may kill their victims by the score or hundred, yet seldom is any effective precaution against them adopted, and they continue year after year. It is the same in regard to crime. An innocent man may be murdered by a gang of roughs on an excursion steamboat, and no one ever be punished for it. A young immigrant woman sets out alone to find her friends in the city, and is never heard from again, but no effort worth mentioning is made to find her. A little girl is murdered and her mangled body thrown into the marsh within sight of houses where people live, and the police do not so much as find a clue that is worth tracing. A man's life is of small account, a woman's less, and her virtue scarcely anything, while the body of a poor man's child may be thrown to dogs; no appropriate effort is made in either case to bring the guilty to justice. Had the general public possessed any more than the mere rudiments of a conscience, any proper human feeling, a thousand detectives if necessary would have been put upon the search for the lost and for the criminals; and no lawyers tricks, or stupid generosity of the law itself would have been permitted to let the villians escape. As it is, the law is so made and construed by the lawyer class that criminals often escape from it more easily than innocent persons, and thousands of them infest society, preying upon it with little danger to themselves, and constant benefit to the lawyer. Each individual leaves everything but his own immediate concerns to be looked after by somebody else. He votes once a year perhaps, for the officials who are to do everything that is just and right, and that is as much trouble as he can afford to take. "Every one for himself and the devil take the hindmost," once a witty proverb of occasional application, has now become so universally applicable it is quoted only as a serious expression of the truth.

"It is time he was dead when he cannot support himself," is an expression I have heard regarding an old man, from one not so hard-hearted as the average of people, and it went without protest from half-a-dozen others to whom it was addressed. No doubt it seemed to them entirely in harmony with the actual state of things.

Now, it may be again said, this is simply the selfish feeling that would exist whether we had any knowledge of Natural Selection or not; but it is well to notice clearly that the free-competition sentiment, reënforced of late years by Natural Selection, justifies or excuses it and makes it worse. In this country we have had that sentiment instilled into us from childhood, because everything in our earlier condition has suggested and encouraged it. Our new soil and other resources, with boundless opportunity for every one to take his own way in making a fortune, has developed that sentiment and its corresponding action. Craft and cheating come to be gloried in by men of no conscience, as proofs of superior intelligence. To discover, and take advantage of, some particular ignorance or weakness, is to them a wonderful thing to do; while the public opinion of the business community does not condemn them for thus glorying in their shame. The end of the process is now beginning to appear in speculating combinations of all sorts, for exploiting, not the workingman only, but the professional class and the rich as well, indeed all who have wants to be supplied.

Every man is opposed to his neighbor or to more than one. All are constantly baffling each other's efforts, using up time and energy in preventing another from getting something wanted for self. Besides the *waste* of time and strength, there is a constant wear and tear upon the physical system from the friction and discord, the irritation, disappointment, defeat and loss endured; still worse, there is a hardening effect upon the moral sensibilities, making one unfeeling, rough, obstinate, cruel and revengeful. Much kindness and good nature, it is true, exist in spite of this; for whatever honest and natural trade there is is conducive to friendship. But the conflict of interests and antagonism of feeling is what every one experiences in some degree. Jealousy, the fear that some one else may get a desired something, often causes men to defeat even their own selfish interests. In extreme cases it renders them unsocial, miserly and base.

In the Kingdom of the Unselfish, that Empire of a more far-seeing Wisdom, all this tendency will be reversed by a sentiment, policy, and conduct which enables all the kind and friendly impulses to flow forth freely under all circumstances. Mutual help and coöperation will be the rule. No one will try to appropriate all he can get, because no one will assert a right to possess more than the average share. The use of the earth and all it contains will be acknowledged as the common possession, in which every one has an equal right or claim. Every one will be industrious, and make due exertion to obtain whatever is necessary for comfort or convenience; but no one desiring more than the rest can have, all are free and willing, yea glad, to assist the one who is less successful than his fellows. All will be ready to submit to friendly criticism (by the way, there will be no other kind), and by this means each will be aided to find the occupation best suited to his or her capacity and acquirements. All employments will be held in honor, because of the superior importance or necessity of what are now commonly called the lowest ones. The consciousness that these employments are thus looked upon will take away much of their unpleasantness, will enable one to respect himself in spite of the most offensive work, and will enable all to treat him with that equal respect which is his due, or allow themselves to take their equal share of such work. But even this is not the crowning glory of the industrial system that is to be. Equal labor for labor,—equal endurance or suffering in return for the hardship of toil,—this will be the only acknowledged just rule for labor's compensation. Under this rule the most disagreeable work will receive the highest pay. Nothing can be more self-evidently just and right; and the people here contemplated will have no selfish interests or feelings, no bigotry or mental cowardice, sufficient to prevent their seeing a just principle, and acting in accordance with it. An average amount of work, of average hardship, will then be entitled to an average income; and work of other kinds can be judged of by this standard. When every one is as desirous to do justice as to exact it, there will be no dispute about wages or prices; and when every one knows he will not be cheated or taken advantage of, there will be no effort to obtain too much. In agreement with the same principle, knowledge will be cheap, and education easy to get. Trades and occupations may be learned at much less cost of labor or money than now; for the pay of the teacher will be but little greater than that of the learner; and experiments made years ago have shown that occupations can be learned very quickly, when one person has an attraction for learning, and another for teaching. Mutual good will will take away the annoyance, friction, and tediousness of ordinary labor; while ability to change employments and surroundings occasionally, in consequence of having skill in several kinds of work, will render it so interesting that scarcely any of the disagreeable features now belonging to it will remain.

Partnerships among such people, or rather combined management of business affairs, for there will be no partnerships of the present kind, will be easy and pleasant; because with every one willing to do his part, and to receive criticism when he undesignedly fails, they could not be otherwise. Indeed every person will be operating for the benefit of the whole as much as for himself, without any special arrangement or combination. Where all are trustworthy no watching will be needed, nor will there be any expense for law. Credit, if any shall be necessary, will be as free as cold water, and equally safe to give or take.

Here is where the mechanic, the farmer, the worker at any work, no matter how simple, can become the artist as well as artisan. For with the right feeling in regard to labor, shown in all around him, and knowing that he will be fully paid, the drudgery now attached to it will disappear; he will choose what he can do best, will take interest in it, will perform it in the best manner, and feel pleasure and pride in it as an artistic accomplishment. The "dignity of labor" will obtain a higher meaning than ever before, and will come to be a realized thing. This can never be under the regime of Competition; for the artisan can have no motive to do well, either in friendly feeling to others, or in the consciousness of being well paid for it; he must aim to do his work just well enough to retain his employment, and as much as he can of that quality, in order to earn good wages.

When no one is idle, but all are self-sustaining, having sufficient means to satisfy their rational wants, with all kinds of swindling in disgrace, and credit universal, there will be no lack of employment; while with subsistence assured, by the admitted right of all to equal shares in whatever employment or opportunity there is, with sympathy and aid to be depended upon in case of accident or other misfortune, no one will be tempted or impelled to overwork. All will labor nearly the same amount of time; in the ordinary occupations all will receive nearly the same pay; all will be likely to realize nearly the same yearly income; all will have sufficient wants to keep them busy. No hard times will be known there; for there will be no over-trading or speculation, no monopolies, no excessive wealth to waste, no distinction or honor to be gained by senseless display and extravagance. Wealth will have no more power than so much dirt.

There will be no communism in the old sense of that word, but a common management of the natural resources belonging to all. Every one's right to control and use the property produced by his or her own labor will be sacredly respected. No one will wish to interfere in the least, nor will any one have any excuse for such desire; because the outcome will be the possession of property by every man and woman, and in a comparatively equal amount, with all the benefits thus implied. It will be substantially the condition the communist desires, but the whole achieved without the least infringement of personal liberty or personal ownership.

Neither will such people be so unthoughtful of the wants of posterity as to allow the reckless waste now going on everywhere to continue where they can prevent. When persons have become so far unselfish as to have a true regard for the welfare of others, now living, it will be easy enough for them to consider the rights of those who are to come. They will scarcely more think of wasting the materials belonging to the future than of throwing away the bread of their own children.

Because all will be sufficiently unselfish to constantly bear in mind the liberty, rights, comfort, convenience and welfare of all others, they will be able to live in unitary homes, or practice any method of close association that may be advantageous. They will do it without discord or serious disagreement; an achievment never accomplished, I think, under any scheme of living yet tried.

Still further, though every one will try to do his unselfish best, yet when he fails to come up to the ideal, as every one will fail in some degree, instead of meeting the harsh, exacting, selfish criticism of the competitive world, he will meet a generous spirit, exacting less than it might. He will be referred to his own sense of justice and duty, allowed to set his own standard, to make his own excuse, to judge and condemn himself, as the one best capable of doing so properly. In a word, our standard will be set up for ourselves as much as for another. And in this atmosphere of charity and generosity even the vilest criminal, were he taken into it, could hardly fail to improve; certainly not the kind of person contemplated.

Those who have followed me through the earlier chapters well know what my justification is for believing such a state of things to be possible. To those who have not let me repeat that the people who are to bring about this condition have themselves first been brought into that stage of mental and moral growth which I have compared to the blossoming stage in the plant, or the pubescent period of the animal; when the intellect is mature and the conscience full-grown; when the individual is able to criticise all his beliefs, prepossessions and assumed knowledge; when he is ready to investigate new claims, and accept new truth from any quarter; when his conquest of the selfish feelings is complete, so that no conscious wrong-doing is possible to him, or conscious leaving of duty undone. To persons of this character nothing here described will be impossible; on the contrary there is nothing in it they will not desire to do, and to assist others in doing. That condition of society will be as natural to them as the present competitive strife is to the selfish man of this time, the stout-bodied, broad-headed man who eats and drinks, builds railroads and makes money, runs for office, and tramples down his opponents, as though such work were the grandest performance a human being could do.

That hard problem of how justly to decide what part of industry's product shall be allowed to talent and skill, is here seen to be solved like that of inherited wealth. When once the selfish spirit is given up, it is easy to acknowledge that talent is an inherited possession—a piece of good fortune—a share of that fortune which, good or bad, is the endowment of Nature, from which none should profit, and none be allowed to suffer, so far as prevention is possible. Being a part of that which Nature has furnished the possessor without cost of labor or suffering, he has no moral right to take advantage of it; he has no better right to use it for profit than he has to use inherited wealth to monopolize opportunity. What costs him nothing does not belong to him for selfish uses. He can justly ask a return only for labor performed or suffering endured; and this he receives in equal labor or hardship endured by others for him. In the moral condition referred to the man of talent will rejoice in the superior ability it gives him, and be satisfied with that, having no desire to use it for putting a greater separation between himself and his fellows.

Skill that has been acquired by labor or study—mechanical or professional skill—is entitled to something more than crude, untaught exertion could obtain, in order to reward the exertion spent in acquiring it To a greater amount than this it has no just claim.

Everything is determined by the one simple principle

that what Nature furnishes free of cost should be enjoyed alike by all; and that when Nature takes away, as by drouth, flood, earthquake, tornado, pestilence, fire, or unavoidable accident, all should help to bear, or to make good, the loss. This is true sympathy; this alone is the complete ideal of justice; this is what high souls everywhere and always instinctively know to be right.

In this new social state every possession becomes moralized, or as I prefer to say, unselfish; every faculty of mind and body, as well as material riches. Our Positivist friends have talked of the moralization of wealth as something possible under the rule of competition and selfishness, by the natural progress of opinion. By the rich becoming more enlightened they are judged likely to become so far moralized as to use their wealth for the world's good. But the Positivists have never given the rich man any reason why he should do this—that is, any new or better reason than he has had always. They have never shown him the justice of it, neither, in a complete way, have any of our socialists or reformers. They expect him (except the socialists) to become generous, at the same time that all their theories justify him in being selfish. All the economists, without exception, allow him a complete right to the selfish use of his property. The great religious Teacher condemned the rich, and required them to distribute to the poor before they became the followers of him; but, so far as recorded, he set forth no grounds on which they could see the requirement to be just. When the justice, as well as the generosity of it, shall be once perceived, many of them will act according to conscience.

The propriety of moralizing talent, or rendering it unselfish, is yet harder to understand, under present teachings. Not long ago I read an elaborate argument from a radical American Individualist in defence of perpetual property in inventions,—that patents and copyrights should be capable of being owned as long as a person lived, and then transmittible to his children. Now, this is the strict logical inference from all the most orthodox instruction concerning property. A thing legally gained and possessed, becomes absolute property, however acquired, and may be transferred by sale or gift forever. Knowledge, trade secrets, discovery or invention, that can be made profitable by sale or purchase, is equally property forever by the same law. Whatever falls to a man's possession by the good fortune of inheritance, or accidental discovery, is by the right of first obtainment, his to turn to his selfish account in the best way he can. If others want any share in his good luck they must pay for it,—is what modern economists and moralists tell us to be the true doctrine, conservative of morals and property, of industry, order and peace.

In contrast to all this, in the new Kingdom or Empire all good or bad fortune will be the good or bad fortune of every one so far as all can partake. An accident that disables or destroys will call effectually for the sympathy and aid of all; an accidental good fortune, a discovery, an invention accomplished through the help of knowledge already existing, or present materials turned to a better use by means of existing talent or skill,—these are shared by all. They cost nothing except the time, thought and labor expended in making them available for use. Except this labor put into them, they are what Nature, or natural law and force, operating through human nature as well as outside of it, has in some way produced, without cost to the inventor or finder, and are no more his than any other man's. The fully moralized or unselfish person will consider them the good fortune of all, like soil, water, air and sunshine.

"How if the inventor, the thinker, the student, spends years of his time to bring out what he believes will be a thing of use and beauty, yet fails, and finds his effort wasted? Should there not be some extra compensation for success to make up for loss of time and effort in failure?" Ah! in this new mode of life there will be so little occasion for failure that it need not be taken into account. In the first place, no one will consider that he has a right to waste his time and labor; it is all consecrated to the useful service of humanity; and he thinks of this before he begins upon any doubtful project. Secondly, he is open to criticism and suggestion; he will have no selfish pride to stand in the way, no selfish interest to demand privacy; he will avail himself of all the counsel offered, or that can be obtained by the asking. With all this prudence and this help he cannot seriously fail or waste his time.

But now let this be observed, that if one has talent for discovery, invention, thought, or artistic production, and there is any surplus wealth in the community, that wealth, instead of being wasted on stately houses, extravagant living, and ostentatious luxury, will be placed at his service to enable him to develop or produce what he could not without it. All the obscure genius, which the present selfish regime allows to fret itself away in helpless poverty, will then come to the surface, will have its chance, and achieve its highest possibilities, where all alike, without envy or jealousy, will rejoice in the accomplishment, and in the common benefit that is to result.

In a word, in this ideal condition the reign of Natural Selection will be over. It will have ceased to operate toward the extinction, the injury, or the depression of any person; for, the less fortunate individual being found capable and worthy of equality, every one assists in bringing him up into line with the best; and whatever social selection there is acts only for the benefit of all, in the way that has been explained.

"Yes, and in your community all the invalids, paupers, drunkards, drones, imbeciles and idiots will be as well off as the very best and wisest," some one in his haste may wish to reply. But in fact, none of these except invalids, and the poor who have become such by undeserved misfortune, can possibly get into such a society, for lack of intellect and character. Every one able to work will find his or her opportunity. And invalids, after the present generation of them have had their natural chance to get well or die, will not be found there any longer. The people of that society will know the causes of invalidism, and will be both wise and unselfish enough not to become invalids, or bring into the world feeble and sickly children. No one will be compelled to injure himself by overwork in order to support a family, nor to expose himself to danger from cold, heat, or accident. Unavoidable accidents there will be, but those that come through carelessness or indifference, that is, three-fourths of all we now have, will be escaped. Invalids, under the new moral and social influences here contemplated, will become well and strong, who otherwise would never be anything but a burden to their friends. New views, new feelings, new occupations, new prospects, new aspirations, change and variety, better environment, and a new spirit such as the race has never fully known, surrounding, permeating and inspiring all,—these will together constitute a condition and means of health, the happy influence of which cannot previously be estimated. No depressing ennui will be there, no repression of worthy ambitions, no aristocratic idleness, no general debility for want of useful work, no nervous weakness from excessive pleasure or suffering, no anxiety concerning hard times, no sadness from overwrought sympathy, no perpetual irritation and complaint. On the contrary, the nervous force now wasted by these various forms of misery will be converted into happiness, and overflow in good spirits, in gentle sport, and quiet joy, subdued only by the knowledge of misery existing in the world outside their own.

No, you may depend upon it there will not long be any sickly, or poor, or unhappy people there. The complete enlightenment and moralization of the individual spirit will regenerate the physical body, along with making a material paradise in which to live. All that is needed is the intelligence to see the way, and the moral determination to follow it, that leads into this new Eden of the future.

It may be well to add the caution, always to be remembered, that nothing can be absolutely perfect, and therefore some imperfection will exist in the perfect society. But the difference between that state of things and the present is so great that I feel justified in making the statement of it strong. The sharp contrasts of the new and the old, taken with this caution, ought not to convey any wrong impression.

Is there any one in the present, competitive society so rich in true felicity, as the poorest of those here described? No, verily. There is no man so rich as he who shall feel in every fibre of his being that he has a real and actual brotherhood in all the humanity around him—an eternal claim to their sympathy and aid that can never be dishonored. No insurance can render him so safe from poverty and want. No safe-deposit vault can keep his treasures so securely as the enlightened human conscience can keep its sense of duty to him. There is no government or police so strong to protect him as the almighty truth that all men are by nature entitled to equality in the means of happiness. There *is something* too valuable for any money to buy, something too high for any selfish ambition to reach; it is the sincere respect, the pure good will, the affection, the deep, reverent love of his fellow beings, and even of the happy dumb animals about him,—a wealth far too precious to be adequately described in words, but which the occupants of this new world will possess, and with it will be able to look with calm contempt upon all the money and the enjoyments the pampered millionaire can boast.

CHAPTER XIII.

LOVE.

"LOVE is life," say a certain class of romantic persons, "Love and life are one; the same child of the one parent source whence emanates all good. All that love produces or effects is good, and good only, tending toward happiness and life."

"Love is death," say certain other persons; very unromantic people these, medical men and scientists. Love to them means reproduction of the species; and studying the facts connected with it they discover that reproduction uses up the vital force of the organism and tends toward death. They observe in some of the lowest forms of animal life how the mature creature develops itself into a mass of reproductive cells, and then, bursting the outside skin that remains to it, lets loose a multitude of progeny by its own destruction. They notice certain species of insects which live but a day or a few days after their maturity, in which time they do their work toward continuing their kind and then die. They see that fish, after their breeding season, have become weak and poor. They know by a thousand facts in human life as well as animal, facts familiar to medical men especially, that exercise of the generative function reduces the natural fund of vitality. The idea, in fact, seems so well established that certain thinkers, who speculate upon the possible continuation of human life beyond any limit hitherto reached, count on the absence of this function as one of the necessary conditions.

Here, then, we have two sets of notions regarding love, that are as completely opposite as can be. Must one of them be discarded as false; or is there some way in which both may be true? I shall try to show how, in spite of all appearances, they can be harmonized.

In the first place we must examine closely into the nature of love, in all its manifestations and qualities, from lowest to highest. Physiologists tell us that all its various forms spring out of, or are dependent upon, a class of organs possessed by all the higher animals and man, whose primary function is the continuation of the race or species. If this organism be taken away or mutilated, while a creature is young, all the feelings and desires called love fail to manifest themselves, or if at all only in the mere rudiments of their natural strength. Not only physical qualities, but grace, beauty, manliness and womanliness of character, are in such case unable to appear.

All this is strictly true, and yet the difference between the love of the mere animal, and that of the highest human being, is so great that all comparison of human love with animal, or reasoning from one to the other, becomes a means of delusion. I venture to assert that there is as much difference between the mere physical love impulse of the animal, and the love of a highly developed human being, as there is between the brain of the animal and that of the well-developed man; or between the animal and human intelligence, or the animal and human character. We have been able to find an immense difference in all the animal and human qualities except love; and now we are about to find that in regard to love also the animal and human are very much *unlike*.

The love of the low, coarse and undeveloped man may be but little if any superior to that of the brute. But that of the civilized and cultivated human is very far superior. Instead of being a mere reckless impulse, bent only on its own satisfaction, it comes to spread its influence over the whole mind, and to be qualified in turn by its connection with every other feeling. The regard for children, home, and friends are most closely associated with it; the ambitions and hopes depend upon its fruition; the spiritual sympathies of religion become involved; and finally the intellectual tendencies and aims come to be interested in the one great complex passion. The whole man or woman may be so completely absorbed in it that when it is disappointed and broken up the person becomes temporarily, if not permanently, a shattered and helpless wreck.

It not only associates itself with all the other feelings, but it enlivens, expands, and glorifies them; at the same time becoming itself glorified, exalted, refined, romantic, eloquent, poetic, and tender; making a charmed atmosphere around its object, delusively elevating it to an undeserved height, and worshipping it with a true devotion. This is what love may be in the better part of our species; and to compare it with that of the animal, either the animal brute or the animal man, is monstrously unreasonable and unjust. Thinkers who have a purpose in so doing can discover in the human mind or soul an immense advance beyond that of the brute; and can draw from it inferences which make man the special favorite of his Creator, and endow him with immortality. But the same superiority belongs to all the faculties of the human, and is as true of his constructive and destructive powers, his ambitious feelings and artistic capacities, as of his thought and his religious emotions. His loves are of the same superior character, that is, in the superior individual. The animal man, and the inferior races of the human family, know only the physical. The highest know all of the high motives, delicate sensibilities, and enthusiasm of energy that have been indicated. The animal, or the low-grade human being, has only one way of manifesting the passion; the high-grade man or woman has a thousand. Let this distinction between lowest and highest forms, or inferior and superior qualities of love, be remembered; for it is one that has never before been insisted upon, and will prove to have important consequences.

How much of this love is selfish, and how much unselfish? is the next point; and in order to decide this it is necessary to show plainly what is the true interior nature of love itself. It is one of those things of which poets and romancers assert that nothing can be known, and of which books and teachers give no explanation.

A great part of the legitimate activity of a civilized community is described in the word *exchange*,—exchange of commodities and exchange of services. The merchant, manufacturer, farmer, miner, hunter, and fisherman exchange the products of their labor for the products of other men's labor, or for the money that represents them. Others exchange their labor only. The teacher, lawyer, clergyman, physician, give mental labor, or the results of it, for the proceeds of physical labor,—a spiritual or mental product for a material one. Each gets as much as he can for what he gives, and the more he obtains the better he enjoys the exchange. One party may thus be very much pleased while the other is very dissatisfied. But when the exchange is pretty nearly equal, the buyer obtaining what satisfies him, and the seller making a profit, there naturally springs up a friendliness of feeling which brings the same parties together again, when there is another occasion for trade. On the contrary, when the trade is unequal there is dislike or hatred by the victimized party, however much the other may be satisfied, and may try to convince the first that there is no wrong. The wrong is proved by continued dissatisfaction; and we see that satisfaction or discontent, friendship or dislike, attraction or repulsion, depends on the *justice* or *injustice* of the exchange.

Take notice still further how the same law holds good: The clergyman or teacher may be well satisfied with the salary he obtains for his labor, and be well disposed toward all the members of his church or his class. But to those who give him special attention, who admire his ideas or his oratory, the preacher pays special attention in return, conversing with them freely, and manifesting for them an exceptional interest. They give to him appreciation and praise; he is disposed to give them more freely of the same attractive qualities, or it may be of others. When one brings you a present of something nice, at a time you need it, and you have an opportunity to return something good, you are not particular if you give a little more than you received. Then if he makes another present it is likely to be larger than yours, and so on for an indefinite time. It is the same with this clergyman and his admirers, only the things they give are spiritual, instead of material, and are not always the same. But each gives something the other wants, and they are not displeased if they give somewhat more than they receive. One thing or quality may be given for the same or for something different; and so the spiritual exchanges may run into the material ones and vice versa, from one party or both, thus becoming very much mixed, till one admirer may present the clergyman his only daughter, and another one a house and lot, along with their mutual admiration. The whole of this spiritual and material exchange is summed up in the word *friendship*.

The teacher, too, finds that some of his pupils have

unusual appreciation for what he takes pleasure in imparting, and the better it is appreciated and learned the more he takes pains to give. Their admiration is an acknowledgment of his superior advancement or talent, which pleases him, and he makes return for it in extra attention. Both parties give and receive various other little attentions and favors that are pleasant; and this spiritual barter of thought and good feeling may come to include physical things, or any kind of service, and terminate in an exchange of presents. The whole of it is nothing but the mutual friendship of the teacher and scholars.

In the family it is the same. Here all the parties are engaged in exchanging a great variety of services, with the result that every one is made happier. This also—the family affection—is but another form of friendship. Or if any one chooses to say their exchange of service and of spiritual good is not friendship but the operation of friendship, that makes no difference; friendship is both the desire to do it, and the satisfaction of having it done, with the intermediate action of doing.

In each case the exchange of goods and services runs from one kind into another, each leading to something else, without limit; just as two boys may begin by swapping pocket knives, and end by giving real estate for moonshiny railroad bonds, or helping one another get elected to Congress.

It is well also to observe that when the parties are disposed to give more than they get the friendship is increasing in intensity; when they give less it is decreasing; and on the whole the values given and received are about equal. After they begin to be unequal they will not long continue.

Now, all this mutual transfer of good and pleasant things, in the family, the church, the school, and the market, which is called friendship or love indifferently,—

is it in character unlike the love between the sexes? or is it substantially the same, differing a little only in the character of the thing exchanged?

In answering let us take notice that the whole of this barter of material and spiritual goods is accompanied, more or less, by an exchange of what is commonly called the *personal magnetism*,—something imperceptible to the eye or ear, but plainly enough perceptible to the touch. When we see two school-girls going along with their arms about each other, we know they are conscious of something pleasant to the touch, and pleasant even from near proximity. When we see two old friends with their four hands tightly clasped, while they gaze in each other's faces, we may be sure they are conscious of something pleasant to the touch, that is passing between them. It is the same when the child nestles close to the parent breast, when the cat and dog hold up their heads for the friendly stroke, when all animals manifest gladness at the kindly touch of a loving hand. It is what every one is familiar with, though few know how it is to be explained. The noteworthy fact is that it is not limited to persons of opposite sex, being common to friends and lovers, parents and children, pet animals and men, and even animals between themselves.

On the principle that the merchant becomes friendly with his customers, all those who exchange material or spiritual goods tend to become friendly, and to make mutual transfers of this personal magnetism. One sort of exchange leads to another. Not that the personal exchange depends on that of other things; for love, of one kind or another, may appear when two persons see each other for the first time; and then, conversely, this may lead to physical or mental transfers. In this respect the personal exchange is like all the rest. It differs only in what is exchanged; and this is the finest force, the choicest product of the human organism, a something no money, no labor, no sacrifice can buy, except to a very limited extent. It passes most freely when the return is of the same nature; yet this too must be adapted to the recipient's wants, else there is no exchange,—only a one-sided transaction, an offer not accepted.

Like some other forces, the personal magnetism possesses an attractive and a repulsive character or manifestation.

Between persons of opposite sex there is opportunity for a more extensive exchange of spiritual qualities, and of personal magnetism, than between persons of the same sex; because there are more unlikenesses of character; there is greater difference between male and female than between male and male or female and female. The greater the number of these unlikenesses the greater number of exchangeable things they possess (mental qualities and unlike services) and therefore the more intense the consciousness of the personal magnetic force exchanged with them. Not only is there more of it, but the magnetism itself, partaking of the quality of the individual and of the sex, is more unlike than in persons of the same sex; hence it is more needed and more strongly desired,—within certain limits of practical assimilation. When it is remembered that the sexes are as different in mental characteristics as in physical, the correctness of these statements will be readily apparent.

Attractive, that is, excellent, physical and mental qualities render the personal magnetism generally attractive; repulsive qualities make it repulsive; for it seems to take on and represent the whole nature of the individual, and is good, bad or indifferent accordingly; though the infinity of variations in persons makes that which is attractive to one indifferent or unpleasant to another in special cases.

We see then, that the manner in which love between the sexes differs from friendship, or from filial, parental, or fraternal love, is in its being richer in quality, from greater unlikeness, and larger in quantity from greater capacity for exchange; the desire for this and enjoyment of it being what constitutes love.

Knowing now what love is, and having such a complete analogy to reason by, we can tell when it is selfish or unselfish, and shall have an explanation of some strange exhibitions of it that appear about us every day. Much of it is called unselfish when in reality it is as selfish as anything possibly can be. In fact it is rarely otherwise than selfish. The test of unselfishness is not *love* at all, but *duty*. An unselfish love can be willing to give up its claim on the loved one, for the sake of duty, right, justice, the welfare of that one or of others. As long as it claims the love of some person as a reward for devotion—for so-called unselfish acts or self-denial—so long it is selfish only, enduring and suffering for its own sake, or doing so for another's happiness only because that is the way to obtain the love desired. We reason so unconsciously it seems instinctive, that in order to obtain the love of some individual we must do something to make that person happier; therefore we plan and labor, suffer and forbear, risk life, perhaps, in some desperate undertaking to gain or keep that love. Yet in all this there is nothing unselfish. Any wild animal will do the same. "But suppose a man not only risks, but deliberately sacrifices his life for the woman he loves,—is not this unselfish?" Hardly. The consciousness of having her gratitude, her admiration, is a partial reward for his love and his efforts. That may be something so sweet to him that, in the absence of it from any other quarter, he will take all risks, and be reconciled to die if necessary. When, on the contrary, he thinks of her happiness equally with his own, and for her sake gives her up to another, taking her admiration of his generosity only as a part of that which comes to him from all who know his course, then he is truly unselfish. But shall we call it unselfish love, or rather, unselfish duty and generosity?

"How is it with the mother whose love follows her wayward boy, in the fond hope of doing something to make him happier, or to recover his love for herself? Is not this unselfish?" If her predominant purpose is to make him happier by making him better, then her love is unselfish, that is, controlled by an unselfish motive. But if her object is to regain an affection for herself, then her love is just as selfish as any other person's, no matter what she may do. The test of a mother's unselfishness is her willingness to give up her children for their own welfare or happiness.

So with the sister's and the brother's love. It is not how much they may love when everything is in accordance with their wishes, that shows their unselfishness; but how much they can surrender their love, or their pride, or it may be, their property, when the happiness of the loved one requires a course to be taken which they do not like. This brings out the true character of the person, and the love, so plainly there need be no mistake. "The loved one's action may be unwise," you will say, "and it is this fact, not selfishness, that causes disagreement and opposition in such a case." But please remember that it is just as selfish to assume one's own superiority of judgment or purpose as to do any other selfish thing. The unselfish person is the one who can willingly admit that another's judgment or motive may be as good as his own, and probably is so. Only with this willingness can one be just. It is not always one can decide what is right or best for another, even when it seems so plain.

"When, however, the poor heartbroken wife clings to her drunken, disgraced and brutal husband, spite of all the misery he compels her to suffer,—then surely," you will assert, "it is an unselfish love that is thus manifested." No, it is not certain to be such, even in a case like this. The poor woman may have no ability to make herself useful, and obtain a livelihood, except by keeping house for this poor wretch of a husband; and no prospect of any sort of love from any one else. While her course *may* be one of pure self-abnegation, it is more likely she is doing the only thing possible for herself.

Test all the ordinary love of the sexes by the same rule, and we readily see that it contains very little of true unselfish feeling. Occasional instances may show it, as when a woman marries a man deformed by accident, after engaging him in a sound condition, or when a man proves faithful to a wife who becomes unfortunate. But even in some of these cases the motives are mixed, and in great preponderance this kind of love is like all the rest. "When a man commits suicide because he is rejected does that indicate unselfishness?" Not at all; the unselfishness would be on the part of the woman who should marry him to prevent his doing so. It is altogether probable that he loved one superior in development to himself—that he possessed too little of the higher mental and physical qualities to pay for the love he desired to obtain. Those he did possess were not of the kind that could make her happy; therefore not such as could win her affections. Though her qualities render her attractive to him, his are repulsive or indifferent to her, and there is little exchange or none. He might as well have offered to exchange copper for gold, or a pound of lead for a pound of silver, with a banker; and to blow his brains out when the exchange is declined would be no more wise or unselfish in one case than in the other.

Or suppose, instead of a difference in degree of development, it is development of a different kind on the same plane, that separates the parties; still it is like one man's offering another a bushel of apples for a bushel of potatoes, when the other wants nothing but onions. The one who offers and the one who declines are equally selfish in what they do; but neither thinks of making any complaint, or of being seriously disappointed; nor would anything of that kind occur in the other matter if the nature of the love exchange were equally well understood. Indeed, it would not then be desired; for every one would know it could give no permanent satisfaction.

With the woman who breaks her heart under similar circumstances the case is the same. There is no unselfishness; on the contrary, the man or woman who loves most, and is most disappointed, is, unknowingly, selfish to an extreme degree, in desiring such an unequal exchange. The unfortunate person makes a terrible mistake,—a mistake deserving the utmost pity and gentleness of treatment; but we cannot truly give it any better name.

There is yet another species of love, which passes for a worthy feeling, but really is not; it is the mere clinging dependence of the weak upon one who is stronger. It is not the natural preference of the physically weak woman for the strong man; but that of a childish and indolent helplessness, which clings and exacts, but gives nothing in return,—an over-prolonged babyishness, which maturity of years does not outgrow. It may fasten on an unworthy object, just as a little child clings to a brutal father; but is selfish only, and cannot be otherwise till the immature character is outgrown.

Those who may wish to criticise the theory of love that has here been announced will say that love generates or inspires love, when first offered, and even after one of the parties has at first repulsed it. This is quite true, except in those cases when one can too plainly see in the other the evidence of disagreeable qualities. So parties who have goods to exchange in trade are, as a general fact, glad to meet, and to compare the offered stocks, and disposed to be friendly, till one finds that the other has nothing that he wants; after which the disposition to be friendly, unless there is some additional cause for it, soon disappears. He may discover this very quickly, or be some time in doing so. If at first he thinks there is nothing desirable, but is afterward convinced by the other that there is, he is like the woman who is finally persuaded to love the man she at first dislikes, or like persons of the same sex affected in the same manner. But if the trading man finds himself deceived in the value of the thing for which he has given a genuine good article, he is then in the position of the dissatisfied lover or friend; and the analogy, or whatever the likeness may be called, of love to other exchange still holds good.

Now that we know the nature of love, and are also able to see what its moral quality is, let us next inquire into its purpose. All our old teachers, the priests and moralists, have taught us that its only natural purpose is the reproduction of the race. All other use for it has been considered base and vile, either openly or by implication. Although in later times some have claimed marriage to be a divine institution, it was so only for the sake of the family, and because unregulated love was degrading. Even reformers of the present century have taken the same ground, and earnestly contended that no other use than reproduction should be allowed to it. The scientists have been scarcely wiser, with few exceptions, chiefly in the medical profession.

The race itself being generally low, this view did not of course make love appear noble. It had always been

mainly that of the animal, and experience did not give
the teachers any higher light. All the great religions originated in Asia, where from time immemorial woman
has never been considered anything but a slave, and a
minister to man's sensuality; hence it was but natural
these religions, and their adherents, should assume love
to be as base by nature as it was in actual practice. One
of these religions, by a strange inconsistency, offers a
sensual paradise as a reward to the faithful; but all the
rest banish love as a vile thing, belonging only to the
earth and the condition of evil. And so their prophets
and priests, their monks, nuns, ascetics and saints, all
holy men and women, all indeed who have endeavored
to reach the purity of the spiritual life, have taught the
impurity and meanness of love, from the earliest times
to the present day. From the whole long line only
one prominent exception stands out; that one Emanuel
Swedenborg, who honored himself and his doctrines by
asserting the intention of love and marriage to be the
creation on earth of a race of angels, to form the heavenly
societies of the spiritual world; and who glorified it still
further by affirming a more unselfish type of love to be
the central delight of the joys of heaven, the first and
greatest source of happiness to all eternity. Leaving out
his influence, which is yet small, that of all other religionists has been toward making love base, and keeping it
so. And they have succeeded. All the manners and
customs, the literature and conversation, of our own
time, attest how thoroughly the common mind is saturated with the notion that love is something mean. The
talk to little girls and boys, the joking practiced on lovers,
the ostentatious celebration of weddings by the rich, the
coarse merrymaking on such occasions by the poor,
the obscene jests and stories current everywhere, the
commonness made of the whole matter, the profane
treatment of everything belonging to it,—all show how

lightly it is regarded. The carelessness of most women, and of nearly all men, about preserving their natural beauty, the red arms and hands of the housewife and kitchen girl, the sunburnt face of the farmer, the griminess, dirt, coarse dress, and slovenly bearing of mechanics, operatives and laborers, the stooping shoulders and ungraceful carriage,—all this has the same significance. It means that love is a fraud, a thing of no account, a dream of happiness for a few weeks or months, and afterward too low and contemptible for any thought or care about preserving the physical beauty, or spiritual graces, by which it is gained.

In a different direction, the shame with which the young girl, and the older prude, treat everything that hints of physical love is but another witness, telling how the indelicacy and brutality of their ancestors degraded this passion and made it shameful.

Still another evidence of the same great fact is the sentiment against *divorce*, in the Roman church, and the more conservative portion of the Protestant. Love is considered a feeling of such inferior character that its existence or non-existence between the married parties is a small matter. They may hate and torment each other during their whole lives; but that is not taken as a good reason for divorce. The external marriage of the church and the law is held a far more sacred thing than the happiness of the married couple. Unregulated love has its evils, and if these can be avoided by a legalized union, love itself may be crushed out entirely, or replaced by hatred, wrangling, and strife; yet the church looks on with entire indifference; it is concerned only when the suffering couples tear themselves apart. Love, in *its* view, is too much tainted by original sin to be worthy of any serious effort for its preservation. With the individual also, the viler he believes the passion to be the more unsparingly he will condemn any variation from the indissoluble marriage of the church.

But why has love been always base and profane? Because, like all other motives of the unprogressed man, it has been selfish. Why has it been a source of discomfort, misery, crime, disease and death? Because it has been morally unprincipled. Why has it been looked upon as merely animal, having no decent use but reproduction? Because man has been ignorant and unspiritual, having his childish eyes so fixed upon the sensual that he could see nothing else. He is now beginning to reach his mental maturity, and will soon discover not only that love has a purpose of infinite importance in reproduction, as taught by Swedenborg, namely, the generation of a race capable of regeneration into the perfect or angelic society, but also that it has other purposes, and that by becoming unselfish all its immense power, so long operating to cause misery and death, can be converted into a grand primary source of happiness and life. Then all the old notions and feelings regarding it will be changed. A revolution, greater than has ever occurred in religious or political ideas, will banish obscenity and shame and sexual profanity, and make everything belonging to this part of his nature, with the one exception of his conscience, his choicest and most sacred possession.

As to the first purpose, as stated above, no words can add to the solemnity of its importance, whether the lifetime of the race extends beyond the present physical bounds or not. No nobler function can the human organism be made to perform; no nobler motive to performance can possibly be imagined. Nothing could be better calculated than such a motive to transform into decency and honor the ignorant, unprincipled, and vile manner in which a large share of humanity is now generated and born for hell, as truly as if predestined there by a malevolent and merciless deity, as once believed.

But what additional purpose is there to this function, already ennobled by such a lofty one as the generation of a race having angelic capabilities? Is it another one equally important? No one can yet say *how* important it is, or may prove to be in the future. It is spoken of only as it appears at the nearest view. In a word, it is the vitality and health of the nerve system. And though this cannot be so fully proved as to make it demonstrable, there are indications so many and so plain as to put it almost beyond doubt.

First, the personal magnetism is itself a nerve force. It may or may not be the only one; but it is at least one. It radiates from the end of every nerve that comes to the skin, and makes itself perceptible to the touch, perceptible even in the clothing a person wears. It is felt by another through the extremities of the nerves in the skin, and is absorbed, conveyed, or transmitted inward by a movement the reverse of that which carries it out. What one gives out another absorbs, and this constitutes a large part of the exchange which is the satisfaction of love. But it may also develop hatred; that is, when so adapted and suitable as to be of use to the receiver it is agreeable or attractive, and is called love; when so unadapted or unsuitable as to be injurious to the recipient it is disagreeable or repulsive, and gives rise to hatred. The more close and complete the contact of persons the more intensely it is enjoyed if agreeable, and the more thoroughly disliked if repulsive. That from the unselfish person is always pleasant; that of the selfish is liable to be or to become unpleasant or repulsive in various degrees under varying circumstances.

Although a force it thus becomes a food for the nerves and brain, supplying them with something of which they make constant use, but which possesses some quality different from that generated within themselves. Every person is more or less conscious of needing it, that is, of needing the company of the opposite sex, from whom it is obtained. Few, perhaps, will admit this in so many words, their old ideas of love having made it an impropriety to do so; the conduct of almost every one will prove it nevertheless. Everybody, too, is in some degree conscious of receiving it; and some persons have professed their consciousness of its reception from parties at a considerable distance. That it furnishes an element which is necessary and healthful, when of the right kind, is abundantly proved by the eagerness with which every one accepts it, and by the renewed brightness, cheerfulness, energy and good nature manifested afterward, as well as by the dullness, indifference, gloom, and irritability of those who are deprived of it. The facts of this kind are universal, and well known to all who observe closely. Another confirmation of its healthfulness comes from the numerous cures of disease by "magnetic healers," with whom it is an open secret that patients of opposite sex to the physician are more easily affected than those of the same sex, and respond more quickly to its healthful influence.

Aside from this kind of evidence, familiar to all as soon as they take time to think, there is another sort, better known to men of science. All the natural secretions of the body are by a happy love, or other happy state of mind, rendered pure, sweet, bland, and healthful; while grief, hatred, disappointment, outrage, despair make them sour, acrid, bitter, and poisonous. The virus of hydrophobia, and that of syphilis and scrofula may yet be found to have this kind of origin.

In both conditions the *secretions* are the bearers of a magnetism agreeing in character with their own. In their pure and wholesome state, as produced by love, certain of them are designed or adapted to be absorbed by each sex from the other; and then, passing into the blood, they become in a double sense food for the brain and nerves, consisting as they do of both force and material substance. If the established proprieties of the subject did not forbid, in such a place, an argument from anatomy could be brought, which would furnish a strong support to this position. But without aid from anatomy the general position that love feeds, supports, gives life, health, and strength to the nervous system, has abundant proof in that negative kind of evidence furnished by the unwholesome, even deadly, effects of unnatural, selfish, and depraved love; and by the weak, shrivelled, distorted mental character of those who endure prolonged affectional starvation. For, who are those wrecks of men who suffer from general debility in middle age, and those hosts of nervous women still younger, that are capable only of lingering misery and torment,—who are they mostly but the victims of abnormal, selfish, sensual, oppressive, and debasing love, either in themselves or their parents? Does the reader think there is some slander in that? Possibly there is; but if the medical men, the confessors, the husbands and wives would all testify I should have little fear of being condemned for the statement. And if an unprincipled, degrading love can give origin to such a vast amount of weakness, disease, misery and death as we see around us, and known by the well-informed to be so caused, why should not the same mighty influence become wholesome and life-giving, in every sense, when it is natural, clean, conscientious, unselfish and ennobling? It does. The man or woman who possesses the enjoyment of a true love is not weak, sickly, peevish or depraved. He or she knows, as quick as it is mentioned, what is the central source and cause of the mental and bodily health enjoyed. And predominantly that health is mental. It is brightness, activity, wit, clearness, sanity, hope, energy, determination—all the powers that belong to a healthy brain.

The persons here referred to are of course those in middle life, not the young whose natural fund of nervous vitality has never been exhausted. I cannot give illustrations, or make exceptions that may be required, but am willing to leave the general statement to the experience of all good observers for confirmation.

There is still another kind of proof worthy of notice in regard to the second purpose of love. It has already been stated that some of the lowest living things cease their existence at the time of reproduction; and that some even as high as insects live but a short space afterward. Of many of the higher animals we do not know whether they reproduce all their lives or not, and of the domesticated ones we cannot tell how long they would live after ceasing to reproduce if allowed to live. But the human female is known to live twenty, thirty, forty or even fifty years after childbearing has become impossible. In a long life nearly or quite one-half of it belongs to the post-reproductive period. Now, in the masculine half of humanity we know that neither love nor the power of generation ceases at middle age, nor for a long time afterward. But if reproduction were the only object of love why should not the power of reproduction cease in man as soon as it does in woman? We are aware of no such peculiarity in animals; it is in the human only that the male retains this ability long after the female has lost it. It scarcely need be said that love endures still longer. How is it with the woman,—does love die out in her along with the power of childbearing? It does, and it does not. If her experience of it has been with the selfish and base kind, quite likely she is willing to forget that she possesses any such faculty. In other cases she has been compelled to crush out the feeling as far as possible, because it could have no satisfaction. But every woman who has had a pleasant experience of love, who knows that it can be pure and honest and unselfish,—every such one, I presume to assert, is capable of love to old age, and as long as man. There are numbers of old people of both sexes who are consciously aware of their need of love as the one thing which more than all else would conserve their waning strength, and enable them to die comfortably of old age. Furthermore, it seems to me probable, almost certain, that in some few fortunate cases love has been an important factor in renewing the youth and restoring the special senses of sight and hearing in such old persons. Everything we know regarding the post-reproductive period of life is in harmony with the supposition that love has for a secondary purpose the support and renewal of nervous vitality; while without such a theory all this class of facts is without explanation.

In addition to the above might be cited the testimony of various medical men, and other parties, to confirm the doctrine here put forth. The best confirmation of all, however, is the fact that every one is instinctively conscious of needing, desiring, and enjoying love without any thought of its primary object. Every honest man who ever felt the attractiveness of a sweet little ten-year-old girl; every mother who ever discovered that her twelve-year-old boy was dearer to her than any of his sisters; knows that love, in civilized people, may get far away from its primitive animal character, that it is comforting, delightful, precious, notwithstanding all thought of the original motive and object out of which this more human love has grown, is entirely put away from the mind as impossible. So it is with the little boy who may not be more than seven or eight years old when some stranger little girl child becomes pleasanter to him than any other, and far more so than any of his own sex. This is the beginning of that romantic feeling which is the inspiration of so much song, story, and art, and which changes the life of every man and woman who is touched by its sacred fire. These men, women, and children now spoken of are those who have been described as well sexed; that is to say, some fortunate and happy experience of love in their parents or previous ancestry has so modified the organization they inherit that their whole thought and character is changed or sexized, so as to render them capable of perceiving and appreciating every peculiarity of the opposite sex, whether in the mature person or the child; and ready to manifest the proper responsive qualities. This, if love were unselfish, would be a very happy organization; as things are it is liable to make its possessor very miserable. But here is a hint which parents, if they are wise, may turn to good account. Though love cannot have its full satisfaction in a complete exchange of personal influences, it may have it in part. If every father had sufficient of this sexized character to bestow on his young daughter some of those little attentions, sympathies, caressings which she instinctively desires from some one, she would not be so ready to fall in love with the first young fool or scapegrace who should show her any partiality. If every mother would treat her growing boy in the same manner he would not become a stranger to her and to his sisters, homelessly seeking his companionship wherever he can find it, better or worse as may happen, and often bad. Both parents would retain an influence over their children, which now they lose before the child is fairly in its teens. Ah! how many homes are made dreary or even desolate, how many young lives are ruined, by that devilish old notion of ignorant piety that love is base and shameful, and that all manifestation of anything resembling it in the family must be suppressed as silly or wicked. Truly, it has turned the inner sanctuary of the human heart into a den of wild beasts and creeping things. And though intelligent people have outgrown and escaped it, the masses of men, women and children are still affected by its baleful influence; and we see its effects about us in homeless families, and read of them in all the newspapers, in accounts of elopements, divorces, jealousy murders and suicides, and all sorts of foolish, desperate, and criminal love-making.

Love, then, has two main purposes,—one the giving of life to a new generation, the other to give vitality to the more highly developed parts of the whole organism. It is thus life-giving in a double sense. It is a source of life to the child and to its parents—not a necessary dissipation of the parents' life, like reproduction in the lowest animals. The contrast of its effects is as great as the difference of development between the lowest animal forms and the highest human. This is the great point, and it nullifies the validity of all the old notions upon the subject. Although the human experience of love has been of an ignorant, selfish, and degrading kind, ruinous in all its tendencies, yet the effects of a truthful, conscientious, unselfish and intelligent love will be as unlike those of the old as heaven is unlike hell. In this respect the experience of the past gives no indication of the future. This is to have a glory and success equal to the failure and disgrace of that.

CHAPTER XIV.

LOVE.

Continued.

YET a third purpose or end, of the love passion, is the reconciliation of the sexes; a thing much to be desired, but which can never be effected so long as love is in disgrace, or held in little esteem. Friendship can exist only with equality and mutual respect; but as long as love is mainly sensual, and woman is looked upon as a minister to man's pleasure, with an unfortunate liability to bear children, so long will men treat her with contempt and injustice, all the worse because she is so dependent on him for the means of living. But when the generation and birth of a child shall come to be viewed as unselfish work of the noblest character, and be entered upon as a matter of high generosity and duty to a possible human being; when love, along with its beauty and charm, shall be seen to have a *use* of the utmost importance as a means of health and long-continued life; then woman becomes of equal value with man, her functions of equal necessity, her contributions equally precious with his. Her industrial dependence will still for the present give man the superior power; but it will be less arbitrary and unjust; the equality of sex value will do more than any other one thing to secure that peace, re-, spect, and mutual sympathy between the sexes which ought naturally to exist in abundant measure.

Some minor results will likewise follow. The sense of shame, and the blush which outwardly signifies it, will disappear along with the coarse, ignorant sensuality from which they were born, when love shall take on its unselfish phase. So too will that shameless and profane *frivolity*, which now tells how contemptible a thing love is in the estimation of the masses of men and women. Delicacy, respect, appreciation, even reverence, will take the place of both, as one effect of the new ideas and better motives that are to come. Another result will be *charity* in place of the present merciless severity, manifested by a society having little of the social spirit, toward those who break its rules, especially when the offenders are women, and incapable of self-defence. There are women of highly developed organization, fine feelings and good purposes, persons who would save the life of the meanest insect under their feet, or risk their own to nurse some sufferer back to health, who, because they are fine-grained and sensitive, are susceptible to every kind of tender sentiment—individuals who in an unselfish society would become worthy, loved and happy members of it, yet who have been tempted or provoked into taking without society's consent the love they could not otherwise obtain, and then have been fairly hounded to their death by the heartless persecution of both women and men. Not untruly has society been called "a monster devouring its own children;" and this is one mode of exhibiting its ferocity. Let us believe that when a nobler and wiser society makes its appearance, persons capable of so much goodness will be understood as they are, and saved to lives of usefulness in spite of their errors or faults.

"But is not this a generosity that encourages to evil?"

is the ready objection. Not at all. The kind of people referred to are not those whose natural tendency is toward evil, but good. If society were half just to them they would be quite as just toward others. Society deliberately shuts out all unmarried women from love, no matter what their character or circumstances may be, but allows all men to get it wherever and whenever they can, by any means short of the most brutal physical force. To suppose such injustice as this to be good for society, or that the abolition of it would be bad, seems to me the grossest kind of delusion. The method of correcting it has been already pointed out, in Chapter XI.

What will unselfish love do for the married? is another question which many people will wish to have answered. Will it make them all contented and happy? No, it cannot make them all happy; no power in earth or heaven could do that. First, because some of them are too badly mismated to be otherwise than miserable; and secondly, because many of them have the selfish nature too strong relatively to be brought under its influence, and such can never be happy very long. But many others, those who can surrender to it, would be made happier, and enabled to obtain whatever happiness is possible to them in their present relations. The amount of it they cannot know till unselfish thought and conduct has brought it all out. In some cases there might be better results than could previously be hoped for; and in every case there could be nothing less than good feeling. For no one can avoid giving respect and admiration to true unselfishness. But it must be true; there must be no fraud about it, conscious or unconscious; no incompleteness in the work of repentance; no lowering of the standard a true unselfishness sets up. This repentance, like any other, requires a conviction of sin, a consciousness of guilt, a sense of the meanness, dishonesty, tyranny and slavishness of a selfish love, of the wrong done, the suffering caused by it, and the justice of resistance to its demands. No promise given in ignorance or delusion must be made an excuse; for no person can certainly promise love beyond the present; the utmost one can say is, "I love you now; if you are sincerely conscientious I cannot hate you, whether much or little I may love." No honorable man in trade would hold another bound to deliver goods promised in such entire ignorance of the conditions necessary to their production as young people are in when they promise to give each other love, an exchange beyond comparison in importance. When all demand or claim is given up, when nothing is asked but what can be honestly attracted, won, and paid for by equally attractive qualities in the person who seeks, then and then only has either party a right to ask forgiveness, to speak of reconciliation, or expect any genuine good will. Such a position is the only honest, and manly or womanly one that can be taken; and whatever sacrifice of pride or of hope it requires must be made. Nothing less than complete justice can completely satisfy. Nothing less than perfect liberty can take away all fear; and where there is fear of tyranny or selfish exaction true love without alloy cannot exist. When fear is gone and freedom takes its place, if there are any gems of affection they will spring up and grow. No person can withhold respect for one who thus proves his or her nobility of spirit; and respect is the first stage toward something better. Then if no love is asked for but what is for the benefit or pleasure of the opposite party as much as for that of the one who seeks it, no further injustice will be done; and if the parties ever truly loved at all they will be likely to find their love renewed, in a way that will make it a permanent thing. If not love there will at least be peace and comfort. If such a spirit and purpose could get into all our discordant homes it would turn very many of them into abodes of joy.

A few additional matters, however, need to be considered in order for these reconciled parties to avoid all future discord. One of these is politeness. The unselfish spirt is that out of which all sincere politeness grows; it possesses it in purpose or intention; but it should be put into form, should be expressed, should show itself plainly, not remain to be guessed or assumed.

A more important thing of a similar kind is the right of privacy, of seclusion, of separation, whenever desired. The habit so many married people have of always occupying a room together, of always eating at the same table, always being tied to each other's company, is enough to destroy the strongest affection that ever existed between two persons. They become tired of one another inevitably. When charged and surfeited with the magnetism from each other's presence they cannot avoid being indifferent; if forced to endure more they become repulsive and quarrel; while every disagreement, criticism, or impoliteness makes their condition perpetually worse. For a couple to place themselves in such a situation is as irrational as if they sentenced themselves to eat one kind of food only, during their lives, and to eat of that continually. Under such circumstances the wonder is not that marriages are unhappy, but that they are endurable at all. Each one should have an apartment so strictly private and sacred that the other would never think of entering it without invitation or permission. This is a simple natural right, which nobody should be expected to lose by being married. No unselfish person could object to it; and without it it is doubtful if even the most self-sacrificing spirit can enable the married to escape some friction and annoyance.

But assuming that peace and good will, with a certain degree of love, are assured to the married parties, and they desire to increase that love, then this is to be done by an increase of spiritual sympathy. By this I mean religious, moral, and intellectual sympathy. Without it there can be no very strong love. Every man and woman desires a companion that he or she can love more supremely than any other one of that sex; and the ideal of their conduct is that neither shall ever willingly say or do aught that can give the other pain or regret. Such a love and companionship is what most people attempt to realize when they marry; but very·few actually obtain it. In order to possess it there must be a unity of religious and philosophical views, an agreement in motives and purposes, and a simultaneous learning with and from each other of all that either one may know or learn separately. The last requirement is the most important of the three. Those who without pride, conceit, or self-righteousness can learn together the same truths, can accept candidly from each other whatever either one has to impart, thus travelling the same intellectual road in close company, will be almost sure to realize a sympathy in regard to nearly all the great concerns of life. The deepest source of trouble in this world is that there is so little honesty, so little unselfishness, in people's thinking; in the marriage relation as in all others. Besides, love is that one subject of which less is known than of any other; and there is less willingness to learn about it than about anything else. The native selfishness of the human heart clings so tenaciously to a desirable love once obtained that no criticism is allowed, no reasoning submitted to, in regard to it, or to the marriage institution; though the latter may be little better than a whited sepulchre. Yet love is the very thing a married couple should have the same knowledge about, the same aspirations concerning, the same determination to render as perfect as possible. An agreement here is more essential than anywhere else; and a mutual high appreciation of love itself ought to be the very first article in the mental sympathy of those who love.

Spiritual love and physical are the two opposite poles, or hemispheres rather, of the whole complex thing. When it is selfish, a spiritual sympathy having for its objects wealth, ambition, popularity, power, is unworthy, disappointing, and morally degrading, as truly as a selfish physical animality. It is an ignorant or an unprincipled *selfishness* that makes either kind of love unworthy. There is no need of disparaging the physical. Body and spirit are equally holy or unholy. Unselfish physical and spiritual love are both equally pure, equally honorable, equally excellent and happifying. A sensuality that is natural and honest, that is enjoyed for its *uses*, that has wise and noble purposes underlying it, is not inferior to any spiritual enjoyment. The conscientious spirit behind it sanctifies the whole, rendering it pure, righteous, wholesome, vitalizing, and morally improving. It has been well contended that in a true state of things physical love is the natural basis out of which spiritual sympathy, and all the higher forms of love and generous sentiment, should rise by spontaneous evolution, till the very highest was reached. And I have no doubt that the reverse process, from the spiritual to the physical, is equally effective and equally excellent in both physical and mental results. Each kind of love naturally inspires the other, and contributes to its development; a most appropriate evidence of the nobility of both.

The prevalent views regarding all these things are so egregiously imperfect or unscientific as to be almost worthless. Old thinkers and religionists have had their eyes so fastened upon a senseless and debauched love, which they found to be demoralizing, that they never conceived of it with any better character. Hence they gave it a bad name, and shut it out of their heaven. But when unselfish love makes its appearance in this world both phases of it will possess such a heavenly aspect that pious people will be glad to take it into heaven, or to stay on earth for its sake; while all men and women will discover that it is the selfish spirit associated with love that makes it vile, and that unselfishness renders it worthy of an archangel. Nothing impure, unclean, unwholesome, unrefined, or in any sense demoralizing, need ever be associated with love, any more than with an angel's holiest thought.

There is yet one other point, however, remaining to be discussed before this whole subject of love can be properly and fully understood; and that is the position which men and women as sexes naturally occupy toward each other. Are they equals, standing on the same level, but doing different work, for different ends? Or are they superior and inferior, one standing higher in the scale of development; and if so which is the superior? These are questions which cultivated women of our time have brought into debate, though formerly women and men alike had but one opinion, and that unfavorable to women. Without attempting to review the ideas that have been put forward, I will here only offer the bare outline of a theory, leaving it to prove itself as it may to the minds of thoughtful observers.

This theory arises out of biological facts, and so far as I know agrees with all of them that have any bearing. It is that the feminine or germ-producing sex is primary, and that the male, or one that produces fecundating material, is a secondary or later development. Like all other later developments, it is a higher or more complete development. Attention has previously been called to the fact that the primary, the original, the basic thing has a superiority in intrinsic value, as being more indispensable than that which proceeds or evolves from it; while the secondary or later growth has a superiority of rank or quality, in other words, a higher degree of evolution. Furthermore, this later and higher evolution of the male *is itself what constitutes masculinity*. There is nothing in the differences existing between the sexes but what is produced by this more complete evolution; this alone is all that is necessary to explain whatever needs to be accounted for in their unlike pecularities.

The facts that sustain these positions may be found in the various Biological departments of Genesis, Embryology and Growth, as exhibited in all forms of life, from the lowest to the human. Briefly, it may be said that the lowest animal and vegetal forms produce germs capable of such trifling evolution as they possess, without the aid of any material from unlike germs, either within themselves or in separate individuals; these last arising in higher forms at a later period. Also, that whatever renders embryologic development slower and more difficult tends to produce the male sex in *physique*, just as the education of hard circumstances, and the slow, persistent overcoming of obstacles, generates the heroic character, or *spiritual* masculinity; and as wrestling with difficult intellectual problems develops the *mental* penetration that discovers the secrets of Nature, and exhibits them in new inventions and generalizations; this latter faculty being manifested, to any considerable extent, only by the male human, and being the surest evidence of his superiority of development. All three of these are essentially the same process, namely, that of development under difficulties, and by virtue of the stimulation that obstacles produce upon the growing physical germ, or upon the expanding intellect and character.

This superiority of development makes man, in a predominant sense, the teacher and leader of woman, while woman's superiority in the primary qualities she has retained makes her the conservator, the prudent, careful protector of what is already possessed. By natural instinct she is a timid, blind conservative, merely; but by acquiring the knowledge which man has exploited from Nature, she becomes a more far-seeing and efficient protector than before. In a subdominant sense she teaches man, and renders him more effective in his own mental functions.

On the self-evident principle that woman has a natural right to whatever of good man enjoys, man is morally bound to elevate woman into his own superior development as completely as possible. This, in short, is the duty of the superior to the inferior of his or her own sex, or of any race, class, or condition whatever, according to the same moral principle that every one is equally entitled to happiness so far as one is, or can become, capable of enjoying it. The rule applies without limit, and is the highest standard of justice.

Man is thus bound to communicate his knowledge to woman, and she in return to accept it and impart to him what she has to teach in her own department, which he is as much bound to accept, each on the supposition that to teach confers happiness on the teacher. The reverse proposition should also be true, and learning as agreeable as teaching; but unfortunately the selfish spirit seems to stand in the way.

Comparing this mental proceeding to a physical one easily understood, let us suppose a man and woman setting out on an excursion toward the top of a high hill not too difficult for either of them to climb. The woman expects the man, he being the strongest, to find the best way, and lead in it, to help her over the difficult places, to do whatever requires muscular strength, and to point out whatever he finds that is beautiful or interesting, for her entertainment. What does he expect of her? To be willing to keep in his company, to follow when he finds a path, to make some effort herself when he tries to assist her through a hard spot, to show some appreciation of the landscapes that come into view, and the small objects of beauty or utility, seen as they pass along or gathered up for future enjoyment. She contributes to his entertainment by the conversation that springs as a reaction from the appreciation of all these things, and is stimulated to discover some that he does not.

This is a not unfair type of the *mental* progression which man and woman together should make; a companionship in all learning, all thought, and in the feeling and action consequent on learning and thought. The direction to be taken, and the end to be sought, must of course be agreed upon before they set out.

The man who is not desirous to take the woman up this mental elevation, into his own highest and best thought, is not a spiritually masculine man,—his masculinity is only animal; and the woman not willing to accompany the man up the intellectual heights as far as he can aid her to go is yet in spirit only a child, and an animal in her femininity. And this mental upgoing includes the moral; for notwithstanding her claim, often made, of moral superiority, woman is not the moral superior of man except in the negative sense, and so far as weakness or timidity prevents her being immoral. The mind must have intelligence of a high order before it can have true morality.

But suppose the man lies down at the first comfortable spot, and refuses to aid the woman, or to go any farther on the trip? Or if he goes must be coaxed or urged to make an advance? Can the woman love or respect such a man?

Or if the woman has to be urged along in spite of indifference or timidity, and carried wholly by the man's strength over all the rough and steep places, with no interest taken in the pleasant things found on the way? Will not the man lose his respect for woman, or wish he had taken some other individual of the sex for his companion? Certainly; both of them will manifest the feeling so easily seen in ordinary marriage.

Suppose further, that he is anxious to advance so rapidly he does not take time to see all the beautiful things, or gather up all the treasures on the route, to be carried along. Or if she is so slow that she dallies over a thousand little nothings, wasting time that might be more usefully spent in going on. Then here is occasion for mutual remonstrance, persuasion, and exhortation that shall modify the disposition of one or both, and enable them to go on together peacefully if not happily.

Now, the mental excursion, through the fields of science, and up the hills of moral difficulty, is substantially the same. The man and woman must keep together, he to make easy the path and help her along, she to follow and keep as near by his side as possible. She is not by nature a thinker, and cannot be to much extent a discoverer of new truth; but once found she can be enabled to understand it, just as the mechanical invention, though it can be made only by one in a thousand, can be understood or learned by all persons of ordinary mind. The best female minds are at least capable of following where the ablest men may lead. And of the best male minds I have no doubt that each one would be glad to communicate to some woman all he learns, and thus endeavor to keep her abreast of himself in his progress.

But if either one of the parties is unable or unwilling to do his or her part toward maintaining an equal pace in their mental progression, and sharing in all the difficulties and achievements of it, then there is no true marriage worthy of the name between them, whatever it may be called by such a society as originally made the institution.

Of course, if neither one has arrived to a state of mental growth where there is desire for such mental excoursing, it can make little difference who their partners are, and they may as well be tied together irrevocably in the manner of the Catholic church.

As a slight digression it may be added, that conservatism being a womanly sentiment, much of the general idea here expressed has its application to Conservatism and Radicalism. The Conservatism that acknowledges progress, but seeks to preserve whatever of good can be carried along, or with wise prudence aims to make progress safe, sure, and solid as it goes on, should not need to have any quarrel with Radicalism; for Radicalism needs all its aid, and should court its good will. The mere miserly instinct that clings to everything, good, bad or indifferent, and the lazy inertness, or blind timidity, that refuses to move in any direction—these will not wed with Radicalism, or have any joy in its company. Neither will a radicalism that is reckless and bigoted have any influence with Conservatism. The two parties are as sadly at variance as the generality of men and women. They are opposites that should be counterparts instead of antagonists. And as the germ of progressiveness exists in all persons, the more masculine element should not refuse all effort to stimulate this kind of life into activity, in even the most inert. When Radicalism, knowing its own position, shall approach Conservatism in the same mental tone with which man approaches the merely passive or indifferent woman, some good not now anticipated may be the result.

"But we are afraid, notwithstanding, that your doctrine will tend to destroy marriage, scatter families, and overturn all domestic arrangements,"—the timid ones will still object. Yet it is self-evident that to teach justice will not make conditions worse, but better, to all who accept it. Even if there be danger, let us see what this instituion is that some people consider so sacred no word can be allowed against it. Here is what is written concerning it by a man well in years, whose profession as a clergyman, and his acquaintance with new social experiments, gave him unusual opportunities for observation and correct judgment.

"The most stringent, vigorous and durable of social institutions depends for its stability on a love which is a mere ephemerality. The tyrannous attraction that draws natural couples together is usually the beginning of a long enforced captivity. In the majority of instances the decease of one of the parties is soon felt by the other as a relief.

"The natural man is tyrannical, the natural woman capricious and exacting. Union after a time results in coldness, and with coldness, and knowledge of each other's infelicities, passional attraction is succeeded by indifference. The relation is maintained afterward by external considerations and stringencies, by law, by custom, by the church, by material interests, and by the family circle.

"Natural marriage is not an inter-freedom, but an inter-slavery. It is not to be criticised on solely natural grounds; for it is the best and highest institution possible for the mere sexual creature, framed in selfishness and obsequious to animal desire. Yet when stripped of its fine illusions it is commonly an ignoble fraud.

"The natural man is educated by a succession of illusions. * * Married partners with the advance of life generally discover that each possesses a private individuality in which the other does not share. When this revelation is opened there is an interior divorce. * * Then begins the solitude, then the experiences of a hidden life. * * In almost every case, by the very force of their latent virtuousness, the millions of married associates press apart from each other. Where there is no essential fitness there is no permanency of relation. Natural marriage begins by attraction, but is maintained by cocercion. The result of all this wedlock of unfitness is that men and women drag out existence in the midst of perpetual tortures."—T. L. HARRIS.

So far as I am able to judge, this statement is correct. Of such unions as I have had opportunity to observe, very few appeared to be really happy—less than a dozen in all. How could it be otherwise? Society, in its policy regarding love, is almost wholly selfish, caring little except to make sure that children shall be supported by the parents. The young are left to grow up in ignorance, and in vice if it so happens. The unmarried are forced to steal or starve; the married, except in a few extreme cases, are bound together for life, whether happy or miserable. Christian legislators follow Jesus or St. Paul, neither one of whom, probably, knew more than his contemporaries about love. The medical profession has been scarcely wiser than the priestly and the legal; all blind leaders of the blind, having learned nothing for a thousand years. No wonder the general result is misery, with frequent occasional ones of seduction, rape, jealousy, murder and suicide.

Will a little new truth be likely to make such a condition of things worse? It is hardly possible. Like that of an old sore, the sensitiveness of the institution to being touched is a symptom of the corruption within; which can be let out only by the keen lance of critical thought. Marriage, like every other human arrangement, must submit to criticism finally, and the sooner the better. As for the married themselves, their only true and honest course is to reconcile the past if possible, and begin anew with higher views and purposes. It is the selfish spirit, principally, that has made them miserable; it is the unselfish that is to make them happy.

In the Kingdom of the Unselfish there will be no heart-burning, no jealousy, no sense of wrong from unrequited love, no seduction, no adultery, no affectional starvation. No one will attempt to deprive another of his or her happiness; no one will claim any love that he or she cannot attract and keep by his or her own worthiness. Parents will not try to escape from their children, nor to murder them before they are born; for they will be the children of love, brought into the world for their own well being, quite as much as for the pleasure of their creators. The unmated and unfortunate will not be deserted; for when love is acknowledged as the right of all some effort will be made to secure the possibility of their obtaining what they need; and they will at least receive something better than heartless derision and neglect.

What all the developments of an unselfish love, enlightened by science, will be it is too soon to predict. All the data for conclusions do not yet exist. It is sufficient to know that they will be only good. An impulse that is both just and wise can do no harm, and is not to be judged from experience of such love as the world has hitherto possessed. Of the old ideas, we are sure that they have led to the most debasing of all tyranny and slavery, and in frequent occasional instances to the most fiendish of all crimes. The new, being opposite in character and tendency, may be expected to have opposite results. As the old doctrines, habits, and purposes generated disease, misery, and death, the new truth, and the unselfish spirit, will evolve health, happiness, and life. Of all the changes brought about by the evolution of unselfishness those connected with this master passion will be the greatest and most important. Of all the gospels ever brought to mankind this one of a love redeemed from ignorance, brutality, and sin will be the most joy-giving and precious. Whoever, after bringing the other departments of his nature into harmony with the law of unselfishness, as previously explained, shall finally convert and subordinate the love feeling, and thus come to understand the full meaning of this new evangel, and to experience its full effects, may expect to realize the joys of the third heaven in the life on earth.

CHAPTER XV.

RELIGIOSITY AND RELIGION.

IN adding one more to the innumerable discussions on Religion, I do so with the excuse of believing there is still something more to be said from the scientific point of view, before any substantial agreement among thoughtful minds will be reached. Until such harmony shall be arrived at, the importance of the subject will render discussion inevitable.

The main point to be presented here has regard to the religious feeling. What is the precise nature of that feeling, and what the end to be attained by its operation, —its real purpose and its accomplishment? Can these be stated any better than they have been stated a thousand times already? Perhaps not, but they can at least be stated differently, if not more rationally.

Let us see if we can discover anything by an analogical process.

When we find a plant rapidly putting forth healthy leaves and branches, preparatory to blossoming and fruiting, we say it is thrifty, it will get a good growth, and produce a crop of wholesome fruit, it is having its natural development, it is *doing well.*

When we see a young animal in the same healthy and growing condition we speak well of that also; it is doing all that could be expected of it, and gives good promise of becoming a perfect animal. We do not accuse it of anything wrong.

If it is a child, growing a strong, well-proportioned, graceful body, not necessarily large, eating and sleeping, playing and working, doing these heartily and regularly, we praise it as a good-looking, healthy child. If it is bright and wide awake, quick to see and hear, to remember and understand, cheerful and well disposed, we say it has a healthily growing mind, and promises to be an intelligent, capable man or woman. It is doing well, doing all it could be asked to do. We do not bring any charge against it, nor, ordinarily, speak of it as being irreligious.

Now, what are mature men and women doing when they are doing their best? Is it making money, getting office, becoming leaders of fashion, racing yachts, studying art, or acquiring culture? Not at all. No one takes either of these things to be the noblest vocation of a human being. If we ask the religionist what it is he says *religion;* if the agnostic or freethinker be questioned he answers *morality*. If these two were acknowledged to be one, as I hope to show that they are, and that both parties unknowingly mean precisely the same, then the answer is that man is doing his best work when he is becoming religious, or cultivating true goodness. The desire to do that is his highest aspiration; that is the blossom and fruit of the human plant.

Supposing this to be correct, what is it but to say that the religious feeling is the desire to become moral, the aspiration to be unselfish—to be just, generous, humane, magnanimous, benevolent, and all the rest, the longing after moral perfection, the desire to *grow* in all the peculiarly *human* qualities? And what is this but the same impulse in man which in the plant is the tendency to grow, to blossom and bear fruit, and in the animal to become the full-grown, perfect, reproductive animal? This tendency is what I mean by Religiosity.

But the religionist will immediately insist that religion is something more than morality, and different from it; something more even than "morality touched by emotion." Prof. Drummond in that remarkable work, "Natural Law in the Spiritual World," refers to the Sermon on the Mount as an embodiment of the religious spirit, and triumphantly asks, "What moralist ever proposed to advocate such monitions as rules of morality?" We may admit that no one ever did, that the distinction between religion and morality has always been kept up, and still the two things can be shown to be in essence one. Perhaps the Sermon on the Mount will furnish as suitable a test as could be named.

No one will deny that justice is morality. I have previously exhibited it as equality, and the love of equality as the love of justice. Now, to be *meek*—to be mild, patient, peaceable under the infliction of evil—we may have three kinds of motive, one, that of duty to God, which is a form of gratitude, and springs from a sense of justice, as does gratitude in all cases. Another motive comes from the enlightened consciousness or reflection that the person who does evil is more unfortunate than we are, in the fact that he desires to be, or can be, unjust to us. Our willingness to be patient and gentle with him is then prompted by benevolence, which is a semiconscious acknowledgment that he is entitled to generosity because he is entitled to better fortune or greater happiness; this again being a sense of what is just, as it is all the while assumed that the wicked, mean, or unjust man is an unhappy one. The third motive is aspiration, the desire to possess both justice and generosity because they are right in bringing greater happiness to both self and others. The result coming from all three is the same, that there is an advance toward greater equality of happiness between the doer of wrong and the sufferer, because the latter has been meek. The fact that he can be meek is the proof of his previous moral superiority, and the good effect of meekness on the wrong-doer is an indication that he too has made an advance.

To be "poor in spirit," what is it but to avoid arrogance and haughtiness, to invade no one's personality, to assume nothing, to claim no more than the poorest and humblest can share, to willingly submit to what is just and right, however mean the claimant may be, to ignore superiority and make the lowest, the weakest, the most unfortunate the equal of oneself as nearly as possible, to take these along abreast of us in the same rank, in appearance, or go down to theirs if necessary. You may call it lowering ourselves if you will, or a raising of them; morally it is a raising of both, and lessens the distance between superior and inferior, in both character and happiness.

Those who "hunger and thirst after righteousness," in the best sense of the word, are they who love justice and equality for all, and aspire after freedom from all wrong-doing. The same feeling is enjoined by a high morality. The merciful and the peacemakers are they who aim to lighten the misery of others, suffering from their own selfishness or unjust conduct. The same peaceful and merciful ones, when they see an individual who has been too happy to have any understanding of misery, would willingly see him suffer enough to render him conscious of what suffering means to others, and dispose him to sympathy; all which shows that these classes of good people, acting from benevolence or generosity, have at bottom an unconscious desire to see an equality of happiness.

The "pure in heart" are they who shall become thoroughly and permanently dominated by the spirit of unselfish goodness, and thereby shall come to have a knowledge of God. Their whole natures are moralized. I shall speak of them more at length in a separate chapter, on Conversion.

The teaching that deadly anger is murder, that lust is adultery, and intended crime of any kind is criminal, needs no discussion; it is equally true whether the offence be called moral or religious, and has no peculiar religious quality. The condemnation of ostentatious prayer, alms-giving and fasting is in accordance with the same idea; for as guilty purpose makes guilt, and absence of it takes away guilt, so absence of true virtuous purpose from alms-giving or prayer prevents it from being true prayer or charity. The self-righteous criticism that would pull a mote from a brother's eye while a larger one was in its own, has been condemned everywhere and always; and it will hardly be claimed that such condemnation is more specially religious than moral.

"Blessed are they that are persecuted for righteousness sake." Yes, truly blessed when they can feel the persecution, yet know that it comes from an unfortunate state of mind—the ignorance, error, and selfishness of undevelopment—and hence have no desire to return evil for evil; when they can accept it as a parent accepts the wrong-doing of a child, in a spirit of magnanimity, believing there is some germ of goodness in the wrong-doer, and trusting to its future outgrowth to make the suitable return. Generosity and forbearance in such case is a giving of moral credit to the morally weak, and is an encouragement to goodness.

Is generosity morality? To some extent at least it is so considered. The generosity of the parent to the child is held to be a duty to the child. The state acknowledges a duty to the poor, and other unfortunate ones, in providing almshouses and asylums, to prevent the inequality of these unfortunates from being as marked as it would be otherwise. But the distinction of religion from morality is that it enjoins a conduct more generous, more magnanimous, more unselfish than any required by morality, in the ordinary sense. This transcendental generosity exhorts us to resist not evil, to turn the other cheek when assaulted on one, to give to him that asketh and from him that would borrow to turn not away, to allow him that hath taken our coat to take our cloak also, to forgive the repenting offender an unlimited number of times, to love our enemies and pray for them that persecute us, to heap burning coals of kindness on the heads of them that injure us in any manner, to labor for the good of the unthankful and the evil—the mean, the lazy, the vicious, degraded and criminal—to do for others as we would have others do for us, and do nothing against others we would not have done against ourselves. To the ordinary man of the world these injunctions are rank nonsense; to the religious their apparent irrationality may be a proof of their divinity. But there is really no mystery here, no lack of rationality. When I consider that the man who smites me on the jaw is one who believes I have seriously injured him, in some indirect manner if not directly, then, if it be true that I have, my only honest and just course, however contrary to custom and to the selfish impulses of the natural man, is to bravely take any punishment, not outrageous, he may choose to inflict, provided he cannot be satisfied otherwise. When he perceives that I have this willingness to do him justice it will probably not take long to make everything satisfactory between us; evil will be overcome with good, and the correctness of the injunction verified. The difficulty is that our daily life is under such a perpetual teaching of selfishness, in its various forms, that we never imagine it possible to follow the directions given. Even an indignant *complaint* is pretty sure to meet with a return of wrath. This is all a mistake. We can learn to calmly accept harsh criticism when it is deserved, we can learn even to accept a blow without becoming angry; and one is not a *thoroughly* honest man till he possesses this ability.

There is as good a reason for giving up one's coat or cloak, for lending money, or giving to him that asks. The social system under which we live, and under which Jesus and all the great religious teachers lived, is one that generates inequality and perpetuates it. Poverty is a necessary concomitant of great wealth, ignorance goes with high culture, and criminality with goodness. Through this arrangement the poor, ignorant, and wicked are as much sinned against as sinning, and the comparative neglect of all of them by society is quite as reprehensible as their own conduct. What Jesus meant by our allowing one to take both coat and cloak through the law I do not know, and it may be uncertain. But when we remember that he who steals a coat is one whom society has allowed to grow up neglected, without learning any useful method of supporting himself, without being secured an opportunity to labor, or taught that labor was a duty; that moreover he may have inherited weakness or laziness from idle parents; and that in consequence of all these disabilities he is in want of clothing or food or money, though by natural justice entitled to an equal opportunity to obtain and enjoy,— considering all this, I say, it is not so very difficult to tell the robber to take your cloak also if he needs it more than you do, or to lend him money or credit, or to give the poor tramp a good breakfast and a kind word. Jesus, Gautama and Moses may not have perceived how severely social injustice affects the less fortunate; but their utterances recognize that there *is* an injustice, and virtually acknowledge much of the wrong the modern socialist claims in his indictment of society. And looking at these requirements in this light they lose their superhuman quality, becoming simple exhortations to do such justice as we can to those whom society has neglected, and allowed to be deprived of their rights. Call them religion or morality, they imply the duty of doing something for the weak, depraved and inferior, which if practiced would operate to raise them, and tend toward the equality of all. In essential character the feeling demanded is the same as that of the parent for the child, the desire of the morally superior to benefit the inferior, and a willingness to suffer in order that it may be accomplished. The parent has more patience with the faults of the child for knowing something of the causes of them in the child nature; and when we as fully understand the causes of feeling and action in the adult man or woman the generosity that is kind to the unthankful and the evil, and which labors for the benefit of the offender, will be much less difficult, and will be seen to involve no different morality. The transcendental generosity converts into a transcendental or finer *justice;* which unconsciously recognizes the right of the poor, the weak, the criminal, and the unhappy to an ultimate equal share of happiness with others,—a present right to what they can enjoy, a prospective right to a better capacity of enjoyment.

"Do unto others as you would have others do unto you" requires both justice and generosity, and both sentiments aim at equality as a final result; for every one wishes to be treated justly, every one wishes to be treated generously; every one when in trouble desires to be raised out of it; every one wants to be helped along toward the attainment of as much happiness as the more fortunate ones possess. The command is,—Do all this to others.

How many people ever thought whether the Golden Rule was religious or moral? "How would you like it yourself? Put yourself in his place,"—these are expressions common everywhere, with all sorts of people, and they mean precisely the same as the Golden Rule. To irreligious persons they are not supposed to express a religious feeling, but a simple common perception of justice, or that what is right for one is equally right for another.

The only noteworthy criticism of the Golden Rule is that it forbids the punishment of the criminal. But when we have learned that the criminal's nature is the product of conditions, causes and circumstances, which have made him what he is; that he is really the most unfortunate of all unfortunates; and when, acting on this knowledge we have provided efficacious means for instructing, reforming, and morally educating him, his punishment will be the very thing the Golden Rule demands, what he will thank us for, what we should rationally desire for ourselves or our children.

The advice given to cast away an eye or other member of the body that causes one to offend, if really the utterance of Jesus and not the forgery of a priest, is the teaching of that asceticism common to all religions, and growing out of the old spiritualistic philosophy they all rest upon, which makes body and soul antagonistic. Though to some degree excusable, and perhaps necessary in a time of ignorance, yet when carried to the extreme here commended it becomes barbarous and horrible, unworthy the religion of a savage. The command to the disciple to take neither purse nor scrip, nor make any provision for food, clothing, or shelter, which the Master himself so well obeyed, is but another instance of that counsel the prophet, seer, medium, mystic and devotee always gets, to rely wholly on the spiritual power controlling him for everything.

The outcome of this hasty examination of the Sermon is, that the transcendental *generosity* of religion, and the transcendental *justice* of a high morality are one. "When thou makest a feast call not thy friends nor rich neighbors, but bid the poor, the maimed, the lame, the blind," the mean, wretched, despised and outcast, "and thou shalt be blessed,"—that is the language of Religion. "Do such justice in the earth that all the poor miserables will be able to make a feast for themselves, and then we shall all be happy together,"—this is what Socialism would say. The spirit of both is a spirit of unselfishness, a willingness to consider the happiness of others as readily as one's own. Unselfishness is a designation all can understand, and about which there need be little dispute.

Another point made by Mr. Drummond in the book referred to, is that morality is limited and unprogressive, the difference between it and spirituality being like that between crystalization and life; that in morality we have got as far as we can go, whereas, spiritually " we do not yet know what we shall be." The unprogressive character of morality was also asserted by Buckle, a materialist thinker, a quarter of a century since; though the progressive element with him was intellect, not spirituality. But if morality and spirituality are in nature and purpose one, as above pointed out, no other argument is needed to prove this notion mistaken; if there were need the history of the progressive races would show that morality has been always changing in both character and amount, and as a net result improving; the standards set up by the socialist, and by various reformers of the present time, are higher than ever were know before. The progressiveness of intellect makes progressive everything connected with it. Morality is subject to the law of Evolution. And if we do not yet fully know what we shall be, it is at least allowable to believe that some of the more advanced are approaching the point where a higher conception of our future moral state will be possible.

I have defined religiosity as aspiration, the desire to be perfect in this unselfish morality that looks upon every human soul as of equal value, or as entitled to opportunity for *becoming* equal to the best. But this, be it observed, is religious manifestation only in its highest form. The religion, so called, of barbarous tribes and half-civilized nations exhibits little if any of this feeling; there is little worthy motive of any kind, mostly fear and selfish prudence, seeking safety from the displeasure of some fearful god. The good that finally comes out of it I have before stated to be a forced cultivation of unselfishness through the habit of sacrifice, which at length generates an ability to do unselfish acts without compulsion. I think there is a question of race connected with this, and doubt if any of the yellow, black, or red races have ever reached anything very high save in rare individual instances. The Semitic and Aryan peoples manifest religiosity proper as moral aspiration. And yet the masses of the Mohammedans I judge have little of it; neither do the Brahminical and Buddhist Hindoos possess it in high degree. Individuals among all these have exhibited its tendency to goodness, and have become saints to those below them. But it is only in the Christendom of Western Europe and America that it has become general, and mostly in those divisions that are Protestant. Wherever it is most abundant there is the least religious formalism and ritual; where it is least there ostentations ritualism and multitudinous observances constitute what is called religious worship. The progress from one of these states to the other shows the increase or decline of true religiosity; and by this criterion the religiosity of our time is decreasing, being gradually overcome by the frivolity, pleasure-seeking, and general selfishness that goes with great wealth and luxury.

The formal observances of religion probably have some usefulness to the wholly selfish person, through their suggestion of various better feelings; thereby, as we might say, planting the germs of the religious faculty.

We may then look upon sentimental or meditative religion —that state in which unselfish goodness is thought upon, or talked about, and the enthusiasm of it dissipated in prayers, songs, and exhortations, with no result of good deeds—as comparable to the germinating stage in the life of a plant, when it puts forth the beginnings of a root and stem, in preparation for more active growth, after the upward shoot shall have reached the open air and sunlight. We do not see any growth till the shoot has appeared above ground, though it has been slowly going on; and in a similar manner, we may hope that the good works of justice and benevolence will in time grow out of sentimental religion, though no signs of them be apparent when we look.

Swedenborg tells us that a man has neither faith nor charity before they exist in works, apparently counting sentimentalism for nothing; but I see no reason against assuming that the germs of the unselfish feeling get their first impulse to growth in the contemplation of unselfish *ideals* till they become strong enough to eventuate in action or good works. It is no less true that "it is only in working for *mutual* satisfaction and happiness that man arises to moral perfection." as said by one whose religiosity manifested itself in producing the Social Palace or Familistere at Guise in France.

Dr. J. R. Buchanan, in a noteworthy book on a new treatment of disease,* will not allow that persons of mere unselfish amiability—sentimental goodness without energy to act—can have even robust *health;* "our conception of virtue should be that of a *positive power*, acting with that broad sympathy and intuitive understanding which realize that happiness cannot be an isolated condition, and that he who would enter the sphere of true happiness must make a sphere of happiness around

---

*"*Therapeutic Sarcognomy*, a scientific exposition of the mysterious union of Soul, Brain and Body, and a New System of Therapeutic Practice, &c. by Joseph Rodes Buchanan." Published by the author, No. 6 James St., Boston, Mass.

him in human beings, and never relax in the pursuit of those noble aims to which his life is devoted."

Sentimentalism, with its accompaniment of creeds and observances, though it may be helpful to the child, is to the more mature person an encouragement to moral indolence and indifference, an excuse for backsliding and demoralization, a substitution of the inferior for the superior; hence such a one naturally dislikes it, and if not already strong should avoid being under its to him unwholesome influence. It is like a muscular man's losing his strength by doing the work of a child.

Out of this sentimental state, as we may well believe, the religious feeling grows by little acts of self-sacrifice, generosity, magnanimity, kindness, into the ability for greater and greater deeds of the unselfish order, till finally religion becomes in practice, what James Martineau called it, "the culminating meridian of morals," or as I should express it, the culmination of unselfishness,—the ability to live the precepts of the Sermon on the Mount and the Golden Rule, with all the similar requirements to be found in various religious systems, all of them having an ultimate purpose to recognize and realize the equal right of all human beings to such happiness as they are capable of experiencing, under the best conditions, and in their best state of development.

Religiosity then is the aspirational *feeling*, theoretical religion is whatever *doctrine* of duty is conducive to moral growth, practical religion is the unselfish *life* in its higher aspects.

With this conception of what true religious feeling is, as the aspiration after moral perfection, in deed as well as in sentiment, let us compare it with some other doctrines of religion, or morality, to see what it is not, and how far they are true or false as tried by this standard. The religion we are contemplating is the religion of the heart or feelings. But there exists a similar desire to perfect the body,—to acquire physical strength, activity and endurance. Would it be proper to call this a religious feeling, and its outworking the religion of the body? If so this was the religion of the old Greeks, and was manifested at their games instead of in their temples. Having it they endowed their gods with physical strength and beauty, and the passions of the animal man. In our time and country it is exhibited mainly in boxing, and base-ball. The religion of the heart, by antagonizing that of the body, shuts away all its own refining influences from the latter, so that it readily becomes associated with drunkenness, profanity, and brutality, especially after being corrupted by the possibility of turning every contest of strength and skill into a means for obtaining money.

Moreover, we possess a desire to grow intellectually, to cultivate observation and the reasoning or classifying faculty, and to discover new objects or new truth. The speculator, the scientist, the mathematician, the logician, the debater, have this form of religiosity, if we call it such, and its operation might be called the religion of the intellect. The love of truth for moral uses belongs, however, to the religion of the heart; this, instead, is love of investigation for its own sake—for the satisfaction of discovery.

Still furthermore, there is an aspiration broader, deeper, higher than any of these, and including all of them. It is the desire for the perfect in every direction, in all kinds of capacity, thought, feeling and action. It aspires to make the man perfect, his actions perfect, and his surroundings perfect. It is not alone the art feeling, as ordinarily understood, but a vastly larger one of similar character; for it takes in the self, the neighbor, and the public, the home, the village or city, and the whole nation; and will finally take in the whole world.

It is the passion for universal improvement. Not knowing any better name, I will call this desire for a universal artistic perfection Artosity, and designate it as the most perfect aspiration of our whole nature, superior to the religious because larger, the very noblest feeling of them all.

Returning to religion proper, the religion of the heart, the contrast of this with the old religions, appears to be, as stated in the first chapter, that in the old, characterized largely by revelation, their doctrine is of the nature of the instruction given to a child; it comes claiming the authority of a superior wisdom, and is accepted mostly with a child's ignorant credulity, mingled with superstition, without knowledge of its true nature and ultimate purpose. The new has the scientific character of the mature thought of the man. It grows out of his intellectual development, as the race becomes thoughtful, scientific, and critical. As the old are adapted to the child-stage of mental evolution this is adapted to its full growth or maturity. As they are the religion of the past, this is likely to be the religion of the future.

All former religion is conservative; aiming to retain and preserve the primitive innocence, dependence, and simple goodness of the child, and by teaching from spiritual authority cultivate those qualities. It resists material science because, in ordinary human blindness, that becomes antagonistic to spiritual knowledge, and tends toward sophistication of the childish religious mind, as does all contact with worldly affairs.

Religious books and teachers generally exhibit the same spirit toward science that the ill-informed parent does toward a precocious child that takes to new and strange studies and pursuits, which the parent imagines to be hurtful or dangerous, because they are beyond the parent's experience, and are liable to beget contempt for it. But though hitherto the childish or religious mind in passing through its stages of growth to maturity becomes hostile to religion, in the future times, when Religion and Science, or spiritual and material knowledge rather, shall have become harmonized, through a better understanding of both, and of human nature, the mind will become intellectual and critical without becoming antagonistic to spiritual knowledge; just as under the wise head of a family the child outgrows the customs and restraints of childhood, and the parental authority, without antagonism, without losing respect and affection for the parent, or any of the inherited goodness; but on the contrary having all its good qualities increased.

What has this religion to do with doctrine? Nothing at all. It has no doctrine of its own, only a science of human nature and human destiny, which it draws from all other science. Like the Pietism of the Seventeenth century, its vitality consists in the actual moralized life, —in "holy living," not in beliefs. It is a new Pietism, having positive knowledge for its inspiration, not the revelation of a scripture. But this pietism of science is superior to the pietism of religion in that it asks for no faith in a scheme of salvation, in immortality, or in a personal deity. Without either of these one may still be a pietist. By losing faith in immortality or God man does not lose his human character; he still has religiosity; he can no more lose the tendency to grow than can a willow tree. If he has believed that all goodness comes from God, and then loses God, he may be tempted into moral indifference, and a foolish or wicked self-indulgence; but unless a mere animal he will be a discontented and unhappy man till he again finds some motive for moral growth and unselfish activity. This pietism does not ask him to spend his life for God, but in unselfish work for the human race; thereby to achieve his own moral perfection along with that of others, and his own greatest happiness along with theirs. The materialist and atheist may possess it therefore as truly as any believer; for with either of them it does not depend on belief but on degree of mental development. In the succeeding chapter it will be shown that without any of the peculiar beliefs of the christian, the atheist or materialist may yet come to know all the christian's peculiar experiences. Notwithstanding his claims, honestly made as they are, the christian has really no monopoly of any spiritual experience, knowledge, or acquirement; nothing but that all may know and share, independently of all belief or unbelief. The basis for human unity is absolutely universal in the human capacity and aspiration for goodness.

All religions are said, by those who have made comparative religion a study, to be characterized by *spiritualism*—a belief in spiritual persons and a spirit world. All those mysterious experiences and happenings that belong to Modern Spiritualism are found equally in Christianity, Judaism, Mohammedism, Buddhism, and Brahmanism. All the mystic powers of modern mediums were equally possessed by the ancient prophets and seers. The modern spiritualism differs from the ancient principally in discarding the mystery and the superstition, in attempting to make the spirit world natural, in endeavoring to show that it and the material are both parts of one connected whole, governed by the same law and order that we know to exist in the physical. But a belief or disbelief in such a spiritual world, either of the ancient or modern type, has no necessary connection with religiosity or religion. It could have such connection only when immortality was supposed to be a gift of God, and religion involved an effort to obtain it through God's favor. Religious feeling however, arises from human nature; and the religious life depends only on a society of human beings, toward and with whom it can be manifested. Whether this society has a continued life in another world, or is confined to this, makes no difference in the actual outworking of the religious impulse. It must show itself here and now, as well as then and there; for its purpose is to live the unselfish life without regard to time or place.

I well know what the orthodox religionist will object to all this. He will say that religious feeling includes a vast sense of gratitude to a personal God for all he has done for us—our creation, and all we enjoy in life, with all the possibilities of immortality; a deep reverence for a being in power and capacities far beyond what we can conceive, and a loving worship and imitation of the infinite excellencies of such a being. But if it be shown that whatever has been done for us, aside from the wilderness of land and water furnished by Nature, has been done by those of our own race, the occasion for an outflow of gratitude will be the same. The being of infinite perfections is in reality only an enlarged human copy of the worshipper himself in his best moments; for that is all any one can conceive of a personal deity, according to the law that we can conceive of nothing beyond experience. The constant familiarity with which christians of all degrees speak of and to their deity, is a sufficient evidence that the ideal conceived and worshipped is not so high a one as the words describe. An ideal of some kind will be worshipped, and the best embodiment of it that is known or imagined; but whether a human hero or superhuman makes little if any difference. It is the imitation of superior excellence carried into actual life, after the sentimental contemplation and admiration of it, that enables the human soul to grow toward righteousness, and to become godlike. The religious instinct will thus find an object, whatever may be the ultimate fate of the dogmas of God and Immortality. Whatever doctrine most favors any person in the progress toward unselfishness is a true doctrine for him in the stage he has reached. At a higher level a more complete form of truth will become necessary. The complete and harmonious truth, however, can be attained only along with that complete unselfishness which, in spite of all bigotry or personal preference, can accept it in its entirety.

Let me not be understood to say, however, that the religionist's love of a personified Goodness or God, so far as it is a personified Good and not personified Evil, and the doing of his will because it is right, and for the sake of being in sympathy with him, is not a true religious manifestation; for it is; and the motives and purposes will be substantially the same as above described; the object of worship will be an unselfish person, and the imitation of him a doing of unselfish work.

It is hardly necessary to say that religiosity is not wonder nor awe. If there is any satisfaction in contemplating an almighty and incomprehensible power, or an insoluble mystery, I know nothing of it, and cannot conceive of those feelings as having any possible value. An unknowable mystery as the background of the universe, and an object of worship, seems to me an unmitigated fraud upon the religious sentiment. Wonder, as well pointed out by Lester F. Ward in his "Dynamic Sociology," is a feeling belonging to the ignorant, not to those who understand. And it is no different whether the object of it be a small thing or a great one. A source of wonder will always be present, no doubt, in the fact that the materials for a universe exist incapable of being either created or annihilated; but the contemplation of it brings no pleasure, nor any moral improvement.

Awe is the consciousness of a possible danger from some uncontrollable power of uncertain action, like a thunder-storm or an insane person; but probably no one ever found it either satisfying or ennobling.

Having compared this religion of growth with Pietism as a religion, and shown that it has no regard for doctrine, I will next compare it with Stoicism as a morality. "He who forsaketh morality despiseth his own soul," was written by one of the old Hebrew wise men, and this might well have been the motto of the Stoics, whose religion or morality was one of self-respect. With them "to be virtuous was to be godlike;" not after the likeness of the Greek gods, but after that of the Supreme Good of Plato. So this religion I am endeavoring to expound is a religion of self-respect,—a self-respect that is honest enough to discard all the false claims of pride, conceit, and self-righteousness, all show and vainglorious pretense; assuming only what the keenest criticism allows to be our own; admitting in all candor that what we are is what we have been made, and that what we possess is what has been bestowed upon us, under the reign of natural causation; yet knowing the *capacities* of the human soul, and determined to do everything to make it strong, pure, bright, and beautiful in the future.

The *superiority to law* claimed by the Stoics was but the natural result of moral evolution that had reached a certain high stage; and has appeared in various religious sects at various times in the world's history. Though none of them may have attained to that stage completely, the fact that they came near enough to it to form this conception is a fact full of hope for future Humanity, for it is the capability of being a law to oneself.

I might here be expected to pay some attention to the Positivist religion, only that to do so would require a discussion of the proper limits of unselfishness, a theme not desirable to take up, further than to say that to entirely ignore or completely abnegate self, as Positivism seems to teach, is to make unselfishness irrational. For, underlying all altruistic motives and purposes there is this hidden selfish one,—that by present self-sacrifice there is to be an ultimate greater gain of happiness. This is a motive of which no one can divest himself. Unselfish feeling and conduct, carried to its highest rational limit, thus becomes a transcendental selfishness, wiser, more far-sighted than any selfishness, as the word is commonly understood.

The satisfaction of the Stoic in self-respect, or the devotion of individuals to a high ideal of duty for the sake of its own nobility, regardless of personal interest or pleasure, is like the satisfaction of the artist in his best performance. It each case it is the satisfaction that comes from realizing an ideal of what is right, of accomplishing a perfect work. The pleasure of benevolence to animals, and unfortunates who can make no return, is of the same kind. We are in the habit of calling it selfish or unselfish as the motive is low or high. The artist's work may be of little importance and his pleasure in it we call selfish; that of the moralist may be of supreme importance, and we speak of his satisfaction as unselfish. The final reason for satisfaction, unconscious perhaps, is that the accomplishment of the most perfect ideal, with the most complete thoroughness and grace, brings the greatest result of human happiness. It is this which makes it high, noble, praiseworthy, that which *ought* to be.

But the apparent necessity that takes the life of an individual for the good of the multitude, like the conscription of an army, or that which compels the laborer to toil in the midst of danger for his bread, is a fearful wrong; and the virtue of submission to it is very doubtful. The continual or complete sacrifice of the superior for the inferior is certainly not commendable, for it is not just. There may be a foolish non-resistance as well as a wise one. And the idea, occasionally appearing among sentimental religionists, that we should be willing to suffer and be cursed for God's glory, that being the prime consideration, and human happiness secondary,—this is worse than irrational; it is the product of a mind stultified by its own slavery to a false and inhuman conception of God.

In regard to *Asceticism*, always, even to the present time, associated with religion, I must express my conviction that however necessary it may have been in the past, the enlightenment of the future will abolish it utterly. We shall eat, drink, and do everything we do with a worthy motive, and a conscientious regard for the Universal Good. And when we *can* do so there will be nothing to prevent the complete normal gratification of all the normal desires of the animal man; not only as a matter of justice to the physical nature, but also as a help to true spiritual progress; for all parts of the human nature will be then in harmony, and all acting in healthful mutual coöperation. Until that time comes however, the warfare of the flesh and spirit will go on, and the triumph of the spirit will be won through more or less oppression of the body.

What now is the ultimate object of religion, and its true reason for existence? The rationale of the whole thing is that man's happiness comes mainly from society. The most perfect society, and the most complete adaptation to it, brings the most perfect happiness. The Christian church seeks blindly, under the guise of salvation, to prepare men for a society of "the just made perfect" in a spirit world. Its true saints or holy ones are its most unselfish individuals, those capable of harmonious and loving union with such a body. A wise and benevolent deity in creating the race (assuming that such a one did create) could have no other object than such a society. This only could make his action rational. A god creating with any other motive would be only a selfish god, seeking his own adulation and glory, like a weak, ambitious human. And so far as Christian leaders have taught that God acted simply for his own good pleasure, like an almighty despot, they have attributed to him the despotic disposition that still lingered in their own hearts. Only a social purpose could be godlike. And only sympathy with such an end can make religion rational, and redeem it from being merely a scheme by which selfish men attempt to save their individual souls.

Morality aims at the same object openly and consciously. To improve society, and fit the individual for life with his fellows, is the whole purpose of all its teachings, barring that small portion that tells him his duty to himself alone, and which properly ought not to be called morality at all, but *prudence*. The state attempts the same effort, at first in a negative way by legal suppression of immorality, and later in a more positive manner by education, and measures to promote the general welfare. I have previously exhibited morality as the vital element of political society, which the state must foster in order to continue its existence. The state has additional functions, it is true; but after securing protection from external dangers, this appears to be its most important work.

Socialism is making its own attempt at the same achievement, in a more direct and immediate way, through a reformation or reconstruction of present society, or by planting the germs of a new one. To its advocates it is the embodiment of morality, and a religion in the sense of being the highest object of their devotion, that which commands their most unselfish efforts. Of course this is hardly true of those few over-zealous and impulsive ones whose extreme estimate of their cause or of themselves leads them to look upon their opponents as villains, and to take unjust, reckless and cruel means to accomplish the good they have in view.

It is also a fact that the more advanced Christianity of the time is becoming tinctured with socialism of a moderate type,—Christian Socialism some of it is called. To me this seems a natural evolution. Another marked characteristic of the present age is the formation of associations for moral culture, and of so-called religious bodies having no creed, and pledged only to cultivation of the higher life. This too, is a sign of progress. The tendency of religious sects toward a closer union on the basis of agreement in essentials, ignoring the minor points of doctrine, is yet another indication of the same kind. The one supreme objective point of both religion and socialism—of the church and the state—is a happy condition of society, characterized by the practical embodiment of justice, and by devotion to the highest rational ideals of unselfish conduct. Dimly perceived or more clearly, located in one world or another, sought directly or indirectly, pursued with more or less sincerity and earnestness, with more or less wisdom in methods and means, this perfection of society has ever been the end that was to be accomplished. It is the condition toward which the human race grows as truly as a plant grows toward its blossoms and fruit.

What then shall we say of the religion that has no sympathy with the objects of socialism? except that it is a very poor and diluted, or else corrupt one. When a great preacher insults the laboring man of mere muscular endowment by saying "he is entitled to his fodder" but no luxuries,* entirely forgetting that such a one has

---

* In a lecture in Music Hall Boston, Nov. 20, 1884, the distinguished clergyman referred to, according to press report, made use of the following language.
"'The root of socialism, in its malignant form, is the idea that the vast mass of men have the same rights as those at the top. They have not. They have the right to live; the primary conditions of life are universal; but the right to all

a right to grow, to develop, to possess the means of *acquiring* intelligence and the taste for better things, above all to educate his children into something better than himself; and when the preacher's sentiment is applauded by a "cultured" audience, the facts indicate anything but the presence of religious or moral feeling. A true sense of justice thinks first of the most needy. Every person who possesses aught of true religiosity acknowledges the higher claims of equality; and admits the duty of doing something to elevate the less fortunate into better views of social life, and into nobler aspirations and enjoyments. To say they are entitled only to the bare means of living is the most outrageous infidelity. And when the old Mother Church herself takes the position that men can rightfully be deprived of their common inheritance in the soil of the globe, as apparently she has done in the well-known case of Dr. McGlynn, then the orthodox and the heretic are equally shown to be lacking in the kind of spirit here taken to be religious. It is not strange that the intelligent workingman cares little for what is called "religion," or that the most conscientious persons are not found within the church membership.

A few paragraphs upon the means of cultivating unselfishness will close the present chapter. And first let me again contradict that common notion, taught by the teachers of religion, that intellect has little or nothing to do with morality. On the contrary the attainment of the unselfish character, like the attainment of any other good thing, depends upon knowing *how* it is to be acquired,— upon the knowledge of means, gained by the intellect, after it has already perceived the superior happiness to be secured, which is the incentive to effort. The mind

---

the things belonging to civilization depends upon what a man is. The man who is merely bone and muscle has no right to that kind; he has a right to fodder certainly.' (Applause and laughter)."

must first have an ideal, created by the intellect, and must be able to see how that ideal is superior to the present reality. Then, recognizing the ideal as right and the actual as wrong, it necessarily makes an effort for improvement. It is the same with a moral ideal as with any other. In a previous essay (Chap. III) I endeavored to show that a consciousness of duty comes from perceiving the superiority of right or ideal conduct, as being most conducive to happiness; that it has the same foundation as an artist's love of the perfect in his art, or the mechanic's sense of right regarding his work,—because it is the realization of the perfect that brings complete satisfaction. And if there should be a dislike to admit such humble origin for that sense of duty which superstition has made so wonderful, the dislike springs only from pride or superstition, and will give way before some natural cause for the sense of right.

Having some conception of what is just, or unselfish, or morally right, the ability to make this ideal actual is gained through a struggle with the selfish impulses, which is appropriately called a spiritual warfare. The well known fact has previously been referred to, that an army of soldiers, by winning a succession of victories over equal or greater numbers, acquired such a degree of courage and determination that they can be beaten only by a much superior force. Conversely, a series of defeats so disheartens or demoralizes an army that it can be beaten very easily. It is in a similar manner, as I conceive, that the moralization or demoralization of human beings in *every respect* is accomplished. The successful effort at a small sacrifice of property, comfort, pride, reputation, or affection, for conscience sake—to do some good, some duty, some right thing—makes the succeeding one easier. Two or three of these may make it possible to achieve a greater one. In the process of time, with the additions of moral capacity that come by inheritance, and the conquest of one selfish feeling after another, a civilized man finally becomes capable of giving up his dearest wishes, his ruling passion, the strongest, most vital point of his selfish nature, anything and all but life itself, and that he will risk, to accomplish what he believes to be some great good to others, and thus an ideal of duty.

If in this connection a word more is required concerning the effect of religious exercises—ceremonies, exhibitions, prayers, fasts, music, preaching, pilgrimages, etc. it may be said that this is precisely the same that harangues, exhortations, patriotic music, banners, etc. have upon an army going into battle, or a political party before an election. In religion such influences do not ordinarily confer new power. They keep alive the sense of duty, of gratitude, benevolence, justice, whatever there may be of these feelings—not necessarily very much—thus keeping the religionist on guard against temptations and difficulties with such degree of ability as he possesses. With sufficient excitement he gains a stimulation from the impulses communicated by others, and for the time being is able to do more. But whether with or without excitement, it is the successful meeting of temptation, the triumph over selfishness, that gives additional moral courage and strength. Just as the conquering of one difficulty after another makes a man conscious of increased energy for the next, so the success of one effort at self-conquest, and the realization of a new benefit or new happiness therefrom, renders him conscious of ability to do it again more easily, or to make a greater sacrifice of selfishness in some other way, when different circumstances call upon him for more public spirit, keener sympathy, or stronger sense of justice. In a word, it is the *habit* of meeting moral trials successfully that develops morality.*

---

* See also Chap. 2, pp. 39, 51 and 52.

In all this conflict or struggle the intellect has its function to perform, not only in determining the ideal right for any given case, but also in tracing out all the probable and possible benefits to result from a right course, and all the bad effects of a wrong one, direct and indirect, proximate and ultimate. And it is here that the wisest person, the one best equipped with scientific knowledge of a high order, that is, an understanding of human nature and social evolution, has an advantage over all others. Ordinary religious teaching and training do not supply it. Teaching by authority gives no reason for a commandment, and without knowing the reason for it a thing is scarcely known at all. Hence the graduate of religious instruction goes wrong in certain directions as readily as any one else. There has been no use of the intellect.

Whatever subject one has knowledge about has interest for that person; and this is as true of the study of morality, and of progress toward the unselfish life, as it is of any other subject. Just as the ship-builder who is to build a fast yacht studies carefully to perfect his ideal of it in a model, and then brings all his knowledge and resources to bear in overcoming difficulties, and embodying the ideal as completely as possible, so should every individual endeavor to make the best use of his intellect to perfect his ideal of unselfish feeling and conduct, and then to successfully carry it into practical realization. The more he studies and learns, both of the ideal and of the means of living in accordance with it, the more he desires to learn, and the better he will be able to do, as truly as the best mechanic or artist will be he who best knows what the perfect thing is, and the best ways that can be taken to produce it. Though never perfect in his action, never as good as his knowledge of right, because the reality is never quite equal to the ideal, and one can be expected only to come as near the requirement as possible under the circumstances, still it will remain true that the better the knowledge the better the performance.

Here, then, is what the moralist has to do,—to elaborate or discover the highest ideals of unselfish feeling, thought, and conduct, in all departments of human activity; and the best methods for overcoming all the thousand and one difficulties and defects that prevent the complete realization of those ideals in actual every-day life. This is what the child and the youth are to be taught, and the practice urged and encouraged, not principally by emulation, still less by authority, but by clear and earnest appeals to the reasoning faculty, till through that and the experience of superior happiness from well-doing, the conscientious feeling, and the moral habit, are at length firmly established and become organic, the most vital, active, persistent and powerful element of the whole constitution.

Neither the struggle of the soldier, nor the labor of the artist is alone the true type of the moralizing process; it is better represented by both combined, and then they are insufficient.

The next best thing to successful struggle in actual life is the imaginary one set forth in fiction having a moral purpose; in description of the lives of heroic men and women; and in accounts of heroic moral conduct in occasional instances. Reading of this character has a lighter effect of the same kind as the actual experience would have; and besides furnishing good ideals, prepares one to some extent for meeting similar realities in one's own life when they arise. There should not, however, be so much of it at once as to prevent the good impressions from being strongly fastened on the mind. The literary world is doing its duty in this respect better than ever before; which fact may be counted as yet another indication of progress.

The old religions assume man to be free yet depraved,

born into evil and prone to it as the sparks to fly upward; the new will show him to be born into the selfishness of the child, a normal, not depraved condition, and with a natural tendency to outgrow it into the full stature of unselfish goodness, but capable of doing so only through the aid of a high order of scientific knowledge. The intellect, appropriately subordinate in the childish religions of the past, based on the authority of inspiration, will in future be itself the fountain of all authority, the leading and dominating influence in all things, guiding the helpless, blind goodness, that has always despised it, into its own true completeness, and the permanent conquest of evil.

The intellectual equipment must include a knowledge of society such as only the very few now possess. Spite of all we can say or do for the cultivation of morality, there still exists the very serious fact that the industrial system of civilization—the whole business world—is conducted on principles of injustice. So long as men are taught that these are right or excusable, and are compelled to get a living under them, no thorough or complete moral education will be generally possible. The promising Sunday-school boy will still become the embezzling clerk or cashier, and defraud in a thousand ways. The defrauded criminal will take his revenge in crime. "Ye cannot serve God and Mammon," nor obtain wealth conscientiously, without seeking first the righteousness of the Kingdom, and then embodying it in the institutions of the world.

CHAPTER XVI.

CONVERSION AND SALVATION.

SALVATION, to the old Hebrew meant salvation from his external enemies, and safety in enjoying the comforts of the present world. To the ancient Hindoo it meant escape from the miseries of a life that had too little happiness to be worth living. To the Christian it means rescue from the liability to future punishment for sin. To show what it means in the light of scientific rationality is the task of the present essay.

What *conversion* means to the evangelical Christian every one has some idea; and this also must be made understandable to the rational faculty, so far as is possible without one's passing through the experience so named.

The philosophical doctrine that nothing can be known except through experience is disputed by one half the world's thinkers; yet almost every person knows that he or she has had experiences that no one can understand who has not also had them; a sort of universal confession of the truth of that doctrine. Every genuinely converted christian is one who knows his experience can be rightly understood only by another true christian. The unconverted christian, and the materialist or agnostic, know nothing of this peculiar experience; and the materialist, especially, finds difficulty in believing it to be anything better than hallucination. So the proviso must be made that its explanation can be *fully* understood only by those who have gone through *some degree* of the experience. In this respect it is like all other experience whatever; religious or secular, material or spiritual, the law regarding it is the same. Hallucination there may or may not be in connection with it; but the thing itself is so truly real that one who has ever had a fair degree of it will never speak lightly of it afterward; for it is one of the most sacred experiences, if not altogether the most sacred, of his whole life; one never likely to be forgotten, because it is one, and the first one, that brings into action all the best feelings of the soul in a battle against the worst, strong or weak, many or few as either of them may be. I do not, however, attempt to say how many conversions are of this character, and have no doubt that many of those called such in "revival" excitements are entirely unworthy of the name.

Ordinarily the experiences called conversions are passed through in the church or under its influence. And it should also be understood that they do not all occur in times of excitement, but are brought about under various circumstances of trial, sorrow, and danger adapted to produce them. In rare cases they occur even without any unusual cause. The instances of moral reform that take place outside of ordinary religious influences are less noticeable, but in their essential character, the triumph of good over evil, they are the same.

The illumination by which we perceive spiritual things has been said to be the light of the Holy Ghost. But what is the Holy Ghost? In the Hebrew and Christian scriptures the name seems to have several meanings, but for our present purpose we need only two of them. One makes it that very condition of the mind, or disposition of the heart, which results from the most thorough conversion—the spirit that makes one holy, to a degree; in the other it is an unseen and indescribable influence coming from a holy source, inspiring in the recipient of it holy thoughts or sentiments, and a conviction of wrong doing, gently impelling him to obey the dictates of conscience, to forsake his sinful ways, to sacrifice his dearly cherished forms of selfishness, and faithfully devote himself to living the higher life. The christian calls it the spirit of God, sent down to human hearts to influence them; the more rational statement is that the spirit generated by conversion tends to communicate itself to others, to bring them into the same state; in other words, the good feeling in certain persons sends out an unseen influence, that tends to induce the same good feeling in others who may be susceptible to it. But let us examine it more at length.

The spirit of goodness which makes the saint, the conscientious christian, the truly good man or woman, can be partially understood by nearly every one, for almost all may have at one time or another some consciousness of it in themselves. It is not this, but the unseen force given out by it, that is mysterious.

We are familiar with the effect of excitement upon one coming within reach of it, when it is perceived by the ordinary senses, in looks, tones, words, gestures and actions; and this effect is produced by religious excitement as readily as by that of patriotism, or anger, mirthfulness, gambling, or partizanship. But the influence referred to is not that of excitement at all, in this sense, because it does not act upon the ordinary senses.

Certain persons, however, without seeing, hearing, or reading about any particular excitement near them, will yet have an indistinct consciousness that there is such an excitement, and be able to tell what the predominant character of it is. The ability to do so is known among those familiar with it as the *psychometric* power, and facts in sufficient abundance exist to put its reality beyond doubt. It is also sufficiently well known that some persons, without addressing the senses, can voluntarily communicate their feelings to certain other persons. I have little doubt that they can thus impart their thoughts also, though in regard to, the present matter the feeling alone is sufficient. This latter kind of ability may be called a *mesmeric* power, as the ability to receive is a *psychometric* one. Excitement that increases any special feeling may increase the mesmeric power which carries that feeling to another; and its effect will thus be an increased one, though not accomplished through the ordinary channels of sensation.

A point to be specially noticed here is that a *good* state of feeling can be communicated as readily as one of opposite nature. And if we assume that good feelings, along with the superstitious ones of awe and fear, *are* thus communicated, we can account for most of the phenomena of religious conversion without resorting to influences from another world. Still, I would not deny that, if there be a spirit world, the beings there may exert upon persons here the same kind of power that I am supposing ourselves to exert upon one another. Religious excitements have often been accompanied by strange mesmeric and spiritual phenomena, such as the dancing manias of the Middle Ages, the wonderful endurance of the Convulsionaires of St. Medard, the falling in trance of the Methodists, with various others in private experience, all of which it would not be unreasonable to expect among people whose principal dealing is with a spirit world and occult influences, and especially when those who experience them have no correct knowledge of mesmerism, nor any at all of modern Spiritualism, by which to understand, and to counteract, prevent, or control them.

A fact more difficult to believe, however, is that the

communication of feeling here spoken of may take place between parties separated by a considerable distance. As an instance, I once heard a distinguished temperance advocate tell how three women agreed to pray for his conversion at a certain hour, and how at that very hour he felt the working of the Holy Spirit so powerfully that it resulted in his conversion as desired. Many similar instances are known, too many I think to be mere coincidences, and possibly in some cases with the consciousness of the affected party that some good friend *was* praying or earnestly wishing for his or her conversion at that precise time, and *who* the good friend was. Such concentration of thought and earnest desire upon a particular one, or even upon a number, by some friend, or by a number of good persons, is just the state of mind calculated to send out a mesmeric force, and produce the effect that actually is produced, and attributed to the Holy Ghost. Coming from a number of the best people in a church, along with considerable excitement of the better impulses of the congregation, and directed upon subjects within reach of sight, hearing and touch, it ought to be still more effective.

Here another special point is to be made, namely, that when the nature and origin of this occult influence is understood, it can be brought to bear upon the unbeliever as readily as upon the believer, either by good religious or good unreligious persons. I have one instance at least, where influences from outside the church and ordinary religion produced effects equal to any usually produced in revival meetings upon one individual. I am not, therefore, speaking beyond knowledge when I say that in this respect the church has no power that the agnostic, infidel, or atheist may not possess equally well. It is moral goodness, goodness of heart, *the good spirit*, that endows its possessor with the power of the Holy Ghost.

But in the more rational conversion now contemplated there will be no occasion for excitement or strange occurrences, although there will necessarily be deep earnestness. Everything connected with the change will be understood, and if the kind of mesmeric force here explained to be the Holy Ghost should be brought into use, it will be done consciously and deliberately. Whatever belongs to this hitherto mysterious realm is to become a matter of science,—spiritual science if you choose—but none the less truly science.

The facts of religious experience are not to be ignored, whatever theory may be taken to explain them. The one here given seems to me sufficient; but if not, the fact of an unknown subtle influence still remains, and also that under the stimulation of it the affected party overcomes a portion of the selfish nature, greater or less, and takes a step in moral progress, which may be permanent, or from which he may afterward recede.

It is this mysterious power of the Holy Ghost, and the change it affects, which give to the sincere christian his firmest faith in the truth of his doctrine. This influence he knows by experience to be a reality. Its effect in a greater or less change of feeling and purpose he also knows to be real; and as there has been no explanation of the facts except the religious one, he infers that because this much is true all the rest is according to what he is taught. His consciousness of having a satisfied conscience, and of being more in union with the Universal Good than ever before, convinces him that he is forgiven, accepted, saved, in agreement with the method made and provided. The Bible deals largely with spiritual experiences, and in it he reads a confirmation of his own, while all is interpreted by one general theory. The skeptic knows nothing of his experience, and can therefore do very little to change the christian's belief. He may point out the absurdities of Christian doctrine from one year's end to another; but the true christian will still know that he has a knowledge the infidel has not, and will only pity his ignorance in return. The change of heart, of will, and of life is to the true convert the vital core of the whole religious system, and commands his abiding reverence; whereas, nothing in Materialism or Agnosticism can do so to the same extent. Among those who have never felt the change rationalism may grow and spread; but upon those who have, its power is only like that of a gentle breeze upon the branches of the sturdy oak.

The believer rejects the criticism of the skeptic for the same reason that the skeptic rejects what he considers the delusion of the believer. Each party insists that the other shall give up what the other knows in order to accept what he knows; and each refuses to do so. It is now to be seen what each will do when he finds it possible to accept the knowledge of the other without giving up his own.

But why does any one fall back? Simply because the ignorant and perverted selfish nature is still strongest, and when outside the good mesmeric and other influence of superior persons, only waits for the right opportunity to reassert itself. A second period of excitement, or of unusual circumstances, may again convert the "backslider," and carry him to a higher moral plane. At length he may reach a condition in which he begins to think of the possibility of holiness, or complete escape from the power of sin,—the state of sanctity of the Roman Church, and believed in by a considerable portion of the Wesleyan Methodist. In all cases however, the sanctified person is still under the protecting influence of the church, or the spirit world, or both, never anticipating a time when he can be able to stand alone in his innocence, and use his moral power to assist others, without being liable to fall from his present estate. He still clings to the hand of his Saviour as necessary to his safety, and believes that if he succeeds with God's help he is doing well. It is God's grace, and the consciousness of spiritual presence, that enable him to fight the good fight, and he expects no final victory, no lasting peace, till he shall reach that happy country where temptation will assail him no more. I ask particular attention to this fact, as I shall interpret it to mean that the decisive conflict between the selfish and unselfish impulses has never been fought.

I must now make the assertion, unaccompanied by any proof except its own inherent reasonableness, that when once the great stronghold of the selfish man has been conquered, his peculiar besetting sin, his dearest indulgence, his ruling passion, that which he loves best of anything except continued existence,—when this is given up, sacrificed and cast out, the victor feels conscious of being victor over all the rest, and knows by what he has done what he can do again with smaller effort. He knows it is the most vital point of his selfishness (of his unregenerate affections) that has been taken possession of, that his work is done deliberately after full conviction of the guilt, sin, injustice, meanness, of the former life; while his present consciousness of a happier state, and his certainty of having done a wise thing, still further assure him that his liability to fall back is past forever. Having gained a consciousness of superior happiness, and greater power of self control, he cannot voluntarily return to the inferior condition, or even be returned to it by any provocation, except for the moment. Suffering the step has cost him, a terrible agony it may be, but that is subsiding, and a degree and kind of happiness never more than partially known before has taken its place, and the new satisfaction overbalances all it has cost.

His work is far from finished, but in a comparative

sense he is at peace. The great struggle of his whole existence being fought and won, what remains will be but shorter and easier ones of a similar kind. He renews the combat against his weaker enemies knowing he is able to vanquish each and all of them. Though not wholly at peace he is able to rest, conscious of being accepted by the God in all good souls, and of being united with them in a sympathy and a brotherhood that can never be broken.

I speak of it in ordinary language, in the soberness of science, well knowing that an enthusiasm, not noisy but deep, is a sure attendant upon the change.

That the church has never produced this radical change in any considerable number of people is indicated by the fact that it has never, even in its own headquarters, drawn together any group of such persons into an unselfish community, having some resemblance to the imagined Kingdom of Heaven; though all their inclinations and sympathies must impel them toward each other, and dispose them to give the world an example of heavenly life. The best men of the church have been engaged in missionary work, but these have done no differently in this respect from the rest. The nearest approach to the life of the Pentecostal time has been made by those new Protestant sects who have founded small societies, with industrial arrangements more or less communistic, and a state of general equality and sympathy most resembling brotherhood. But these have all felt obliged to isolate themselves from the great world of humanity, not being able otherwise to escape its contamination. Nevertheless they are slowly dying out; not one, I think, has vitality enough to hold its own and make progress.

And yet, all the various brotherhoods and sisterhoods, monasteries, societies and communities that have existed, at all times and in all civilized regions, especially in all Christian lands, are but so many evidences that a perfect society is universally felt to be the appropriate outcome from true religion; and that the most religious people in every age and country instinctively try to realize some approximation toward that ideal state. The ancient political thinkers like Moses, Lycurgus and Plato, aimed at the same result, as did also the socialistic ones of modern times.

Let us inquire why it is that the Christian church, and the older religions, have never been able to effect such a thorough change in men's hearts as would enable them to inaugurate a kingdom of heaven in the centers of religious influence,—to plant a germ of new society so vital it would live and grow in spite of worldly opposition, uniting all hearts within itself so strongly they could not be separated. Why is the improvement of Christian society so slow; why so much sin and misery in Christian communities; and why is the Christian himself so little different from his irreligious neighbors?

The Christian has his answer ready,—the depravity of the human heart, the difference of God's ways and man's ways, the counterfoil of the devil's power, and so on; but mine is an entirely different one and is this. It is because the church has never possessed a true philosophy, a true understanding of human origin and nature, a true science of society. It was impossible that she could have; and for want of such knowledge she has never been able to preach a *thorough* conviction of sin, to effect a *whole-hearted* repentance, and secure a *complete* salvation. Holding free-will as a part of the theological scheme, necessary to justify man's condemnation, she could never inculcate the ideas that produce a true unselfish humility; never could show the equality of human souls, even in a comparative sense or at any time, never could banish the remains of pride, conceit and self-righteousness from those disposed to be humble. Never teaching that belief depends on knowledge instead of choice, and hence that honesty in thought was a virtue, she has allowed humanity to indulge and foster its prejudices and hatreds against all who ventured to think unlike the way of the majority; and in consequence she for long centuries filled the earth with the blood of persecution, and still justifies unfriendliness, bigotry, contempt between those who differ over a petty detail of worthless doctrine. For want of social science she repudiated the example of Jesus and the early disciples, adopted all the institutions and customs of a selfish society, and accepted the gifts of the wealthy and tyrannical, till her priests and teachers themselves became addicted to luxury, anxious for wealth, and indifferent to the object of true religion. She had no truth by which she could convict the rich man of his injustice, or support the poor one in his efforts to obtain the means of comfort and improvement. On the contrary she taught the poor to be content in their poverty, ignorance, and helplessness, and required of the rich only a dole of charity instead of justice. With her false and base conception of human nature she had no respect for it, but degrading all the passions connected with the body, she made love a vile thing, discarded it for her priesthood, and insisted that young men and women who had made a wrong choice in marriage should live out lives of sin and misery without hope of separation, compelling children to be generated in wickedness, and to grow up in an amosphere of discord, thus producing more tendency to evil than all her good influences could correct. Quarrelsomeness, jealousies, revenges, and heartburnings of all kinds she could not prevent or reconcile, because she had no doctrine by which to point out the injustice of each party, nor did she teach the duty of submitting without anger to the criticism of the injured, and of removing the cause of it without delay.

Last, but far from least, for want of a rational conception of the purpose of repentance and conversion, she has directed it mainly toward a far-off, inconceivable deity, whom the sins of man could not injure, and failed to show the sinner that his wrong-doing was against his fellow men and women, that the forgiveness he was to seek must be *their* forgiveness, and that without this no atonement could possibly be made, no final peace or happiness could be obtained.

To crown all her shortcomings, and render her infirmities perpetual, she set up the priest and his holy book as authorities not to be questioned, whose wisdom was to be sufficient for all the needs of human life. Then she taught her children to learn nothing further, to stultify their brains, stifle all reasoning, and become the stupid slaves of the Book and its Interpreter. For all this, with all her other faults she deserves—not immediately to die, but, like some harsh old mother, to be patiently shown the error of her ways, and gently set aside to give such care and teaching as she can to some of the youngest and weakest members of the race, till in process of time she becomes entirely superannuated, and her charges able to receive, from more trustworthy teachers, a higher grade of instruction.

What I have said is mostly true of all other religions as well as the Christian ; but keeping the latter still in mind, the reasons given seem to me to account for its failure to fully change the human heart and accomplish the purposes desired. Without rationality, without science, without being purified from all superstition, the church can only labor on as it has done, blindly and feebly, with no substantial improvement over the success of the past. It is not enough even to cast out superstition, or the greater part of it, as a few of the most progressive sects are doing; there must be an active practical effort to abolish injustice, by such a revolutionary reform as will put all institutions on a basis of justice, and make the whole operation of society tend toward equality instead of inequality.

To make still clearer the difference between the conversion here meant and the ordinary conversion of the church, let them be contrasted a little more in detail. The conversion of the Christian is a less difficult thing. To believe that old Adam's transgression was the cause of ours, and that Jesus Christ made atonement for all of it, is less repulsive to the selfish heart than to think that we ourselves are responsible for it, that no other person can relieve us of the consequences to the least extent, and that we must inevitably suffer, till by our own efforts, aided perhaps by some kind soul, we are able to right every wrong in the spirit of true contrition and humbleness. But this more repulsive truth is precisely what we must come to accept. To ask forgiveness of a mighty deity, so much above us that we are really almost nothing, does not humiliate the selfish pride as it does to confess our villainy, our cruelty, our extortion and robbery, our treachery, our abuse of those who never injured us, our pettiness, our vile meanness of whatever kind it may be, to the victim of it, who is no greater than, and perhaps inferior to, ourselves; asking forgiveness of him or her with a full consciousness of how mean, how cruel, how unjust we have been, and knowing that the other party has looked upon us in the same light. This is what will try the soul. But this is what must be done, and done with every one we have ever wronged in deed or in purpose, before a full pardon can be obtained, before full peace of mind can be secured. Not only must pardon be sought, but whatever wrong can be righted by making compensation, by retracting false statements or impressions, by giving up what is not ours by the law of pure justice, by making satisfaction in any way that remains possible, and in accepting criticism to learn what that way is, must be so righted. The consciousness of guilt that does not feel the duty and the necessity of doing this is no true conviction of sin; the sinner who cannot do this has not yet repented to the bottom of his heart, and is not yet sure of his salvation. No other proof of the change can take the place of this. Yet how often is it ever required by the church? How many instances can any one tell that he or she has known?

The consideration of duty to God is to be understood as held in abeyance, if one duty is to be set against another. The ordinary christian, especially in the beginning of his new course, puts his duty to God so far above every other consideration that he forgets his duty to human beings; and though it seems a strange thing to be said, yet the fact appears to be that when they have attended to the former duty, the majority of church people consider that nothing more is required. If impelled by benevolence to do anything for the neighbor, it is to preach to him the necessity of saving his soul, according to the cheap and easy plan of having all his sins expiated by one who was never guilty, leaving to him only the duty of gratefully accepting the arrangement. The serious work of making restitution for all wrong-doing is seldom entered upon for oneself, or even urged upon others, a much easier task.

But the demand made by a full conversion is just the opposite. If a man believes in a personal deity, to whom he owes a certain duty, let him perform it without fail; but I venture to say to him in all seriousness that God can wait without suffering; whereas, human beings suffer constantly, in one way or another, from the effects of wrong done by others, and every moment they are made to wait for reparation is an addition to the original injustice. Moreover, the God who does not require the correction of this wrong, as the first duty of the convicted sinner, is no true God; and such a conception of him as allows neglect or postponement shows a sad lack of true conceptions of justice. A just God can never forgive till all the sinner's offences against his brother man have been forgiven, and washed out of the memory of the injured; then the offender will be likely to find himself at peace with God.*

The peculiar trial of one's faith and conscience will come in various ways, no doubt, as it already does in the partial conversions of the church. With some the special form of selfishness that is deepest rooted in the heart may be ambition; with others the greed for wealth; with others still a selfish love for some man or woman who has no inducement to return it; with many it will be the pride that refuses to see, or when seen refuses to acknowledge and correct, the wrong committed against some man, woman, or child. With yet others it may be the bigotry and self-righteousness that obstinately shuts the intellect against all views of truth but the one, or uncharitably declines to believe any good of those outside the one sect, party, or race. Whichever of these it may be, it will be the one thing more difficult to surrender, or to perform, than any other. Not, however, that it will necessarily be in all cases so very difficult absolutely. In persons whose education, habits, and course of life have not engendered strong impulsions or tendencies, whose minds are comparatively balanced, it may for aught I can see be relatively easy. Young men and women entering upon life's work, with serious minds not obstinately fixed upon certain notions, nor grown depraved by a career of vicious habits and unjust practices, seem to me not unpromising subjects for this

---

* In speaking of God I use the word in various senses, most commonly the one attached to it by the church, and do not see how I could well do otherwise. My own conceptions of deity, however, will be found in the chapter on that subject.

discipline. Children, born with no unusual adaptations to evil, and with good capacities for the higher kinds of instruction, could probably be educated into the fully unselfish state of mind by the time they entered the state of mature manhood and womanhood. This is the time when Nature herself seems to make an effort to perfect them morally as well as physically; the time when women are more amiable and lovely, and men more generous and heroic than most of them ever are in later years. It is the time when they get their first strong impulse toward good and noble things; and with wiser teaching might in many cases be able to reach the moral grade corresponding to the physical. At least I know of but one reason why they cannot. That is the old, old reason that men will not learn until they must; that they must travel through purgatory to reach heaven; must be broken to pieces by suffering before they can be molded anew; must be purified of the uncleanness of depraved nature by repeated sorrows and torments; must be subjected to God's will by the disappointment of all their own ambitions, hopes and plans; till when utterly defeated, and crushed into lifeless nothingness and despair, they submit to be regenerated, or remade into the likeness of the ideal perfect man and Savior, fit for the Kingdom of God. The necessity for such crucifixion of the soul is taught by all religions, old and new. None can escape it but the child and youth; and the youth, educated in the existing school of religion, is likely to be perverse, and to insist upon living a selfish or unconscientious life, refusing to believe the warnings of Religion, or what is more strictly true, refusing to give up the full measure of worldly enjoyments, which religion, even the most liberal, insists must be given up to some extent. The spiritual and material satisfactions have been placed in antagonism, and the animal nature, not willingly submitting to die, has had to be crushed down, and more or less destroyed, in order that the higher one might be developed.

The conflict is a feature in human history that could not have been avoided. It is made necessary by the lack of sufficient knowledge, forethought, and self-control in the masses of the race during its immature stage. The belief in natural depravity and other doctrines, originating in the ancient East, has served to maintain it for ages, and will continue it for a good while to come, aided by the actual moral condition of humanity. For, the highest *truth* can come only with a good degree of the *unselfish spirit;* the two things assist each other in their development; and the unjust character that could willingly believe a discipline of torment to be necessary, was accompanied by the delusive theories that demanded it. Thus it is that religion has always been associated with asceticism, and the saint or holy man has been a recluse, tyrannizing over the body, depriving it of its natural wants, or torturing it, to kill out all the instincts and appetites that belong to its healthy state. The modern Christian saint however, practices self-denial but little to what his ancestors did, and in the future will do so still less. With the progress of intelligence the wants of the body and soul will come to be better harmonized, and in time asceticism will cease to stand in the way of the unperverted desires of the young. Then, with a different education, it may be possible to make philosophers at the age of twenty years, and not difficult to effect the entire change of moral character at a similar age.

To prevent all misunderstanding however, it is probably necessary for me to repeat in plain language, what is already implied, that no one has a right to drink wine, for instance, till he has proved his ability to do without it, and to take it only as conscience allows, that is, for its proper uses, not for pleasure alone. And the same prescription is correct in regard to all other gratifications of the senses; use for a definite good purpose to be accomplished, must be the predominant motive; pleasure the reward for such a wise and conscientious use, but never the primary object.

It is not merely sensual pleasure that is thus ignorantly placed in antagonism with religion. All the feelings associated with worldly enjoyment, including even the social and family affections, are assumed to act in opposition to God's will; and all the disappointment of them, with the consequent fearful suffering, is represented by modern religion as so much discipline to prepare the human subject for heaven. This, in the view of things I am setting forth, is mostly pure superstition. A large part of human suffering of every kind is due to selfishness of motive and conduct, and such suffering, when regarded as natural punishment, has an effect in improving the character. It is that dear school of experience said to be necessary for those who can learn in no other, and is the primitive teaching of the whole race. Another installment of misery comes simply from ignorance, without any wrong motive; while still another portion results from the wrong-doing of others—of individuals and society—and for which, in pure justice, the perpetrators, not the victims, are to blame. The teaching of the priest that all of this, without distinction, is under the superintendence of a personal deity, a benevolent despot or a cruel one as you prefer, is calculated to prevent or retard all improvement of the social condition, and the acquirement of that useful knowledge necessary to guard against every kind of ill success, accident, failure, and despair. It is one way in which religion has shown its weak or evil side.

The present generation of young people, already partially or wholly educated into the false habits, wants, tastes and whims of a selfish society, will probably follow the course entered upon till an experience of defeat, failure, disappointment, shall have somewhat broken down the willful selfishness, and aroused the indolent thought, before they will be prepared to learn wisdom and accept righteousness. With those whom a longer life has confirmed in selfish practices, or made strong in selfish ambitions, there will be still more to counteract and overcome through the intellect, and stronger resistance from the lower feelings; so that it is hardly possible they can be radically changed without a great deal of suffering, as the primary inducement to make the effort required. Under the education received they have become like a tree that has grown warped, deformed, and straggling, needing to be straightened up, pruned into shape, and perhaps replanted into better conditions, before it will mature and bear fruit. With such an education as will sometime be given they would be like the tree set at first in its proper place, and trimmed when young into its best form, requiring little attention afterward to grow into a thing of permanent beauty and use.

But the same means that can prevent the child from taking on bad habits and practices can make it easier for the adult man or woman to cast them off. The more clearly a possible reconciliation of the natural man and the spiritual, of the individual with society, of a true normal worldliness with morality and religion, can be demonstrated; and the more people can be taught to understand of the superior happiness belonging to the superior state; the more readily will the old be abandoned for the new, and the less will be the suffering connected with the change. It is a wiser teaching, and a deeper intellectual perception in the taught, that are to be the means of its accomplishment.

Nevertheless, practically, it will be impossible to escape a certain amount of pain; and as already said, this will center upon the point where the selfish personal desires cling with the most intense force. In the present generation there may be in many cases a trial that will involve a sacrifice of what is dearest of all except continued existence. The struggle will arise from newer and clearer perceptions of what is right and wrong, in other words, from higher ideals of what life should be for all, and of what our own conduct should be in view of such standards; followed by a necessary conviction of present wrong-doing, and an aspiration for the higher, purer, happier condition that is to come from sincere repentance.

If it be desired to know further who are most, and who least susceptible of this radical change, there is one test that appears almost absolute in its certainty. This is the existence of a thoughtfulness regarding the happiness of others, for the good indication; and for the opposite a feeling of cruelty, heartlessness, or indifference to the suffering of other conscious beings, human or animal, which is the index of the very lowest human state. Kindness and cruelty are the poles of moral feeling; and whoever exhibits the most of either, separate from affection or interest, and regardless of belief, seems to me the nearest to or farthest from the possibility of salvation.

Here it may be well to refer to that late Eastern movement known as Theosophy or Occultism. Do I mean to prescribe all the hardship and trial that is hinted at in Occultist books as indispensable to the reaching of the highest condition? No, most certainly not. The highest state aimed at by the theosophist is, almost certainly, an Oriental conception of what is here called the Kingdom of the Unselfish. But the manner of arriving at it, like all other Oriental plans of salvation, involves asceticism; and the soul when saved is only a one-sided soul, the less human part being left behind. The asceticism may not be the most severe, but the prohibition of wine and the injunction of celibacy, which according to such information as I have gained are two of the requirements, show the spirit of the method adopted. With only this much, however, the theosophist, I believe, retards, instead of aiding, the development he seeks, if it is really moral strength, and not mere occult spirit power. In the view here advocated asceticism of any kind is needless, and occult power, whatever there is of it, is more likely to be obtained after the Unselfish Stage is reached, when it can be wisely used. In regard to ascetic self-denial then, the present scheme demands less; though as to the abandonment of the selfish life nothing can be more thorough.

It should also be well understood, if not sufficiently implied already, that the mental state here contemplated does not depend on the cultivation of spiritual senses, or mediumistic faculties of any description. Such acquirements may be valuable when we have become able to reduce the knowledge of them to a science; but they are not necessary to the attainment of the Unselfish Condition; and so far as I have observed, the persons who most readily exhibit those occult faculties are not the ones most likely to manifest the reasoning power, so closely connected with unselfishness.

No more necessary is the belief in a spiritualist philosophy. Not only is the old religious and spiritualistic teaching of the sort adapted to the immature mind, but further, the discipline and culture required by it, especially all that is meditative, dreamy, and occult, seems like an effort to reverse the natural progress of intellectual growth, and reduce the adult back into the mental condition of the child.

To restate now a few points, some of them already repeated, the conversion here discussed, as distinguished from the ordinary conversion of religion, is a crisis period in a whole course of moral development, a time when the strongest desire of the selfish nature, the ruling passion, the central and most vital point, the tap root of its whole growth, is reached and destroyed, conquered and cast out; not by destroying or suppressing any part of the human mental constitution, but by destroying its liability to perverted action, and turning it instead to good and happifying uses. It is a change which carries the subject of it into an ideal better and wiser condition, where all his motives, thoughts, words and acts are dominated by unselfishness and a conscientious purpose. It may come on through meditation, induced by various considerations and circumstances, or, like the conversion of religious excitement, may be prompted by a mesmeric influence proceeding from certain good people, friends or others who may have a benevolent interest in the party acted upon. This, which Superstition calls "the saving power of the Holy Ghost," may in some cases be felt very distinctly and have a marked effect. Any one may exercise it who possesses within himself a sufficient degree of the unselfish character, by which it is generated and from which it outflows.

The passage through this crisis, severe to many, but not necessarily severe to those who have been prepared for it, and the entrance upon the stage beyond, is what constitutes salvation. But salvation is not salvation from all sin or wrong-doing; it is salvation from the *power* of sin, and from the *power* of the selfish disposition. No one can be so perfect he cannot do wrong by mistake or want of thought; but the peculiarity of this condition is that he cannot do wrong by *design*, and that he *can* repent, and seek to right the wrong of which he has been guilty. In repenting he seeks pardon, not of God, but of the person injured. If he has a personal deity there is certainly nothing to prevent asking forgiveness of him also. Then, having already conquered his strongest disposition to evil, he is thereafter able to master that and every other, and to make rapid progress toward that state where even involuntary sin will be of rare occurrence, and only venial in character. For, be it observed, this person has sacrificed pride, and is willing to accept criticism or ask advice in order to guard against wrong-doing. His willingness to learn the right is as marked as the willingness to do.

Moreover, this person who has passed from the power of sin by conquering it in its strong-hold is for ever after capable of standing alone. He is not dependent on the presence of the Holy Spirit, on the study of sacred books, or on the influence of the church; though all of these may at times be of service to him. From being dependent on a source of grace outside himself, he becomes himself a perpetual fountain of good influence to others. He is not fearful of being contaminated by the company of sinners, but is able to take hold and lift them up without being dragged down himself in so doing. He is able to resist the whole world of evil by virtue of having already vanquished, within himself, all that it can bring against him. His conviction of the unwisdom of all selfishness for himself is as strong as his hatred of it in others. His moral state has become organic, a part of his constitution, which he can no more lose than the full-grown man can become a child. He is radically and completely saved—saved from ever again coming under the dominion of evil, and therefore capable of securing for himself all the happiness of such a superior development.

With this clear understanding of what the change is that determines the future happiness of a soul, a few words may be said concerning those religious developments that most resemble it in the past, and of which we have become able to form a better judgment.

Something similar there has been, a condition near enough like it to give a crude conception of the nature of the feeling involved, and of the extent, degree, or comprehensiveness of the change; this conception exhibiting various degrees of imperfection at various times and places during the world's history. As according to the view here taken the condition is a natural product of evolution, it is but natural we should find the germs of it existing, with more or less of immature growth, and prophecies of a completer growth to be attained in future. In a few rare and isolated instances there may have been a close approach to it. But that a clear, full, and comprehensive idea of it was never arrived at I am fully satisfied, for the reasons before given, and especially the fact that no vital, germinating points of a society, such as persons in this state would form, have ever existed.

One of the first of these imperfect conceptions of it may possibly be found in the *absorption into Brahm* of the ancient (and present) Vedanta system of Hindoo theology and philosophy. Its imperfection consists in the selfishness which looks upon it as the salvation of the individual, to be accomplished through meditation and asceticism, comparatively regardless of unselfish work to be done for others. The union with deity contemplated is somewhat like the feeling of a lost or wayward child restored to its father, and who, in its reconcilation to him, with expectation of being a favorite, is really devoted and means to be good to him, but has little design of being good to any one else.

The *Nirwana* of Buddhism, the final complete union of perfected souls, was another such incomplete idea of the state, to be reached partly through asceticism like the first, but unlike that, by a large degree of genuine benevolence in feeling and action. This feature, illustrated by the immense missionary work which has spread the Buddhist religion among more than half of the earth's population, marks its superiority to that of the Brahmin, by necessarily making it a union of more unselfish natures.

Whether the old Persians had a similar idea, to which a definite name was given, I am unable to say. The Paradise of Zoroaster was to be gained, not by asceticism or meditation, nor even by benevolence; but by active effort; by fighting long and faithfully on the side of Ormuzd against Ahriman, or of justice and right against wrong. This, it may fairly be contended, is a higher grade, if not of religion at least of morality, than either of the others; and its unselfishness is further proved by its associating with itself the final triumph of the good, and conquest of the whole world to righteousness, when even Ahriman himself shall be saved. The better minds among this people aspired to be "pure in thought, in word, and in deed;" and it is not improbable some of them may have believed they had actually attained to such a state of purity—a purely conscientious state, not inferior to that of Nirwana, and in which there would exist a high degree of harmony.

Our modern Theosophists inform us, with much reason for the statement, that the "descent of the Spirit," the "incarnation of God in man" was a belief held and taught by the comprehending few, in ancient Egypt, and over all the civilized parts of Asia, at the same time. What this really meant could only be the acquirement by man of a godlike spirit, the raising of the human till it became divine.

This may likewise be the forgotten meaning of the Sabbath, in the Hebrew Story of Creation, assuming that story to be allegorical, and to have reference only to spiritual creations or changes.

Was it also what was meant by Jesus when he talked of the Kingdom of Heaven? I cannot answer. The record of his utterances is too confused, and too much corrupted by fraud, for me to decide what they meant, or what they really were. The larger part of them can be given that interpretation. The Essenes possessed the most unselfish society of the ancient times; and if Jesus had been one of their body, as some believe, it seems probable that this condition was the object of his view. If he was their ideal man only, and not an actual person at all, as some others have hinted, it still appears likely that an imperfect idea of it existed among some of their number. That some of the best spirits among those who have called themselves his disciples have had such a conception I have no doubt. St. Paul's description of Charity is a description of the unselfish character; and certain things written in the first epistle of John, in the New Testament, indicate that the writer had probably made as near an approach to the unselfish state as was possible, under the intellectual conditions of his time.

The Gnostics, of a little later period, conceived it more perfectly perhaps than any before them; for they claimed to teach the *Knowledge of God*, and the *Liberty of the Spirit*, two things that can be fully understood only by coming fully into the Unselfish Condition. The *Unity with God* of the old Mystics and the Neo-Platonists was still another instance of belief in the possibility of a much higher than the ordinary human state, and of efforts to attain it through spiritual agencies. One or two of the Christian sects that started into life during the middle ages may have had a dim idea of this condition, but mixed with so much error that they became notorious only for folly and indecency. The early Alchemists, for aught I know, may have been striving to transmute the base metals of selfishness into the pure gold of unselfishness, and teaching the few more capable ones under the guise of allegory. The condition was sought by Fenelon, Molinos and other Roman Catholic saints, under the name of Perfect Love or of Quietism; still later by the Wesleyan Methodists as

Holiness; and last of all by another Protestant sect as Perfectionism. As complete a view of it as any was that possessed by Emanuel Swedenborg, which he called the Celestial State. It is the true "peace of God that passeth understanding" to all but the few who have experienced it, though often talked of much by those who have felt a mere breath of its celestial influence, in times of religious excitement. It is the true Illumination by which spiritual things are discerned, the true Gnosis by which we know both God and ourselves.

With none of these parties, I must repeat, was the ideal perfect, or the state sought for completely attained. The reason I have already once given in explaining the failure of the Christian church, and of all religions, to prepare men for it. It is that they lacked the knowledge that science and modern thought have given to the present age. They had no philosophy able to harmonize thought and make it equal to the truth. Without these aids they could do no more or better than they did. It remains for us, with our richer resources, to accomplish what they could not. They had dim visions of the pure ideal; they made out some of its outlines; they attempted, in their imperfect way, to realize this imperfect ideal, among imperfect men, and failed. As with other and minor good things, the germs of it are in the past, the full growth and fruition in the future.

Is it necessary for me to speak of the happiness belonging to this new state further than is already expressed in previous chapters? Has not every enthusiastic religionist and socialist protrayed some of its glories as they appeared to him? Do not all of us imagine some rare perfection this world of ours is to take on at some distant future time? Certainly all who ever think much have done so. To these fancyings I have only to add what is to me one of the very firmest of all convictions, that all the good and happy things that both these parties have believed to be possible of obtainment *are* possible; not separately but together; not the spiritual without the material, nor the sensual without those of the spirit; but both combined and harmonized, reconciled and united to each other in eternal peace. All that can give pleasure, either of a high order or a low one, belongs to the Kingdom of the Unselfish or Empire of the Wise. Nothing low in the sense which the drunkard, the glutton or the libertine understands; for not one of these ever conceived of the meaning now in view. It is that every organ of the physical frame will be seen to have a noble use; every function that gives sensual enjoyment a wise purpose; everything pertaining to the body will become holy; all will have a sacredness and value now unknown; for its instincts, appetites and capacities, when enlightened and moralized, controlled by high motives, and directed only in conscientious ways, will be found to possess powers of life, health and happiness unsuspected so long as devoted only to selfish enjoyment, or looked upon as by nature impure and unholy. "There is no end to the evolution of enjoyments in our progress toward God" (or in God) "when once it has become safe for us to trust ourselves."*

---

*——————————"If a soul depart
Instructed—knowing itself—and knowing truth,
And how that Brahma and the Self are One—
Then hath it freedom over all the worlds.
And if it wills the region of the Past,
The Fathers and the Mothers of the Past
Come to receive it; and that Soul is glad!
And if it wills the region of the Homes,
The Brothers and the Sisters of the Homes
Come to receive it; and that Soul is glad!
And if it wills the region of the Friends,
The Well-beloved come to welcome it
With love undying; and that Soul is glad!
And if it wills a world of grace and peace,
Where garlands are, and perfumes and delights
Of delicate meats and drinks, music and song,
Lo! fragrances and blossoms, and delights
Of dainty banquets, and the streams of song
Come to perfect it; and that Soul is glad!
And if it make its bliss in beauty's arms,

The *moral* satisfactions of a higher life have been described by many persons, and every one is supposed to be familiar with such descriptions; though the reality of their truth can be known only when the experience gives it. The conflict with the world and endurance of its persecutions, which is the counterpoise of spiritual enjoyments, has been portrayed in too strong a light to remain true of the unselfish condition; for that state implies, not a conflict with the real world, but with the false one created by selfishness, ignorance, and sin. The real human nature needs enlightenment more than resistance, comprehension more than abuse. The unselfishness of spirit that can meet the world with candor and justice will meet far less of its ill-will than did the saints of old.

For the positive part there will be a sympathy, a harmony, a unity with all good beings, whatever they may be called or wherever they dwell, with the better part of every human soul, and with the universal good as manifested in all high motive and true endeavor. The peace of God and the peace with man will not be separated. If there shall be misunderstanding, suspicion, dislike, slander and reviling from the world of less fortunate humanity, there will also be abundant charity with which to neutralize its bitterness; while the perpetual satisfaction, and the continually increasing joys, of this bright new world, wherein no serious discord can remain, will much more than compensate for all disagreement with the old. For a new world it truly will be,—so new, so changed, so unlike the past that one may even wish to change his name, to forget his history, to deny his former opinions, to throw away nearly all his previous

---

    "Finding most wonder, most release, most rest,
    On the soft bosoms of the Maids of Heaven,
    Lo! The bright Maids of Heaven—more loving-sweet
    Than loveliest earthly beauty—come to him,
    Rejoiced—rejoicing! and that Soul is glad!"
                  From "*The Secret of Death*," by *Edwin Arnold*.

mental possessions, and baptize himself outwardly and inwardly with the pure waters of a new fountain of life. Wealth, ambition, power, fame, of the old and selfish order, will be as nothing against the new ambitions, and the spiritual wealth of the higher state. There can be no temptation to go backward. And as the incomer to this new state may desire to leave his past behind him, so his associates will be willing to do the same. Goodness will be remembered; the imperfection of one's life will not be perpetually talked of. Friendship will need no cultivation; brotherly love will be a genuine thing; because no one can be untrue, no trust can be betrayed, no confidence can result in any harm. A spiritual kinship, more binding than any ties of blood or race, will take the place of all previous obligations. The goodness and wisdom apparent in each individual will be the superior attractive power to those who love such qualities; and their warmth and light, shining through the countenance, will prevent even the plainest face from being unlovely. Sincerity and frankness must be perpetual where there is no necessity for deceit or dissimulation.

When all work together for good there will be no loss of effort, no misspent energy; all will go to increase the common sum of happiness; and how much this means may be imagined when we observe how freely it is now wasted in foolish efforts to take from one another, or to enjoy in a life of selfish individualism.

Here then, is sufficient ground of appeal, both to the rationalist, who cannot understand the mysteries of religion, and to the religionist, who dare not be rational for fear of losing his faith. The Intuition, when it attempts to build a philosophy, assumes the work of the Understanding and fails. Its highest function is the *prophecy* born of aspirational feeling, and to be realized through the understanding. By its mistake it has kept up a perpetual warfare between the two sides of human nature, elevating one, and degrading the other without cause. For, be it again said, it is not the spirit or the body that is holy or unholy, but the motive by which they are animated or controlled. It is not the body that is to be abhorred, but the ignorant selfishness which dominates both body and soul. It is not spirituality that is to be desired, but the wise unselfishness which can turn everything in body and soul to a sanctified and beneficent use. At last the point of misunderstanding can be made plain, and the two mental factors can be united without harm to either. The intuition can prophecy, and all that it imagines in its brighest dreams the understanding can bring forth into reality.

CHAPTER XVII.

ARTOSITY AND ART.

THOUGH the above terms must be defined in the sense here given to them, it is not necessary for my purpose to enter upon any very extended discussion of the nature of Art, or the definition of Beauty, subjects that have been already discussed by many distinguished minds without coming to a definite agreement. A certain proportion of the artistic world will unite with me in considering Art to be *perfect work*,—function skillfully performed, purpose effectively and gracefully carried out. Whether the work accomplished produces a building, a statue, a picture, a song, an oration, a piece of diplomacy, a business operation, a manufactured article, or a construction of any sort whatever, matters not. Even destructive work may be artistic, may be easily, gracefully and effectually done, when set about in the right manner. And thus everything we do, say, or think becomes artistic or slovenly, thorough and finished or crude, graceful or awkward, to a certain degree. There is nothing done to which these terms do not apply. Whatever is beautiful or perfect without man's conscious agency, that is, a person, an animal, a plant, or a stone, a mountain, a lake, is so because the forces existing in nature have acted in such a manner as to create the perfect thing instead of the imperfect, or along with the imperfect as an exceptional instance. It is the effect of work done, of force acting upon matter. In a general way at least, we may call it Nature's perfect work.

Is Beauty always perfect work? are perfection and beauty one? Perhaps it will be found that all beauty that can stand the test of criticism is beautiful because it is perfect. Many things that seem perfect or beautiful to one person may be imperfect and unbeautiful to another, who can see what the imperfection is. The beauty in the color of a flower may mean the relief that comes to the mind when no fault can be found in it. It is clear, bright and uniform, and we know no reason why it should be otherwise. The flower may be variegated, and we may still call it beautiful. But if the variegation were known to be a symptom of disease or weakness in the plant, would it still be beautiful in the flower? A rich deep red in the lips and cheek of a human face is beautiful to many; to one who sees in it the sign of a scrofulous constitution it is far otherwise. The peculiar features of the negro may be considered handsome in some parts of Africa; to the ethnologist, looking upon them as indications of imperfect development, they have no beauty.

The flower has also a perfect form, symmetrical and regular, which gives us another negative pleasure from not being able to find fault with it, a pleasure that quickly disappears if we discern some imperfection at first overlooked. The flower is therefore beautiful for having two qualities, color and form, neither of which we are able to say is imperfect. On the contrary, the impure or uneven color, and the unsymmetrical or irregular form are in very many things imperfectious; they are indeed so strongly associated wtth imperfection in our minds, that unconsciously we assume the first-named, or beautiful characteristics, to be the marks of perfection.

A clear, steady, resonant tone we call musical and perfect, in distinction from one of an opposite kind, which we know to be imperfect. It may have still another admirable quality, which we are in the habit of calling *sweetness;* not the clearness that represents the perfect health of the vocal organs, but a quality of the timbre, belonging to the voice habitually, and is called sweet only because it indicates the sensibility of a fine-grained organism, and the sweetness of tender, humane feelings, the characteristics of the most perfectly humanized person. We certainly do not expect to find it in the voices of the coarse and brutal. And it is sweet, beautiful or perfect because those more perfect human qualities it represents confer the most happiness on their possessor, and all with whom he or she may be related.

Why the musical tone, and the harmonious combination of tones, are agreeable to us no one can say, except that they make a gentler impression on the auricular nerve than do the harsh sounds we call noises and discords; just as the higher grade colors of light, the green, blue and violet, consisting of finer vibrations, leave a gentler effect upon the eye. If so then in music there is a negative happiness, from the lessening of disagreeable labor in sensation, just as in contemplating the beautiful flower there is a lessening or absence of the disagreeable thought connected with the imperfect.

If grace of movement is not commonly understood to be *ease* of movement, it has at least been tolerable well proven to be so in one of Mr. Spencer's essays. Unconsciously, perhaps, we discover or infer that there is in it such a lessening of muscular effort, and therefore give to it the same admiration we give to beauty.

Mr. Spencer has also done something to show that poetry, the music of words, is pleasant to us for the reason that it demands less effort of the attention. In oratory it is the easy combination of simple, well-understood, expressive words—aside from the appropriate metaphor and the fine adjectives, which adorn both oratory and poetry alike—that gives to eloquence its beauty and effectiveness. It is furthermore a well-known rule of art that in a picture or a statue having a sentiment or an idea to express, the ease with which it makes its design evident forms one of its strongest claims to beauty, or to excellence as art.

Regarding all of these there is no question that beauty or perfection is a means of happiness; and in all there is a strong intimation that the happiness is of that negative kind which consists in an escape or relief from what is disagreeable, or such a lessening of it as we call ease. Beauty, grace, excellence, perfection, ease, pleasant feeling, happiness, is a series of terms that seem to have a natural affiliation. I see no reason to doubt that beauty means perfection in the accomplishment of design or end, that end being the attainment of some form of happiness, negative or positive.

In drama, and in various other artistic works, it is not beauty, as commonly understood, that we are called upon to admire, but expressiveness—the intensity or force of expression—and we have to consider only their appropriateness, in other words, their perfect adaptation to express. The perfect adaptation constitutes the beauty, the gracefulness, the excellence, the artistic and admirable quality.

What connection is there between the artistic sense and the intellect?—is a question that may next be considered.

Among the ancients, Plato made Beauty to be one with the Good; Aristotle was the first to associate it with Truth. To Aristotle it was that which makes the parts, order, and proportions of an object easily comprehensible; and comprehension is the truthful or correct understanding.

Simplicity, order, and systematic character are still

considered necessary to render a thing artistic. They make the contemplation of it easy to the mind, and easy comprehension gives pleasure. Those qualities, so essential to art, involve more or less of rational thought; but they are not all, and do not include all the thought, that is necessarily involved in artistic production.

St. Augustine is quoted as seeing beauty in unity of relations; that thing to him was beautiful whose central principle and organic relations we can perceive,—a definition which is substantially the same as that of Aristotle. But, expressed in other words, this central principle is the one thing among many different relations, qualities, or adaptations belonging to the beautiful thing, —a something common to all of them; and its perception is by a generalizing process, the same as that by which an induction is made from many diverse facts. As all the species of a genus manifest the genus characteristic, so each quality, relation, circumstance or adaptation of the perfect thing possesses or exhibits the *general* characteristic manifest in all the others. It is that which, in common language, renders them all harmonious or appropriate. And when we find fault with some one point, in a thing assumed to be perfect, we say this particular point does not agree with the rest, is out of character with them, does not harmonize, is not appropriate like the rest, and is out of place or does not belong with them. It has not the same propriety, the same quality, or the same adaptation to a purpose. When the common unity can be discerned in *all* the diverse parts, qualities, and operations, then we call the thing artistic, graceful, beautiful or perfect. We have no other criticism to make.

The combination of *unity with diversity* is the definition which Victor Cousin, the modern Eclectic philosopher, gave to Beauty; while *harmony*, the term more especially associated with art, is the word that Edgar A. Poe, the poet, applied, in a philosophical essay of his, to what present thinkers mean by *unity of law*, or of generalization. Unity, in this sense, and harmony, in art, are the same. Appropriateness is a word quite as strictly belonging to art as either of the others. When everything pertaining to a production of art or artisanship is appropriate to its design, plan or purpose, it is the perfected or artistic thing, possessing unity and harmony.

Truth possesses the beauty of consistency; and without this harmony or agreement of every part with every other, it is not the complete or perfected truth.

I see no necessity for the distinction made by some writers between intrinsic or absolute beauty and relative beauty. The first is that produced by nature, such as a flower, a pearl, or a precious stone, and in which there is something pleasing, while we are not sufficiently acquainted with all its parts and qualities to discover any fault. The latter is the perfection of things having a purpose, and which we understand well enough to see whether they are perfect or imperfect. When we know more of the real ends served by nature's beautiful things we shall probably find them not altogether perfect; while in some others, not considered beautiful, the beauty of adaptation may be as great as in any. For, if in the flower its gay color may be the means of attracting the insects that enable it to continue its species, in some insect the lack of all bright color may be an equally good adaptation, enabling it to live by escaping the notice of its enemies. The perfectness of this *adaptation* is that which gives pleasure to the art sense, this being the most perfect work of Nature.

The addition of perfect forms or colors, or both, to adaptation constitutes the enrichment of decoration or adornment.

But what then is the relation of Beauty to Goodness?

The same as Plato saw it, a unity. Moral goodness is moral beauty, the perfection of unselfishness. Moral quality extends to everything so nearly we may well question if there is any exception in an act or utterance that affects nobody. And as happiness or the greatest good is the supreme end of all activity, whatever is out of harmony with this supreme purpose lacks one element of appropriateness, and cannot be completely artistic, perfect or beautiful. Though a disagreeable scene, or a painful subject may be perfectly represented, and therefore artistic in a minor sense, unless it be designed to teach a useful lesson, or convey a needed warning, for human benefit, the thing as a whole becomes inartistic in the higher sense, and unworthy the name of true art. The art feeling, as claimed by Ruskin, is associated with the moral conscience; and the morally unprincipled man cannot be the great artist. Truth must possess the unity of consistency, Beauty that of propriety, Goodness that of equality or justice. And when Mr. Ruskin said that ideal beauty is alike the aim of the artist, the moralist, and the religionist, he might have added that it is equally the aim of the thinker or scientist. Truth makes everything beautifully consistent, harmonious, systematic, simple and admirable.

According to Schopenhauer the intellect has nothing to do with art or taste, the beautiful being discerned only by intuition. On the contrary, intellect has everything to do with art, as I have before shown that it has everything to do with goodness. The words, however, may be so understood as to give no real contradiction. The kind of intellect that only *learns and memorizes* does not perceive the beautiful, except so far as taught. But that kind of intellect that can *classify and organize* its stores of knowledge, and thus be able to draw from them a *higher truth that it has not been taught*, this is what perceives beauty or the lack of it. Another writer has said that "one of the necessities for high art is imagination or invention, the genius or faculty for producing that which is unexpected, an object, a harmony, a perfection, a thought, an expression, of which we had no idea, could not forsee or hope to find, and which we perceive with delight when exhibited." This originating power, or genius for invention, is the same that discovers a new truth. Schelling, an earlier German thinker, called it the "intellectual intuition." It is simply the finer sensitiveness of the developed intellect, which perceives likeness or unlikeness where the more ordinary grades of reasoning faculty cannot. The same kind of reasoning "genius" gives the ability to criticize, —to see what is appropriate or inappropriate, harmonious or inharmonious, how many things agree in some one particular, and how many are unlike the rest in this respect. The most complete art is, then, the combination of eclecticism with originality, the learning or doing of all that is true and right in what others have learned or done, and then by originating power going beyond it.

This, however, refers to works of design, planned and executed by human skill. But, furthermore, there is reason to believe that all *inherent* beauty possesses utility or adaptation to some end, as its essential characteristic when fully analyzed. Utility and beauty are thus one, and that one utility. Otherwise beauty will have no reason for existence, no harmony with other purposes or adaptations, nor with the universal purpose of happiness.

In agreement with the current opinion it is said that there is no standard of *human* beauty; and further, that if the Evolution theory is correct no such standard is possible. But I venture to predict right the contrary, that the future scientist, the anthropologist and ethnologist, will discover a true standard of human beauty, with good and sufficient reasons for every item of beauty or grace in form and carriage of the body, and every beautiful feature in the shape and expression of the head and face. Some hints toward it have already been offered by Mr. Spencer, in one of his essays, and more definite ones will hereafter appear under the guidance of the same theory of Evolution.

It may not be entirely needless to say that Art has little compatibility with Fashion. Fashion, uninfluenced by reason, continually changes everything. Art is as unchangeable as truth itself; for art is rational, and depends on rationality. If all people were artists there would be very little of fashion, though a richer variety in all that fashion now controls. The changes made would be determined by art, and the effect of them would be improvement.

The new word Artosity is defined in defining art. The perfect work of art consists in the harmonious coöperation of all things to the artist's purpose of realizing his best ideal in creations of utility or in expression. Otherwise stated, it is the agreement, congruity, fitness or propriety of every part with every other in regard to form, quality or aspect; and of the whole with its design or end, and with the conditions, surroundings or circumstances under which the purpose is fulfilled. Whatever has this is artistic in the fullest sense. It may be grand art or commonplace, simple or complex; but of either kind it will be complete. Artosity, then, is the art feeling, the aspiration to realize this complete art, the desire for it, the appreciation and love of it when attained. It is to art what religiosity is to religion.

But Artosity is a larger or more inclusive word than Religiosity, and indeed embraces religiosity itself. For while the latter is concerned with what is right in the moral world, and aims at unselfishness in all things commonly supposed to have moral quality, Artosity is concerned with what is right in every possible domain of human activity, and even in the organic world below man. It feels the consciousness of *ought* in regard to whatever is great or small, high or low. It acknowledges the duty of doing whatever is done in the best manner, and of improving everything that can be improved. It is pained by the perception of what is wrong in anything and everything, everywhere and always. It is the Universal Conscience. It will be satisfied with nothing less than perfection in morals and manners, in social customs, in dress and adornment in industry; in the home, the village, the city, the nation; in law, in religion, in art. It cannot be indifferent to slovenliness, awkwardness, bungling work or inefficiency, any more than it can to injustice. It is saddened, grieved, disgusted, or outraged by the ten thousand senseless, brutal, and villainous things that occur about us every day, every one of which is out of place in an artistic world, a world wherein art should be carried into everything. It perceives that in all the million items that go to make up human life there is a possibility of pain or pleasure to the human sense of right; and aspiring to please this artistic sense of right regarding all possible conditions, and every kind of action or expression, it aims at a more universal and more perfect unselfishness than Morality or Religion has ever dared to include within its widest aspirations.

To repeat then, there is no mistake in calling it the Universal Conscience, the sense of duty regarding all we feel, think, say or do, in order to avoid giving pain to the artistic sense of others, or to confer pleasure by its gratification, and by the increased happiness that results to all by the realization of a near approach to the perfect. It is thus not lower than the religious feeling, but higher; not smaller, but larger; including the moral conscience as a part of its own universal sense of right.

Respecting its origin I can scarcely do more than refer

to what has already been said about the origin of its moral part—moral artosity—in Chapters II and III. It is not an inherent sense, but a cultivated one. Both art and morality begin in the intellect, and to be true, in the highest sense, must be firmly based on positive knowledge. Only through the intellect can we learn what is the right, the perfect, the ideal, in all the multifarious concerns of life. The more fully the intellect is informed the stronger and clearer will be the sense of artistic right, including moral right. The moralist has but to consider how much stronger the sense of political right is in our own country, where it has been discussed for generations, than it is in countries lacking such discussion, to understand what the intellect has to do in creating that moral sense of right concerning the relations of the individual and the state. Every artist, and person who has learned a trade or business, knows how the learning of it creates the feeling of what is right, fit or proper within it; and how the desire to realize that right is strengthened by such knowledge. Of course the way to its cultivation is made plain by knowing its origin.

If every one possesses somewhat of this universal sense of right, and desire to see what *is* right, proper, suitable, congruous, equal, true, harmonious, artistic and beautiful in things, conditions, and persons around him, then certainly every one is of right bound to recognize that feeling, and so to conduct himself as not to outrage, or even give offence to it. For, it can scarcely be denied that in some degree, and regarding some matters, it does exist in all; as indeed it must wherever there is any considerable amount of intelligence. No one is so obtuse that he or she does not know when another is awkward or graceful in carriage, slovenly or neat in dress, ill-mannered or polite in behavior, whether work performed is

botched or workmanlike. Without any knowledge of
architecture or of anatomy a person can still tell whether
a house or a town is dilapidated, dirty, and ill-arranged
or the reverse; whether he sees a fine horse, or a miserable, crippled old skeleton, driven by a miserable, ragged,
half-starved human. One class of these things gives
more or less pain to every beholder who is not himself
too stupid to care; the other class gives pleasure. And
the willful individualist, who insists on his right to do
what he will at his own cost, does not reflect that the
cost of all inartistic proceedings falls, not on himself, but
on those around him, all of whom have to suffer pain,
disgust, or disagreeable feeling of some kind, that his
selfish individuality may be gratified.

Here is a species of immorality, practiced by almost
everybody, and yet scarcely any one takes the trouble
to condemn. For whatever little may have been written
by artists and moralists, and more especially by socialists against it has produced no effect; and not one
person in a hundred of the average mass of civilized humanity knows what an artistic sense, of a general character, means. Artists and mechanics have an idea what
it requires of them in their own particular work, and but
little further; for though, as just said, when the offense
against it is extreme he perceives botchwork, slovenliness,
awkwardness, he does not condemn it as an offence
against moral right, against justice, against all persons
who are sensible of the wrong. Individualism has taught
people that they have a right to transgress all rules of
taste, and even of decency, so long as they do not openly
insult one or knock him down; after which politeness
and law begin to make a protest. They can offend his
eyes, ears, and nose with all sorts of disagreeable things,
yet the right of the individual to offend is so much more
strongly fixed in the general mind than the right to pro-

test, that people submit to a great deal of ill usage before they feel justified in making any quarrel, or even complaint. The disagreeable things become accepted as a matter of course. In reality it could not be otherwise. So long as present ideas of individual freedom prevail, and individualism remains the law of the industrial world, and of the world of thought, the individual must be permitted to wreak his fancy upon everything he does, and exhibit his lack of sense, taste and propriety in every possible way. He could not be sufficiently individualistic unless he did. And individualism must continue till men have become strong enough to have no fear of losing their petty liberties by closer association. This is more especially true in our own country.

Yet some of the more cultivated acknowledge the claims of art generally. Decoration of all kinds is attempted by everybody; but decoration is not art in the sense here intended. It is work which may be artistic, if so done as to harmonize with the character and surroundings of the decorated object, without obscuring its merits by being too elaborate, abundant, or pretentious. Or, like any other, it may be inartistic, if done without due regard for a rational taste. It may be the beginning of art; for at least it has beauty or improvement as its object. True art, however, shows itself in the constant improvement of manufactured articles, in landscape gardening, and in the architecture of ordinary buildings. It will do no harm to mention some things in which there is still too little, and toward which the artous feeling should be directed. No attempt to criticise the fine arts will be made.

The idea of village improvement, as a sort of reform, is sometimes advocated. The straightening and grading of streets, planting of trees along their sides, and making a solid, well-drained roadbed is a work of art as well as of utility; and could scarcely be one without being the other. But trees with crooked stems, and scattered, straggling limbs are not artistic; they give more pain than pleasure to the art feeling, and are less useful for shade. Some of those that have brightly colored foliage in spring or fall might be made as handsome as flowers by shortening in the branches when young to make them grow thick, and the whole tree of good shape; while without such care their color scarcely renders them pleasing. To set them so thickly their shade causes dampness is not artistic because not rational, unless in a very hot climate.

Farm villages, that could be pleasantly arranged and laid out, have been thought of; but no one has proposed to make the farm itself artistic. Rich men who own a few acres of ground with a house on it will spend a great deal to make it beautiful, and commonly succeed. But the farm grounds, the place where delicious food is produced, or what should be such, is never supposed to be capable of artistic treatment, or the man who works on it capable of being an artist. So far otherwise is it that in many localities the farmer is the very embodiment of slovenliness, anything but neat in his manner of raising the delicious products of the soil, and the farm itself is a sort of slovenly hell. Yet the farmer could be an artist if he possessed the requisite intelligence, to give him both aspiration and capacity. It is no more difficult for him to be one than for the mechanic or architect. Neatness, plan, system, regularity, order—everything in its appropriate place, and out of a place where it is not appropriate—good fences, ground clear from weeds and bushes, regularity in straight or curved lines, fully-decayed and odorless fertilizers, thorough cultivation, work of all kinds well done, plain but tasteful buildings, shapely trees with fruit on them, wood-land clear of useless underbrush and rotten wood,—these are what will make the roughest farm beautiful, a pleasure to every eye, and an education in taste to every child that grows up on such a place. Cattle? no, cattle do not render a farm more artistic, but the reverse. They may give a pleasant appearance at a distance; the poets and romancists have written so many pretty things about them, that we try to imagine something beautiful; but closer contact with them in their ways, and the places where they live, shows nothing of the sort, and it is only in their wild state, roaming over the woods and plains, that a true taste can find them beautiful. The family horse, cow, dog and cat, may be tolerated, partly for their friendship as well as for their necessity. Of course the individual animal may be a handsome one of its kind, only not as a part of the ideal farm as it may sometime be. At present necessity makes animals allowable.

And the farmer's home,—is that artistic? Scarcely. There are plenty of old farm-houses that get into pictures made by artists; some of them quaint, curious and interesting; but these qualities, even with age added, do not render a thing artistic; they only make it an object of curiosity—picturesque. And the artistic farm-house itself is not often seen. Yet it is not difficult to build it in form and style corresponding to the location where it stands, with an interior appropriately contrived for its uses, and without any slovenly surroundings at the rear, sides, or front; but on the contrary, with tastefully arranged grounds, trees, shrubs, hedges, vines, or flowers, pleasant to the eye in every direction, most of them useful as well as ornamental. As to the interior there are certainly many farmers' wives and daughters capable of furnishing and arranging household things, suitable to the conditions, in an artistic way, when once they have learned that decoration is not art, and that the art of arranging consists in taking things out of a place where they do not belong, and putting them where they are not only appropriate but the *most* appropriate; so that any one can find them by simply thinking where they properly ought to be, and with what other things they are most naturally connected. This is simply neatness or tidiness, the opposite of slovenliness, and gives to everything an agreeable appearance. The practice of it is not only a duty we owe to all around us, but an exercise for the cultivation of the mind equal to anything prescribed by Dr. Watts or the logicians; for it is a constant reasoning process, set in operation by everything we come in contact with in our homes and our every-day life; not only in the farm-house, but the village and the city house, the store, the factory, and every place where business, work, or entertainment is carried on. It is a classification of things by their likeness or unlikeness, and placing them to correspond, which is the only arrangement worthy of being called *order*. But this is something entirely distinct from cleanliness. That may be artistic or it may not. A good degree of it is necessary; for dirt is certainly matter out of place. But there are persons who are fearfully clean, who spend half their lives, and a vast amount of dirty soap-suds, in perpetually cleaning one thing or another, yet are as continually dirtying every article they touch, for want of thought in the manner of using; who scatter everything about them in slovenly confusion when at work, and waste nearly all the time taken up in replacing them afterward. Similar persons fill their grounds full of flowering plants, wherever a vacant spot, suitable or unsuitable, can be found, without regard to the time, character, or appearance of the flowers. And some of them may imagine they possess a love of the beautiful; when they have merely the child's delight in bright colors, the bare rudiment of what may sometime, by due encouragement, develop into a love of art. Though doing better than to do nothing, neither of these classes have any conception of art proper, or of the beautiful except in a slight degree.

Coming to the city, we find it hardly more artistic than the country. The filthy mud of the business streets in wet weather, and the filthy dust when the weather is dry, with a bad odor almost always,—these are certainly not artistic surroundings for normal human beings to inhabit. They may be suitable enough for a a population bent only on getting "filthy lucre," regardless of time, place or circumstance, of honesty, decency, or humanity, and with scarcely a thought of beauty, grace, or propriety. The buildings of all shapes, sizes, colors and internal arrangements are not things of beauty except a few; but types of an individuality that is blind, selfish and reckless. The confusion generated by commercial speculation, gambling, and swindling, is not the beautiful system of orderly supply and demand so highly praised by students of theoretical economics. The palaces of the rich, and the squalid sheltering-places of the poor in the same town, are not a beautiful combination in architecture. The ash and garbage boxes, barrels, kettles, etc. on the sidewalk are not an artistic sort of decoration; neither are the innumerable signs, of every conceivable variety, that are standing on it or hung above. The everlasting parade of horses, trucks, wagons, hacks, street-cars, pleasure carriages, hand-carts, garbage-carts, etc. etc. before the fronts of houses where people live, is not a decorous and seemly procession. The endless confusion of sounds they make, even when enlivened by newsboys and hucksters, is not music. The utterly heterogeneous character of the human throng, in their figures, faces, expressions, dress, manners, bearing, and occupation—the good and the bad, the intelligent and stupid, the distinguished and the obscure, the young and old, the rich and poor—all mingled together as chance may throw them, does not make them a fine-appearing company of men and women. The manner in which they treat each other, though the best of anything mentioned, is not always the graceful politeness which constitutes the noble art of manly and womanly good behavior. Even the bare-headed and dirty statues, at the street corners, and in little dusty parks, are not in their appropriate places. No, none of all these things is artistic. To sensitive persons who have some dim conception of what they might be, or may be, they are but the immense discord of a million combined inharmonies. The only artistic portions of a city are some of its parks, a few of its best streets, and a part of the buildings on these. It cannot be otherwise till a great social renovation shall have changed the whole method and character of industrial operations.

Of the human race itself, in city or country, only a few individuals are at the same time handsome, intelligent, and good, as art would require that they should be; and these few are the product of chance more than of design. Education and good conditions improve the child after it is born;* but the original production of human beings is still less artistic than the breeding of horses, cows, pigs or dogs. Here, too, there will be no change for some time to come.

But art is still possible in the little things of common life, things which when well or ill done make an importance difference in the amount of happiness or pain one receives or confers. There is nothing so small or trifling that it is not worth doing in the best manner, whenever greater matters do not forbid giving it the necessary time. That was a genuine artist, whatever his vocation

---

*This may be easily observed in the American born children of Irish immigrants of the inferior sort, and how in them the form becomes slimmer and more graceful, the face narrowed and refined, the sunken eyes filled out, the nose raised up and lengthened, the expression brightened, and the whole appearance more human.

who originated the proverb, "What is worth doing at all is worth doing well." To illustrate I quote from an old letter of Mrs. President Garfield, which without her design got before the public, and does credit to her intelligence.

"I am glad to tell that, out of all the toil and disappointment of the summer just ended, I have risen up to a victory; that silence of thought since you have been away has won for my spirit a triumph. I read something like this the other day; 'there is no healthy thought without labor, and thought makes the labor happy.' Perhaps this is the way I have been able to climb up higher. It came to me one morning when I was making bread. I said to myself, 'Here I am, compelled by an inevitable necessity to make our bread this summer. Why not consider it a pleasant occupation, and make it so by trying to see what perfect bread I can make?' It seemed like an inspiration—and the whole of life grew brighter. The very sunshine seemed flowing down through my spirit into the white loaves; and now I believe my table is furnished with better bread than ever before—and this truth, old as creation, has just now become fully mine, that I need not be the shirking slave of toil, but its regal master, making whatever I do yield me its best fruits." * * *

With such a purpose any one can be master of his work, can keep his self-respect, can give dignity to labor, and glorify drudgery, so long as he does not feel unjustly compelled to it, whether building ships, digging ditches, writing a book or weeding a garden. Thought makes labor art; for thought generates the ideal, the conception of what perfect work will be, and art gives the satisfaction of realizing the ideal. However humble it may be, the artist or laborer may then take pleasure in seeing that his work is thoroughly, neatly, handsomely done. To every one who can do some particular thing well there is a satisfaction in doing it. The same satisfaction may extend to the doing of various other things, when sufficient knowledge and thought have given the ideal, and practice has generated the ability to make it actual. And though every one has not the capacity to learn the perfect doing of many things, yet any one can learn to do something well, and that something will be his art.

A limit exists, however, past which monotony will become tedious; but it applies to all varieties of work, the finest and roughest alike.

The particular art which includes breadmaking, the commonest of all, and one of the most important, has never yet been cultivated with a worthy motive, or a due appreciation of its value. When attempted as an art it has always been with the poor motive of giving pleasure only, and hence strong flavors, concentrated sweets or sours, and pungent spices, have been resorted to to stimulate the sense of taste, and force appetite to its most gluttonous accomplishment, aided further by stimulating drinks; all with the result of deadening taste, making greater stimulation necessary, exhausting the power of the stomach, and finally bringing sudden death to the high-liver. The vegetarians, and other hygienists, administer wholesome food, but seldom make it as attractive and refreshing as it should be. Nobody essays to do artistic cookery with the conscientious purpose of nourishing the body and brain to the fullest extent, by the method of satisfying the appetite with pure materials, and the best natural flavors, so combined as to render everything pleasant, sapid, and delicious, without the rank, rich, harsh tastes of concentrated fat, sugar, vinegar, and spice,—a diet that will strengthen the appetite and digestion, with all the physical and mental functions, and furnish at the same time the greatest amount of permanent pleasure to the sense.

With the advent of the new Kingdom will come the

conscientious treatment of every sort of human performance. If Religion has been the mother of Art, inspiring the Greek sculptor and the Christian painter with their best ideals, then the higher religiosity of that new state will grow, and broaden itself out, into the universal conscience of Artosity, and apply ideas of right and duty to every variety of work, entertainment or accomplishment. Whatever will give pleasure, or lessen discomfort, to a human soul, without injury to another, either through the sense of art or otherwise, is the thing to be said, done, or striven for; because that is the right, the just, the rational, the proper, the beautiful or graceful thing, which increases the sum total of happiness. Every one within that domain will possess that motive—he cannot be there without it; and that motive will develop him into an artist, and create a paradise of grace and beauty in his surroundings, his home, his conveniences, and in the dress, carriage, habits and manners of those with whom he most associates. This motive will render every one capable of improvement. And the desire for improvement will render every one attractive, every one industrious, every one willing to aid in the achievment of a universal artistic condition.

The Ideal it is that man worships in his God. It is the ideal person that he admires and imitates. It is his ideal of right for which he will sacrifice time, money, health and life. Give him a better ideal and he becomes a better man. Give the boy an ideal of true manhood, and he will grow into manliness, not blackguardism. Give the young man a better ideal of social duty, and he will be more conscientious, and faithful to his work or his trust. Let the young girl form an elevated ideal of love, and virtue need never be mentioned in her hearing again. Let any one fully conceive of the high possibilities that lie before the developed human soul, and he or she will aspire to reach them, as surely as the shaded plant grows toward the sunshine. A more perfect ideal means a greater good, a wider, deeper, purer, and more certain happiness. We can no more avoid the effort to realize it than we can avoid drawing our breath. Let every one who wishes well to humanity aim to conceive of the most perfect ideal possible, and study the art of placing it with all its attractiveness, and all the steps by which it is reached, before those he desires to raise.

Finally, it should not be forgotten that as goodness done without a good motive in the love of it, is no goodness; as repentance without a conviction of guiltiness (which also implies an appreciation of the right) is no repentance; so an effort to imitate grace or beauty without a sincere desire for it is no virtue. The ideal must be admired for its own excellence, after the reason of its superiority is well understood, before an imitation of it becomes art, and can command the sympathy of the art feeling in others. And as there is joy in good souls over the sinner that truly repents, so there is joy, sympathy and friendship in the soul of the artist when he finds another doing his work in the true art spirit, as perfectly as he can. Whatever good thing is done, whatever wrong is righted, whatever artistic work is accomplished, must have this love of the good, the true, and the beautiful behind it, else, if it can be done at all, it brings little of the proper reward of well-doing, either in direct self-satisfaction, or in the reflected satisfaction and admiration which others should feel. Having the right motive, there is a way to find pleasure in everything we undertake to do. That which is true of doing right in the most important matters of life is true, in a less degree, of doing right in the smallest.

CHAPTER XVIII.

GOD.

IN announcing this subject it seems more necessary even than in treating Religion, that some apology should be made. "Can you produce anything new in regard to this oldest, most cogitated, and most bewritten of all subjects?"—is the skeptical inquiry that quickly comes into the mind. Possibly not; but I shall attempt to give the reader's mind a cant in one or two directions where it has not commonly been turned. It is so difficult to say when a conception is really new that I shall not venture to claim any novelty.

The name God is the same as the Norse-Gothic-Anglo-Saxon word meaning *good*. Though the original meaning to the Teutonic tribes was probably not the same, it is still a noteworthy point that in all modern religions God *is* the good deity, not the evil one. Whatever evil qualities one may attribute to his God, this god is still a better one than the other, the one Christian people name the Devil. However poor one's conception of a good deity may be it remains true that his God is an embodiment and representative of his ideal good.

This however, is the God of the present time and of civilized peoples. To find the beginning of the conception we must go back and down to Fetishism, in which the savage attributes life and personality to everything that he in his childish reasoning believes to be a cause, and pays special regard to it as having a power to aid or injure him. With partial civilization, and increasing knowledge of the universe, he comes to discard the little fetishes of wood and stone, trees or animals, and adopts larger gods, representing the forces of Nature, and its grandest objects, thunder and lightning, the winds, the sea, the mountains, the earth, moon, sun, and sky. With yet further intelligence, men cease to attach personality to any of these things; but they still attach a personality to the universe as a whole, and to this personality they attribute all the powers of all the previous inferior ones, making him the Almighty Creator, Preserver, Ruler, Manager and Supervisor of all things. This they will continue to do till, through the still greater advance and dissemination of knowledge, they become able to perceive that the deity over all has no more reason for existence than the former deities over every special part.

Nevertheless, when the anthropomorphic deity over all is laid aside as unnecessary, yet the tendency to fetishism still lives and manifests itself. "How is that?" will be enquired, "what can fetishism cling to now?" It still has a hold in Idealistic philosophy; more especially in the Absolute idealism of Germany; for the English idealism of Berkeley was in fact only the ordinary personal deity in another mode of manifestation. The German philosophy however, without attributing a consciousness to the universal Thought, yet held it capable of coming to consciousness in man; thus making the conception as much as possible unlike the primitive fetishism, but claiming the original and universal cause to be something similar to our own personality, just as does the primitive man every little cause of events in his daily life.

This highest and most subtle form of fetishism may

never be wholly abolished, till we come to understand the nature of intelligence so well we can conceive how it becomes an attribute of matter. To all appearance it does become such; but the explanation, the likening of it to some quality of matter we already know, is the thing to be accomplished. The idealist declares this impossible; but it may prove to be no more so than once was the explanation of heat as the vibratory motion of molecules.

In all these conceptions, from the most fetishistic to the most idealist, the deity is not necessarily a good one. It is a superior being, but whether predominantly good or evil depends on the character of the devotee. Only when he becomes predominantly good does the deity becomes so likewise. Compare the old Hebrew or Greek deities with the best Christian conceptions, and this is sufficiently evident. In nearly all religions the good and evil characters are represented in the same person. In only one of the old ones, Parseeism, is the representative of evil invested with some of the attributes of a god; and the indications are that from this source was derived the evil deity of Christianity. When the two opposite qualities exist in two separate persons, it becomes possible for the better one to be thought of as more purely good.

The philosophical argument concerning God is useless except to the few persons who can think clearly and believe honestly, in short, who are philosophers. To these there is no evidence sufficient to prove a personal deity. Yet the belief in such a being is no less prevalent for want of evidence. The fact seems to be that people who desire, or feel the need of, a personal god will have one, whatever the proof for or against. And among these may be put the class of divines or theologians. It will seem to many unjust that they should be. But the point is that the theologian's anxiety to have a deity is sufficient to prevent his reasoning candidly. He is much more partial to one kind of proof than to the other, and is biased by his desires. I do not mean to intimate that the opposite party is free from bias; but only to emphasize the fact that the theologian, as a rule, is like the great mass of humanity, governed in his thought by his feelings.

The sentiment of the majority is well expressed in this quotation:—

"It unspeakably lightens the burdens of life to believe in an almighty God; to be firmly grounded in the faith that whatever comes, all is for the best; that a masterhand is at the fore. The need of such consolation has been and is so great that the human mind accepts the faith eagerly; and shrinks from proof to the contrary as the body shrinks from a hurt. It is terrible not to see sufficient evidence on which to base confidence in the kind intention toward man of such a power; and to be convinced against one's will that such an intelligence would place man, weak, ignorant, and undeveloped, upon the earth to shift for himself among the terrible forces by which he is surrounded, is like believing a mother would leave her two-year old child to play unwatched with fire, edged weapons, and wild beasts."

The individual whose feeling is like that here expressed is truly like a little child clinging to its father, even though the father is harsh, abusive or brutal to it; the child knows of no way to live without him, and must cling to him in spite of all abuse.

It is only a scientific knowledge of the universe, and its human life, that can change this helpless, dependent feeling, and enable one to think regarding God. So long as men know nothing of the world and of themselves, they will inevitably cling to some imaginary superior power, for fear of drifting away into the darkness and being forever lost. If nature is to them a mystery, they will seek for light from the supernatural. If they know little of their own origin and history, they will believe some mighty person has created and guided, and will finally dispose of them eternally. With little knowledge of natural forces, and no conception of the nature of a true cause, they can only reason like the savage, and attribute everything to a personal will like their own. Unable to trace their mental operations to natural causes, they imagine them to be produced without cause or motive; and in like manner they imagine a great Creator, without cause or means, ushering a universe into existence by the mere fiat of his will. The undeveloped human mind, whether savage or civilized, can think in no other way. It can get no farther back than its own will, so-called, for a final cause, and to explain what is beyond itself can only resort to a similar will. And even if a different method of thinking were possible to minds in this condition, the great majority of them are too inert or indolent to make any suitable effort.

So long as great philosophical questions remain unanswered there remains some excuse for such beliefs, even among the intelligent. Yet the theological and speculative class have too little acquaintance with scientific thought, too little ability for self-guidance, and hence too much of the disposition to depend on something outside themselves; while the less cultivated part of the race are so entirely helpless they have no alternative but to accept whatever kind of deity, of supervision, and of disposal their superiors may adopt and present to them. Thus the belief in God comes to be more an indication of the intellectual quality of the believer than of any inherent probability in the idea itself. And so we may expect this faith in an anthropomorphic deity to continue as long as ignorance, weakness, and indolence exist in the average man to the degree they are found in him at present. We may suggest to him the improbability of his being made a pet of in the next life by one who subjects him to such rough usage in this; or to the more enlightened we may exhibit the immense fact that this planet of ours has been the scene of misery for ages,—that an inexpressible amount of agony, of every possible kind and degree, has been endured by animal and human organisms, day after day, month after month, year after year, for thousands, yes, millions of years without cessation,—and still both of them will believe in a God of infinite power and goodness, who created and controls everything, and who might have made the whole aspect of the universe different from what it is. They cannot do otherwise. There is nothing to be said against the fact itself; the child must become a man before it can have a man's independence, and ability to think. Moreover, no one ought to attempt to destroy the idea of God in the immature mind, or force upon it ideas of the more mature; the change from one to the other should be as gradual, easy, and natural as that of the physical child into the physical man. Criticism, urged before its proper time, if received at all, will only confuse, disturb, and torment; and to offer it is more of a vice than a virtue. The natural change comes only through the possession of scientific knowledge, including history and comparative religion, supplemented by an ability to deal with philosophic conceptions.

Since we cannot prevent the belief in a personal deity, who has designed, caused, and arranged everything, let us see if we cannot criticise, and improve, the conception of such a being, so that we may have as good a one as possible. If there appears to be any profanity in this proceeding it is not so; for a god is assumed to be a perfectly good being, and if we conceive of him otherwise, that mistake does him injustice. But the appearance is that believers in God do not dare to criticise their beliefs concerning him for fear they are irreverently criticising him. One of the most effective arguments against a personal deity I have ever seen was that such a god was a great "Slave-maker,"—that those who held the belief became slaves and cowards, and that thus the conception was degrading. It seems to me that the indictment is true; that believers in God *are* cowards and slaves to a degree at least, afraid of a monster of their own creation. He is to most of them a great, almighty despot; a benevolent one some will say, to others far from being so; doing his own will in heaven, earth and hell, for no other reason than because it is his will; using his creatures as the potter his clay, making some to honor and some to dishonor; and taking them through a career of happiness or misery, as his own sovereign choice may happen to be; if happy well, if otherwise there must be no remonstrance no complaint; he created and he disposes of them; they are his property to all eternity, and there is nothing to be done but submit, patiently and happily if we can, hoping all will be right somehow, but patiently or not there is no alternative.

Here is a good place for criticism to begin. Nothing more utterly despotic and arbitrary could be thought of by a selfish, proud, arrogant king than such an exercise of unlimited power. Is it possible a God, a good being, could act like such a man? Does a good person desire to have control over others, and to direct their destiny without their consent, or their knowledge of what it is to be? Not at all; on the contrary he would leave them an equal freedom. Would a good father wish to hide from his children their future career? No; he will wish them to have faith in him, and to submit willingly where they *cannot* know; but he is ready to teach them all they desire to know and can understand. Does this ideal God give his creatures all they desire to know and can understand? Is there any religious person who does not wish to know more? Is there any one who does not believe he could understand more if it were given him, even though his finite ability cannot comprehend the deity, who is assumed to be infinite? Would he be satisfied with a good human father who knew, but would enlighten him no more? Then is it a good God who leaves him so much in the dark, yet demands his confidence and submission? Put a human person in the god's place and he is at once condemned. The absurd reasoning of the old Christian Father who accepted God's ways, and believed them to be God's because they were absurd, irrational, incomprehensible, outrageous or impossible, is the only reasoning that can enable one to believe such a god to be the perfect Good. He is the conception of men who could think of nothing nobler than an absolute king. Blind, ignorant submission to such a being is in perfect truth submission to a great slave-maker.

This being, who in the common language of religion *is* the Universal King, is of course a god of infinite *majesty*, as an earthly king would be if he could be almighty. Grand and splendid cathedrals are built of carved stone by his worshippers, as "monuments to his *glory*," like the palaces of kings. But does this imply goodness? On the contrary the good person has no majesty, no airs, no dignity but what his moral character necessarily endows him with, and is approachable to the humblest tramp. And as to the costly temples, the god that could accept such offerings, while millions of human creatures are suffering for need of the treasure lavished upon them, would be but a poor specimen of deity, little if any superior to the men whose ignorant devotion builds the structures. This again, it will be said, is judging the infinite by the finite, which cannot comprehend it; but in reality the infinite would only posssess infinitely more of this humility than the human, not anything different from it in kind.

Then as to his justice and holiness. Saying nothing of

the so-called justice of condemning a race to suffer for the sin of its first parents, even through hereditary transmission if it were possible to avoid it; nor of the similar justice of allowing the innocent to die for the guilty; I call attention to the special idea that God's absolute holiness could not tolerate sin, or allow any of it to go unpunished, even though the punishment must be suffered by his own innocent son. Is this the way a holy and just human person would act? Do the best persons we know feel and act thus? Or do they tolerate the sinner, and forgive the penitent, with no desire to punish, but only to secure what compensation is possible to the one who has suffered wrong? Are they the best people who are afraid of sin and sinners; or are they those who have but a little goodness, who are so weak they dare not trust themselves within reach of contamination, and cry out against even the appearance of evil? It is easy to see what sort of people have given this character to the personal deity; that it is not the morally best class, but a class who could not conceive how the best would feel. They made an infinite being having their own feelings, and called it God. A God conceived by better men would show his abhorrence of sin, not by the punishment of an infinite person, nor by an infinite (eternal) punishment of the finite sinner; but by infinite efforts to abolish it in the present, and prevent it in the future, with as little punishment as possible.

The belief that a God of infinite goodness could punish the wicked forever is dying out so fast there is little need to hurry it; but the idea that an infinite God has the moral right to create beings, foreknowing that they are destined to a career of misery, as Calvinistic Christians believe, is so abhorrent to all true sense of justice that a few words regarding it are excusable. I know not how much has been said or written against it by theologians; but the simple fact that a numerous body

of Christians can compare sensitive human beings with
the unconscious clay of the potter, and call him a just or
righteous God who could treat one like the other, regardless of the sufferings of those human vessels made to
"dishonor," merely because it was so asserted by St.
Paul, seems passing strange, a marvelous phenomenon
in human psychology. The better grade of human
beings do not admit that a parent has a right to create
children who must suffer from disease or deformity; and
the man who would knowingly be guilty of such a crime
would be looked upon as a monster of brutal selfishness.
Yet here are millions of men and women, many of whom
are gentle and humane in their every-day life, who still
try to believe that a God has been doing what is much
worse than that, for the unfortunate soul created by him
is supposed to be unhappy for ever. Truly, if such a
deity is not one of infinite injustice, then I do not know
what he should be called.

Let us pass to another conception of the God who is
supposed to be good. This is the god who takes away
bright, healthy, promising, happy children by some disease or accident, in order to save their souls from danger
in this world, or to attract the attention of their parents
to a better one, that they also may be saved. He likewise takes away the happy husband or wife from the
partner who is in danger of being too happy, or of forgetting this god, who apparently is as jealous of the attentions paid by human beings to each other as he is
careful of their souls' good. He takes in the same way
the father or mother of a family of little children, leaving
them exposed to all the dangers of the world, starvation
included, that some indiscernible good, shall in some
strange way, accrue to somebody. If any *man* does this
he is taken for a criminal, and put out of society by death
or imprisonment. But when the great god does it no
question must be asked; it is assumed to be done for a

wise purpose, and that good will come out of it contrary to all appearances. No man would admit the right of another human being to take one half such liberties with him to do him good; every one hates the maxim attributed to the Jesuits, that the beneficial end to be reached justifies the evil means of gaining it; and no truly good person would wish to violate another's liberty by following such a method; but instead would try to obtain the consent of the one to be benefitted, by assisting him to see the wisdom of the proposed means. A parent will often allow a child to learn by experience rather than violate its liberty by force; and so would a benevolent deity. Here, however, the old objection that the infinite wisdom is not to be compared with man's, will again be offered. But it has no validity. Let God be sufficiently wise, and his results ultimately good; yet he is not good in subjecting men to the suspense and torment of a blind, compulsory trust for months and years, before any satisfactory result can be known. If it be that such suffering is necessary as a contrast, to enable the sufferer to appreciate happiness more keenly, then it is like a discord in music, long continued and repeated in every chord, when the inharmony of a single short note would answer every purpose. Finally, supposing the assumption of his adherents to be true, that all is for the best to those he favors with his chastisements, what shall we think of a god who in his partiality thus saves a part of his children, but leaves the rest to go on and destroy themselves for ever, without the check of a single heavy stroke from his merciful rod? Surely such a god is nothing but a demon, invented by weak, ignorant and heartless humans, themselves incapable of understanding how an unselfish being, divine or human, would act. An unselfish and wise parent, we all know, would interfere to prevent his children's rushing into ruin, while he allowed them to learn by sad experience what they could not learn otherwise, so long as their future welfare was not seriously endangered. But an infinitely wise and powerful being who does not withold his creatures from destruction, even by depriving them of liberty till they are able to use it more safely,—it is absurd to say this is a good God. A god, finite or infinite, who does nothing while men are constantly falling into everlasting misery, is certainly far inferior morally to an average human parent, less benevolent and less impartial. And it is a helpless fear of the great slave-maker that prevents men generally from making this criticism. A truly good God would find means to bring home all his willful, wandering, unhappy children, where not a single sigh for a lost one should mar the universal joy.

Still one more of the popular conceptions is that of a *forgiving* god, one who is constantly forgiving the sins of men against himself. Nothing could prove more clearly how little the human masses think, and how little they have yet imagined of the true nature of a good God. The whole doctrine of propitiation and forgiveness is a relic of barbarism, a part of that great mass of heathenism which Christianity inherited from a previous age. Its deity is the barbarous god of half-humanized men, jealous of his honor and his dignity, like a weak, empty-headed dude, or a fierce, rough cowboy. A true God would be nothing like this. The senseless profanities of senseless, ignorant people, which form one class of these offences, could no more move him to anger than the unconscious irreverence of the little child that calls its father Pop, or Governor, and orders him to do some little service, arouses the ire of the parent. Why should it? The ignorant and thoughtless man is but a child, with no better conception of the real character of a God than the prattling youngster has of the father's superiority to itself. When the child becomes old enough to comprehend, and is sufficiently taught, it is ashamed of such talk and abandons it. So when the childish man or woman acquires sufficient intelligence to form some idea of what God is or should be, he or she will become more reverent; more reverent indeed than some of those who now take his name in such a flippant or business-like way in their ministrations at some of our churches. And when the settlement is made with the individual's own conscience, God is sufficiently satisfied. He has no more desire to punish than has one of us to punish the little child.

But does not the anger of God burn against the sinner who commits a wrong upon his fellow-man? If he deliberately violates his conscience to do it, or does it recklessly, the indignation of God and of all good men and women must burn against him till he is punished enough to have some consciousness of the suffering he has caused to others. But this deliberate crime of the morally ignorant and short-sighted is not very common, I judge; and that which is provoked, in greater or less degree, seldom calls for much vindictive feeling in men, still less in gods. And whether provoked or unprovoked, it is something no deity can forgive, or remit the consequences of, nor can any person, except the one or ones whom it was designed to injure. No amount of prayers to God can make any difference. The one offended is the one that must be reconciled. The forgiveness of a God, or of any other person, if it could be had, would amount to nothing so long as the victim still feels that a designed or reckless injury has been done to him, and is not repented of for its own sake. Nothing can make peace and good will between the wrong-doer and the wrong-sufferer till the former has become fully convinced of the wickedness or meanness of his conduct, and so strongly impressed by the heinousness of it, that his pride and self-righteousness are broken down, and he is able in all humility to ask forgiveness of the injured, and to prove his sincerity by making whatever compensation remains in his power. This is much harder than to ask the forgiveness of God; that may be almost as easy as it is useless. But when the sinner has secured the reconciliation of the injured one, then all good beings are ready to be at peace with him also. No prayers or outward sacrifices are needed; but instead a righting of the wrong from a true conviction of its wrongfulness. Never till this is done, no matter how long, can the sinner be forgiven, be at peace, be happy. After it neither a God, nor any good person, could wish to punish, or do otherwise than forgive, and that gladly. Jesus said that there is more joy in heaven over one sinner who thus repents than over ninety and nine just persons who need no repentance. He then knows to a limited extent what it is to be at peace with his brother and at one with God. The sacrifice required is that of his own selfish perversity, and his prayers are to be addressed, primarily, to the one who has suffered most from his offence. When this is done, however, he may appropriately ask God and all good beings to forgive the sin, which is at the same time one against all who have had any consciousness of the wrong done, and their sense of right pained by such knowledge. It is in fact against all who can be in any manner affected by its influence. In the same sense that the fall of a pebble jars the whole planet, we may say the whole race is hurt by the injury done to one individual; there is no impropriety therefore in praying for a universal pardon, the forgiveness of all humanity.

The superstitious fear of unforgiveness with which many Christians torment themselves is a demonstration of that low moral state in themselves which prevents their conception of the feeling that would animate a truly benevolent deity. When they shall have come up into a higher one, they will be able to understand that after having thoroughly criticised and condemned themselves they will have been sufficiently punished already; and will be in that condition in which forgiveness is proper, and to all good beings natural.

It is perhaps still necessary, though it should not be, to say that God—a good and wise deity—is not the author of human suffering; nor of the human selfishness that manifests itself in wars, crimes, oppressions, and every sort of villainy; neither of the poverty, disease, and wretchedness that have always afflicted the larger part of humanity. If any being were it would be absurd to speak of him as being good. Evil may effect a good result, some of it; and more of it will after it has forced man to develop a degree of intelligence that can get good out of it; but that a good God made human nature and evil both, with such possibilities of resulting human misery as we see actually produced, is but little better than sheer idiocy. The god who could do that is the same old monster of a blind and cruel imagination that we find in all the other popular conceptions of God. On the contrary, the true God is a savior; one who suffers for others; not to expiate their sins, a thing impossible even if it could be exacted or accepted, but who suffers that they, by being aided into a better moral state, may sin and suffer less. Every man or woman who makes sincere and well-directed efforts for the improvement of humanity, in any way, is to some degree such a savior; and millions of Christians waste gratitude on an imaginary, impossible savior, while many of the real saviors, who do unselfish work and suffer for it, are allowed to go without any proper acknowledgement of their deserts, or any thought of gratitude.

Here again I must repeat that if anything in the above seems profane, it is not so. No good God need be feared for doubt concerning the wonderful stories of a sacred book, or skepticism regarding anything contrary to natural reason. Such a fear would be the fear of a devil or fiendish being, for a good one could have no wish to avoid criticism, still less could he wish to punish any one for a natural doubt.

In all these conceptions of God we see plainly that he is always thought of as a man. It is the anthropomorphic god only that is concieved of as personal; for no personality but the human kind can be imagined. At the same time no god but a personal one is of any value to those who wish to have a god at all; and so long as men must have a deity they will insist on his being a person. What the religionist worships in reality is the highest human ideal he can conceive. It is this toward which he aspires or desires to grow; and its embodiment in Jesus or Buddha is what renders those names so sacred. As mentioned in a previous chapter, an Unknowable, an inconceivable and everlasting mystery, can give him no satisfaction. Let us therefore try to imagine such a personal being as *may* be an actual existence; one in whom he may believe without any violation of his rationality.

We must first assume the existence of a spirit world, and locate him in that world; for a personality must have a location and a home somewhere. Assuming further that that world has been inhabited since men began to die out of this, then some kind of society has existed there as long as here. If we assume yet further that the spirit world is composed of finer materials than this, and that the human organism has finer senses, then we may reasonably suppose its people to know each other's true character better than we do, that they attract and repel more readily and completely, and thus separate themselves into groups having similar characteristics, and finally into two great classes, of good and evil, who with their abodes constitute Heaven and Hell. If the evil ones cannot be easily destroyed as here, they necessarily, when separated from the better part, form some sort of loose aggregation among themselves. As their selfish natures render them unsocial and discordant, no steady and permanent headship can be maintained; but such a one as there could be might temporarily be held by a person similar to him we are in the habit of calling the Devil.

The better part of the total humanity, having predominant tendencies to good, are easily organized; they naturally select their best and wisest men for the leadership of the minor societies, and these, acting on the same principle, as they come to form larger and more complex organizations, put the superior men of their own number into the highest places. Finally, it is not impossible to suppose, the more unselfish portion of the whole Earth race in that world would become consolidated into one grand body, with a single leading mind at its head. Being already the superior of all, and placed in his position without having sought it, the same true civil service principles which put him there would continue him in it, as long as his superior fitness continued; while every additional experience given him would qualify him still better for the office, and enable or require him to hold it indefinitely. No one wishes to compete with him for it, nor asks for rotation; because humility, not ambition, is the dominant feeling among his near associates, and the effort to obtain a position would prove a person's unfitness to occupy it. Thus the chief, once established in the "highest heavens," that is, among those of the most superior virtue, would be virtually "enthroned for ever and ever;" yet with no aspiration for a place above his fellows, no desire for a better fortune than all may have, but only with a willingness to be most useful in the position where others believe that he can be. Because a more unselfish spirit and purpose dwells in this man and his nearest associates than among any others, he holds an influence over all below him that nothing else could give. The goodness dwelling within himself he radiates abroad over all to whom it can reach, and it is returned again in impulses of gratitude, admiration and affection from every heart. He becomes a spiritual sun radiating its heat and light, receiving them back from millions of his fellows, as the material sun receives the gravitating impulses from everything attracted toward it as the mighty center of all.

The most perfect organization implies an executive Head and Center so perfect in his justice and benevolence, so wise theoretically and practically in his administration, that every subordinate center, and even every individual, will spontaneously elect to be guided or controlled by his method and decisions, notwithstanding a temporary inability to perceive the goodness or wisdom of them. Such free election of the chief, and complete submission to his rule, is the result of the individual's own free judgment. He voluntarily accepts a despotism, so far as it may be necessary, because he sees it to be benevolent and wise; and says "Thy will be done,' feeling assured that no power thus given will be abused, that no surrender of freedom will be used to take his freedom away, that no needless arbitrary action will be taken, that nothing but good can come from the superior goodness and wisdom of his accepted chief, leader and guide.

Let this spiritual chief be supposed to continue in his office, and his organizing work, for some centuries or thousands of years, till the great masses of well-disposed human spirits become arranged into harmonious coöperating bodies, more closely bound together as they approach toward the center, and he is then able to wield all their combined power for any beneficent object. He becomes, in his world, a *Consciousness of the Race*, analogous to the Self or Ego, the head-center of the individual mental and physical organism, which, except in case of insanity, retains its official headship during the organism's whole career. We then have in this Personality all the attributes that are actually conceived as existing in God. What he lacks, the infinity, absoluteness, creative power, omnisciense, omnipotence, omnipresence, etc., commonly attributed to the deity, are those which cannot,' except by the delusive process of forming pseud-ideas or counterfeit conceptions, be given to a personal being.

It is the moral quality of the spiritual Head, his superior goodness in every sense, that gives him power over the depraved and vicious; which enables the single one to put ten thousand to flight, and to conquer all the powers of hell. There are few so vile but they are conscious of the rightful superiority of goodness, and this it is that makes the ten thousand surrender to the one when the struggle is forced upon their consciences. But why, then, can he not subdue the hells, and change their tendencies to evil into tendencies to good. Surely there must be a desire to do it, and a good reason for the failure. Let us speculate a little further, and see if we can find what it is.

For a large mass of human kind to become organized into a harmonious, coöperating body, there must be harmonious thought—an agreement in fundamental ideas— what Dr. John W. Draper called an "organization of intellect." This philosophy will naturally be a spiritual one, with a personal cause and creator at the origin of the universe, because the primitive mind necessarily assumes a person to be the cause of whatever is not known to have a natural cause. All the primitive philosophies and religions were of this character, and only a very few of those able to think proposed materialism as a substitute. Spirit was everything and was good; matter, if anything at all was nothing but evil, and whatever belonged to the material body of man was unworthy and base. Man himself, when he came to possess any goodness, became conscious of the vileness into which he was continually led by an ignorant selfishness, and to himself confessed that he was naturally depraved and evil. Thus on earth or in the spirit world, wherever the human race was, the ideas of the spiritual philosophy, and the dogma of natural depravity, grew up. Moreover, the dogma of human free will is nothing more nor less than the habitual reasoning of the savage and the child, that all human action not seen to have a natural cause must be referred to a personal one; which, as it is not discovered outside, is taken to be the man himself, as an original cause or god, able to act in either direction, and therefore meriting reward or punishment.

Now, with a belief in his mind that the wicked man is evil in all his tendencies; that all the appetites, passions and propensities connected with the material body are naturally vile; and yet that he is rightfully punishable for all his unsocial conduct, while the good man is entitled to credit for all his goodness; how can the good man approach the wicked one with any hope of making a good impression? The wicked one, though he may be taught the old doctrine so thoroughly that he may sometimes acknowledge the justice of his punishment, yet knows constantly and vividly that it is not as easy or as possible for him to be good as to be bad; he knows there is in most cases a fearful inequality in the conditions under which the good and bad come into existence; that often the circumstances are different in which they act; and that their inheritance of natural character is not the same. He can scarcely avoid an instinctive consciousness of being insulted, or nearly so, and of an undesigned effort to degrade him still more by the assumption of superiority which the righteous man carries with him in his face, his speech, and his manner. The very fact of the present moral inequality between them may suggest to him that there has been injustice somewhere. He knows, furthermore, that the pleasures of sense are worthy of respect, as a means of happiness, equally with those of the spirit; and till some one comes admitting these justifications of his course, he will feel and believe that the teaching offered him is a fraud, and will reject it. Knowing nothing of the joy of unselfishness, he will cling to that he is familiar with; and thus with some disposition for improvement, that might be cultivated into good impulsions, he continues in his selfish course of life, till it becomes false, unnatural, and ruinous.

That, it seems to me, is the main reason the hells are not converted, either in this world or the other; and why the whole united goodness of the better part of Humanity, instead of attracting repels. It is itself vitiated with injustice, and meets the natural result of failure. The causes that originate hells are too many and various to be considered here, and human society will have to be renovated to the very bottom before all of them are removed.

Now again let me say that the god here imagined is not known or asserted to be an existing reality. The only assertion is that for aught we know he *may* be. He has been spoken of in the more common way as masculine, which is correct enough, but I judge it altogether probable that some female deity will be closely associated with him, one sufficiently developed to do a woman's work equal to his own, with equal worthiness and grace.

Such is the personal god we may believe in if we prefer. We may never behold him, or yet we may. If we do it will not be upon a great white throne, or surrounded with ineffable majesty; we may find him in the councils of the wise if we are able to get there; or, quite as possibly, in some time of sore distress he will be at our side with some word of comfort and aid, and we shall know him only by the beauty of the halo about his head, or the wonderful benignity of the expression on his face.

Having thus sketched a *personality* that might with sufficient propriety be called God, I will now put aside all old and new speculative conceptions, and try to describe the real and true God, which does exist, and will as long as human intelligence shall exist on any planet of all the vast universe. This true God is the spirit of Good, which lives in all human hearts everywhere throughout the race, in all times and places, in the past, present and future, in the material world and the spiritual, in the child and the adult, the savage and the civilized, with varying degrees of power in each one of the immense multitude, yet with a germ in the lowest barbarian or criminal, and in the most fortunate with an imtensity sufficient to control and harmonize all the energies and faculties of the man into one constant influence for good. It originates with intelligence, increases with mental evolution, and belongs most to those who possess, not the largest quantity, but the highest order, of knowledge. It is the force which society exerts upon the selfish individual to bring his action into harmony with the good of all. It is the power not ourselves, that is, outside of the separate individual, that makes for righteousness. Its influence may pass from one to another, from the better endowed to the less, or from the spiritual world to the material and the reverse. It is that which in the future will make human solidarity possible and actual, the crowning result of all human effort. Idealized, it is that which all noble souls worship, and embodied in a person becomes their God.

This is the God in whom, or in which, all nations and races have believed; which all religions have taught men they should love; which all men, even the bad, respect if nothing more; which the atheist or agnostic admires and seeks to imitate as truly as does the theist, the materialist investigator as truly as the spiritualist ascetic. It is the Good about which Socrates and Plato philosophized, and which the speculating religionist has always associated with inconcievable notions of the infinite, the unconditioned, the unknowable, etc., making up an incomprehensible jumble of counterfeit and real ideas, terrible to contemplate, and which no logic has ever been able to untangle and separate, or to harmonize into a consistent whole.

Whether mixed with the traditions of mythology, and the speculations of theology, or separate and clear as I have given it, this is the true God that no one can deny, nor any one hate, nor any refuse to admire and worship, with such degree of aspiration as his state of moral growth will allow. It is the being in temporary unison with this Good that the mystic has enjoyed, and called union with God; a description true, in its degree, whether he be in sympathy with some idealized person, or only with himself and the indefinite whole of human goodness. The young convert and enthusiast has felt a partial union with this Universal Good, and by the vivid impression of a first experience it has convinced him of the truth of religious dogmas, and made him an evangelist to those who know it not. It is the consciousness of this real thing, mainly, that gives sacredness or respectability to all else called religion, and supports churches, priests, monasteries, convents and all the paraphernalia of sacerdotalism. For the sake of this, man has accepted the delusions of dogmatic teaching, the impositions of priestcraft, the self-denial and torture of asceticism. It is the knowledge of this one reality that blinds the religionist to all the reasonings of the critic, and separates him from his materialist brother; and conversely, it is the ignorance of it, with the usual religious accompaniments at least, that separates his materialist brother from him.

We cannot speak of this deity as being infinite, absolute, omniscient, omnipotent, omnipresent, unknowable, incomprehensible; none of these adjectives apply. It is a quality of human nature, a state of the human soul, a product of mental evolution, and as universal as the race. It exists inherent within every one, potentially if not actually, and because it does the false inference that the individual is a part of an infinite being has been drawn by spiritualist thinkers, from the ancient writers of the Vedas down to the teachers of the Mind-Cure in the last decade of our own time.

The Universal Good is a *providence*, to some extent, and will be more so in the future, when every one shall feel that its power is over and around him, to shield him from evil and aid him toward happiness.

When the individual reaches a point of development where he can surrender the last item of his dearly-beloved selfishness in obedience to this Power, represented in, and speaking through, his own conscience, then he will know God, will know what it is to be a Son of God, begotten of the Spirit, and destined to a high condition of happiness of indefinite duration. He will have entered into the Empire of the Wise, and will begin to realize from experience how much of beauty, and glory and blessedness is possible to a perfected humanity.

Nature, including man, creates gods, and will create higher and better ones than any yet known, both in the ideal and the real. It has been observed by Max Müller that its conception of Deity becomes the foundation of a *people;* and that all its institutions become organized in accordance with that idea. If this be correct, as seems probable, let us hope that the Universal Good will become the prevalent conception of the American people, and that, uncontaminated with belief, doctrine, or sectarian opinion, of any kind whatever, it will spread from our country to the whole human race.

CHAPTER XIX.

IMMORTALITY.

IN most of the ancient religions there is a story of a Tree of Life, of which men ate and became immortal, like the highest gods. Christian tradition has it that man was once immortal by nature, and lost his immortality by transgressing his Creator's command. Even after this the first men lived well nigh a thousand years. According to Hindoo legends they lived a fabulous number of thousands. And this wonderful age, too, was lost through sin and gradual degradation.

What the real meaning or true interpretation of these old traditions is no one has yet fully discovered; though their wide prevalence, and the sacredness attached to them, makes it reasonable to suppose that they once conveyed some portion of truth, and had a value. Perhaps they will appear more worthy of respect after some considerations developed from modern knowledge have been presented.

The race has always tried to believe it was to be immortal in a dim, uncertain spirit world, after the death of the body in this. What is called *intuition* has clung to this faith or hope, despite the lack of evidence, and does so still. Yet though commonly held as a faith or hope, there is a certain amount of evidence for it. There is the universal belief of all uncultured races; there is the story of the disciples of Jesus; there is the systematic statement of Swedenborg; there is the positive testimony of many clairvoyants and mediums of later times, who have experienced various evidences of its reality. Others, not mediumistic, have seen enough to convince them there is truth in the theory of the spiritualists; enough at least to show that the materialistic thinkers who have tried to account for modern manifestations by other theories have done so without a full acquaintance with the facts. But after admitting a spiritual existence of some kind, it must still be said that one can hardly find in Spiritualistic writings any account of the spirit world, or of the nature of the life there lived, that is generally agreed upon by those who give information about it. There is no systematic and positive spiritual Astronomy, Geology, Geography, Biology or Sociology, or what would correspond to these sciences. The confused and contradictory statements are a serious defect in Modern Spiritualism; and much as one would like to believe in the solidity and permanent value of the spirit life, it still seems more like a dream life than anything else.

The majority of scientific men, probably, have given up all hope of an immortality in a spiritual state; and in this material world the longest life they think of is from ninety to a hundred years. But such expectations or opinions decide nothing. The same people condemned Spiritualism as about equivalent to astrology or sorcery, and all who believed in it as incompetent to judge of its true character; in both of which suppositions they were much at fault. The scientific man has never given the subject of immortality any attention at all proportionate to its importance. All that we have in regard to it is the belief of the barbarous races, the tradition of the church, the argument from intuition, and the evidence offered by Spiritualism. About Spiritualism every one forms his own opinion; and about the New Testament statements I am far from desiring to make an expression of any kind.

But concerning the argument from intuition a few thoughts will be offered.

When we come to examine this intuition argument, looking clearly at every phase and form of it, we find that in all cases it is an inference drawn from the existence of our own needs or desires. Because we are too weak to go alone, too blind to see our way through the world, too ignorant to know much of its origin, progress and destiny or of our own; and also because we are too indolent to learn what we might, we want a deity to fall back upon; one who knows everything, controls everything, and who will lead and train us till at last we come out all right in a world of eternal happiness. In proportion as we become humanized our reasoning from within will not allow us to believe he can be less generous or beneficent than ourselves. Most of us wish finally to land in a place where will be little work and a good deal of rest, and so our heaven is a place of that kind. The Arab and the wild Indian want a different sort of heaven, and their beliefs give it to them. We, having become capable of the higher or finer feelings, have naturally disgraced and suppressed the lower appetites, so we are contented, or try to be, with a heaven in which the latter are unknown.

So with immortality, which is the foundation want of all the others. The human family everywhere, in all times, and in all stages of progress, have believed in some sort of continued life after consciousness ceases in the body. Only the few who have learned to reason in spite of their feelings, have ever given up this belief. We cling to it as the one best thing among all our hopes, the great comfort for all the disappointments and miseries of the present world.

The reasoning from intuition is in substance like this. All our lower desires have their natural gratification, to some extent at least, and if they could not thus be satisfied there would be no propriety in having them. Why should we possess others if there were not some future provision for their satisfaction also? They are higher, nobler, better than those we can gratify in this imperfect state; why not a more perfect condition for them? This is the reasoning of the priest and theologian always. The great founder of the Transcendental philosophy also had to fall back upon it for God, Freedom and Immortality; for this is all his judgment of the Practical Reason means. Men of science resort to it when they fail to find any evidence in their own field of research. A few years since a book was written by two English scientists to prove an "unseen world" of spirit by showing that it was required by intellectual *consistency*. The rational consistency of all else would not be perfect without that, and our intellects cannot be satisfied without consistency. John Fiske, of Harvard University, has lately taken the same method in an essay before the Concord School of Philosophy. Only on the supposition that the human spirit will by evolution become perfect enough to endure forever, he says, can the *reasonableness* of the universe maintain its ground. Otherwise the highest spiritual qualities of man, the outcome of all Nature's creative work, will be wasted and lost; which to all human feeling is certainly not reasonable. Once I saw an elaborate argument to show from intuition that every man and woman was ultimately to find his or her soul affinity and eternal mate, perfect in every characteristic, and perfectly suited to each ones desire for companionship. Certainly, the inference was, it must be so; that is what every one wants, and Infinite Perfection will see that the want shall be satisfied.

The unintuitive thinker replies to all this that our inferior wants are satisfied very imperfectly; that most of us reach the end of life with more of disappointment than satisfaction of such desires; that we want money, home, friends, love, respect, honor, and a comfortable finishing up of our existence here, and that few of us get these things in any satisfactory degree, while with some the fulfillment is not more than one tenth, and the disappointment nine tenths of all their ambitions and hopes. From such result the prospect is poor for the gratification of all those high, refined, and noble aspirations that require a perfect world and perfect people.

Well, every one will make his own estimate of these reasonings for and against. But whatever they may be worth in regard to a spirit world and spirit life, the point I ask attention to here is that intuition, or reasoning from the feelings, is of some value in regard to life in a future age on our own material earth. If, instead of a universe controlled in all its details by the arbitrary will of a personal deity, we come to see our world as subject to a great law of unfoldment, under which the present amount and degree of progress has been attained, with intelligence and morality as the result of that progress, then further advance may bring to us some portion of those good things our ancestors hoped to realize only in a different world. We began in the imperfect, we may end in the perfect. This is but a formula of complete evolution. Society, like all else, begins low and works up. Man, from being a brute may come to be an angel, without the necessity of shuffling off the mortal coil.

In this light the argument against intuition comes to mean simply that, in our present state of imperfect evolution, the difficulty of realizing our wants and aspirations is so great that most of us fail oftener than we succeed. But that implies nothing against what we may do in the future. With the more complete development of society and of the individual, the difficulty will be less; because intelligence and morality will be more advanced. Society will be more just to the individual, and the individual more just and generous to his fellow. Where we now realize only one fourth or one third of our ordinary wants, we may come to realize two thirds, three fourths, or nine tenths of them. There is no need of assuming that we must go into another state of existence to do it. To our fathers, who had no idea of a law of progress, that assumption was necessary. To them it was natural enough to adopt the old Asiatic view that this world is a villainous place at best and inevitably; the only hope of future happiness being in another and better one. Since we know the fact and the law of progression the case is vastly altered. Even religionists, some of them, now believe the Kingdom of God is to come in this world by natural means; and though it is not supposed to imply immortality, it includes almost everything else we hope to find in Heaven; is, that all that depends on human character.

Now, if this is to be true, it will be only a more complete carrying out of the process by which we realize somewhat of our ideals of common things. If it is a house, a business, a farm, a machine, a joint-stock company, or a work of art that we desire, we have our idea of what it ought to be to be perfect, and succeed in realizing that ideal, sometimes poorly, sometimes pretty well, according to the amount of our intelligence and our good luck. In some cases success depends almost entirely upon what we know, and our power of self-control; in other words, upon ourselves. And whatever we obtain through good luck, that also we must *keep* by our own ability; else it soon leaves us, like the spendthrift's inherited fortune. What we achieve through our own exertions we can keep in the same way. But if we cannot *make* a heaven by our own efforts and acquirements, we could not *keep* it if one were bestowed upon us. It will be as near the ideal perfection as we are able to make it, no nearer. If, therefore, we possess the angelic spirit, the willingness to learn, and the personal accomplishments that give pleasure to others, we can realize a heavenly state as easily and completely as a sculptor does his ideal of a statue, a mechanic his of a machine, or a general his of an organized army.

I am now ready to take the same position regarding immortality. It, like all the other ideal good things we hope for, may be ours if, through our own development, we are able to achieve and to retain it. Mr. Fiske believes intuitionally that in the spirit world an immortality, as the result of development, will be attained. And my position is that through the same means an immortality, or an indefinite approximation to it, may, for ought we know, be possible in this material world.

To those who are entirely unfamiliar with the idea of a physical immortality it will seem utterly preposterous. "Men always have died out of their physical bodies, and they always will," is their ready answer to such a suggestion, and any one who thinks differently is in their wise opinion a fool or a lunatic. But somehow the possibility of it has crept into the heads of a good many people, most of them intelligent, some of them scientific persons, physiologists, men who have made the human constitution a life-long study, and are qualified to have an opinion worthy of respect. A few of them will be quoted; but first let me meet the common objection that such a notion is absurd or insane.

It has always been held that because man always has died he is mortal necessarily. And St. Paul, who is responsible for most of what the Christian world believes, says it is appointed man once to die. But St. Paul is of no greater authority regarding a matter of science than any other man of his time, and may be set aside without hesitation. As to the experience of the past, and the death of all those who at one time or another have believed they could continue their lives, that no more proves that man will always be mortal than it proves that he will always be diseased; or that the rich and poor, the ignorant and the educated, the free and the enslaved will always exist together. Disease, poverty, ignorance and slavery always have existed, yet all of them are capable of being lessened, and we all hope for a time when they will disappear entirely. Already the average lifetime has been considerably lengthened, and if it is now shortening again we know what are the causes. If disease shall be finally conquered, the balance between life and death will be reduced to a very small matter. It will still be claimed however, that the unavoidable friction of the human machinery will insensibly wear upon it, till finally, without any perceptible disease, we shall die gently and pleasantly of old age, after living much longer than we do at present.

But now what if some new and strong influence should come in to turn the close balance in favor of life? Would it require very much to make the life power strongest, and enable it to constantly repair and renovate the animal structure so thoroughly as to render life perpetual? Is there any impossibility in this? Already the physiologist is so impressed by the perfect working of the human organism that its perpetual operation has been suggested. Some years ago Dr. John Gardner, an English physician, wrote a work upon "Longevity, or The Means of Prolonging Life After Middle Age," one of the most useful books ever written, and one which every physician will speak of with respect. In this he writes:

"Before the flood men are said to have lived five and even nine hundred years; and as a physiologist I can assert positively that there is no fact reached by Science to contradict or render this improbable. It is more difficult on scientific grounds to explain why men die at all than to believe in the duration of life for a thousand years."

Nothing could be more explicit than this.

Dr. Homer Bostwick, an American author of several medical works, published in 1851 a book upon "The Causes of Natural Death, or Death from Old Age," which was devoted to a method for "*indefinitely* prolonging vigorous, elastic and buoyant health." He asserts unqualifiedly that "time or the number of years has nothing whatever to do with old age or death;" and that there is no law of nature that limits human life. He quotes Dr. Southwood Smith, as saying that "though when fully come, the term of old age cannot be extended, the coming of the term may be postponed. To the preceding stage (the middle-age life) an indefinite number of years may be added." And he endorses the statement of Dr. Monroe, a distinguished English anatomist, that "the human frame as a machine is perfect,—it contains within itself no marks by which we can possibly predict its decay; it is apparently intended to go on forever."

These, too, are sufficiently plain.

Says Herbert Spencer in his Data of Ethics:

"It is demonstrable that there exists a primordial connection between pleasure-giving acts and continuance or increase of life; and by implication between pain-giving acts and decrease or loss of life." (p. 82.)

What is this but to say that if we could avoid our miseries, and sufficiently increase our pleasure-giving acts or happiness, we might increase the life power and prolong our lives for a time no one can tell how long?

Again in another work, Mr. Spencer says, though in different language, that death from old age, like death from disease or accident, is a result of inadequate intelligence, (Biology, Am. ed. 2-393.)

In other words, with greater intelligence we could postpone it longer; and with a sufficient degree of intelligence could put it off indefinitely.

Says Dr. B. W. Richardson the author of several useful books on medicine and hygiene:

"Healthful brain work, by development of the nervous organism during generation upon generation, may give to mankind an increase of health and the possession of a

longer natural life ; may indeed by continuous evolution lead to an *unthought of birth of human existence.*"
"This for the possible future." * * *(Field of Disease, p. 446.)

Among earlier authors I could quote similar opinions from Descartes, Condorcet, Von Baer and Hufeland, all of them men of high reputation, and even from Benjamin Franklin, the prince of common sense. But confining myself to the latest thinkers, men equipped with all the results of our present knowledge, I will refer to two distinguished French scientists, Dr. Charles Robin, and Charles Letourneau.*

Robin is quoted by Letourneau, in his "Biology," as saying :

"No scientific contradiction would hinder our conception of a *perfect equilibrium* between assimilation and disassimilation, indefinitely repeated in all existing beings, without interrupting the continuity of the molecular renovation, and without a decomposition of the organized substance ensuing. * * The anatomical element or organism once produced, once born, may be supposed to present a perfect equilibrium of *indefinite duration* between the process of assimilation and that of disassimilation."

Letourneau himself then proceeds as follows :

"To dare now to assert that it is not impossible to conquer death, is to expose ourselves to an accusation of madness. The Animist and Vitalist doctrines fail; they have lost all credit with science; but a yoke borne for a long time always leaves a permanent impress, and in the domain of opinion the effect often long survives the cause. For centuries life has been considered as a mysterious, miraculous fact, beyond all investigation. Each organism was regarded as a monarchy despotically governed by a metaphysical entity. It was believed that the problem of life must eternally defy the power of human science. It was a *fatum*, against which it was useless to

* Within the present year (1888) Dr. William A. Hammond of N. Y. has in a magazine article repeated the idea first expressed by him in 1863 (Treatise on Hygiene) that "there is no physiological reason why man should die." He attributes death to man's ignorance of all the laws of life, with unwillingness to obey those he does know ; and believes there is only a question of time when the life period will be vastly lengthened.

struggle. Such is the prevailing opinion; but it exists only by force of habit. The phenomenon of life has been analyzed. We know that it is the result of simple molecular exchanges comparable to those that take place in an electric pile. That there is in the vital phenomena something immutable, predestined, no one can now maintain. Every living thing conserves itself as long as there is in it a certain nutritive equilibrium—as long as assimilation and disassimilation are almost equally balanced. Now, it is certain that the duration of this equilibrium depends upon an infinity of causes, internal and external. Of two children born one may live an hour, the other half a century. There is neither law nor rule when the course of life is abandoned to the hazard of events, as always happens. *A priori*, it is surely not impossible, an organized being given, to maintain indefinitely in it the tide of life at a *constant watermark;* and it seems to us that science is now sufficiently armed to attack boldly this great problem." (Biology, Am. ed. pp. 296-298.)

When the foremost scientific men of the world give such testimony as this what becomes of the contemptuous charge of lunacy or idiocy? Though nothing else could be expected, yet how plainly it shows the old propensity to judge before knowing anything of the question, and to assume the stupidity of those who differ from us.

I have chosen to bring forward only those who by their profession are familiar with the science of life, and have made a study of the human constitution. Other names might be cited, persons of intelligence and repute in various professions, who are equally convinced that we know nothing as yet about the possible duration of human life. One of these, a well-known educator of the State of New York, has within a few years written two small works upon the subject,* while magazine articles further show that the opinion of thoughtful people is not so entirely one-sided as commonly believed.

Presuming that the ordinary objections may now be withheld for a time, I will go on to offer some further

---

* " *The Possibility of Not Dying*, and ' *When Age Grows Young*," by Hyland C. Kirk Published by C. T. Dillingham, New York.

suggestions, with indications of what may appear in the not very distant future. As to the conjecture that the world will become too full of population if all are to live to a great age, well-informed persons already know how to dispose of it, and others may be assured that no serious difficulty will arise on that account.

Every recovery from disease may not be a renewal of life, because there may be a reserve force, active all the while, and capable of replenishing its natural reservoir as soon as opportunity is afforded. But we see children lingering along for years, barely alive and expected to die any time, apparently with not vital power sufficient to improve; yet afterward they begin to grow strong, and finally acquire enough vitality to carry them through an ordinary lifetime. So in middle age we see those who are broken down in constitution, whose vitality seems to be exhausted, who still by some lucky turn acquire new vigor in all their vital organs, becoming even stronger than in their youth, and living to a good old age. Such cases are not numerous, it is true, yet many people can think of some one of this kind they have known. In old age, even, the same tendency to renewal of life is manifested. Under certain still more favorable conditions and influences certain old persons put out a new growth of hair on their bald heads, or they recover their lost eyesight, or what is yet more remarkable, find a new set of teeth pushing off the artificial ones of the dentist. In all these instances there is renewed health and vigor of the body and mind all through. They are less common than the former, but everybody has heard of them, some few have known of them by better evidence, and in medical and other works a considerable number of authentic cases have been published.

Quite a list of persons might be cited who are reported to have lived to great ages—one hundred to a hundred and fifty years—while newspapers of the present day report some of a hundred and seventy or eighty. Though such ages are seriously doubted, and one scientist who investigated in England was not convinced of any person having reached more than a hundred and seven years, to me there seems as much evidence for as against them. Certainly there is no impossibility. If some of our young people, by having good original constitutions, good conditions, and superior knowledge, should carry their life terms up from a hundred and seven to a hundred and fifteen or twenty no one would feel surprised, no one would consider such lives unnatural or strange. If by still better constitutions, and still wiser living, the children of these should reach a hundred and thirty or forty or fifty, still no one would see aught but natural reasons for such longevity. Even if those old persons who recover their eyesight and hearing, with new teeth, hair, and general vigor, should find out what is the cause or condition of their renewed youthfulness, and if by the proper means they should resume their youth a second or a third time, still there would be in this nothing but natural causes and effects, and surely no one can say it is impossible. Nobody has ascertained the circumstances attending these cases, apparently because no one supposed them to indicate a possibility of continued life renewal. The idea of death being inevitable has so occupied men's minds they could see no evidence to the contrary, although in every such instance it is thrust right before their eyes.

To the ready objection of the skeptic that instances of old age are exceptional, and furnish no ground for the inference that others can become like them, there is an equally ready response that they are exceptional only on condition that all our present circumstances remain unchanged. On the contrary, whatever is exceptional can be made regular, normal, or ordinary when we come to know the causes and conditions that render it exceptional. To acquire this knowledge may be difficult, but not impossible. Once the crossing of the Atlantic in a steamship was exceptional. All our great mechanical inventions and improved processes in industry were the same. All those superior qualities which constitute genius of one kind or another are exceptional in certain persons; yet we are constantly trying•by education to make them more common. Every improvement made by one person is exceptional till others adopt it, and so, therefore, is every step of human progress. It is the same with long life as with all the rest.

Now, with all this possibility, arising from a knowledge of the most perfect hygiene—the most perfect ways of eating, drinking, breathing, sleeping, thinking, feeling, working and resting; from a knowledge of all means of restoring the sick; from the inheritance of constitutions untainted with the almost universal curse of scrofula; from a scientific knowledge of the conditions under which renewals of life and vigor occasionally happen;— with the possibility inherent in all this, let us suppose a new element to be added, one that is thoroughly healthful in its nature, to turn the balance in favor of life. This new element is the moral force,—the influence of new moral motives, new purposes and aspirations, a complete change or rejuvenation of the whole moral nature. And this new influence acts upon the most central and vital part of the whole constitution. It gives new life and strength to the body because the man is purified and renewed in his *conscience*, the centre and stronghold of his mind, and hence of his entire being. A new happiness and new hopes bring in new energy and determination, and stir up every vital organ to its very best performance. Every observer knows how powerfully the mind can act upon the body; and when the mind itself is purified, renovated and strengthened all its influence goes toward producing the same effect upon the physical part. Already this power is so well known to a few persons that it is turned to account in healing the sick. I have known a health institution where a moral change (called spiritual) was distinctly made the precedent to any promise of restoration. In the "faith cures" now so frequently reported, and also in healing by the new method of Mind Cure, though the results are most commonly produced through either the expectancy or the determination of the mind, yet the moral or spiritual influence is often brought in, with additional good effect.

Well, the moral renovation that is now contemplated, as an important new factor in creating vitality and continuing life, is such a complete moral victory as will cast out all the great enemies of the soul, and carry the victor into the Kingdom of the Unselfish. The joy of conquering in the great and decisive battle that substantially ends the hitherto perpetual conflict of good and evil in the soul, the new aspirations, ambitions and hopes, the new affections that grow out of this result,— all these constitute a new fund of happiness which in every way ministers to life. Besides this there is the healthful influence of rest, of peace, of the calm, quiet harmonious soul working out its new destiny without friction, anxiety, or complaint.

All the good results of the change however, are not yet named. There will be a moralization (sanctification the men of the church would call it) of all our physical instincts and appetites, which will turn every one of them to a good use instead of a bad one, a wise use instead of a foolish one, in all cases. To conceive what benefit will come out of this it should be understood that the largest half, if not three-fourths, of all our diseases, besides numberless correlated horrors and sufferings, arise from sensuality in its selfish and unprincipled character— from gluttony, intemperance and lust. Then let us remember that all the forces now acting in furtherance of disease and death can be made equally effective to aid health and life, when we shall have gained the wisdom and moral strength to use them rightly, and we find ourselves in possession of a conservative power that has never been properly estimated. Judging from the evil effects of unprincipled courses, we may well believe that a vast amount of vitality can be saved, and made to lengthen human life, by habits of living that shall be fully controlled in every respect by a thoroughly enlightened conscience. It is not at all certain but that death could be arrested and held at bay by this power of a moralized sensuality alone.

But there is still another new element to be reckoned in, before we determine this question of life's possibilities. This other factor is the rest and satisfaction of the intellect, that comes from the acceptance of an ultimate philosophy,—from a conviction that solid rock is at last reached in the foundations of thought. The Christian may here set out his system of doctrines as being to him just what is wanted, a something on which the mind can rest undisturbed. Yet it does not satisfy the requirement. For there is no Christian, or if any only as a rare exception, who is not sometimes troubled by doubt; whereas, that I refer to is something that will enable its possessor to set all doubt at defiance. It is a fundamental truth that can challenge criticism to the utmost, and come out stronger and brighter, more fixed and unquestionable, after every examination. The intellectual confusion and unrest of the present time is alone enough to kill men who, if free from it, would live to a hundred years. Its uncertainty haunts one from the time he begins to think till he breathes his last breath. It perpetually tires the brain with a perpetually disappointed search, till the baffled and wearied seeker for truth is resigned to die, in the hope of finding the object of his quest in a world and a life beyond this. All the great questions the soul puts to itself have ever been met with silence or falsity; and the wearing effect upon the brain is communicated to the whole physical system. The possibility that answers may be found to all these great problems, the consciousness of possessing a key to such solution if not also the solutions themselves, brings a satisfaction nothing else can give,—not joyous or lively, but deep, calm, solid, and lasting. The tedious search is ended, the harassing struggle is over, the brain, like the heart, is profoundly at rest. No need of saying that such a rest will lengthen our term of life.

"*Is* there any such ultimate philosophy," every one will enquire. It would be useless for me to say there is or there is not. My word in regard to it would be worth nothing to one who knows the history of thought, and of philosophies fondly believed by their inventors to be final. If my conception of its nature and effects, and the language already used does not command some degree of belief nothing would; and so I leave it till a time arrives when something more can wisely be uttered.

I will take occasion to say however, that I believe there are means of increasing the vital force that can never be utilized successfully until the moral regeneration referred to has been attained, and the intellectual element of a truer philosophy has been united to the moral. The best hygiene, one that will furnish the body everything it needs, and calls for through its instincts and appetites, without asceticism of any kind, without intemperance or any wrong use, will not previously be learned, or if learned not accepted. Neither will all the best means of restoring the health that is lost. The most valuable truth can never be acquired till we are morally worthy and intellectually capable.

Here then are three new influences, bearing upon duration of life,—the perpetual rest of a satisfied intellect, the equally perpetual peace and calm of a satisfied conscience, and the reconversion of all the forces now generating misery, disease and death, through the natural appetites and passions, into such a use that they shall generate happiness, health and life instead. Each one of these influences alone is powerful; what they may accomplish when combined no one is yet able to say.

Immortality, it has been said, is the despair of the philosopher, but the hope of the Christian. What if it should become the despair of the Christian, but the hope of the philosopher? According to the speculation I am now setting forth it is likely to be the outcome of human evolution, the last grand result of intellectual and moral development. A number of thinkers have already looked upon it in this light, and I cannot do better than quote the two great chiefs of the Evolution doctrine; Mr. Fiske having been mentioned as one who takes the same view, except that he transfers the scene of evolution to a spirit world.

Says Mr. Darwin: "The fact of man's having risen to the very summit of the organic scale, instead of having been originally placed there, may give him hopes of a still higher destiny hereafter." ("Descent of Man," last paragraph.) Mr. Darwin makes no conjecture about what this higher destiny is to be; but when we see how much the highest man has already raised himself above the lowest aboriginal man, it need not be surprising if he should finally achieve an indefinite continuation of life. Mr. Spencer has no doubt that evolution is to end in the most complete human happiness. He tells us that "if man could anticipate all the changes to occur in his environment, and never fail in providing efficiently against them, he would have eternal existence and universal knowledge." And though this implies an absolute perfection of knowledge never to be acquired, yet a *comparatively* perfect knowledge and adaptation will necessarily be the result of evolution; and how large a step toward the eternal existence it may prove we do not know. Certainly, according to his authority there is nothing against, and everything to favor a greatly increased life period. (See Biology, Am. ed. vol. I. 88–9. vol. II. 393.)

From what has now been presented one can see that it is not the mere speculator, not the religionist with an old mystery from a sacred book, not a seer with some new revelation, not a visionary or enthusiast of any kind, who is the new believer in the possibility of a life indefinitely prolonged. It is the man of science—the biologist, the physiologist, the anthropologist, who discovers this possibility. It does not result from the inherent quality of the mind; it is not the reward for faith in any particular religion; it is not to be realized without means. It is to come from the increase of knowledge and of moral worth; it is to be earned, achieved, and preserved by effort, like every other good thing we obtain. There seems to me nothing at all unreasonable in believing that when we reach the Wisdom Period of our mental growth we shall be able to retain or increase our stock of vitality, and perhaps to renew it an indefinite number of times. A lifetime twice or thrice the ordinary length of seventy years seems almost certain. And an extension of even this long life, which shall be terminable only by ultimate accident, and accompanied by almost the vigor and beauty of youth, is scarcely beyond a rational conception of what is possible.

If this last grand result shall appear it will be, like all the beatitudes we intuitively try to expect in some far-off, imaginary heaven, one of the ultimate glories of human perfection; hinted of, idealized, and dreamed over in fancy, longed for and sought in our times of supreme suffering, centuries and ages before we acquire the power to realize them; the desire and aspiration for them being different from the ordinary wants we can supply only in their higher character, and the greater difficulty of realization.

Only those who are making some approach toward the Higher State, or developing some capacity for it, are able to make life worth living, either to themselves or others. To the ordinary selfish man of the world, therefore, these speculations will have little interest. His quality of mind does not understand the conditions, or appreciate the motives, that belong to its continuation. But those who have been sufficiently impressed with what is here offered will now wish to enquire what more practical considerations can be suggested, what direct and immediate steps can be advised, to one who wishes to advance as rapidly as possible on the road toward an exceptional long life.

In regard to *moral development* what is already told in previous essays of this course is the best that I can say; to learn it and act accordingly the best that any one can do. The *intellectual* part of the work includes science in general, and especially all those kinds of science that deal with life or living things, still more especially those of the anatomy, physiology, psychology and hygiene of man himself. It is useful also to know something of the essentials of Medicine, and the various methods of medical treatment, as practiced by the ordinary and extraordinary medical sects. Whatever has a bearing upon health must be candidly investigated. From all schools and theories something of value may be learned; and the outcome of the whole study is likely to be an abandonment of the main part of the old system of stimulation by drugs for disease, and by prophylactic means in hygiene; while in place of it will grow up a faith in the *unconscious intelligence of the body*,* a confidence in its tendency to preserve life and health, and in its natural power of healing or self-repair, which will trust it to take care of itself under all ordinary exposures. It will also trust it to right itself when slightly disordered, and when seriously diseased the same faith in instinctive self-healing will furnish it whatever hygienic conditions are instinctively called for, and give a true assistance by re-enforcing the natural powers with additional supplies of force in the forms of heat, sunlight, electricity, and vital magnetism. In short, through the increase of this sort of intelligence, the body, like the soul, is likely to regain its natural liberty, self-control, and self-regulation.

In connection with this matter, one must know enough of the philosophy of science to understand the theory of the Conservation and Correlation of Forces. Without a clear conception of force, and of this law, a person cannot realize the folly of wasting vitality or the necessity of saving it; cannot secure the best results from the conservative power of the system, nor make the best use of the physical or mental energies; but on the contrary, is liable to waste more vital force in bad habits, anxious feelings, or overwork than the best conditions can supply. Indeed the whole question resolves itself into the simple one of the gain or loss of force.

It hardly need be repeated that all knowledge of a high order, all the more important conclusions of modern research, everything that strengthens the grasp, or broadens the comprehension of the mind, will be in some manner useful for the purpose in view.

And when the necessary wisdom has been acquired it must not fail of being carried into practical effect. It is to be made use of in the same spirit, with the same ap-

---

*Unconscious intelligence of the *Sympathetic nerve system*—would be the more correct expression to one familiar with anatomy. The *vis medicatrix naturae* is the medical phrase for the same thing in part.

preciation, and the same interest that an artist applies principles to his work, or an engineer makes use of mathematics and mechanics in constructing a bridge or a tunnel. All we can learn must be applied in downright earnestness to the one Grand Art of Living.

To the doubt that will still arise whether it is practicable for us at the present time to acquire this knowledge, and this moral and physical cultivation that have been specified as requisite to success, the proper answer is that when we have put forth our best efforts, and gained what we may, we shall probably then be able to see our way clearly to the attainment of whatever else we may need. So the question of practicality comes home at last to each individual, and it remains for him or her to decide how great an intellectual and moral effort he or she is capable of attempting.

Still further, and finally, *motive* to live gives *power* to live. With faith in the possibility of living indefinitely; with the moralized passions and intellect belonging to the Unselfish Stage, which makes us conscious of being able to secure our own and others future happiness; and with the wisdom to harmonize and combine all selfish and unselfish purposes in one great object; we then have the strongest possible motive to live; and this, by the utmost stimulation of all our faculties, becomes a mighty motive *power*, and adds yet another effective influence toward a final victory over death.

CHAPTER XX.

HUMAN PERFECTIBILITY.

WHEN we plant a seed, or set a young tree, we expect it to grow up into its normal form, with healthy and beautiful foliage, and when it has attained its natural limit of growth, to produce its natural seeds or fruit. If it becomes deformed we know that some external cause has forced it out of shape; if it shows disease we suspect it has been compelled to absorb filthy substances for its food; if it lacks its proper color, and vigor of growth, we know that it is starved for want of sustenance or water, is robbed of its juices by insects, or has lost its vitality in contending with disease. If when healthy and full-grown it fails to produce fruit, we attribute the failure to lack of fertilizing substance, or destruction of blossoms by untimely frost. Though some species of trees may make a straggling growth, it is not for them an abnormal one; and we do not suspect the tree or plant of any tendency to perversion or depravity in either form or product. We always look for a cause of its failure, in whatever respect.

Likewise when a young animal begins its growth we expect it to continue, and to develop its normal size, form and other qualities. If dwarfed in size we know it has lacked sufficient sustenance, either since birth or before. In its wild state we never expect to find it deformed unless by accident, and if so when domesticated we still know there is some cause. If under man's care it exhibits disease (as it never does when wild) we suspect that unnatural surroundings, filthy or damaged food, or contact with diseased men, has been the cause of such disease. We never accuse the animal of a natural disposition to get diseased, even though it eat poison mixed with food when hungry; nor of any perverse unwillingness to attain its full size, and reproduce its species. If when domesticated it lacks gentleness and docility, well-informed people are pretty sure it has been brutally treated by man, or that it inherits its viciousness from ancestors that were so treated; that it has acquired them in spite of a natural disposition to be gentle, patient and friendly. Even when it devours its young, it is easy to discover that it has been deprived of the animal food natural to its wild state.

The human child too is generally supposed to be born with a natural tendency to grow up into a healthy and good-natured man or woman, if allowed to do so. And if man had never acquired any moral qualities, perhaps he would never have been accused of any more perversity than the animal. But somehow, before the child gets up to maturity, as the innocence of childhood passes away, it is imagined that a moral perversity comes in; and by the time it is full-grown there is no difficulty in believing that an evil disposition is his or her natural inheritance. What renders this belief still easier is the old notion that man is so very different from, or superior to, an animal; an opinion which also comes easily enough to a state of ignorance and its accompanying conceit. Both these beliefs are very old, perhaps nearly of the same age, that of natural depravity at least, so ancient no one knows its origin.* Being adopted by Christianity as one of the vital points, it has been taught

---

*See " Bible Myths and Their Parallels in Other Religions." Chap. XX.

to the whole Christian world for fifteen centuries, and beaten into people's heads so thoroughly in a thousand ways, either openly or by implication, that persons who have positively discarded the belief, and all those associated with it, still unconsciously assume its truth, and act upon that assumption.

The explanation of this universal mistake is not difficult. Man begins life as an animal, and like all other animals is selfish in all his instincts and dispositions, therefore selfish in all his thoughts—his manner of looking upon the world and its inhabitants. When he comes to have a taste of the superior happiness of the unselfish life he believes that to be the truer life, and his previous more selfish one to be largely false. The inherent selfishness which still dominates him induces him, whenever he distinguishes two ideas or sets of ideas, to believe his own to be wholly true, and that which is not his to to be wholly false. So likewise, if his own present one is normal the other must be depraved. Moreover, he finds that much of his selfish life really is depraved or abnormal,—all his criminality and vice, which makes him enemies, adds to his troubles, and shortens his days, if it does not end them by violence, is an unhealthful, and morally insane life. All unwise selfishness is of this character. Depravity is also associated with purposes that are in themselves more or less unselfish. All that Jesuitism of the Christian church, and of all kinds of Reformers, which is willing to do evil that good may come out of it, from the persecutions of the earliest popes down to the Anarchism of the present day, is a depraved manifestation, a fruit rotten at the core, a goodness often more than half wickedness. All the asceticism of the religious world, and of good persons not religious, is no less truly a form of depravity. But the depravity of good and of bad people is alike said to be natural, an inherent perverseness attaching to all human kind. The true explanation is in both the same; it is that the natural selfishness is only partially enlightened, and therefore only partially good.

Animals and plants are depraved by man's imperfect intelligence; but in their wild or uncultivated state no such fault is to be found in them. In the case of animals, their intelligence is not sufficient to overcome their instincts; and these keep them physically undepraved. They fight, steal, kill and break all the commandments of morality; for this is the normal action of a blind, instinctive selfishness under conditions such as we find. So it is the natural action of the blind animal man, normal to him so long as he, like the animal, is unenlightened by knowledge, and lives in similar conditions; but changing as he becomes wiser, and secures for himself a better environment, till finally he comes to look upon it as entirely abnormal or depraved. What is normal to him in the primitive state becomes entirely otherwise in the cultivated. The fact, however, furnishes no reason to conclude that he possesses an inherent tendency to evil; on the contrary it proves just the reverse,—that his natural tendency is toward a higher state than he is born into. The supernaturalist of course will say that religion is to be credited for all the moral improvement he makes; but it is quite as believable that he adopts religion, so far as there is good in it, because he has intelligence to see that good conduct is better for him than bad; and that he accepts the superstitions of religion because the childish beginnings of knowledge and thought lead him into all sorts of queer fancies and delusions, generating the superstitious beliefs, and an expectation of finding wonderful things in what is unknown. In his primitive mental state he thinks very much as the child thinks, as all the old mythologies prove. He accepts the paternal care, wisdom and providence offered him by religion for the same reason the child accepts it from its parents;

as is indicated by the fact that religion at the present time has its adherents mostly in women, and in those men who are least capable of battling with the world, of thinking for themselves, and working out their own happiness in their individual ways. Thus it is quite as easy to explain how religion originated from man's nature—the superstitious part from his weakness of intellect, the moral part from his increasing intelligence—as it is to suppose that religion created his tendency to goodness; though, as stated in a previous chapter, religion after becoming established, and itself acquiring some goodness, assisted by its own action in perpetuating, if not increasing, the moral tendency. And this explanation of the genesis, action and effect of religion is the same whether man exists in two worlds or only in one.

The animal not having sufficient intellect to dominate, delude and derange its instincts, and therefore remaining undepraved, in the physical sense, is for the same reason unable, except in a small degree, to discover the advantage of unselfish conduct, and so remains in the selfish, unsocial or unmoralized state. Man's intelligence is enough superior to partially control his instincts, and with imperfect knowledge to delude and pervert them, so that he becomes physically deformed, and full of disease; while the same intellectual superiority enables him to learn the greater happiness of a social life, to outgrow the blind selfishness of the animal and the child, and to acquire the moral feeling and action belonging to society. He is thus in a fair way to become entirely human (what some would call divine) while he will at the same time restore his instincts to their natural freedom, and thus recover his natural health of body.

Already in medical science the *vis medicatrix naturae*, or natural healing and renovating power of the body, has long been recognized as a leading influence in its restoration to health when diseased or mechanically injured. The most capable physicians and surgeons appear to depend mainly on this power for restoration, and less on remedies than formerly; while some of them go so far as to deny all virtue to medicines, and claim that all cure of disease is self-cure, with the aid of favorable conditions.

What is there to prevent us from believing in the existence of a moral *vis medicatrix*, and its healing power over the mind? We see how the discouraged person in time regains energy, the frightened recovers courage and selfposession, the crestfallen again comes to hold up his head. Sometimes a prison convict, when he returns to society, leads a better life and secures the respect of his fellows. From some of the better conducted prisons there is quite a proportion of such. Why should we not expect that all sorts of criminals and conscienceless people will turn toward goodness when they can be so enlightened as to understand the nature of society, and the obligations of one to another and to the whole? Would not this be a natural result from man's desire for a greater happiness? When he can be convinced that morality is better for him will he not take to it instead of crime? I believe he will, and that he has never had a fair chance, by right instruction, to show how much tendency to good there is in his constitution.

In the chapter on Religion the religious feeling is defined as the desire for moral growth, the aspiration for a state of more perfect unselfishness. If this desire exists to a strong degree in some persons, as it certainly does, then it should be needless to say, to those who understand the superiority of natural causes to inconcievable ones, that this feeling so intense in some must have its germ in all; that it is not planted by some outside power, and by some inscrutable process, in minds where everything of the kind was before unknown; that a *capacity* for it, at least, must exist in the very lowest.

If this reasoning can now be confirmed by an explanation of those manifestations of evil spirit, which in some cases appear so fiendish to our ordinary perception, there will be little excuse for continuing to harbor the old notion of inborn wickedness. That the fiendishness actually exists is not denied. It has been asserted or implied in this book more than once. No believer in innate villainy could adduce more proof of it than I am willing to admit. Nothing more utterly inhuman can be conceived than occurs about us every day, in isolated instances at least, and in all parts of the earth, during this last and best century of man's existence. The stupidity, too, is equal to the brutality. The new-born child, nevertheless, is always innocent. If its inherited structure of brain allows it to easily become depraved, it also allows it to be educated into virtue; and its ancestors, a few generations back, were born with no worse brains than the average. The inferior endowment of brain is still only exceptional.

When a little child tears valuable things to pieces, or throws them in the fire or the water, we say that it is gratifying its curiosity or desire to learn, not that it acts from a desire to do mischief. It may well be believed that the child has no wish either to do or to avoid mischief; it simply wishes to observe and get acquainted with things around it. Its mind is beginning to grow, and the disposition is entirely commendable; the more curiosity it has the better, if only some older person watch over its explorations and prevent it from doing harm. Without any instruction, it may come to do wicked things, and yet have no consciousness of wrong. I once heard a full-grown man, whose education had been better than the average, tell how he had not long before picked up a little ground lizard, sometimes called a salamander, and thrown it into a fire of brush or rubbish to see if it would endure fire according to the old fable. No one had ever taught him that an inoffensive wild animal has a right to its life till man needs the ground it occupies; nor had his education given him sufficient scientific knowledge to make him sure that all animal flesh would burn. Therefore he had no conscience regarding the matter; and though possessing no more propensity to be cruel than most young men, he tossed the innocent and struggling creature into the fire with the utmost indifference merely to satisfy a doubt no child should be left ignorant enough to possess.

When half-grown children torment animals there may be a double motive,—one the curiosity to see what an animal will do, the other the desire to see something laughable that is expected; and still oftener perhaps the curiosity to see if it will not do something funny that is not expected. As long as any laughable action results the torment will be continued, for the child or half-grown boy has no natural conscience, and unless taught has not even a suspicion that he ought to have any feeling except enjoyment of the sport. The same is generally true of those older persons who say irritating things to tease their own companions.

The young man who goes shooting wild animals for sport or game has been taught just the contrary,—namely, that it is perfectly right for him to kill anything he finds that is not claimed as some one's property. The thought that the animal can have any right to live never comes into his head. Civilized boys may be taught that they must spare the nests and the lives of singing birds, not because the bird has a right to its eggs or its life, but because it is pretty and sings. The sportsman kills because there is a satisfaction in knowing that he possesses a new power—the ability to shoot—and he enjoys seeing the proof of it when the animal falls. He also gets credit and admiration for it, like the sharp-shooter who shoots for a prize, and in this is another satisfaction. But neither the child nor the man does what he supposes to be wrong, unmanly, or in any way unnatural or depraved.

In offences commonly known as crimes, though there may be a consciousness of wrong-doing, there is often a way found to overcome it, and in part at least to justify or excuse it to the criminal's own mind. And this is a fact that should count for something in refutation of the depravity doctrine. I judge that very few criminals fail to find considerations that give some sort of excuse for what they do. It is also true that they sometimes act, as do many who are not criminals, on excuses that do not satisfy themselves, and then they are conscious of being degraded. When such a person has wronged another it is generally, if not always, the case that he hates him; because the presence of the injured one is a continual irritation of the offender's conscience; another fact against the idea of depravity.

What the excuses are that allow one deliberately to commit the greatest crimes I confess my inability to understand; but I am satisfied there are such with every criminal possessing much intelligence, or else that a long-continued habit of violating conscience has made him cease to desire them. If he has but little intelligence then he acts from the blind impulse of the moment, like a drunken man or a savage. If such deeds come not deliberately, but from provocation, they are simply the reflex action generated by the provocation, and in direct ratio to the amount of it. Even if the provocations are but small, they may be so often repeated, or so long continued, that the subject of them at last becomes frantic with desperate rage, and like a mad dog or a Malay running *amuk*, strikes viciously at every one within reach, or with less excitement singles out his worst tormentors and kills them if he can. Many a desperate murder and suicide is the result of a long series of little torments, which finally become unendurable, and end in the most fearful deeds. They indicate no more natural depravity than does any little movement in self-defence of the most common kind. Even if the perpetrator be what we call insane, he still reasons himself into the belief that he has a right to commit the crime,—that it is the best he can do for himself, and for others who are to be affected.

One of the first indications of so-called depravity in a child is its disposition to be untruthful. Deception is the resort of the weak always, and in the child is no more an evidence of depravity than is weakness or imperfection of any other kind. Children are taught to lie, by seeing how their parents do the same thing, and again by being made to suffer for telling the truth when they have done something wrong and confess it. Moreover, some of them do not readily learn to distinguish between what they imagine and what they really see or hear. For this the parent makes no allowance, and when the child reports falsely, owing to such a weakness, it is scolded or punished with as little charity as if it were a full-grown, thoughtful person. There is nothing here so bad but with wise teaching it may be easily outgrown; though with such teaching as is given, the child may live seventy years, and still, like the majority of those now living, not be truthful on all occasions.

Envy is a so-called bad quality common to both childhood and maturity, and belonging full as much perhaps to the latter period. I have never known it to be thought of as otherwise than bad, mean, and intolerable; yet I shall promptly take the position that it is neither one of these. On the contrary, envy is just as natural as breath, and is no more depraved or evil. The essential nature of the feeling is a desire for equality—for an equal possession, or an equal happiness in some way. Of course it is the feeling of the weak or inferior. In those who have sufficient energy and ability, it excites emulation, and prompts an effort to acquire that which is coveted. But in those too weak to make much effort, it creates a wish to obtain a part of what the more fortunate have, or dislikes them for exhibiting good things the inferior cannot share. In minds that have become embittered and irritable, it may impel to the tearing down of an envied person's reputation, or an injury of his or her property. When the envious person cannot gain an equality by his own efforts to rise on the ladder of fortune, he is very likely to attempt it by dragging the one above him down to his own level. In children, not yet taught to conceal their feelings, we can easily see its operation. When one of a group has any good fortune all the rest want a share, and call the possessor bad names, perhaps, if they do not get it. We all have a conviction, formed by a reasoning so clear and simple we take no notice of it, that one is rightfully entitled to as much happiness as another. If I am capable of enjoying as much as some one more fortunate why should I not have it? There is no answer. "You can have it if you are able to get it," most people will say; but why should I not be able? is the real point. What propriety is there in one's being richer in all sorts of good things than another who wants them just as much, and could enjoy them equally well? And why should not each one be able to obtain them by making the same exertion? Why should not the same opportunity be open to all? Some of the lucky ones will say that is the case already; and these, blinded by their own selfishness, and supported by teachers who are given high salaries and respectability for teaching acceptable notions, will not readily allow the truth to affect their minds. Yet the conscious feeling of the rich man that he ought to do something for the poor with his money, is a testimony that he does really admit to himself privately, in an indistinct way, that the less fortunate ought to have something better. The public sentiment that demands it of him means the same. The true missionary, carrying his good tidings to the poor savage, is animated by something more than the injunction of his Master,—it is a consciousness of right and propriety in the gospel's being given to every one. Culture, too, makes an effort to popularize science, to spread useful knowledge, to make good literature easily obtainable by all. Every one, almost, who gets hold of something good, no matter what, wishes somebody else to know how good it is; and thus truly confesses that others ought to be as happy as himself in its enjoyment. This is precisely what the envious person feels or thinks. It is a truth so self-evident that all of us perceive it without any conscious reasoning. There is no more depravity in the envious feeling than in the love of life itself. And the lesson of it is that every one, fortunate or unfortunate, ought to do his best to alleviate, to lessen, and as far as possible to abolish, the inequalities of fortune generated by wild, undisciplined, haphazard Nature, and carry the reign of human justice and equality into every nook and corner of the world's affairs, however large or small, and whatever change or temporary sacrifice it may require.

Jealousy is closely related to envy, though it has not always as much justification. It is the effect of the blind native selfishness, determined to retain whatever is possessed, or the opportunity of obtaining what is desired. The jealous person is weak, too weak to have confidence in his ability to hold or to obtain the desired object; hence suspicious of all competition, and full of anxiety when any appears. If he were strong he would feel unconcerned. It is in many cases unjustifiable; but in general it is the fear of the weak that they will be robbed by the stronger,—not only the stronger in purse, but in influence, in personal appearance, in mental or moral character. Sometimes it may be the fear of the rich that they cannot get all they want; a feeling less excusable than the other. But it is no more depraved than the love of life, of food, of comfort, of anything. Foolish it may be, mean often, justifiable sometimes, occasionally enlisted in favor of some good cause; but in its ordinary forms to be outgrown, like all other weaknesses, by an increase of knowledge, of noble purposes, of just conditions and equal opportunities.

Faultfinding is the name given to still another wicked propensity of the natural man. Having the intellectual faculty, he discovers good and bad in his fellows; and if it is right to commend the one it is right to condemn the other. When he is ignorant and reckless he does harm by it; when he becomes considerate and just he will criticise in a way to be beneficial. In his present half-enlightened state he finds fault with the inferior as if he expected him always to remain an inferior; which makes the criticised party his enemy, and prevents the criticism from having its proper effect. The retort is made that the critic is conceited or self-righteous. The real fault to be found with both is their want of thought, and of the unselfish spirit. One is unable to give criticism in the right manner, the other unable to accept and improve by it, because the critic's fault is equal to his own. If both could feel right one would criticise without contempt, and never say aught about an offender he would be unwilling to say to his face; while the other would take it and correct himself, no matter in what spirit it was given.

There are people who take pleasure in faultfinding, merely because they have keen, active minds, and no other employment on which to use up their mental energy. Some useful study for such persons would help them wonderfully, and save them from a really reprehensible use of their faculties. In all other cases probably it will be found that the faultfinder has some excuse for his criticism,—that something does offend his sense of right, of propriety, of rationality.

As envy may prompt one to recover what is injustly taken or withheld from him, and jealousy inspire him to guard carefully what is rightfully his, so this may enable him to protect himself from annoyance or mischief, or to admonish an erring neighbor into a better course of life. Even deceit, the least respectable of the four, can sometimes be made to serve a useful purpose. In neither of them do we find any natural depravity, but only natural infirmity or weakness; that which belongs to the early state of all organized things, whether in the world below man or in the social world he himself creates. It is a necessity of evolution. What is called Natural Depravity means the imperfection belonging to the childhood of the race.

The constantly *suspicious* disposition is, like those already mentioned, an evidence of weakness, indicating a mental condition similar to the physical condition of a young plant just putting out its first tiny leaves, barely able to live and grow at all, needing all it can get, and every favorable influence, to help it along. Or, in other cases it is like that of the starved plant, with strong tendency to grow, but unable to obtain moisture and nutriment from the dry, barren soil that contains it. If we observe the scanty opportunities afforded by the surroundings of these suspicious people, their starved minds and sociabilities, or the poor inheritance of body and brain transmitted to them by parentage, we shall be quite as much disposed to pity as to berate them. If they did not possess this over-watchful disposition they would have no desire to grow, to improve, to become more human.

Irritability too, what is the meaning of this? We know well enough what it means when the cause is physical, when the tired or hungry child cries, when sickness and soreness torment all the nerves of the body, and make us ready to cry out at every slight movement or sound. Isn't there just as much reason for it when the person is spiritually sick and sore, when comforts and enjoyments of every kind are taken away, when disappointments and defeats one after another, small ones only it may be if enough of them, drive one to the verge of despair and suicide, or if less than this still leave the spirit battered and bruised all over and through? Irritability is one's only defence for the last germ of vitality or hope yet left to him, and indicates that an effort is still being made toward recovery.

Quarrelsomeness means that the subject of it possesses a good fund of power of some sort, and wishes to try it against that of another for the satisfaction of finding out that he has the most; for power means happiness in some way, and a consciousness of it gives satisfaction. It shows itself in a love of games, or of a conflict of wits in debate; in a struggle for office or for a prize; and even delights in the fierce excitement of the deadly clash of arms. But under the whole of it runs a current of aspiration for superiority of some kind, however miserable and poor. The bull-fight and the prize-fight are its most disgusting exhibitions; but even in these, there is to those so poverty-stricken in all noble ideals as to take part in them, a satisfied pride in knowing what might there is in human muscle, and in the superior ability to handle the fist or the sword. In the world as it now is such power as this can occasionally be turned to good account; and all that is needed is enlightenment, not change of nature, to make this propensity useful in forms of emulation that in their results shall benefit both victor and vanquished.

For *revenge* it is difficult to say as much. In low states of society where brutality is the rule, and punishment a necessity, this feeling is probably of service in taking the place of law. But certain I am that when men become wise enough to understand the springs of human conduct, and able to reform offenders instead of killing or tormenting them, revengefulness will die out of the mind, as useless parts of the animal structure disappear (or nearly so) when the animal grades up into a higher type.

Pride is one of the old trinity of original sins, (sensuality, curiosity and pride) and a sinful feeling it certainly is when compared with those above it; but compared to a state of mind that has never known pride, it is a virtue. It matters not what special sorts of pride, nor how many, we include in the generic name, the assertion holds good. Pride is better than no pride until one has grown beyond all pride, and discarded it for a true and noble self-respect, which is at the same time a respect for universal human nature, gained by experiential knowledge of its possibilities. The ordinary pride is an evidence that the possessor has already made some upward progress; and because he does not know how or why he has done so he despises those who have made less. He has no consciousness that anyone has a higher development than his own; and treats his superiors just as he does those whom he knows to be inferior. As he acquires a better knowledge of the world and its various grades of inhabitants, he sloughs off some of his pride, becoming more modest, approachable, or sympathetic, and obtains some idea of what is meant by human solidarity. But in the meantime his pride has been to him a source of strength or support in his efforts to rise, though at last it becomes an obstruction to further growth, and must be cast off. It is an indication, not of depravity, but of weakness and immaturity. The love of praise and popularity is the sign of a still weaker or less mature growth, but at the same time better than nothing as an aid or stimulation to improvement.

Of *bigotry* we must say the same as of pride. So long as the individual mind remains unable to think out a scheme of belief for itself, or to form comprehensive and reliable judgments concerning important questions, it must rely upon the judgment of others, or take whatever doctrine falls in its way that seems most rational to its present amount of intelligence; just as it does in regard to ordinary affairs of business life. It judges for itself concerning its own *inability*, and as to which is the best authority, or the safest person to rely upon. It begins by thinking honestly and independently as far as able; but after an authority is found, or a satisfactory solution, it gives up its freedom and its candor, often becoming a mere stupid slave, and a blind foe to all who are not equally slavish and satisfied with itself. This bigoted mind is then ready to persecute the dissenter to his death, or make life miserable in a thousand ways to those who offend less seriously. Thus the bigot is the cause of a vast amount of evil. Yet in the beginning he did the best he could; and after the serious trouble of getting his thoughts once settled he is too feeble and lazy-brained to again arouse himself, to revise the old opinions, or obtain new knowledge for a better judgment or a safer authority. There is no more inherent depravity than before; and the evils of bigotry, what are they but a part of that universal hard fortune the race of man must undergo in passing from the selfishness of the animal life to the unselfishness of a perfected society?

Sensuality is evil only because it is blind. Men have had sufficient knowledge to pervert it, not enough to guide it rationally. When they shall come to understand the true purpose of all instinctive sensuality, as they have never yet done, they will cease to be gluttons, drunkards and libertines. They will discover that their instincts are too noble to be abused in the hoggish manner they have ever heretofore been.

Curiosity, of the mature or thinking person, was in former times condemned because it prompts us to stray away from the simple path of childhood, marked out by simple goodness, and forever followed by the unprogressive Chinaman, but deserted by nearly all of the white race. In wandering away from it we at length come out in all sorts of skepticisms, and with a disposition to criticise all the rules of the fathers. This of course seems terribly evil to those who venerate the timid wisdom of the fathers; but it is likely to prove itself far better for us than the helpless goodness they sought to make perpetual. Progress, even though attained by passing through error and evil, is better than the stationary simplicity of the ancients. The variation from the primitive path gives origin to the story of the fall of man from his primitive innocence. The child when it goes out from the old home, and the young man who enters alone upon a new business, will make mistakes and suffer; but it is better than to do nothing, and the knowledge acquired leads to success. The start may be made too young, and mistakes may be fatal; this is the evil belonging to it. Nevertheless it is a process Nature requires us to pass through, and the only tendency to evil involved is that necessitated by our ignorance. We pass through it in the intellectual world, and the moral, as well as in the physical; we make mistakes and fall and hurt ourselves, for the same reason the child falls when it first leaves its mother to go alone. The outcome is the same in both cases; we learn by experience, and acquire the ability to do a man's work, and to enjoy a man's happiness, in place of that of the child. But intellectually and morally we have not yet reached the mature stage, and so do not see the full parallelism of the two processes.

What shall be said for the drunkard? Is he not depraved? Certainly, depraved by an unnatural condition of the body, brought about through ignorance, stupidity, recklessness, or by whatever motive induced him to drink. But at first he was not depraved, and in gratifying this abnormal appetite he is still only selfish. If his family could be happy without his being deprived of his indulgence he would be willing. If no one but himself were to be disgraced he would as soon have it that way. It is not others that he wishes to make suffer, but himself that he wishes to enjoy. It is probably the same with the libertine, except that in some cases he takes pleasure in knowing his ablility to seduce.

Yet another illustration. The ill-mannered boy who shouts, whistles or swears in our ears as we pass him on the street has no positive desire to be hateful, but only to satisfy himself. He has no conception of true manliness, or of good behavior; or if a little he still expects credit for smartness, bravery or some other good quality by his lack of politeness. If we consider that when he imitates the smoking, drinking, swearing, shoulder-hitting, and such other habits of his class, he is imitating what he has been taught to look upon as manliness, we may discover in him an aspiration to grow, to improve, to become what seems to him better than he is now. Perhaps if somebody would try to give him a better ideal, without trying to rob him of the old one he now imitates, he might be willing to accept it and improve. By his own conscious improvement the thought will become fastened in his mind that there are people and ideas superior to those he has always known; and thereafter his progress may surprise those who give him no credit for inherent goodness.

And of those who are the very lowest in moral capacity, the wretches who deliberately and without provocation commit murder or rape or both,—Is there a possibility of becoming good in them? A possibility of becoming better there probably is; but the germ of goodness is so small I cannot ask any mercy for them. Their animus is not a love of the crime; for if they could have what they aim to get without the crime they would as soon take it without. There have been those, however, who delighted in slaughter for the sport of it, as the wild small boy delights in killing small animals. But leaving aside all thought of vengeance, is there any reason why such persons as these should have their lives? Are they not like the nearly worthless plants the gardener throws away as of too little vitality to ever repay the trouble of raising? Even if these criminals could become truly good men would not the memory of their crime, and the consciousness that everyone knew of it and could never forget,—would not this consciousness so continually torment them that life would be worthless if they could have it? And though it may be pleasant to speculate on the possibility of their meeting their victims in another life, and of being pardoned and restored to good will, yet this is only conjecture; and as they actually appear in this life, with no more prospect of happiness than we can see, would it not be as well to let them go at once where life will be different if life at all, or else where the materials of their bodies and souls will pass into the great ocean of substance to take the chance of being recombined into more fortunate organisms, with happier careers, than those which have been so fearfully blighted? Let those decide who will; I have no wish to determine the fate of even such as these.

But it must still be repeated, nevertheless, that the conditions out of which such monsters come forth are social conditions,—conditions society has either made or allowed to exist, and over which it has a thousand times more power than any individual. No murder, no outrage, no villainy of any sort occurs in which society has not some direct or indirect share of guilt; how much let everyone estimate for himself.

It is time the old theory born of Asiatic helplessness was given a final go-by. We suffer from it continually and in a million ways. Children are taught deception by being taken for liars, thieves, and mischief-makers by nature, and in being punished regardless of motive or extenuation. Babies even are suspected of natural villainy and abused, when ignorant mothers or nurses can find no other cause for irritability. Animals too must endure an extra share of ill-treatment, because their best qualities are so little known, and they are continually suspected of bad ones. The criminal is supposed to be so full of venomous ill will by nature that very little effort is made to save him from total ruin, still less to reform him by teaching him genuine knowledge, and useful skilled labor, by which he can live honestly. On the contrary he is put into surroundings that disgrace and irritate, and where brutal treatment often outrages all his limited sense of justice, till at the end of his punishment he is again turned loose upon society thoroughly depraved and desperate. In the Christian church the idea has excused persecution, and given origin to celibacy with all its attendant corruptions. Everywhere and with everybody it prompts to suspicion and dislike, and encourages or justifies selfishness in our attitude toward others; for it takes everyone to be a knave or villain till the contrary is proved. It repulses strangers and separates friends. It has thus done much to generate the very depravity it assumes. But this will never be much less, until, while prudent in regard to present evil tendencies, we begin to treat humanity in the faith that it possesses growing germs of goodness, capable in time of becoming fully developed. Evolution is a philosophy of hope, the old is one of despair.

The critical rationalist has professedly disowned the original-depravity idea, yet it is difficult to see how he gives his brother man any more credit for inherent goodness, or good capability, than does his orthodox neighbor. He seldom acts toward him as if he thought he would respond to good quicker and more surely than to evil; though this is the inference that properly comes into his mind, from scientific knowledge, after the old dogmas are cast out. He accuses the adherent of old opinions of harboring bigotry, yet in this very important point is at least slow to discover the truth. It is useless, however, to accuse either party of bigotry, or of any other immorality, without showing him its nature and cause, how he becomes guilty, and how he can improve. When causes are known charity, and true liberality, and self-improvement begin to appear.

There is one special application of this thought that needs imperatively to be made at this time, when a great social renovation is soon to cause serious disturbance in the minds of all, and has in it the possibility of much evil, even if there were a general disposition to be rational and generous. The socialist now makes his claim in behalf of a single class, which, though sadly needing the proposed change, is not the only one that needs it. The rich need it for their own moral good, the professional class to save them from a servile prostitution of their abilities, and the whole female half of society to lift them out of their hereditary slavery, as much as does the laborer for his material benefit. Justice will in some manner benefit every one. But the socialist, in appealing to the workingman only or chiefly, assumes the moral perversity of the whole capitalist class,—an assumption directly adapted to engender all the animosity he predicts. He often speaks as if he believed them to be bent on doing conscious and deliberate injustice;

the accusation necessarily tending to enrage both the rich and the poor against each other. But it is not true. The capitalist does do injustice, of the most fearful kind, by shooting down in the street the men who threaten to damage his property. But he does it, not because he is by nature worse than the less fortunate workingman, but because he has been taught for centuries that property is more sacred than life, and that he has a right to take life in defending his property. So have the priest and the editor, who justify him in this wholesale murder, and the governing lawyer class who allow it to go unpunished and even unprosecuted. The extreme anarchist, who advocates a resort to force to obtain the property he should have been enabled to secure peaceably,—does he not act on the same idea? Justice, it is true, is on his side; but that does not justify him in committing a greater injustice than he suffers, by taking life for the property he is excluded from, through the industrial arrangements of a society in which all have been blind. The rich may be deliberately blind hereafter; because it is for their shortsighted selfish interest to be so, just as it is for the selfish interest of the poor to get their eyes open. Yet that does not prove that if places were changed one class of persons would be more disposed to resist light and justice than another. The perception of justice and injustice is what will make a man a socialist. And though a majority of the rich cannot be expected to overcome all their prepossessions for wealth and luxury, yet a considerable minority of them may do so; and a large majority of that middle class, neither rich nor poor nor ignorant, who make up the body of all progressive parties, must be counted on to do the final work of placing society on a basis of industrial justice. The more faith the socialist has in human goodness, and the more he appeals to it in all classes, the sooner will the social revolution come, the more peaceful will be its advent, and the more glorious the results it will accomplish.

It is precisely because humanity possesses the elements of goodness that the social revolution will triumph in spite of all opposition. That is why the Anti-slavery cause triumphed, and why Christianity itself triumphed in the early centuries. Socialism will not only triumph for that reason, but the same element of good furnishes ground for a hope, that notwithstanding the present holders of power show much of the tyrannical and merciless spirit, the reorganization of industry will be effected through the ballot, and with comparative peace and order. The same enlightenment that has made the socialist must be relied on to convert the farmer, the capitalist, the professional man, and the police. It is fear of natural depravity that generates the sacredness of law, and the dread of disorder or change. The Jesuit who gives his prime allegiance to his church, and the American Protestant anxious to put an acknowledgment of his God into the national constitution, are both alike liable to become bad citizens, and dangerous to their fellowmen, because they sincerely believe that the source of all goodness is outside of human nature. The socialist should be the last one to harbor such an idea, either consciously or unconsciously; but should put his whole confidence in human capacity for good, feeling assured that the more he trusts it the more he will find it exhibited.

Furthermore, the well-to-do conservative is eternally iterating and reiterating to him that the idle, the poor and the starving are the lazy, the thriftless and drunken ones, themselves alone blameable for what they suffer. Though this is to some extent true, the socialist should be ready to reply that the lazy, thriftless and drunken among the rich do not starve; that the thriftless poor spend for the same indulgences the rich do; that the lazy one was never educated by society into industrious habits, as he might have been; that the rich, instead, have by their own example taught him that laziness might be respectable; that every tramp, when he first became one, would have been glad to work; that a poor loafer is morally no worse than a rich sport; that drink is the only comfort, such as it is, that many poor wretches can get; and that even a savage will work for the things he wants. Thus there is nothing in the *natural character* of any of these to prevent their being educated when young, by a better industrial system, into industrious and useful members of society.

The one general statement which harmonizes all we know concerning this matter is that the human being, like the animal and plant, has a native tendency to grow, to develop, to become perfect. Beginning as a mere animal, with no thought, feeling or instinct different from that of other animals, man ends by becoming an angel, with all the noble qualities we can imagine the highest intelligent being to possess. It is not that nature has endowed the human with anything better, at the start, than the higher animals possess, in the way of a mental or spiritual character; but only a finer and completer physical organism, which gives man the capacity for a greater improvement, enables him to make a greater advance, and at length to reach a point where his progress becomes continual.

It is only with the best of humanity however, that its progress is thus continuous, as yet. So far as we can see, many individuals of the white race carry the childish development of mind into old age, and a large number the half-developed state of the half-grown boy or girl. The colored races seem to be arrested in their growth at some one or another of the stages between childhood and maturity. Those who have acquired the capacity for continuous evolution appear as but a small minority of the whole human family, the flower of the white race in

Europe and America. What the other races may be able to do under a better leadership, after one portion of humanity has become capable of leading, no one can say.

But because human nature possesses the *capacity*, in its highest individuals, to become divine, *it* is therefore sacred; the most sacred of anything we know; far more sacred than any kind of art, property or institution, any creed, law or revelation. For these are but its aids, the protections with which it surrounds itself, the means by which it advances, the ladders upon which it climbs. It may cherish or discard any one or all of them, according as its own needs or aspirations may be served thereby. It alone is the one supreme thing in value and importance.

When the human being shall come to realize what the capabilities are within himself no standard raised during his earlier days will be able to satisfy his aspirations, or be allowed to limit his progress. His own soul becomes God. Whatever its origin, however low and brutal it may once have been, he knows from an experience nothing can controvert that by inherent capacity it is divine, and his ruling desire is to make it so in actuality.

Select and replant, and give cultivation, describes the process by which all our finest fruits and flowers have come to be what we find them to-day. *Select and regenerate, and give good conditions,* tells how the noblest domestic animals have been developed from the inferior wild ones of the forest and plain. Without such selection and without the best conditions, man, through his own superior improvability, has civilized himself, and has reached a point where he can see what is yet before him. With improved conditions, and with the selection that will come through better knowledge and greater freedom, he will not be slow to prove himself something quite superior to the poor, miserable, depraved creature, "begotten in sin and shaped in iniquity," that the priests and philosophers of all ages have mistakenly believed him to be.

What he needs most is the wisdom that can secure a good social environment; and when this shall have been obtained his future will be very different from his past.

THE END.